THE *RATIO STUDIORUM*

THE *RATIO STUDIORUM*

The Official Plan
for Jesuit Education

Translated and Annotated by
Claude Pavur, S.J.

The Institute of Jesuit Sources
Saint Louis

Number 22 in Series I: Jesuit Primary Sources
in English Translation

© 2005 by Claude Pavur, S.J.

Cover photograph by J. J. Mueller, S.J., depicting
Ignatius of Loyola studying Latin in Barcelona with young classmates, 1524-26
Frieze at Fusz Hall, St. Louis University

The Institute of Jesuit Sources
3601 Lindell Boulevard
St. Louis, MO 63108
    tel: [314] 977-7257
    fax: [314] 977-7263
e-mail: ijs@slu.edu

Library of Congress Control Number: 2004117289
ISBN: 1-880810-59-X

CONTENTS

Introduction

The *Ratio atque institutio studiorum* is the founding document of Jesuit education. When it was issued in 1599, over fifty years of collaborative academic efforts had gone into its making, along with almost twenty years of committee work and two major trial-program documents (1586, 1591). It formally constituted and established as a unity an international network of schools that had already begun to be put under the auspices of the Jesuit order, that is, the Society of Jesus, founded by St. Ignatius of Loyola and his companions in 1540. The text was slightly revised in 1616. After the restoration of the Society of Jesus, which had been almost universally suppressed in 1773, it was again slightly revised and reissued in 1832, but not with its previous normative and binding status. Similar official academic plans with titles evocative of the *Ratio studiorum* occasionally appeared in later years (for example, the *Ratio studiorum superiorum Societatis Iesu* of 1954); but these were designed for the organization of studies within the Society of Jesus. The document of 1599 stands alone as the most thoroughly elaborated official plan for the full Jesuit system of education, extending from what is now the early high-school years, through the college level (the time of philosophy studies), to advanced professional studies (the course in theology, which corresponds to our professional graduate training).

It was an achievement that Ignatius of Loyola wanted but did not live to see. Had he done so, he would have found in this text the unmistakable marks of his own lived experience and his own spirituality. In fact, the work is of a piece with the other two great foundational Jesuit documents that for the most part he did compose himself, the *Spiritual Exercises* and the *Constitutions*. The *Ratio studiorum* has the same kind of very carefully structured, dynamic, and dramatic qualities that mark the *Exercises*, and the same kind of studied attention to organizational detail and scope found in the *Constitutions*. There is a similar kind of overriding attention to *final ends* in these three documents. And all three exhibit a balance of structure and freedom, establishing a definite plan with specific rules, but allowing a great respect for responsiveness in the Spirit when making adaptations to particular circumstances.

Such is what one might expect of an incarnational spirituality that stresses how the Divine takes on particular historical and cultural limitations. This expression of that spirituality has resulted in a powerful academic vitality, a type of education with character, style, and purpose, having order but not regimentation, allowing ample use of freedom but giving no quarter to drift or dissolution. And that was what Ignatius wanted: not the relatively loose approach followed by the Italian schools of his day but the more systematic one followed in France, the one designated by the phrase *ordo Parisiensis*. At first hand, after his experiences while attending several colleges, Ignatius had seen what saved time, what worked well, what did not.

Because he wanted the schools of the Society to be as productive as possible, he favored the "Parisian" structuring of education, which, as his experience had shown, achieved its ends most economically. There was a great advantage to using distinct educational grades in a differentiated curriculum, and to assuring a deep appropriation of educational content by way of student exercises, with careful oversight for the passage from one level to another.

As the essential code that established the lines along which Jesuit education was successfully conducted around the world for the next two centuries, the *Ratio studiorum* marks a major moment in the history of Western culture and education. It established a tradition that through its widespread influence on famous figures like René Descartes, and on countless less-celebrated but not insignificant persons, can be said to have played a major, even if somewhat hidden, role in the unification of European culture and in the unfolding of Western modernity around the world.

To be sure, it was not the only late-Renaissance attempt at a better organization and a network of schools. Like all significant advances, the *Ratio studiorum* could not have arisen without the preceding and contemporary contributions made by many others, notably those deriving from the Brethren of the Common Life. Neither could it have emerged as it did without the dynamic traditions of Scholasticism and humanism, which it brought into a striking synthesis.[1] But the *Ratio* as a whole is a decidedly original creation: it is the result of a well-documented creative picking and choosing and shaping and testing and reshaping of the available influences. The guiding committee undertook a massive, unprecedented effort of collaboration with academic professionals, above all with experienced teachers from many different countries. They overcame problems of differences on a very wide range of issues, from how much latitude should be allowed to professors of theology to how many holidays should be granted to the students to which Latin grammar should be used. Their work resulted in an authoritative written guide that would allow this type of education to become a tradition in the context of the Society of Jesus' universal outreach. It was a carefully thought-out, detailed "strategic plan" that, promulgated as an official code, helped to assure the delivery of certain goods year after year to generations of students.

[1] John W. O'Malley, S.J., "The Jesuit Educational Enterprise in Historical Perspective."

The story of the creation of the *Ratio* and its implementation is well told elsewhere. I refer the reader to the works mentioned in the bibliography and to the general timeline provided in an appendix. Here I will add only a few somewhat personal comments about the present edition.

My motivations in undertaking this project have been complex: I have wanted to promote the development of Latin studies as such, by calling the Academy's and the public's attention to the wealth of postclassical Latin materials, where so many works of lasting influence like the *Ratio studiorum* can be found. I have also wanted to promote a rethinking of Latin pedagogy today, partly by publicizing Renaissance methods that de facto achieved far more than we can usually manage or imagine today, even with the most devoted of students and the most spacious of schedules. My third desire was to make available this inescapable, foundational text in order to inform present-day discussions on and decisions about Jesuit education. Having recently rediscovered the *Spiritual Exercises* and the *Constitutions* of Ignatius, the Society of Jesus and its collaborators should be ready to rediscover the institutional educational genius expressed in this document.

Perhaps most of all, I have wanted to draw the attention of my contemporaries to one of our greatest needs and to one of our most intractable problems: the question of *order in the educational project*. Despite all of our singular achievements and technological accoutrements, we have failed to attain a convincing model of a coherent, comprehensive, purposeful program of studies, especially at the college level. An effective overall curricular architectonic eludes us. Perhaps in some quarters it is not even considered a value. But this monumental educational achievement from the sixteenth century is something to think about. It can serve as an inspiration, a stimulus to our good spirit of rivalry, and a rousing challenge. The *Ratio* was a gift for its own age. In a different way it can be a gift for ours.

The Latin text translated below is essentially that of the critical edition made by Ladislaus Lukács in *Ratio atque institutio studiorum Societatis Iesu: 1586, 1591, 1599*, nova editio penitus retractata, volume 5 of the series Monumenta Paedagogica Societatis Iesu (Rome: Institutum Historicum Societatis Iesu, 1986). I thank the Society of Jesus' Historical Institute in Rome, particularly Fathers Thomas McCoog, S.J., and Mark Lewis, S.J., for granting permission to make use of this work. Any deviations from Lukács's readings are noted in parentheses in the Latin text. The bracketed numbering follows that of the excellent Belin bilingual French edition of the *Ratio Studiorum*. For easy reference, I have added to the Belin presentation bracketed numbering for the Catalog of Thomistic Questions.

I gratefully acknowledge a huge debt to Saint Louis University's Dr. Clarence Miller, who thoroughly examined an early draft of the translation and brought to bear on it his finely tuned sense of both languages as well as the vast experience that he has gained in reading Renaissance Latin texts over much of his life. His comments notably improved quality, accuracy, and style throughout. I have also gained help, support, and important encouragement from many others at Saint Louis University: Dr. John Doyle of the Philosophy Department, the entire staff of the Institute of Jesuit Sources, Dr. Ron Crown of the Pius XII Memorial Library, Dr. David Murphy of the Center for Medieval and Renaissance Studies, the College of Arts and Sciences of Saint Louis University (which provided me with a sabbatical year), my colleagues in the Department of Modern and Classical Languages, and the Jesuit Community at Jesuit Hall (which gave me companionship, opportunities, and resources in abundance). And of course I have a large debt to all my teachers, particularly those who embodied many of the values embodied in the *Ratio*. I owe a very special thanks to the spirited kindness of a great benefactor, Dr. Virginia Lupo. To her I dedicate this translation in a spirit of lasting gratitude for her generosity.

Claude Pavur, S.J.

Saint Louis University

July 28, 2004

General Outline of the *Ratio studiorum*

Detailed Table of Contents

[H1] Rules for the Provincial

[H2] Rules for the Rector

[H3] Rules for the Prefect of Studies

[H7] Rules for the Professor of Scholastic Theology

[174] Final Goal
[175] Saint Thomas should be followed
[176] With what exception
[177] In doubtful matters it is permissible to take either side
[178] Concern for faith and religious devotion
[179] Opinions that offend Catholics should not be asserted
[180] The course should be finished in four years
[181] Division of the questions
[186] Each year's questions ought to be finished
[187] From which questions they should stay away
[188] From matter proper to Sacred Scripture
[189] From controversies
[190] From philosophical matters
[191] From cases of conscience
[192] The same material should not be repeated
[193] How Saint Thomas's articles ought to be explained
[194] Lengthier treatments should not be taught
[195] Either Saint Thomas should be defended or the question omitted
[196] Monthly disputations

[H8] Catalog of Some Questions
[H9] From the First Part of Saint Thomas

[C1] Question 1, Article 1
[C2]   Article 2
[C3]   Article 3
[C4]   Article 4
[C5]   Article 5
[C6]   Article 9
[C7] Question 2
[C8] Question 3, Article 1
[C9]   Article 2
[C10]   Article 3
[C11]   Article 4
[C12]   Article 7
[C13] Question 4, Article 1
[C14] Question 5
[C15] Question 7, Article 1
[C16]   Articles 2, 3, 4
[C17] Question 8
[C18] Question 9
[C19] Question 11
[C20]   Article 3
[C21]   Article 6
[C22]   Article 8
[C23]   Article 12
[C24] Question 13, Articles 3 and 4
[C25]   Article 5
[C26]   Article 7
[C27]   Articles 8 9 10 11 12
[C28] Questions 16 and 17
[C29] Question 19, Articles 9 and 12
[C30] Question 23, Article 1
[C31]   Article 3
[C32]   Article 5
[C33] Question 24
[C34] Question 25
[C35]   Article 1
[C36]   Article 6
[C37] Question 27, Article 1
[C38]   Article 3
[C39] Question 29
[C40] Question 32
[C41]   Article 4
[C42] Question 39
[C43] Question 43
[C44] Question 53

[H10] From the First Part of Part II

[C45] Question 1, Article 1
[C46]   Article 2
[C47]   Article 3
[C48]   Article 4
[C49] Question 2
[C50] Question 3, Article 1

[H11] From the Second Part of Part II

[H12] From Part III

[H13] On the Sacraments in General

[H22] Rules for the Prefect of Lower Studies

[H23] Regulations for Taking Examinations

[H24] Regulations for Prizes

[H25] Rules Common to All the Professors of the Lower Classes

[H26] Rules for the Professor of Rhetoric

[H32] The Training of Those Who Are Reviewing Theology in Private Study for Two Years

[H33] Rules for the Teacher's Assistant, or the Beadle

[H34] Rules for Non-Jesuit Students

[H35] Rules for Academies

The Official Plan for Jesuit Education

▼ ▼ ▼ ▼ ▼ ▼

Ratio atque institutio studiorum
Societatis Iesu
(1599)

Ratio atque Institutio Studiorum Societatis Iesu

The Official Plan for Jesuit Education

[1] Universa studiorum nostrorum ratio, ante quatuordecim annos fieri atque institui coepta, nunc tandem absoluta ac plane constituta, ad provincias mittitur. Etsi enim propter magnam utilitatem, quae studiis nostris allatura videbatur, eam multo ante perfici atque in mores induci R. P. N. Generalis optaverat, id tamen hucusque commode fieri minime potuit. Decuit enim in re satis ardua multisque difficultatibus implicata, nihil plane definiri, priusquam provinciarum difficultates ac postulata diligenter examinarentur,

[1] Our comprehensive educational plan, first offic years ago, is now being sent to the provinces in finished and final form at last. The plan's apparent usefulness for our studies was so great that Our Reverend Father General had hoped that it would be completed and implemented much sooner, but this simply could not happen in the right way until now.[1] For in a project so difficult and involved in so many troublesome issues, it seemed right not to set down anything definitive before the provinces' difficulties and formal requests were carefully reviewed, so that the result might satisfy all parties as far

---

The notes that follow are intended to assist readers who are encountering the *Ratio studiorum* for the first time, especially those who have only a minimal acquaintance with Christianity, Catholicism, or the Jesuit tradition. The cited sources of material and the works mentioned in the bibliography will provide much additional assistance.

The bracketed boldface numbers at the beginning of each section were introduced by the translator to facilitate referencing. Beginning with p. 7, the indented number in each section appears in the Latin original from which this translation was made.

For a fuller explanation of the title of this work, *The Official Plan for Jesuit Education*, see endnote 1 on page 237. The Latin version, printed in the left-hand columns and translated in the right-hand columns, is taken from *Ratio atque institutio studiorum Societatis Iesu (1586, 1591, 1599)*. The 1599 version followed here is found on pp. 355–454 of this source. Hereafter the abbreviation *Ratio* will be used for the *Ratio studiorum*.

[1] Our Reverend Father General: the leading superior and administrator of the Society of Jesus. The word "general" is not a military but an organizational term (as in the phrase "attorney general"). It indicates a person carrying the responsibility for the overall supervision of a number of local and regional superiors. A religious superior is a person who has been given authority over a community of members of a given religious association.

Specifically, at this time Claudio Acquaviva (1543–1615) was the Father General. He was the fifth general of the Society (1581–1615) and generally acknowledged to be one of the best of the Society's administrators. See *The Catholic Encyclopedia*, s.vv. "Claudius Acquaviva," and also "Jesuit Generals Prior to the Suppression of the Society (1541–1773)." Hereafter this source will be abbreviated to *CathEncy*.

ut omnibus, quantum fieri posset, satisfieret; et ut opus, quod ab omnibus deinceps in usum adhiberi debebat, æquioribus omnium animis reciperetur.

[2] Quare quidquid initio a sex deputatis patribus de omni studiorum nostrorum ratione magno labore atque industria disputatum atque constitutum fuerat, eo consilio ad provincias missum fuit, ut doctores nostri et harum rerum periti cuncta diligenter et exacte perpenderent; ut si quid in hac ratione minus commodum observarent, vel quod institui commodius posset, animadverterent; quid denique de tota hac ratione sentirent, adhibitis rationum momentis, exponerent. Quod cum omnes fere provinciæ strenue atque viriliter præstitissent, omnia, quæ ab iis observata vel proposita fuerant, Romæ iterum a præcipuis Romani Collegii doctoribus, et a tribus deputatis patribus, qui in hunc finem Romæ substiterant, sedulo recognita, R. P. N. Generalis cum patribus assistentibus accurate

as possible, and so that they might all receive in a greater spirit of equanimity the document that they would all have to put into practice from then on.

[2] It was for this reason that the provinces were sent whatever the six appointed fathers had initially debated and worked out with a great deal of energetic effort about the whole shape of our program of studies.[2] The intention was that our academic personnel and those experienced in these matters might consider everything attentively and in detail, so that if they noticed anything not quite suitable in this plan, or something that might be structured more suitably, they might point it out, and so that they might finally express what they thought about this plan as a whole, citing the main reasons for their positions.[3] When practically all of the provinces had vigorously and energetically performed this task, everything that they had observed or proposed was subjected to a painstaking review at Rome by the leading academics of the Roman College and by three appointed fathers who had stayed at Rome for this pur-

---

[2] The six appointed fathers were John Azor (Spain), Gaspar Gonzalez (Portugal), James Tyrie (France), Peter Busée (or Buys, from Austria), Anthony Ghuse (or Guisanus, from Germany), and Stephen Tucci (Italy). No mention is made here of the earlier committee of twelve appointed by Acquaviva immediately after his election as general in 1581 and commissioned to work out a plan of studies. See Allan Peter Farrell, S.J., *The Jesuit Code of Liberal Education: Development and Scope of the "Ratio studiorum,"* 22 ff. The word "provinces" describe the basic geographic administrative units of the Society.

[3] Academic personnel: literally, "doctors." The general word for a teacher of any level in the *Ratio* is *professor*, as the section headings make clear. Considering the text of the *Ratio* alone, we can say that the word *doctor* connotes a high level of academic achievement, but not necessarily a teaching position. Therefore, the semantic field of *doctor* may overlap with those of the current English "specialist," "expert," "scholar," "academic," "person of learning." Hastings Rashdall, in his *Universities of Europe in the Middle Ages*, notes that, in late medieval Paris, the term *magister* was common in theology, medicine, and the arts, and at that university the term *doctor* was used for teachers of canon law, whereas in Bologna teachers of the law tended to use *doctor, professor, or dominus* (pp. 19 f.). See also the note on §16 below.

perpendit, rationemque hoc modo accomodatam iterum in universam Societatem mitti curavit, et ut ab omnibus exacte servaretur, præcepit.

pose.[4] Our Reverend Father General, with his fathers assistant, carefully examined it, and once it had been suitably modified in this way, he had the plan sent back again to the whole Society, instructing everyone to follow it in detail.

[3] Monuit tamen provinciales omnes, ut quoniam novæ institutiones ab experimento solidiorem firmitatem accipiunt, in suis quique provinciis, quid quotidianus docendi usus ostenderet, adnotarent, et Romam postea mitterent, ut extrema tandem operi manus admoveretur, et studiorum nostrorum ratio, post tantam, tanque diuturnam discussionem, certa aliqua firmitate stabiliretur.

[3] But he pointed out to all the provincials that, since new policies and procedures gain strength from actual use, they should note in their own provinces what the day-to-day practice of teaching revealed; then they should send their observations to Rome, so that the finishing touches might at last be put on the work, and our program of studies rather firmly established after such a thorough and such an extended discussion.

[4] Cum vero provinciales, qui ad quintam generalem congregationem venerunt, ex suis provinciis, quæ ex quotidiano usu minus commode accidere animadversa fuerant, attulissent, ac plerique omnes maiorem in hac ratione brevitatem præter cætera desiderarent, magno sane labore factum est, ut tota ratio iterum diligenter examinaretur, et perpensis rationum momentis, quæ a provinciis afferebantur, quid tandem firmiter constituendum esset, diiudicaretur, et omnia, quoad fieri potuit, ad breviorem commodioremque methodum redigerentur. Quod ita

[4] But when the provincials who came to the Fifth General Congregation had reported from their own provinces what day-to-day experience had shown to be not so suitable,[5] and since almost all of them desired, among other things, that the plan should be shorter, a careful reexamination of the entire document was undertaken, with no small effort, to be sure. After a deliberation on the most important issues raised by the provinces, there emerged a judgment about what was going to have to constitute the plan's final content, and, as far as possible, everything was reduced to a more concise and serviceable method.

[4] Roman College: the college founded by Ignatius in 1551 in Rome. See Farrell, *Jesuit Code*, 65.

[5] Fifth General Congregation (1593–94). General congregations are meetings of representatives from the leadership of the Society and from all its provinces. Their principal responsibility is to elect any new Father General. They also compose and issue major documents for the Society and make important decisions affecting the Society's life and mission. For extensive information about historical general congregations, see *For Matters of Greater Moment: The First Thirty Jesuit General Congregations*.

præstitum est, ut sperari merito possit, postremum hunc laborem ab omnibus comprobatum iri.

This revision has been accomplished in such a way that there is good reason to expect that this last effort is going to win everyone's approval.

[5] Quare hæc studiorum ratio, quæ nunc mittitur, omnibus aliis, quæ ante hac experimenti causa missæ fuerant, posthabitis, servari in posterum ab omnibus nostris debebit; in eoque sedula doctorum nostrorum opera collocanda erit, ut, quæ postrema hac ratione præscripta sunt, facile suaviterque executioni mandentur. Quod ita futurum esse mihi facile persuadeo, si omnes intelligant, rem hanc R. P. Nostro maxime cordi esse.

[5] For this reason, the educational plan now being sent supersedes all the others sent earlier for experimental use, and all Jesuits will be obliged to observe this version for the coming years.[6] Our academic personnel should energetically devote their efforts to making sure that what is prescribed by this last plan is put into effect in a smooth and trouble-free manner. I am quite ready to believe that this will happen if everyone realizes that Our Reverend Father has a special personal interest in this project.

[6] Superioribus vero, quibus præcipue hoc onus incumbit, graviter sane atque efficaciter R. P. N. Generalis commendat, ut quanta maxima possunt animi contentione enitantur, ut res hæc, tantopere in nostris Constitutionibus commendata, et quæ nostris auditoribus uberes fructus allatura creditur, ab omnibus alacriter et exacte servetur.

[6] And turning to the superiors on whom the chief burden of this work falls, Our Reverend Father General advises them with the utmost seriousness to strive with the greatest possible personal involvement to get everyone to enthusiastically and faithfully follow this undertaking that is so strongly called for by our *Constitutions* and expected to produce such abundant results for our students.[7]

Datum Romæ 8 ianuarii 1599.
Mandato R. P. N. Generalis

Jacobus Dominicus secretarius

Issued at Rome, January 8, 1599
By order of Our Reverend
Father General

Giacomo Domenichi, Secretary

---

[6] Jesuits: literally, "Ours." The term "Jesuit" was not used by Ignatius.

[7] *Constitutions:* the foundational text of governance for the Society of Jesus, primarily composed by Ignatius and given shape between 1551 and 1558. For a detailed discussion of the development of the *Constitutions,* see *The Constitutions of the Society of Jesus,* trans., ed., and annot. George Ganss, S.J., 49–54. This source will hereafter be abbreviated to Ganss, *Cons.* Though many adaptations and annotations have been added to it over the years, the *Constitutions* has maintained from the beginning its status as the privileged document for the administration of the Society.

For the relationship between the *Constitutions* and the *Ratio,* see endnote (endn.) 2.

[H1] Regulæ Præpositi Provincialis

[7] *Finis studiorum Societatis*

1. Cum ex primariis Societatis nostræ ministeriis unum sit, omnes disciplinas instituto nostro congruentes ita proximis tradere, ut inde ad Conditoris ac Redemptoris nostri cognitionem atque amorem excitentur, omni studio curandum sibi putet præpositus provincialis, ut tam multiplici scholarum nostrarum labori fructus, quem gratia nostræ vocationis exigit, abunde respondeat.

[8] *Præfectus studiorum generalis*

2. Proinde non solum id rectori valde commendet in Domino, sed ei etiam præfectum studiorum, vel cancellarium adiungat; virum in literis egregie versatum, qui et zelo bono et iudicio ad ea, quæ sunt ei committenda, polleat; cuius sit munus, generale rectoris instru-

[H1] Rules for the Provincial

[7] *The final goal of the Society's studies*

1. Since one of the leading ministries of our Society is teaching our neighbors all the disciplines in keeping with our Institute in such a way that they are thereby aroused to a knowledge and love of our Maker and Redeemer,[8] the provincial should consider himself obliged to do his utmost to ensure that our diverse and complex educational labor meets with the abundant results that the grace of our calling demands of us.

[8] *General prefect of studies*

2. Accordingly, not only should he, in the Lord, present this task to the rector as one of high priority,[9] but he should also assign him a prefect of studies or executive assistant, a man with outstanding abilities in the arts of written communication, who is capable of managing his assignments en-

---

[8] [O]ne of the leading ministries of our Society: a significant phrase, revealing a self-understanding of the order that developed quickly and powerfully, but nevertheless later, than its founding in 1540. The idea of the Society as a teaching order was an organic development from the first charter of the Society, *The Formula of the Institute* (1540, slightly revised in 1550), which, though it does not envisage an educational network, mentions lectures, education, doctrinal formation of the believers, and the defense and propagation of the faith. For the relevant text of the *Formula*, see endn. 3.

Neighbors *(proximi)*, as in the Gospel of Mark 12:31, which in the standard Latin translation is "diliges proximum tuum tamquam te ipsum" (you shall love your neighbor as yourself).

"Institute" is an important word that connotes (1) the basic idea of what has been established in the founding of the Society; (2) the way of life and manner of proceeding, in light of certain larger purposes; and (3) the particular foundational documents of the Society that express and define the particular form of Jesuit religious life. See Ganss, *Cons.*, 43 f.

[9] [I]n the Lord: a phrase recurring ten times in the *Ratio*, suggesting that the action is taken before God, in all religious sincerity, on the basis of one's conscience, with best intentions, and with an indifference to one's own immediate advantages or disadvantages.

mentum esse ad studia bene ordinanda; cui professores et scholastici omnes, tum qui in eodem collegio, tum etiam si qui in convictorum et alumnorum seminariis
forte degunt, et præfecti ipsi studiorum in seminariis in rebus ad
studia pertinentibus ea, qua par
est, humilitate pareant.

thusiastically and judiciously. This
man's duty should consist in being the
rector's general administrative agent
for getting and keeping the course of
studies in good order. In academic
matters, he should be obeyed with all
proper humility by all the professors
and the students, both those in the
college and any that happen to be
spending time in the seminaries of
boarders and day students, and also by
the seminary prefects of studies themselves.[10]

[9] *Præfectus studiorum inferiorum et atrii*

3. Quod si ob gymnasii
amplitudinem ac varietatem per
unum studiorum præfectum non
videatur scholarum omnium rationibus satis esse consultum, alterum
constituat, qui ex generalis præfecti præscripto inferioribus studiis
moderetur; quin etiam, si ita res
exigat, adiiciatur tertius, qui scholarum atrio præsit.

[9] *Prefect of lower studies and of the
courtyard*

3. But if it does not seem that a
single prefect of studies can take
sufficient care of the orderly management of all the classes because of the
school's large size and diversity, he
should appoint a second one to manage the lower studies under the direction of the general prefect. In fact, if
the situation so requires, he should
add a third, to take charge of the
school's courtyard.[11]

[10] *Professores quomodo
comparandi*

4. Multo ante provideat, quos-
nam pro unaquaque facultate

[10] *How to acquire faculty*

4. Well ahead of time, he will plan
which professors he might be able to
get for each academic unit, taking note

---

[10] College: in the *Ratio*, this term covers a wider semantic field. Ganss lists the five types of Jesuit colleges that had evolved by 1556: (1) houses without lectures, for Jesuit students; (2) houses with lectures for Jesuits and non-Jesuits (usually called externs in Society documents); (3) academic institutions founded mainly for non-Jesuits, even if some Jesuits were present; (4) residences or boarding colleges for those preparing for the priesthood and taking courses at some other school nearby; and (5) boarding colleges for lay students (*Cons.*, 174 f.). Also see endn. 4 for Farrell's elucidation of these terms.

Prefect: the word designates someone put in charge of a given domain.

[11] Countyard *(atrium):* in §294 below we hear of a "room that looks out onto the court-yard." This was a space in which students could gather before class (§287). Newer schools departed from the medieval structures by including a central courtyard, called the *atrium*, which served as a space for physical exercise and recreation, as schoolyards do today. See Aldo Scaglione, *The Liberal Arts and the Jesuit College System*, 91–93, drawing on François de Dainville, *L'éducation des Jésuites (XVIᵉ-XVIIIᵉ siècles)*, 518–25.

professores habere possit; observatis iis, qui ad eam rem videntur aptiores; qui docti, diligentes et assidui, ac profectus studentium tum in lectionibus, tum in aliis literariis exercitationibus, studiosi sint.

of those who seem more fit for this work—those who are knowledgeable, diligent and energetically dedicated, and who are keenly concerned about the students' progress, both in the lessons, and in the other literary exercises.

[11]   *Sacræ Scripturæ studium et magister*

5. Magnam diligentiam adhibeat in promovendo sacrarum literarum studio; quod perficiet, si viros ad id muneris eligat non solum linguarum peritos (id enim maxime necessarium est), sed etiam in theologia scholastica, ceterisque scientiis, in historia, variaque eruditione et, quoad eius fieri potest, in eloquentia bene versatos.

[11]   *The study and the teacher of Sacred Scripture*

5. He should very diligently promote the study of sacred texts. He will accomplish this if he selects for this task men who are not only expert in the languages (for this is absolutely indispensable) but also well versed in Scholastic theology and in the other branches of learning, in history, in intellectual culture of different kinds, and, to the extent that it is possible, in the art of eloquence.[12]

[12]   *Auditores et tempus*

6. Hanc autem Sacræ Scripturæ lectionem per biennium, hoc est, secundo fere et tertio theologiæ anno theologi audiant quotidie per tres circiter horæ quadrantes, ubi duo sunt theologiæ professores; ubi vero tres, vel singulis diebus breviorem, vel (si magis placeat) longiorem alternis.

[12]   *Students and time*

6. For a two-year period (generally in the second and third years of theology, that is), the theologians should attend a class on Sacred Scripture every day for about three-quarters of an hour where there are two professors of theology; but where there are three, they should attend either a briefer class every day or (if preferred) a longer one every other day.

[13]   *Hebrææ linguæ professor qualis*

7. Linguam hebræam, si commode possit, doceat Sacræ Scripturæ professor, vel saltem aliquis, qui sit theologus; optandumque, ut esset etiam linguarum peritus, non solum græcæ propter novum Tes-

[13]   *Qualities of the professor of Hebrew*

7. The professor of Sacred Scripture should teach the Hebrew language if he can do this properly. Or at least some person who is a theologian should do this. And it is desirable that he be expert in the languages, not only

---

[12] Scholastic theology: theology based upon the *quaestio* and the dialectical methods of the medieval Schoolmen. It is distinguished from positive theology, which bases itself on primary materials like the Bible, councils, canon law, and patristic writings. See Ganss, *Cons.*, 188n5.

tamentum, et versionem Septuaginta Interpretum, sed etiam chaldaicæ et syriacæ, cum ex his linguis multa in libris canonicis sparsim habeantur.

Greek on account of the New Testament and the Septuagint, but also Aramaic and Syriac, since many phrases from these languages are scattered throughout the canonical books.

[14] *Auditores et studium*

8. Ab hac lectione per annum audienda, hoc est, secundum fere vel tertium theologiæ, theologi non eximantur, nisi qui ad eam inepti penitus censerentur. Præterea, ut monent Constitutiones, deliberare debet, quinam sint huic studio addicendi; qui vero addicti fuerint, biennio, quod repetendæ theologiæ præscribitur, plus studii in hebraicis ponant; imo in ipso cursu theologiæ privata academia, saltem in vacationibus, si fieri potest, iuventur.

[14] *Students and their study*

8. Theology students should not be exempted from this course of study, which generally ought to be taken in the second or third year of theology, unless they are judged thoroughly unsuited for it. Moreover, as the Constitutions point out, he should deliberate about who ought to be assigned to this study. And those who have been assigned should put more emphasis on Hebrew studies in the two-year period that is prescribed for the review of theology. In fact, even during the ordinary course of theology, at least in vacation times, they should be supported by a private academy if possible.[13]

[15] *Theologiæ cursus et magistri*

9. Quadriennio ex Constitutionibus theologiæ cursum absolvi curet; idque a duobus vel, si omnino aliter commode fieri non posset, a tribus ordinariis professoribus, pro diverso provinciarum usu. Illud autem in primis meminerit, non esse ad cathedras theologicas promovendos, nisi qui erga S. Thomam bene affecti fuerint; qui vero ab eo alieni sunt, vel etiam eius

[15] *Course and teachers of theology*

9. He should see to it that the theological course is completed in a four-year period, in accordance with the *Constitutions;* and it should be managed by two professors of the regular faculty, or, if it could not be properly done in any other way at all, by three, according to the different practices of the provinces. He should especially keep in mind, however, that only those who are well disposed towards St. Thomas should be promoted to theological chairs.[14] But those who gener-

---

[13] Academy: *academia* is defined in §481 below as "a group of committed students, chosen from the entire student body, who join together under the charge of a Jesuit to hold certain special exercises pertaining to studies." Since an academy had officers and rules, it was more formal than a study group is today.

[14] Saint Thomas: Thomas Aquinas (1227–74), a Doctor of the Church and the preeminent Scholastic theologian. His *Summa theologica (Sumtheol)* has been used as the fullest authoritative synthesis of systematic theological thinking. For the *CathEncy*'s discussion of a Doctor of the

parum studiosi, a docendi munere repellantur.

ally disagree with him, or even those who are not very enthusiastic about him, should be kept out of an academic post.

[16] *Biennium ad theologiam repetendam*

10. Initio quarti anni cum rectore, præfecto, magistris, suisque consultoribus designet aliquos, qui et probatæ virtutis in primis sint, et ingenio polleant, ut ad theologiam privatim repetendam, et habendos actus superioris arbitrio biennio, ut Constitutiones iubent, privatum et quietum studium habeant; de quo privata inferius erit instructio. Ex quibus, ubi regionis mos est, poterunt aliqui, facta a Generali potestate, ad gradus doctoratus vel magisterii promoveri.

[16] *The two-year period for reviewing theology*

10. At the beginning of the fourth year, together with the rector, the prefect, the teachers, and his own consultors, he should designate some students who are both outstanding in tested virtue and notably talented to have private, quiet study for reviewing theology on their own and for participating in Acts at the superior's discretion for a two-year period, as the *Constitutions* prescribe.[15] There will be particular instructions about this later [in this document]. Where it is the local custom, some of these can be promoted to the rank of Doctor or Master, with the permission of the general.[16]

[17] *Promotio ad gradus*

11. Ubi est consuetudo, ut publica fiat promotio ad gradus, Constitutio accurate servetur; nec ullus promoveatur, nisi theses aliquot ex insignioribus Scripturæ locis scholasticis conclusionibus intermisceat. Ratio quoque promovendi, et reliqui ritus (modo ne Constitutionibus repugnent) pro

[17] *Promotion to rank*

11. Where it is customary to have public promotions to a rank, the *Constitutions* should be carefully followed. And no one should be promoted unless he includes some theses on the more important scriptural passages among the Scholastic theses. The manner of the promotion and the rest of the ceremonies (provided that they do not conflict with the *Constitutions*)

Church, see endn. 5.

[15] Acts: academic exercises that were public performances, in which a student's knowledge would be tested and displayed, sometimes through the proposal and defense of theses. Latin dictionaries often fail to mention the special usage of this term in the medieval and Renaissance academic tradition. To indicate that these words are being used in these specialized senses, they will be capitalized in text and notes. General Acts covered almost all theology (see §107 below), and Special Acts focused on particular questions. For further discussion of the questions of Acts, see endn. 6.

[16] The rank of Doctor or Master: for a fuller explanation of these terms, see endn. 7.

cuiusque loci consuetudine statutisque teneantur.

[18] *Casuum professor*

12. Duos in eo collegio, ubi est pro nostris seminarium casuum conscientiæ, casuum professores constituat, qui universas eius generis materias inter se divisas biennio explicent; vel unum, qui binas quotidie lectiones habeat.

[19] *Collatio casuum*

13. Bis in hebdomada in domibus professis, in collegiis bis aut semel, ut melius esse in Domino iudicaverit, sive in iis aliqua sit, sive nulla publica casuum lectio, sacerdotes nostri conveniant ad habendam inter se de casibus collationem aliquo præside a se constituto, qui prudenter ac tuto possit hanc provinciam sustinere; atque is præses regulas professoris casuum, in quibus modus huius collationis præscribitur, legat ac servet.

[20] *Eadem collatio in collegiis primariis*

14. Fiat etiam huiusmodi casuum collatio in primariis collegiis, sive unus duove sint casuum professores, sive nullus, potis-

should accord with the custom and regulations of each region.

[18] *The professor for the study of cases of conscience*

12. In any college where there is a seminar in cases of conscience for Jesuits, he should appoint two to be professors for the study of cases of conscience. These professors should divide all the relevant material between them and cover it all in a two-year period. Or he should appoint one, who should give two classes daily.

[19] *Conference on cases*

13. Twice a week in professed houses, in colleges once or twice, as he judges better in the Lord, whether or not there is some public class on cases of conscience,[17] our priests should gather to hold a conference on cases of conscience among themselves.[18] He ought to appoint as the presider someone who can prudently and safely manage this charge. And this presider should read and observe the rules for the professor of cases of conscience, which include prescriptions for the procedure of this conference.

[20] *The same conference in the main colleges*

14. There should be such a conference on cases of conscience also in the main colleges whether there are one or two professors of cases of conscience,

---

[17] [C]ases of conscience: a practical branch of moral theology based on the discussion of individual cases. The course of studies devoted to cases of conscience was primarily pastoral preparation (see §197 below), set up as a track parallel to the full, technical scholastic elaboration of questions (see §200 below).

[18] Conference: the Latin word *collatio* has a rich usage rarely covered in standard Latin dictionaries. The *Oxford English Dictionary* (OED) provides an extended discussion of the relevant range of meanings conveyed by the English use of collation. See endn. 8.

simum pro omnibus theologiæ auditoribus; sed semel tantum in hebdomada.

[21] *Ab ea non eximendi*

15. Ab his autem omnibus, quas diximus, collationibus præter theologiæ ac philosophiæ professores, et si quos alios excipiendos superior iudicaverit, nulli præterea casistæ, nullique sacerdotes, qui ex instituto vel interdum confessiones audiant, eximantur; immo superior ipse non nisi raro, et graves ob causas absit.

[22] *Philosophiæ professores quales*

16. Philosophiæ professores (nisi gravissima necessitas aliud exigat) oportet non modo cursum theologiæ absolvisse, sed eandem biennio repetiisse, ut eorum doctrina tutior esse possit, magisque theologiæ deserviat; si qui autem fuerint ad novitates proni, aut ingenii nimis liberi, hi a docendi munere sine dubio removendi.

[23] *Philosophiæ cursus*

17. Philosophicum cursum triennio absolvent, non autem minore tempore, ubi sunt nostri; si autem soli sint externi auditores, relinquatur provincialis iudicio; quotan-

or none, especially for all the students of theology, but only once a week.[19]

[21] *Those who should not be excused from it*

15. Moreover, except for the professors of theology and philosophy, and any others that in the superior's judgment ought to be exempted, no students of cases of conscience and no priests who hear confessions (by regular assignment or on occasion) should be excused from all these conferences that we have mentioned.[20] In fact, the superior himself should be absent only rarely, and only for serious reasons.

[22] *The character of the professors of philosophy*

16. Professors of philosophy (unless the most serious necessity demands otherwise) should have not only finished the course of theology but also taken a two-year review of it, so that their teaching might be more reliable, and of greater service to theology. However, if any professors are inclined towards innovations or have too free-spirited an intelligence, they definitely ought to be removed from their academic posts.

[23] *The philosophy course*

17. They will complete the philosophical course in a three-year period, certainly not in less time where there are Jesuits. If, however, there are only non-Jesuit students,[21] this should be

---

[19] Theologians: in Jesuit parlance, theologians often means "those who are in the theological course," theology students, therefore. This same usage is found for philosophers, logicians, rhetoricians, and humanists.

[20] Confessions: that is, the sacrament of penance, which involves a confession of sins to obtain absolution.

[21] Non-Jesuit: the Latin word *externi*, for which some translators use the Anglicization "externs," simply means "outsiders" and can be applied in relation to any group. Because "out-

nis vero, si fieri potest, unus cursus absolvendus, et alter inchoandus.

left to the discretion of the provincial. But each year, if possible, one course should be finished, and the second one started.

[24] *Rhetoricæ et humanitatis tempus*

18. Licet cursus temporis ad humanitatis et rhetoricæ studium definitus esse nequeat, et ad superiorem pertineat expendere, quantum in his literis quemque habere oporteat, nostros tamen non ante ad philosophiam mittat, quam biennium in rhetorica consumpserint, nisi ratio ætatis aut aptitudinis, aut aliquid aliud obstare in Domino iudicetur. Quod si aliqui indole ingenii ad magnos progressus in his potissimum studiis faciendos præditi sint, ut solidius fundamentum iaciant, videndum erit, an operæ pretium sit triennium impendere.

[24] *Time devoted to rhetoric and humanistic studies*

18. Although the time period for the study of the humanities and rhetoric can not be defined, and it belongs to the superior to judge how much time is good for each one to spend in these literary studies, he should nevertheless not send Jesuits to philosophy before they have spent two years on rhetoric, unless they are judged in the Lord to be impeded by age or by aptitude or by something else. But if some are gifted with a special genius for substantial achievements, particularly in these studies, there ought to be some consideration of whether it might be worthwhile to invest three years in order to lay down a more solid foundation.

[25] *De examine logicorum*

19. 1. Postquam cursum philosophicum ingressi fuerint, bis examinandi erunt per designatos examinatores, præfectum videlicetstudiorum, et magistros theologiæ ac philosophiæ, rectore præsente, eiusque consultoribus et ipso provinciali, si posset; primum quidem paulo ante Quadragesimam, vel sub ferias paschales, deinde rursus logica absoluta.

[25] *On the examination of the students of logic*

19. 1. After they have entered upon the course of philosophy studies, they should be examined twice by appointed examiners, namely, the prefect of studies and the teachers of theology and philosophy, in the presence of the rector and his consultors, and the provincial himself, if possible. The first examination will be a little before Lent, or just after Easter Week, and then again when the study of logic is finished.

---

sider" has a negative connotation that the Latin does not carry, and because a phrase like "those who are not in our community" is wordy, the use of non-Jesuit seems preferable in this context.

[26] *Virtutis ratio habenda*

2. In hac autem tota re, quia magni momenti in Domino iudicanda est, et considerate admodum ob maiorem Dei gloriam transigenda, servet in primis provincialis regulas 49 et 56 officii sui, et potissimum rationem habeat virtutis.

[26] *Virtue ought to be taken into account*

2. In this entire matter, since it ought to be judged in the Lord to be something of real importance, and since it ought to be accomplished with quite careful attention to the greater glory of God,[22] the provincial should keep first and foremost rules 49 and 56 of his office, and he should especially take virtue into account.[23]

[27] *Examinis finis et modus*

3. Hoc examen, quo decernitur, utrum quis philosophiæ, an casibus conscientiæ destinandus sit, secretis fiat suffragiis, et quod constitutum fuerit, simul cum examinatorum iudicio scriptum constet in libro ad id designato; serventque rem omnino secretam, qui examini intererunt.

[27] *Purpose and manner of the examination*

3. This examination, which determines whether anyone ought to be assigned to philosophy or to cases of conscience, should be conducted using secret votes, and the decision should be set down in writing, along with the judgment of the examiners, in the book designated for this. And they should maintain complete confidentiality about who took part in the examination.

[28] *Qui casibus, qui philosophiæ destinandi*

4. Ergo in priori examine si qui inepti ad philosophiam deprehensi fuerint, destinentur ad casus, vel ad docendum provincialis arbitrio (sic enim hanc destinationem ad casus intelligimus); de reliquis nihil certi pro tempore statuatur. In posteriori vero examine triplex omnino gradus in iis, qui exami-

[28] *Who should be chosen for case studies, who for philosophy*

4. If any have been found unsuited for philosophy in the earlier examination, they should be sent to case studies or, at the judgment of the provincial, to teaching (for this is how we understand the assignment to case studies). About the rest, nothing certain should be set for the time being. In the later examination, three grades

---

[22] [T]o the greater glory of God: an important phrase associated closely with the Society, appearing here with some variations in §§37, 71, 99, 207, 290, 434, and 441 below.

[23] [R]ules 49 and 56 of his office: rule 49 states: "In each house, he should define the limits of the cloister precisely and see to it that the areas falling under this law are clearly indicated and that the law itself is carefully observed. He should also see to it that all other protections of chastity are attentively applied in such a way that precautions are taken against all dangers in this extremely important matter." Rule 56 reads, "If he allows anyone special books for special studies, he should see to it that they are at the very outset assigned to the designated library." See *Regulae Societatis Iesu*, pp. 98 and 100. For the Latin originals of these rules, see endn. 9.

nantur, animadverti potest; aut enim mediocritatem excedunt, et hi reliqua studia persequi debent; aut infra illam sunt, et hi omnino casibus applicandi erunt; aut denique in mediocritate consistunt, et in his etiam sua distinctio erit.

are possible for the examinees: either they surpass the average, and they ought to continue on with the remaining studies; or they are below the average, and all of these ought to be assigned to case studies; or, lastly, they attain an average rank, and among these also there will be particular differences at this level.

[29] *Talenti ratio habenda, et quibus biennium theologiæ concedendum*

5. Nam si mediocres sunt in literis, et nullo alio talento præditi sunt, hi quoque mittentur ad casus; sin autem horum quispiam simul cum præcipua virtute bonum præseferret talentum concionandi vel gubernandi, tunc quo maiori securitate et auctoritate possit Societas eius opera uti, deliberet provincialis cum suis consultoribus, an præter philosophiam duo theologiæ anni sint ei concedendi. Quod ubi statuerit, aperte moneat eum, non nisi ad hanc mensuram studia continuaturum.

[29] *Talent ought to be taken into account, and who should be granted two years of theology*

5. For if they are average in humanistic literary studies, and they are endowed with no other talent, then they will be sent to the course in case studies as well. But if among these anyone displays real talent for preaching or administration along with distinguished virtue, then the provincial along with his consultors ought to deliberate about whether that person should be given two years of theology beyond philosophy so that the Society might be able to make use of his service with greater confidence and to greater effect. When the provincial has made this decision, he should frankly inform him that he will continue his studies only so far and no further.

[30] *Triennium quibus*

6. Quod si forte iis, qui concionandi facultatem habent, biennium non sufficiat ad eas theologiæ materias in scholis audiendas, quæ necessariæ videntur, ut tuto et sine errore suum munus exequantur (cuiusmodi sunt, quæ in Summa Divi Thomæ in prima parte docentur ante disputationem de angelis, in tertia de Incarnatione et sacramentis, et in prima se-

[30] *Who should be given three years*

6. But for those who have the talent for preaching, if two years are perhaps not enough time to cover in class the theological material that seems necessary for them to carry out their duty safely and without error (such as what is taught in the *Summa* of St. Thomas in Part I before the discussion on the angels, in Part III about the Incarnation and the sacraments, and in the First Part of Part II on

cundæ de gratia), poterit tunc illis tertius theologici studii annus ad eam rem concedi; vel certe iuvandi erunt privatis domesticæ alicuius academiæ lectionibus, quibus vel eo biennio, vel postea suppleant, quæ in schola per id tempus non explicantur, omittendo etiam publicas aliarum rerum lectiones, quæ minus ipsis utiles viderentur.

grace),[24] then they can be allowed a third year of theological study for this purpose. Otherwise they will surely have to get support from some in-house academy whose private classes will enable them, either in the two-year period or afterwards, to make up what is not taught in class during that time, missing even the public classes on other matters that seem less useful for them.[25]

[31]   *Quadriennium quibus*

7. Denique si quis esset, ut ingenio non omnino spectabilis, ita regendi vel concionandi facultate et virtute adeo singulari, ut compensaturus videretur perfectam illam theologiæ scientiam, quam Constitutiones requirunt, atque ita e re futurum Societatis iudicaretur, si theologiæ cursum conficeret, huic sane, re prius cum consultoribus communicata, quartus etiam theologiæ annus concedi poterit.

[31]   *Who should be given four years*

7. Finally if there were anyone who, to the extent that he was not entirely remarkable in intelligence, was distinguished by such special personal virtue and capacity for leadership or preaching that he would likely compensate for that finished knowledge of theology asked for by the *Constitutions,* and if it were judged that the Society would benefit from the outcome if he completed the course of theology, then certainly he could be allowed a fourth year of theology, after the consultors have been informed of the matter.[26]

[32]   *Examinandi qui extra Societatem studuerunt*

8. Eodem etiam examine probandi sunt, qui vel totum cursum philosophiæ, aut eius partem, vel partem etiam aliquam theolo-

[32]   *Those who have studied outside the Society must be examined*

8. Also the same examination should be used to test those who have taken either all or part of the philosophical course or also some part of

[24] *Summa:* Part I of St. Thomas Aquinas's *Sumtheol* deals with God and creation, Part II with human beings, and Part III with the topics involved in the human being's return to God. [I]ncarnation: literally "enfleshment," this word refers specifically to God's taking on of human flesh in the person of Jesus as a child of Mary. [S]acraments: religious rituals that directly communicate the grace of Christ. [G]race: a spiritual gift, often explained as a sharing in the life of God.

[25] In-house: the Jesuit residence had an inward "public" or "common" aspect for group events and official business. When something occurs within the context of the community residence, it is designated by some such phrase. The *Constitutions* mentions that "the scholastics of the Society are apart by themselves without being mingled among the externs, although they may have dealings with the externs as far as the superior judges this suitable for greater edification and service to God our Lord" (*ConsCN* C338[v.5] [pp. 338 f.]).

[26] Consultors: official advisers to a superior.

giæ antequam in Societatem ingrederentur, audiverint, ut idem de illis etiam statuatur.

[33] *Studiorum privilegium humilibus fiat*

9. Maxime autem caveat, ne hac studiorum indulgentia et privilegio utatur, nisi erga humiles et vere pios [Lukács: plus] et mortificatos, qui eo non putentur indigni.

[34] *Qui in ipso cursu a studiis amovendi*

10. Si quis etiam forte ex designatis ad philosophiam, aut etiam theologiam audiendam in ipso studiorum decursu mediocritatem eandem vere non excedere videatur, ut initio existimatum erat, similiter debebit post idem examen casuum studiis addici.

[35] *Mediocritatis descriptio*

11. Mediocritas porro, de qua dictum est, ita videtur accipienda, ut accipi vulgo solet, cum aliquis mediocri ingenio esse dicitur; nimirum ut ea intelligat et comprehendat, quæ audit, quibusque studuit, ac de iis etiam rationem poscenti reddere mediocriter possit, etiam si ad eum doctrinæ gradum in philosophia ac theologia non perveniat, quem Constitutiones designant his verbis "satis in ea profecisse," nec possit assertiones, quarum ibi fit mentio, defendere ea eruditione ac facultate, qua defenderet is, cui ingenii satis esset ad philosophiam vel theologiam perdocendam.

theology before they entered the Society, so that the same decision may also be made about them.

[33] *The privilege of studies should be granted to the humble*

9. He should be extremely careful to bestow this gift and privilege of study only on those who are humble and truly devout and mortified, who are not thought unworthy of it.

[34] *Who should be taken out of studies when the course is underway*

10. If it happens that anyone from among those assigned to study philosophy or even theology does not really seem to be exceeding the average in this course of studies that had been anticipated at the beginning, then he must be enrolled in the study of cases in the same manner as after the examination mentioned above.

[35] *Description of the average*

11. Moreover, the average meant in this statement ought to be taken in that sense in which it is commonly taken when someone is said to be of an average talent: namely, that he understands and grasps what he hears and what he has studied, and he can also render a fair account of these things to someone asking him about them, even if he might not arrive at that level of learning in philosophy and theology that the *Constitutions* designate by the words "to have made sufficient progress in them," and he might not be able to defend the assertions mentioned there with the scholarly learning and ability with which the one who has enough talent to learn

philosophy or theology really well might defend them.[27]

[36] *De talentis quomodo iudicandum*

12. De illa autem bonitate talenti ad concionandum vel gubernandum, quam habere debent, qui per biennium daturi sunt operam theologiæ, itemque de singulari talento eorum, quibus ipsum quadriennium concedendum diximus, serio cum suis consultoribus, et aliis gravibus viris, qui eos bene norint, et de huiusmodi rebus iudicare possint, consideret.

[37] *Iudicium provinciali permissum*

13. Verum, quoniam in huiusmodi examine et iudicio ingeniorum solent haud raro discrepantes esse sententiæ, penes provincialem erit, re bene perpensa, perspectis suffragiis, auditisque suis consultoribus, id decernere, quod in Domino iudicaverit expedire ad maiorem Dei gloriam, et commune Societatis bonum; quod si iudicaret non esse quempiam illis studiis applicandum, notet hoc in libro, ut de priori examine dictum est.

[38] *Mathematicæ auditores et tempus*

20. Audiant et secundo philosophiæ anno philosophi omnes in schola tribus circiter horæ quadrantibus mathematicam prælectionem. Si qui præterea sint idonei

[36] *How a decision about talents should be made*

12. But about that excellence of talent for preaching or administration which those who are going to work at theology for two years ought to have, and likewise about that special talent of those to whom we have said even four years should be granted, he should undertake a serious consideration with his consultors and with other men of character and influence who know them well and can make judgments about such matters.

[37] *Decision left to the provincial*

13. But, since opinions about talent usually differ in such an examination and decision, after the matter has been well deliberated, the votes examined, and his own consultors heard, it will rest with the provincial to discern what he judges in the Lord to be of use for the greater glory of God and the common good of the Society. If he decides that some particular person should not be assigned to those studies, he should make a note of it in the book, as has been said of the earlier examination.

[38] *Students of mathematics and their schedule*

20. In the second year of philosophy, all the philosophers should also attend a forty-five-minute mathematics class. Moreover, if there are any who are suitable for these studies and inclined towards them, they should work

---

[27] [D]efend the assertions: respond formally to challenges made.

et propensi ad hæc studia, privatis post cursum lectionibus exerceantur.

[39] *Scholæ inferiores quot*

21 1. Scholæ studiorum inferiorum (omissis propter rationes, quæ afferuntur in parte quarta Constitutionum, abecedariis), non plures quam quinque esse debent, una rhetoricæ, altera humanitatis, et tres grammaticæ.

[40] *Cur non permiscendæ, nec multiplicandæ*

2. Hi enim sunt quinque gradus, ita apte inter se connexi, ut permisceri aut multiplicari nullo modo debeant; tum ne ordinarios etiam magistros frustra multiplicare necesse sit; tum ne multitudo scholarum et ordinum longiore, quam par sit, tempore egeat ad hæc inferiora studia decurrenda.

[41] *Duo ordines in una classe*

3. Quod si scholæ pauciores sint, quam quinque, ne tumquidem hi quinque gradus varientur, sed poterunt duo ordines in una classe ita constitui, ut uterque uni ex iis quinque gradibus respondeat eo modo, quo dicetur regula octava præfecti studiorum inferiorum.

[42] *Altiores classes potius retinendæ*

4. Illud porro curandum, ut quando scholæ pauciores sunt, altiores semper, quoad eius fieri potest, retineantur, sublatis infimis.

on them in private classes after the course.

[39] *How many lower classes*

21. 1. For lower studies (the earliest stages of schooling being left out for the reasons presented in the fourth part of the *Constitutions*),[28] there ought to be not more than five classes: one of rhetoric, a second of humanities, and three of grammar.

[40] *Why they should not be mixed together or multiplied*

2. For these are five grades, linked with one other in such a way that they must by no means be combined or multiplied, first, to avoid having to increase the regular teaching staff uselessly, and second, to avoid having so many classes and levels that more than the right amount of time has to be spent on completing these lower studies.

[41] *Two levels in one class*

3. But if the classes are fewer than five, not even then should these five grades be changed, but two levels can be organized in one class in such a way that each of them corresponds to one of the five grades, as described in the eighth rule for the prefect of lower studies.

[42] *Better to keep the higher classes*

4. Moreover, whenever there are fewer classes, care should be taken to always keep the higher classes, to the extent that it is possible, and to remove the lower ones.

---

[28] [T]he reasons presented in Part IV of the *Constitutions*: "To teach how to read and write would also be a work of charity if the Society had enough members to be able to attend to everything. But because of the lack of members these elementary branches are not ordinarily taught" (*ConsCN* C451ᵛ·² [p. 180]).

[43] *Multiplicandæ interdum scholæ, non gradus*

5. Quando autem dicimus scholas grammaticæ non plures esse debere quam tres, et omnes inferiores non plures, quam quinque, intelligimus non tam de scholarum et magistrorum numero, quam de numero graduum, quos modo descripsimus. Nam si multitudo discipulorum tanta sit, quantæ sufficere non possit unus magister, tunc geminari poterit schola, data a Generali facultate; ita tamen, ut idem gradus, eædem lectiones, eadem ratio ac tempus docendi in utraque retineatur.

[44] *Ubi liceat multiplicare*

6. Hanc tamen geminationem fieri non oportet, nisi ubi sunt studia Societatis universalia, aut ratio exigit fundationis, ne plus quam par sit, Societas oneretur.

[45] *Præstantes humanitatis magistri præparandi*

22. Ad conservandam humaniorum literarum cognitionem, et magistrorum veluti seminarium fovendum, binos minimum aut ternos habere studeat in provincia his literis et eloquentia præstantes. Quod consequetur, si ex iis, qui ad hæc studia idonei propensique sunt, nonnullos subinde huic rei dicare studet, ceteris facultatibus, quantum satis est, excultos; quorum opera ac sedulitate bonorum professorum genus quoddam ac tanquam seges ali ac propagari possit.

[43] *The classes should sometimes be multiplied, but not the grades*

5. But when we say that there should be not more than three classes of grammar nor more than five of all the lower classes, we mean this not about the number of classes and teachers, but about the number of grades that we have just described. For if the number of students becomes so large that one teacher cannot provide for them, then the class can be split, with the permission of the Father General. But this should be done in such a way that the same grade, the same lessons, and the same plan and syllabus are kept in each one.

[44] *Where it is permissible to multiply*

6. This splitting, however, ought not to occur except where the entire range of the Society's studies is found, or where the institution's charter demands it, so that the Society might not be burdened more than is proper.

[45] *Outstanding humanities teachers must be prepared*

22. To preserve the understanding of humanistic literature and to cultivate, as it were, a seedbed of teachers, he should strive to have at least two or three in his province who are outstanding in this literature and in eloquence. He will achieve this if he regularly takes pains to dedicate to this project some of those who are suitable for and inclined toward these studies and sufficiently accomplished in the other subjects. Through their energetic effort, a certain type and (as it were) a crop of good professors can be raised and multiplied.

[46] *Grammatica Emmanuelis*

23. Dabit operam, ut nostri magistri utantur Grammatica Emmanuelis. Quod si methodi accuratioris, quam puerorum captus ferat, alicubi videatur, vel romanam accipiat, vel similem curet conficiendam, consulto præposito generali; salva tamen ipsa vi ac proprietate omnium præceptorum Emmanuelis.

[47] *Magistri perpetui*

24. Perpetuos grammaticæ ac rhetoricæ magistros, quam potest plurimos, paret. Id autem fiet, si post absoluta casuum, aut etiam theologiæ studia nonnullos, quos magis in hoc quam in alio munere Societatis iuvare posse in Domino iudicaverit, ad id strenue applicet, horteturque, ut se totos in tam salutare opus ob maius Dei obsequium impendant.

[48] *Ab ingressu parandi, nec removendi*

25. Proderit etiam in ipso Societatis ingressu aliquos, qui ad id accommodati viderentur, quique propter ætatem vel ingenium in gravioribus studiis profecturi non essent, hac conditione recipere, ut vitam suam in his literis docendis divino obsequio dicare velint;

[46] *Emmanuel's "Grammar"*

23. He will see to it that our teachers use Emmanuel's *Grammar*.[29] But if somewhere it seems to be too elaborately detailed for the boys to grasp, he should use the Roman grammar or he should have something like it formulated, after consultation with the general superior, as long as the substance and the particular qualities of all of Emmanuel's rules are kept.

[47] *Career teachers*

24. He should prepare as many career teachers of grammar and rhetoric as he can. This will come about if, after their studies of cases or even of theology are completed, he promptly assigns to this undertaking some whom he has judged in the Lord to be capable of being of greater assistance in this than in another work of the Society, and urges them to devote themselves completely to such a good work in order to make an even greater act of submission to God.

[48] *Those who should be prepared from their entrance and not removed*

25. It will also be advantageous to accept some into the Society only on the condition that they are willing to dedicate their lives under holy obedience to this teaching of language and humanistic literary studies.[30] They should seem fit for this kind of work

---

[29] Emmanuel's *Grammar*: Emmanuel Alvarez (Manoel Alvarus; 1526–82), *De institutione grammatica libri tres juxta editionem Venetam anni 1575*, the famous Latin grammar. The author entered the Society in 1546 and served as rector at Jesuit colleges at Coimbra and Évora.

[30] [U]nder holy obedience: that is, under the religious vow of obedience. This expression signifies the Society's most serious, binding acceptance of the individual's authentic self-offering. This is one point at which the *Ratio* clearly seems to assume for itself a very high place in the Society's Institute, since it is here directing the provincial on the constitution and missioning of its membership. This area passes beyond the sphere of the educational plan and seems to belong to other essential organizational matter typically treated by the *Constitutions*.

quod etiam adnotetur in libro provincialis. Hi vero vel ante, vel postquam aliquot annos docuerint, prout in Domino visum fuerit, aliquid ex conscientiæ casibus audire et sacerdotes fieri poterunt, ad idem docendi munus reversuri; ab quo non removeantur sine gravi causa et consultatione; nisi interdum ob defatigationem, ut uno aut altero anno intermittant, præpositus provincialis statuerit.

and not likely to go far in the more advanced studies on account of their age or talent. This also should be noted in the provincial's book. But either before or after they have taught for several years, just as it seems good in the Lord, they will be able to follow part of the course in cases of conscience and become priests, and then return to this service of teaching. They should not be removed from it without serious cause and consultation, unless occasionally the provincial superior should decide that they should have a break for one or two years on account of fatigue.

[49] *A docendi munere non eximendi*

26. Discipulos interim nostros provincialis a docenda grammatica vel humanitate non eximat, nisi aliter ob ætatem aut aliam rationem statuendum in Domino videatur.

[49] *They are not to be excused from the service of teaching*

26. The provincial should not exempt our followers in training from the teaching of grammar or the humanities unless it seems in the Lord good to decide otherwise, on account of age or some other reason.

[50] *Ex cursu ad theologi eligendi*

27. Ex singulis tamen cursibus seligat singulos aut binos ternosve, seu plures pro numero discipulorum, qui plus ceteris profecturi videantur, quos theologiæ applicet; quibus tamen, si necesse sit, vel si videatur, uti poterit, absolutis studiis et tertio anno probationis, ad docendam etiam grammaticam seu studia humanitatis.

[50] *Those to be selected for theology from the course of studies*

27. Still, from each course of studies he should select a certain one or two or three or more, in proportion to the number of students, who are likely to go further than the rest, and he should assign them to theology. Nevertheless, if it is necessary, or if it seems right, he can employ them in teaching even grammar or the humanities after their studies and their third year of probation are finished.[31]

---

[31] Third year of probation: "The period of time required for admission in the manner mentioned should always be more than two years. But if one who was tested for a long time before being sent to his studies or during them; and if he ought to be admitted to profession, he will have another year after the completion of these studies to become still better known before pronouncing it" (*ConsCN* C514 [pp. 194, 196]). This year has come to be known as "tertianship."

[51] *Magisterii tempus*

28. Enitendum, ut scholis nequaquam præficiatur, qui philosophiam, si eam audituri sunt, nondum audierint, cum qui iam audierint, non desunt.

[52] *Initium docendi a qua schola*

29. Curandum etiam, ut nostri initium docendi faciant ab ea schola, qua superiores scientia sint, ut sic quotannis ad altiorem gradum cum bona parte suorum auditorum possint ascendere.

[53] *Academia ad magistros instituendos*

30. Atque ut instructiores sint, quando ad docendum veniunt, pernecessarium est, ut privata academia ad id exerceantur quod rectori valde commendetur, quo, ut est in eius regula 9, diligenter efficiatur.

[54] *Confessarii non desint*

31. Efficiat, ut in collegiis præsertim primariis, in quibus numerus externorum discipulorum copiosior est, plures sint confessarii, ne ad unum omnes ire necesse sit; quam etiam ob causam extraordinarii interdum exponantur, ut magis poenitentibus satisfiat.

[55] *Nec coadiutores*

32. In collegiis vero, præsertim minoribus, operam dabit, ut coadiutorum satis sit, ne magistrorum et

[51] *Time for the teaching assignment*

28. There should be a real effort to put nobody in charge of classes who has not yet taken philosophy, if he is going to study it, when there is no lack of those who have already studied it.

[52] *At which class the teaching should begin*

29. Care should also be taken that Jesuits begin their teaching with that class about whose content they are more knowledgeable, so that each year they may be able to rise to a higher level with a sizeable number of their students.

[53] *Academies for training teachers*

30. And, so that they may be better prepared when they start their teaching, it is mandatory that they be trained in a private academy toward this end. The rector has the full responsibility of seeing that careful attention is given to bringing this about, as it stands in his ninth rule.[32]

[54] *Confessors should not be lacking*

31. He should ensure that in the colleges, especially the main ones in which the number of non-Jesuit students is rather high, there should be a greater number of confessors so that everybody does not have to go to one person. Also, for this same reason, confessors different from the usual ones should sometimes be made available, to better serve the needs of the penitents.

[55] *Nor should lay brothers*

32. But in the colleges, especially the smaller ones, he will see to it that there are enough lay brothers to keep

---

[32] His ninth rule: see §83 below.

discipulorum opera rector ad munera domestica uti cogatur.

[56] *Reditus pro bibliotheca*

33. Ne nostris quantum satis est, librorum desit, aliquem redditum annuum sive ex collegii ipsius bonis, sive aliunde, amplificandæ bibliothecæ attribuat; quem alios in usus convertere nulla ratione liceat.

[57] *Abstinendum a libris inhonestis*

34. Omni vigilantia caveat, maximi momenti id esse ducendo, ut omnino in scholis nostris abstineatur a libris poetarum, aut quibuscunque, qui honestati bonisque moribus nocere queant, nisi prius a rebus et verbis inhonestis purgati sint; vel si omnino purgari non poterunt, quemadmodum Terentius, potius non legantur, ne rerum qualitas animorum puritatem offendat.

[58] *Constantia in scholarum horis et vacationibus*

35. Constituat, quibusnam toto anno horis inchoandæ finiendæque sint scholæ, ubi certis anni temporibus variantur. Quod autem constitutum fuerit, in eo constanter perseverandum; sicut nec facile permittendum, ut dies vacationis hebdomadariæ differatur aut anti-

the rector from being forced to employ the labors of teachers and students for household duties.

[56] *Revenue for the library*

33. So that Jesuits have a sufficient supply of books, he should set apart for the expansion of the library holdings some annual revenue either from the properties of the college itself or from elsewhere. It should not be permissible to switch this revenue over to other uses for any reason.

[57] *Unseemly books have to be avoided*

34. Taking it as a matter of the greatest importance, he should with all vigilance and caution see to it that in our schools we avoid entirely the books of poets or whatever material can injure moral integrity and good character, unless they have first been expurgated of unseemly language and subject matter; otherwise, if they can not be completely expurgated, as Terence cannot,[33] it is better that they not be read, so that the nature of the material does not damage anyone's innocence.

[58] *Keeping to class schedules and vacations*

35. Where seasonal changes make a difference, he should decide the starting and ending times for classes for the entire year. The schedule decided upon should be followed consistently. Just so, it should not be easily allowed that the weekly break day is delayed or anticipated.[34] And care should be taken

---

[33] Terence: famous Roman comic playwright (195–159? B.C.), very popular among the Renaissance humanists for the elegance of his language.

[34] Break day: see §§70 and 93 below. This is a day on which the ordinary schedule is altered or interrupted for free time but some class room activity can also take place, as described in §376 below: "On a break day, a historian or a poet should be taught, or something pertaining to

cipetur; curandumque, ut ordo dierum, quibus docendum et quibus vacandum est, omnino servetur.

to keep in its entirety the calendar of school days and free days.

[59]   Vacatio

36. Ut assiduitas in literario exercitio, sic et aliqua remissio necessaria est; cavendum tamen, ne ullæ novæ vacationes introducantur; et in iis, quæ præscribuntur, constantia servetur. De quibus hæc potissimum dicenda sunt:

[59]   *Vacation*

36. Just as constant application is necessary in literary training, so also is some relaxation from the effort. Still, beware of the introduction of any new vacation times and consistently keep the ones prescribed. About this, these points are especially important to make:

[60]   *Vacatio generalis*

37. 1. Anniversariæ vacationes generales classium superiorum breviores non sint uno mense, nec longiores duobus. Rhetorica, nisi mos universitatis aliud exigat, mense vacet; humanitas tribus hebdomadis, suprema grammaticæ duabus, una tantum reliquæ.

[60]   *General vacation*

37. 1. Yearly general vacations for the higher classes should not be briefer than one month, nor longer than two. The rhetoric class should be free for a month unless the custom of the university demands something else; the humanities class, for three weeks; the most advanced class of grammar for two; the remaining classes only for one.

[61]   *Dies festi*

2. Ut certi statique sint dies festi, quorum numerum minui magis, quam augeri oportet, eorum catalogum conficiendum curet pro suæ regionis ritu.

[61]   *Feast days*

2. So that the feast days are set and sure[35]—and the number of these should be diminished rather than increased—he should see to it that a full list is drawn up, according to the religious practice of his locale.

[62] 3. A vigilia natalis Domini ad festum usque Circumcisionis diem classes superiores, inferiores vero a meridie eiusdem vigiliæ

[62] 3. From Christmas Eve up to the feast of the Circumcision the higher classes should be free;[36] the lower ones, however, should be free

---

scholarly learning; and this should be reviewed."

[35] Feast days: days of celebration in honor of holy persons, institutions, or events, marked with special liturgies for the occasions.

[36] Christmas Eve: December 24, the day before Christmas, which celebrates the birth of Jesus. Circumcision: January 1, a feast in commemoration of Jesus' circumcision, as prescribed in the sacred laws of Israel.

usque ad festum diem sanctorum Innocentium vacent.

from the noon of the eve, up to the feast of the Holy Innocents.[37]

[63] 4. A Quinquagesima vacetur, ubi mos erit, usque ad feriam quartam Cinerum; quo tamen die post meridiem magistri omnes doceant.

[63] 4. From Quinquagesima Sunday, there should be a holiday up to Ash Wednesday where it is the custom.[38] But on that day, all the teachers should conduct class after noon.

[64] 5. A dominica Palmarum usque ad dominicam in Albis superiores classes, inferiores autem a meridie quartæ feriæ maioris hebdomadæ usque ad feriam tertiam Paschatis vacent.

[64] 5. From Palm Sunday up to Low Sunday, the higher classes should be free, but the lower ones should be free from noon of the Wednesday of Holy Week up to Easter Tuesday.[39]

[65] 6. A vigilia Pentecostes in scholis superioribus, in inferioribus a meridie eiusdem vigiliæ usque ad feriam tertiam vacetur, et præterea feria quinta.

[65] 6. From the eve of Pentecost in the higher classes, and in the lower ones from noon of the eve, there should be free time up to Tuesday, and on Thursday besides.[40]

[66] 7. Pridie solemnitatis Corporis Domini tum inferiores, tum superiores a meridie solum vacent; contra vero in Commemoratione defunctorum solum ante meridiem.

[66] 7. On the day before the solemnity of Corpus Christi, both lower and higher classes should be free only from noon. But on the other hand, on All Soul's Day, they should be free only before noon.[41]

---

[37] Feast of the Holy Innocents: December 28, a feast commemorating the innocent male babies killed by Herod as recounted in Matt. 2:16–18.

[38] Quinquagesima Sunday: approximately fifty days before Easter, the feast of the Resurrection of Jesus. In some traditions, it marks the beginning of a period of fasting. The date of Easter varies from year to year, falling sometime between March 22 and April 25. Ash Wednesday: The Wednesday after Quinquagesima Sunday, marking the beginning of Lent, a forty-day period of fasting, abstinence, and penitential practices preceding the celebration of Easter. February 5 is the earliest possible date for Ash Wednesday, March 10 the latest.

[39] Palm Sunday: the last Sunday of Lent, commemorating the entrance of Jesus into Jerusalem in the days immediately preceding his passion and death. Low Sunday: the first Sunday after Easter. Holy Week: the week preceding Easter, covering the important memorials of Jesus' Passion and Death. Easter Tuesday: the Tuesday after Easter.

[40] Pentecost: the celebration of the Holy Spirit's descent upon the apostles fifty days after the Resurrection, recounted in the New Testament in the second chapter of the Acts of the Apostles.

[41] Solemnity of Corpus Christi: the celebration of the institution of the Eucharist (Holy Communion), which is the sacrament in which the Body and Blood of Christ is communicated under the appearances of bread and wine. Until recently, this feast was celebrated on the Thursday after Trinity Sunday, which is the Sunday after Easter. Now this feast falls on the second Sunday after Easter. All Soul's Day: the commemoration of the souls of the faithful departed, usually falling on November 2.

[67]   8. Porro his diebus, quibus scholæ tantum inferiores habentur, nihil de legitimo tempore diminuatur.

[68]   *Supplicationes*

9. Si quando per supplicationes publicas non liceat habere scholas antemeridianas, pomeridianæ certe habeantur; in Rogationibus tamen etiam antemeridianæ, ubi ea consuetudo viget.

[69]   *Hebdomadaria vacatio*

10. Saltem singulis hebdomadis dies unus quieti destinatus sit. Quod si duo dies festi in unam hebdomadam inciderint, nullus præterea erit vacationis dies, nisi forte id sæpius atque ita accidat, ut alter in diem Lunæ, alter in sabbathi diem incidat; tum enim poterit alius dies indulgeri. Quod si unus in hebdomada dies festus fuerit, isque dies Mercurii vel Iovis, eo die vacetur, non alio; sin autem die Lunæ aut sabbathi, cessabitur item die Mercurii vel Iovis; si denique die Martis aut Veneris, tunc si concio non habeatur, et liceat honestæ recreationi operam dare, non vacabitur alio die; si non liceat, vacabitur rursus die Iovis aut Mercurii.

[70]   *Diversa pro ratione classium*

11. Et in superioribus quidem classibus hebdomadariæ cessationi dabitur integer dies. In

[67]   8. Furthermore, on the days on which only the lower classes are held, the scheduled time should not be reduced at all.

[68]   *Supplications*

9. If public supplications ever make morning classes impossible,[42] afternoon classes should certainly be held. Nevertheless, on Rogation Days, where that custom is popular, there should be morning classes as well.[43]

[69]   *Weekly time off*

10. At least once a week one day should be marked out for rest. But if two feast days fall within one week, there will be no extra time off, unless it happens fairly often and in such a way that one falls on a Monday, the other on a Saturday; for then another day can be granted. But if one feast day falls in a week, and that is a Wednesday or a Thursday, there will be a break on that day and not on another. But if it is on a Monday or a Saturday, the same kind of free time will fall on the Wednesday or Thursday. Finally if it is on Tuesday or Friday, if a sermon is not being given, and if time can be given to solid recreation, then there will not be any other break day. If such recreation is impossible, there will be a break again on Thursday or Wednesday.

[70]   *Differences by class*

11. And in the higher classes, to be sure, a whole day will be given to the weekly break. In the lower class-

---

[42] Public supplications: prayers that call for the presence of an entire community in a given jurisdiction.

[43] Rogation Days: "The Rogation Days are the 25th of April, called Major, and the three days before the feast of the Ascension, called Minor." For a fuller explanation of this term, see endn. 10.

inferioribus vero ante meridiem docetur, in rhetorica per horam cum dimidiata, in ceteris per duas horas; post meridiem omnes vacant; ab initio tamen iunii omnes tota die.

[71] *Observatio libri studiorum*

38. Denique, ut totus hic Societatis labor ad maiorem Dei gloriam bene succedat, videat, ut omnes tum superiores tum inferiores perfecte observent suas, quæ ad rationem studiorum pertinent, regulas.

[72] *Varietas pro varietate regionum*

39. Et quoniam pro regionum, temporum ac personarum varietate in ordine et statutis horis studio tribuendis, in repetitionibus, disputationibus et aliis exercitationibus, itemque in vacationibus potest varietas accidere, si quid in sua provincia magis expedire ad maiorem in literis profectum existimabit, referat ad præpositum generalem, ut ea demum statuantur, quæ ad omnia necessaria descendant; ita tamen ut ad communem ordinem studiorum nostrorum maxime accedant.

[73] *Pietatis et morum præcipua cura*

40. Ad extremum, quæ de pietate et disciplina morum ac de doctrina christiana tradenda in regulis inferiorum magistrorum, et quæ de moribus ac pietate in communibus omnium magistrorum regulis præcipiuntur, ut proxime

es, there will be class before noon: in rhetoric for an hour and a half, in the rest, for two hours. After noon, everyone is free; but from the beginning of June, everyone has the entire day free.

[71] *Following the book of studies*

38. Finally, so that this entire work of the Society might prosper well with respect to the greater glory of God, he should see to it that all classes, both higher and lower, perfectly follow their own rules, the ones pertaining to the plan of their studies.

[72] *Diversity according to the diversity of locales*

39. And since, in accordance with the diversity of locales, times, and persons, there can also arise diversity in the order and designation of the study hours, in reviews, disputations, and other exercises, and likewise in free times,[44] if he believes that something would facilitate greater progress in literary studies within his own province, he should report it to the Father General, so that whatever is necessary might be determined in detail, yet still in such a way that they might most nearly approximate our common educational plan.

[73] *Special care for religious devotion and morals*

40. Ultimately, he should think that the following things, stressed so many times in the *Constitutions,* are especially recommended to him as elements that most directly bear on the welfare of souls: whatever the rules for the teachers of the lower classes require to be

---

[44] Disputations: structured academic exercises in which a person presents theses and defends them against questioners.

ad salutem animorum spectantia, et toties in Constitutionibus inculcata, sibi præcipue commendata putet.

[74] Singuli sub anni cuiusque finem serio examinandi erunt per designatos examinatores, rectore præsente, et ipso provinciali, si possit; nemoque a primo anno philosophiæ ad secundum, aut e secundo ad tertiam admittendus, qui mediocritatem non attigerit; hoc est ut ea quæ audivit, bene intelligat, ac de iis etiam rationem possit reddere. Ad theologiam vero scholasticam audiendam nemo admittetur qui mediocitatem in philosophia non superarit; ita nimirum, ut eius assertiones defendere tuerique cum approbatione possit; nisi forte præclara in mediocri aliquo ad gubernandum aut concionandum talenta eluceant, propter quæ aliud statuendum provinciali videatur; cui nulla in ceteris dispensandi sit facultas.

imparted about religious devotion and moral training and Christian doctrine, and whatever the common rules of all teachers prescribe about morals and religious devotion.

[74] *[Attached to the end of 19.1 in the 1616 edition. See [25].]*

Toward the end of every year, they ought to be rigorously tested by designated examiners in the presence of the rector and the provincial himself, if possible. No one who has not achieved the average level should be passed on from the first to the second year of philosophy or from the second to the third. This means that they understand well the things they have heard and also are able to explain them. No one who has not done better than average in philosophy should be allowed to take classes in Scholastic theology; that is to say that he is able to defend philosophical assertions and to support them with proofs. An exception might be made for someone of only average ability if he displays extraordinary talent for administration or preaching. On that basis, a different decision might seem right to the provincial. In other cases, he has no authorization to dispense.

[H2] Regulæ Rectoris

[75] *Studiorum cura*

1. Cum ideo collegia et universitates Societas amplectatur, ut in his nostri commode possint et doctrina ceterisque rebus, quæ ad adiuvandas animas conferunt, instrui, et quæ didicerint ipsi, communicare cum proximis; post religiosarum et solidarum virtutum curam, quæ præcipua esse debet,

[H2] Rules for the Rector

[75] *Interest in education*

1. The Society eagerly undertakes secondary and higher education so that Jesuits can be properly instructed both in doctrine and in the other matters that contribute to helping souls, and so that they can share with their neighbors what they themselves have learned. Therefore, after his rightly

in illud maxime incumbat, ut finem hunc, quem in gymnasiis admittendis Societas sibi proposuit, Deo juvante, consequatur.

foremost concern for religious and essential human virtues, he should devote himself especially to achieving, with the help of God, this final goal that the Society has set before itself in allowing schooling to be part of its mission.

[76] *Præfecti auctoritas*

2. Ad studia moderanda adiutorem habebit studiorum præfectum, cui omnem tribuet potestatem, quam ad rectam eius officii administrationem pertinere iudicabit.

[76] *Authority of the prefect*

2. For managing the studies he will have a prefect of studies as an assistant and delegate to him all the authority that he judges to pertain to the correct administration of that office.

[77] *Literariis exercitationibus intersit*

3. Ita reliqua negotia dispenset ac temperet, ut omnes literarias exercitationes fovere atque amplificare possit. Adeat interdum scholas etiam inferiores; frequenter intersit theologorum philosophorumque disputationibus, tum privatis tum publicis; an et quibus de causis huius exercitationis fructus impediatur, observet.

[77] *He should be present at literary exercises*

3. He should so arrange and regulate the rest of his work that he can foster and promote all the literary exercises. Sometimes he should go to the classes, even the lower ones. He should frequently attend the disputations of theologians and philosophers, both private and public. He should note whether the productivity of these exercises is being hampered and why.

[78] *Præcidendæ discipulis occupationes*

4. Nullo modo ferat auditorum quempiam a disputationibus aut repetitionibus abesse, ut omnes eam rem magnæ sibi curæ esse intelligant; proinde occupationes omnes discipulis præcidat, quæ studiis impedimento esse possint.

[78] *Students' activities to be curtailed*

4. In no way should he tolerate any student's absence from the disputations or the review sessions so that everyone might realize that it is a matter of great concern to him. Accordingly, he should curtail all student activities that can interfere with studies.

[79] *Præsertim biennio repetentibus*

5. Eos qui biennio recolunt theologiam, habendis concionibus in ecclesiis, vel in cænobiis virginum, quam minime potest, occupet; idque consulto provinciali.

[79] *Especially for those in the two-year review*

5. He should occupy those who are reviewing theology in two years as little as he possibly can with preaching sermons in churches or in convents of religious women. If he does so occupy

them, it should only be after consulting the provincial.

[80] *Magistris qui substituendi*

6. Ex iisdem, si quando ordinarii vel philosophiæ vel theologiæ præceptores desint, in eorum loco aliquos suffici par erit;. iidemque poterunt, si opus sit, domesticis tum repetitionibus tum disputationibus præceptorum loco præsidere; immo etiam, consulto provinciali, philosophiam vel theologiam in scholis ad tempus prælegere.

[80] *Who ought to be substituted for the teachers*

6. If the regularly assigned teachers of the philosophers or theologians are ever unavailable, it will be proper for some of those making the two-year review of theology to take their places. And, if need be, these substitutes will be able to preside in place of the teachers in both the reviews and the disputations held in the house. In fact, after consultation with the provincial, they will even be able to give classes for a time in philosophy and theology.

[81] *Linguarum academiæ*

7. Efficiat, ut hebrææ græcæque linguæ academiæ instituantur inter nostros; in quibus academici bis aut ter in hebdomada certo aliquo, puta vacationis, tempore sic exerceantur, ut inde prodire possint, qui harum linguarum scientiam et dignitatem privatim ac publice tueantur.

[81] *Academies for languages*

7. He should have Greek- and Hebrew-language academies established among Jesuits, in which, two or three times a week, at some set time like the break days, the participants should practice in such a way that they might go on from there to safeguard the knowledge and the standing of these languages, privately and publicly.

[82] *Linguæ Latinæ usus*

8. Domi linguæ latinæ usum inter scholasticos diligenter conservandum curet. Ab hac autem latine loquendi lege non eximantur, nisi vacationum dies et recreationis horæ, nisi forte in aliquibus regionibus provinciali videretur his etiam temporibus facile posse hunc latine loquendi usum retineri. Faciendum quoque, ut nostri, qui nondum studia absolverunt, literas cum ad nostros scribunt, scribant latine. Bis præterea aut ter in anno, cum aliqua celebritas, ut renovationis studiorum

[82] *Use of the Latin language*

8. He should ensure that at home the use of the Latin language is carefully maintained among the students. They should not be exempted from this regulation about speaking Latin except for break days and recreation hours, unless in some regions it seems to the provincial that the practice of speaking Latin can easily be kept during these times as well. He should also make sure that when Jesuits who have not yet finished their studies write letters to one another, they should write in Latin. In addition, two or three times a year, during some special cele-

aut votorum agitur, philosophi etiam ac theologi carminum aliquid condant affigantque.

bration, like the inauguration of studies or the renewal of vows, the philosophers and the theologians as well should compose and post some poetry.[45]

[83] *Academia ad magistros instituendos*

9. Ne magistri classium inferiorum docendi rudes ad docendum accedant, collegii, ex quo humaniorum literarum et grammaticæ magistri solent educi, rector deligat unum aliquem docendi peritissimum ad quem sub finem studiorum ter in hebdomada per horam conveniant proxime futuri præceptores ad novum instituendi magisterium; idque vicissim prælegendo, dictando, scribendo, emendando, aliaque munia boni præceptoris obeundo.

[83] *Academy for training teachers*

9. So that the teachers of the lower classes do not begin their teaching unskilled in that art, the rector of the college from which teachers of humanities and grammar usually come should choose some particular expert teacher,[46] and, right before the end of their studies, those who are just about to be teachers should gather to meet with him three times a week for an hour to be trained for their new position in teaching. They will be trained by taking turns in giving lessons, dictating, writing, correcting, and performing the other duties of a good teacher.

[84] *Rhetores nostri quomodo erudiendi*

10. Si nostri rhetores et humanistæ vel ad publicas non accedunt prælectiones, vel accedunt quidem, is tamen, qui scholæ præest, et externos discipulos exercet, non potest nimio fortasse oneri externorum et nostrorum probe instituendorum sufficere, nostros alteri cuipiam idoneo rector committat, a quo ex formula in regulis professoris rhetoricæ præ-

[84] *How our students of rhetoric are to be trained*

10. If our rhetoricians and students of the humanities either do not attend public class lectures, or do attend them but the one who is in charge of the class and trains non-Jesuit students can perhaps not sufficiently manage the task of properly training both Jesuit and non-Jesuit students, then the rector should entrust the Jesuits to some other suitable person to give them in-house practice privately, according to

---

[45] [I]nauguration of studies: special ceremonies to mark the opening of the school year.

[T]he renewal of vows: in some religious orders, the religious vows of poverty, chastity, and obedience, even if they are perpetual rather then temporary, are repeated yearly in a ceremony reaffirming the original commitment, especially for those who are still in formation. "St. Ignatius of Loyola laid down that in his order there should be a simple profession, followed by more or less frequent renewal of vows until such time as the candidate should be prepared for the solemn or definitive profession; this under Pius IX and Leo XIII has become the common law of all religious orders" (*CathEncy*, s.vv. "Religious Profession").

[46] Rector: for a discussion of the meaning of the term "rector," see endn. 11.

scripta domi privatim diligenter exerceantur.

[85] *Quomodo exercendi*

11. Videat etiam, ut interdum aliquæ a nostris rhetoricis orationes aut poemata latine vel græce, tum in mensa habeantur tum in aula, de re aliqua ad ædificationem domesticorum et externorum pertinente, qua ad perfectiora in Domino animentur; aliæque exercitationes non desint, quæ in Constitutionibus commendantur.

[86] *Externi ad rhetoricam hortandi*

12. Curandum est, ut alumni nostri sive convictores annum (quoad eius fieri potest) rhetoricam audiant, antequam philosophiam aggrediantur; eorumque parentibus, quantum id expediat, demonstrandum. Ceteris quoque externis idem suadendum; qui, si volent nihilominus aliam rationem sequi, cogendi non erunt; si qui tamen adhuc plane pueri ad philosophiam velint accedere, ex quibus perturbatio potius timeatur, posset cum iis agi, quod cum illis, qui nollent promissione obligari, vel nomina in matriculam dare, agendum Constitutiones statuunt.

the pattern prescribed in the rules for the professor of rhetoric.

[85] *How they should practice*

11. He should also see to it that from time to time some speeches or poems in Latin or Greek are given by our rhetoricians both at table and in the meeting hall. These should be about some subject relevant to the edification of those residing in the community and of the non-Jesuits, to make them eager to attain a higher stage of spiritual fulfillment in the Lord. And the other exercises that are called for in the *Constitutions* should not be left out.

[86] *Non-Jesuits ought to be encouraged to study rhetoric*

12. He should make sure that our day students or boarders take a year of rhetoric (to the extent that this is possible) before they take up philosophy. Their parents, too, should be shown how helpful it is. The rest of the non-Jesuits should be persuaded likewise; but if they still wish to follow some other plan, they should not be compelled. If, however, any who are still clearly boys wish to pass on to philosophy studies,[47] and there is a reason to fear that there will more likely be some disturbance from them, they can receive the treatment set by the *Constitutions* for those who do not want to be

---

[47] [W]ho are still clearly boys: the *Constitutions* suggests, "The suitable age seems to be from fourteen to twenty-three years, unless the students are persons who possess a basic knowledge of letters" (*ConsCN C*338^{v11} [p. 139]).

obliged by a promise,[48] or who do not want to give their names at registration.

[87] *Tragœdiæ et comœdiæ*

13. Tragoediarum et comoedia-rum, quas non nisi latinas ac raris-simas esse oportet, argumentum sacrum sit ac pium; neque quic-quam actibus interponatur, quod non latinum sit et decorum, nec persona ulla muliebris vel habitus introducatur.

[88] *Præmia*

14. Præmia distribui publice poterunt semel quotannis; modo id fiat sumptu clarorum hominum, eoque moderato pro scholarum numero collegiique ratione. Eorum autem, qui sumptus suppeditant, in ipsa præmiorum distributione honorifica mentio erit facienda. Magna autem cura caveat, ne dis-cipuli, dum se ad huiusmodi res comparant, morum faciant studio-rumve iacturam.

[89] *Oratio in studiorum renovatione*

15. Non committat, ut oratio in studiorum instauratione publice ab alio, quam a magistro aliquo insig-niore, nisi necessitas cogat, habeatur.

[90] *Quæ scriptiones in codi-cem referendæ*

16. Servandum curet, quod est in regulis præfecti bibliothecæ de referendis in codicem his rebus,

[87] *Tragedies and comedies*

13. The subject matter of the trage-dies and comedies, which ought to be only in Latin and extremely rare, should be holy and devotional. And nothing that is not in Latin and proper should be inserted into the action, nor should any female character or cloth-ing be introduced.

[88] *Awards*

14. Once every year, awards can be distributed publicly, provided that this happens at the expense of well-known persons, scaled to fit the college's size and scope. An honorable mention of those who provide the funding ought to be made in the course of the award ceremony. But he should take special care that, while the students are get-ting themselves ready for such an event, they do not lose moral or aca-demic ground.

[89] *Speech at the inauguration of studies*

15. He should not assign the speech at the inauguration of studies to some-one other than some quite distin-guished teacher, unless he absolutely has to do this.

[90] *What writings are to be recorded in the book*

16. He should take care to observe what is in the rules of the librarian about recording in a register the items

[48] [T]he treatment set by the *Constitutions:* "If some should be unwilling either to bind themselves with a promise or to enter their names on the list, the door of the schools should not for that reason be closed to them, provided that they behave peacefully and give no scandal in the schools. They should be told this, but also informed that more particular care is taken of the stu-dents named on the list" (*ConsCN* C496[vv.3, 4] [p. 188]).

quæ publice exhibentur scribunturque in collegio seu extra collegium a nostris; hoc est, dialogis, orationibus, versibus, et aliis huiusmodi, præfecto aut aliis harum rerum peritis dato negotio seligendi.

[91] *Librorum distributio*

17. Bibliothecarium in librorum distributione a studiorum præfecti præscripto iubeat non discedere.

[92] *Consultationes magistrorum*

18. Singulis aut alternis saltem mensibus consultationes habeat omnium magistrorum infra logicam, præsente utroque præfecto; ceterorum etiam interdum, præsente præfecto generali; in quibus primum aliquid ex regulis magistrorum tum communibus omnium, præsertim iis, quæ ad pietatem ac morum disciplinam spectant, tum propriis singulorum ex ordine recitetur. Moneat autem, cuique licere proponere, si quid in iis difficultatis occurrat, aut si quid forte non observetur.

[93] *Hebdomadaria cessatio*

19. Scholæ inferiores hebdomadaria cessatione non careant semel in hebdomada vel per integrum diem, vel saltem pomeridianis horis, prout regionum usus tulerit.

[94] *Magistrorum fovenda alacritas*

20. Studeat etiam diligenter caritate religiosa magistrorum fovere alacritatem; curetque, ne muneribus domesticis gravius onerentur.

that Jesuits publicly present and write in the college or outside of it: namely, dialogs, speeches, verses, and other materials of this sort. The prefect or other competent persons ought to be given the task of selecting them.

[91] *Distribution of books*

17. He should tell the librarian not to deviate from the instructions of the prefect of studies in the distribution of the books.

[92] *Consultations with the teachers*

18. Every month, or at least every other month, he should hold consultations with all the teachers of classes below logic in the presence of both prefects. He should also sometimes have consultations with the others in the presence of the general prefect. In these consultations, something from the rules of teachers should first be read aloud, both those shared by everyone, especially those regarding religious devotion and morality, and from those special to each of the grades, following the levels in order. And he should remind them that anyone may raise any difficulty that is coming up in the rules or anything that might not be getting observed.

[93] *Weekly recess*

19. The lower classes should not go without a break once a week, either for a whole day or at least for the afternoon hours, according to what is allowed by local usage.

[94] *The teachers' enthusiasm ought to be fostered*

20. In a spirit of religious charity, he should also diligently foster the enthusiasm of the teachers, and he should take care not to burden them

Quod autem rectori præscribitur regula vigesima quinta sui officii, id peculiari studio cum iis exequatur.

[95] *Exhortationes ad discipulos*
21. Deliberet, an præter magistrorum hebdomadarias exhortationes, alia insuper a patre quopiam gravi habenda sit singulis vel alternis mensibus in loco aliquo ampliore; in quem inferiores tantum, vel etiam superiores classes cogantur; et an ex usu sit, ut ipsemet præfectus aliusve per classes interdum monita salutaria et propria puerorum tradat.

[96] *Præfecti atrii regulæ*
22. Ubi præfecto studiorum inferiorum a provinciali socius addetur, qui et atrii præfectus dici poterit, ad illum pertinebit regula secunda præfecti inferioris et regulæ eiusdem, quæ ad mores pertinent a numero trigesimo septimo usque ad finem; et, si videatur, regulæ de novis examinandis a numero nono usque ad tertium decimum.

[97] *Congregatio B. Virginis*
23. Det operam, ut Divæ Mariæ Annunciatæ congregatio ex Romano Collegio in suum propagetur; cui qui nomen non dederit, non esset in academiam, in qua recoli

too heavily with household duties. With a particular zeal, he should carry out with them what is prescribed for the rector in the twenty-fifth rule of his office.

[95] *Exhortation to the students*
21. He should weigh carefully whether, beyond the teachers' weekly exhortations, additional ones should be given by some respected father every one or two months in some more spacious setting where only the lower, or the higher classes as well, should be assembled; or it should be customary that the prefect himself or someone else should occasionally impart advice helpful and appropriate for the boys, class by class.

[96] *Rules for the prefect of the courtyard*
22. When the provincial has assigned to the prefect of lower studies an assistant, who can also be called the prefect of the courtyard, the second rule of the lower prefect will pertain to him, as will the lower prefect's rules that apply to morals from number 37 up to the end;[49] and, if it seems good, the rules on examining new students from numbers 9 up to 13.[50]

[97] *Sodality of the Blessed Virgin*
23. He should strive to propagate in his own institution the Sodality of Blessed Mary of the Annunciation, first established at the Roman College.[51] A student not enrolled in it

[49] [T]he second rule of the lower prefect: see §243 below. [T]he rules of the same that apply to morals from no. 37 up to the end: see §§287–300 below.

[50] [R]ules on examining new students from nos. 9 up to 13: see §§259–63 below.

[51] Sodality of the Blessed Virgin: "A confraternity or sodality is a voluntary association of the faithful, established and guided by competent ecclesiastical authority for the promotion of special works of Christian charity or piety" (*CathEncy*, s.v. "Sodality"). The Blessed Virgin is

solent literariæ exercitationes, admittendus; nisi forte ipse rector aliter expedire in Domino iudicaverit. Verum ea, quæ ad congregationem vel academiam spectant, ne fiant eo tempore, quo in templo nostro sacræ conciones seu lectiones habentur.

ought not to be admitted to an academy in which literary exercises are usually practiced, unless perhaps the rector himself has decided in the Lord that another arrangement is more beneficial. But whatever pertains to the sodality or the academy should not occur at a time when devotional sermons or lessons are being given in our church.

[98] *Quædam provinciali permissa*

24. Denique de vacationibus, de gradibus, de nostris, quibus biennium ad recolendam theologiam concedendum erit, deque aliis provincialem consulat; et diligenter, quæ ipse statuerit, exequatur.

[98] *Certain things left to the provincial*

24. Finally, he should consult the provincial and diligently carry out his decisions about breaks, about the stages in the educational program, about Jesuits to whom two years ought to be given to review theology, and about other matters.

[H3] Regulæ Præfecti Studiorum

[H3] Rules for the Prefect of Studies

[99] *Præfecti munus*

1. Præfecti munus est, generale rectoris instrumentum esse ad studia recte ordinanda, scholasque nostras ita regendas ac moderandas pro facultate ab eo accepta, ut qui eas frequentant, quam maxime in vitæ probitate ac bonis artibus doctrinaque proficiant ad Dei gloriam.

[99] *The function of the prefect*

1. The prefect's function is to act as the rector's general agent for achieving good academic order, and to direct and regulate the classes, according to the power received from the rector, in such a way that those who attend them make as much progress as possible in moral integrity and in the liberal arts and learning, for the glory of God.[52]

Mary, the mother of Jesus.

[52] Liberal arts: the long-standing term used here, *bonae artes* (the good arts), explicitly joins the idea of educational and ethical development. The particulars were variously defined at different points in the history of classical humanism, but the general concept derives from antiquity. The standard Renaissance conception of the core liberal arts included grammar, rhetoric, poetry, history, and moral philosophy. According to George Ganss, Ignatius placed language study under the category of *litterae humaniores,* which for him eventually also included rhetoric, poetry, and history. For Ignatius, the arts or liberal arts were logic, physics, metaphysics, moral philosophy, and some mathematics. See George Ganss, S.J., *Saint Ignatius' Idea of a Jesuit University,* 58.

[100] *Præfecti et cancellarii discrimen*

2. Sicubi forte cancellarius est a præfecto distinctus, provincialis erit videre, quænam ex his regulis utrique communes, vel alterutri propriæ esse debeant, pro cuiusque academiæ consuetudine et statutis.

[101] *Præfectus non dispenset*

3. Nihil immutet ex iis, quæ habentur in ordine studiorum, neque dispenset; sed, ubi opus est, referat ad superiorem.

[102] *Liber de ratione studiorum*

4. Librum de ratione studiorum familiarem habeat, et ab auditoribus professoribusque omnibus regulas sedulo curet observandas; præcipue vero eas, quæ de doctrina sancti Thomæ theologis, et de delectu opinionum philosophis præscribuntur; in quo præsertim invigilet, cum conclusiones defendendæ, maxime vero cum imprimendæ erunt.

[103] *Professores materias absolvant*

5. Unicuique ex professoribus tum theologis tum philosophis tum casistis, præsertim si quem paulo tardiorem compererit, in memoriam revocet, ut progrediatur ita, ut singulis annis materias sibi assignatas absolvat.

[104] *Disputationes quomodo moderandæ*

6. Omnibus disputationibus, ad quas professores sive theologi sive

[100] *Difference between the prefect and an executive assistant*

2. If perhaps there is somewhere an executive assistant distinct from the prefect, it will be up to the provincial to see which of these rules ought to be common to both and which proper to each one, in keeping with the custom and the bylaws of each institution.

[101] *The prefect should not dispense*

3. He should change no detail belonging to the order of studies, and he should not grant dispensations; but, where there is a need, he should report it to the superior.

[102] *Book about the plan of studies*

4. He should be familiar with the book about the educational plan, and he should make sure that the rules are observed with consistent attention by all the students and the professors, especially the rules that are prescribed for the theologians about the teaching of Saint Thomas and for the philosophers about the selection of opinions. In this matter he should be especially vigilant when theses are going to be defended, but most of all when they are going to be printed.

[103] *Professors should finish the material*

5. He should remind each one of the professors, the theologians as well as the philosophers and the professors of case studies, especially if he has discovered that anyone is a little too slow, that everyone should make enough progress every year to finish the matter assigned to him.

[104] *How disputations should be managed*

6. The prefect is supposed to be in charge of all disputations for which

philosophi conveniunt, præfectus præsit oportet; signumque det finiendi iis, qui disputant; ac tempus sic distribuat, ut omnibus suus sit disputandi locus. Non patietur, difficultatem ullam, quæ in disputationem veniat, ultro citroque sic agitari, ut non minus, quam antea incomprehensa permaneat; sed postea quam de re quapiam fuerit concertatum, eam ab eo, qui præest, diligenter explicandam curet. Neque enim argumenta solvet ipse, sed argumentantibus et respondentibus potius moderabitur; idque maiore cum dignitate præstabit, si non argumentando (quamvis id aliquando deceat), sed interrogando faciet, ut difficultas magis explanetur.

professors or theologians or philosophers gather. He should give the disputants the signal to stop, and he should apportion the time in such a way that each person has his proper time for engaging in the disputation. He will not allow any problem that comes up in the course of the disputation to be argued back and forth in such a way that it remains less understood than before; but, after a controversy, he should see to it that the issue is carefully explained by the one who is presiding. For he will not resolve the arguments himself but rather guide the proponents and the challengers. And he will achieve this with greater dignity if he does not engage in the argumentation (although from time to time this is proper) but asks questions in such a way that he makes the problem clearer.

[105] De actibus theologicis

7. Suo tempore in memoriam redigat superiori ut, auditis præceptoribus, statuat, quibusnam sive totius theologiæ sive partis alicuius theses defendendæ sint; qui quidem actus ab his, quibus non est tribuendum recolendæ theologiæ biennium, habendi sunt anno theologici studii quarto, aut (si æquo pauciores sint theologi quarti anni) tertio; idque etiam ubi nostri domi theologiam audiunt, externis invitatis, cum aliquo apparatu. Ad generales vero non necesse est, ut omnes admittantur, qui peculiares habuerunt; sed ii, qui ingenio et facultate præstent, eligi poterunt; ii vero qui habituri sunt

[105] About theological Acts

7. At the appropriate time, he should remind the superior that, after the teachers have been heard, he should decide who should defend the theses, either of all of theology or of some part of it, and which Acts should be held in the fourth year of theology by those who are not going to be given the two-year review of theology or in the third year (if the fourth-year theologians are fewer then needed). He should also do this when Jesuits are taking in-house theology courses,[53] inviting non-Jesuits and giving the event some formal setting. It is not necessary that everyone who has participated in the Special Acts be admitted to the General Acts; those out-

---

[53] [I]n-house theology courses: courses given in the context of the community rather than in the more public classrooms of the school.

biennium, biennio ipso actus suos celebrabunt, ut deinde dicetur.

standing in talent and ability are eligible. Those who are going to have the two-year review will celebrate their own Acts in the course of that two-year period, as it will be announced at that time.

[106] *De actibus peculiaribus*

8. Ad peculiares autem actus, quos singuli singulos habebunt, materias ex quatuor theologiæ partibus præfectus cum magistris distribuet; sed ita, ut non nimis frequenter, sed per intervalla quædam habeantur, ac duabus horis et dimidiata minimum circumscribantur; nec nisi mane vel a prandio tantum; et argumententur fere non pauciores quam tres, quorum unus sit, ut plurimum, doctor.

[106] *About Special Acts*

8. The prefect along with the teachers will distribute material from the four parts of theology for the Special Acts that each person will perform individually. But he will do this in such a way that they do not occur too closely together but at certain intervals. They should last at least two and one-half hours, and take place only in the morning or after the midday meal. Generally, no fewer than three should debate, and for the most part one of these should be a professional academic.

[107] *De generalibus*

9. Generales universam fere theologiam comprehendant, et antemeridianum videlicet ac pomeridianum tempus occupent, vel certe ad quaternas seu quinas horas producantur, ubi non nisi mane vel a prandio disputari moris est.

[107] *About General Acts*

9. General Acts encompass practically all of theology, and so they should take up the morning and the afternoon, or they should last at least four or five hours where it is the custom to debate only in the morning or after the midday meal.

[108] *Conclusiones imprimendæ*

10. Generalium horum actuum conclusiones possunt, si videatur, esse communes nostris omnibus eodem anno defensuris; et publicis typis (si loci consuetudo ferat) excudi.

[108] *Theses to be published*

10. The theses of these General Acts can, if it seems good, be common to all Jesuits who are going to defend in the same year, and they can be printed and published if local custom supports this.

[109] *Certum conclusionum tempus*

11. Eorum, qui sunt hos actus habituri, unus in ultimam, si commode potest, reservetur hebdomadam, qua studia finienda sunt; alter in eam, qua scholæ rursus aperiendæ.

[109] *The schedule for the theses*

11. If it can be done conveniently, one of those who are going to present these Acts should be kept for the last week of the term and another for the week in which classes resume.

[110] *De actibus externorum*

12. Ad actus generales haben-dos aliqui quotannis invitentur externi, qui theologiæ curriculum in nostro gymnasio non exigua cum laude confecerint. Huiusmodi autem actus oportet esse ceteris sollemniores, et quanto maximo nostrorum, externorum doctorum, ac principum etiam virorum conventu celebrari.

[111] *Actibus qui præsideant*

13. Præsideant omnibus actibus professores, vel alternis vel simul ambo; ita ut de suis uterque quæstionibus respondeat; præsidere etiam possunt alii doctores nostri.

[112] *Conclusionum numerus*

14. In generalibus actibus conclusiones nec nimis longæ sint, nec plures fere quam quinquaginta; pauciores, si publicus academiæ mos aliter habeat. In peculiaribus vero actibus non plures quam viginti; quam duodecim vel quindecim in menstruis disputationibus; quam octo vel novem in hebdomadariis.

[113] *Respondens conclusionem confirmet*

15. Responsurus conclusionem unam aut alteram breviter (antequam ad disputationem veniatur) paulo quidem ornatius, sed theologico tamen more confirmet.

[110] *About the Acts given by non-Jesuits*

12. Every year, some non-Jesuits who have finished the theological curriculum in our school with an excellent record should be invited to perform in the General Acts. But such Acts ought to be more formal than the others and celebrated by as large as possible an assembly of Jesuits, non-Jesuit academics, and even leading members of the larger community.

[111] *Who should preside over the Acts*

13. Professors should preside over all Acts, whether in alternation or two at a time, so that each one might comment on his own questions in reply. Other Jesuit academics can preside as well.

[112] *The number of theses*

14. In the General Acts, theses should neither be too long nor exceed about fifty in number; they should be fewer, if the public tradition of the school dictates otherwise. There should be not more than twenty in the Special Acts, not more than twelve or fifteen in monthly disputations, and not more than eight or nine in weekly ones.

[113] *The one responding should assert the thesis*

15. Before the disputation occurs, the one who is going to respond ought to assert one or two theses briefly with a bit more rhetorical embellishment but still in the theological manner.[54]

---

[54] [I]n the theological manner: for John W. O'Malley's discussion of the humanist and Scholastic elements in early Jesuit education, see his "Jesuit Educational Enterprise in Historical Perspective," 10–25.

[114] *Disputationes menstruæ et hebdomadariæ*

16. De menstruis et hebdomadariis disputationibus servanda diligenter curet, quæ in regulis professorum theologiæ ac philosophiæ præscribuntur.

[115] *Audiendi et observandi præceptores*

17. Audiat aliquando præceptores, minimum semel in mense; interdum etiam commentarios legat a discipulis exceptos. Si quid animadversione dignum vel ipse observaverit, vel audierit ab aliis, ubi id certo compererit, præceptorem perquam benigne et comiter admoneat; remque totam ad rectorem, si necesse sit, deferat.

[116] *Recognitio conclusionum*

18. Idem servandum, cum in recognoscendis conclusionibus aliquid incideret, quod inter præfectum et præceptorem non conveniret; neque enim eo insciente conclusionem ullam aut delere aut immutare debet; ipsa vero immutatio fiet ceteris omnibus insciis, præter rectorem.

[117] *De actibus philosophicis*

19. Sub finem triennii cursusque philosophici disputationes habeantur de universa philosophia; ad quas deligantur pauci et egregie instructi, qui eius loci dignitatem sustinere valeant, hoc est, qui multo plus quam mediocriter profecerint.

[114] *The monthly and weekly disputations*

16. He should see to it that the professors of theology and philosophy attentively follow what is prescribed in their rules concerning the monthly and weekly disputations.

[115] *The teachers ought to be visited and observed*

17. He should make class visitations now and then, at least once a month. Sometimes he should also read the notes taken down by the students. If he himself has noticed or has heard from others anything worthy of attention, when he has verified it, he should advise the teacher in a quite kind and courteous way, and he should report the entire matter to the rector, if it is necessary.

[116] *Examination of the theses*

18. The same process should be followed when in examining the theses anything comes up on which the prefect and the teacher do not agree. For he ought not eliminate or change any thesis without the teacher's knowledge. But that change will happen without anyone else knowing, except for the rector.

[117] *About philosophical Acts*

19. Near the end of the three-year philosophical course, comprehensive disputations on philosophy should be held. A few excellently trained students should be selected for them, ones who can uphold the dignity of this position, that is, whose achievements far surpass the average.

[118] *Examen nostrorum meta-physicorum*

20. Hi seligendi sunt per examinatores tres aut etiam plures. Examinabunt autem semper præfectus et præceptor proprius; quibus a rectore addetur tertius ex reliquis magistris vel alius, qui recte id facere posse iudicetur. Cum his tribus aderunt præterea saltem duo alii professores a rectore item eligendi, qui vicissim etiam mutari poterunt; vel si id non possit, alii valde idonei, qui cum tribus examinatoribus suffragium scripto ferant; ita ut sint minime quinque secreta suffragia; et ab omnibus rem omnino secretam servari oportet.

[119] *Alumnorum et convictorum*

21. Alumnos seu convictores satis est examinari a suo præfecto et duobus philosophiæ repetitoribus; aut, si ii defuerint, a doctioribus duobus theologiæ auditoribus ex nostris, a præfecto generali assignandis. Verum qui ab his iudicati erunt idonei, non prius ad actum sese comparent, quam sui præceptoris ac præfecti generalis iudicio sint probati.

[120] *Publicum fit*

22. Hoc examen (a quo, et severe quidem agendo, nullus fere excipiendus e nostris; et, si fieri potest, nullus etiam ex alumnis et convictoribus) publicum erit, nisi quid obstet; videlicet si nostrorum est, coram omnibus nostris philosophiæ auditoribus; sin alum-

[118] *The examination of Jesuits in metaphysics*

20. These ought to be selected by three examiners or even more. The prefect and the student's own teacher will always be examiners, and to these the rector will add a third one from the rest of the teachers or another one who he thinks is fully capable of this assignment. Along with these three, there will be present at least two other professors in addition. These are likewise to be selected by the rector, and they can in turn be replaced. Or if this can not be done, there should be other quite suitable persons who, along with the three examiners, should submit a written vote. Thus, there should be, at a minimum, five secret votes. And the matter should be kept strictly confidential.

[119] *Examinations of the day students and boarding students*

21. It is sufficient that day students or boarding students be examined by their own prefect and by two who are making the review of philosophy; or, if those are not available, by two of our own more advanced students of theology, who are to be assigned by the general prefect. But the ones that these judge suitable should not prepare themselves for the Act before they have gotten the approvals of their teacher and the general prefect.

[120] *It takes place as a public event*

22. This examination will be public, unless something prevents this (and from this examination, no matter how rigorously it is conducted, usually no Jesuits nor even, if possible, any of our day and boarding students should be excused). That is, if Jesuits are being examined, the examination should take

norum seu convictorum, coram omnibus sui collegii philosophis; sin externorum (qui tamen ut examen hoc subeant, cogendi non sunt) coram omnibus externis philosophis saltem suæ classis.

place in the presence of all of our own students of philosophy; if the day students or boarders are being examined, it should take place in the presence of all of the philosophy students of their own college; and if non-Jesuits (who, nevertheless, should not be compelled to undergo this examination) are being examined, it should take place in the presence of all the non-Jesuit students of philosophy, at least those in their own class.

[121] *Examinis tempus et forma*

23. Examinandi initium statim post ferias Paschatis fiat; vel etiam ante, si multitudo cogat examinandorum, distributis diebus eo ordine, quem rector, audito præfecto et præceptore, existimaverit commodissimum. Duret examen singulorum minimum una hora; eatque per omnes primarias materias, quas præfectus tempestive ac secreto examinatoribus assignabit.

[121] *Schedule and structure of the examination*

23. Examinations should be scheduled to start immediately after the Easter feast days, or even before that, if the very large number of examinees requires it. The days should be divided up in the order that the rector, after consultation with the prefect and teacher, thinks most suitable. Each person's examination should last at least one hour, and it should cover all the basic material that the prefect will assign the examiners in due time and in private.

[122] *De tempore et forma actuum philosophicorum*

24. Porro philosophici actus totum scholarum tempus occupent minimum vel mane vel a prandio. Tres fere argumententur; quorum unus sit, ut plurimum, aliquis ex nostris magistris sive theologiæ sive philosophiæ; vel doctor aliquis religiosus aut externus. Conclusionum autem numerus ac ratio non discrepent ab eo, quod de theologicis generalibus statutum est regula nona.

[122] *Concerning the schedule and structure of the philosophical Acts*

24. Furthermore, the philosophical Acts should take up the entirety of the class time, at least either in the morning or after the midday meal. Usually three should engage in the disputation. Of these, normally one ought to be someone from our own faculty whether of theology or of philosophy; or he should be some professional academic, either one from a religious order or a non-Jesuit. And the number and order of the theses should not vary from what has been set down in

the ninth rule about General Acts in theology.

[123] *Quibus actibus qui intersint*

25. Theologi non modo auditores, sed etiam professores curet præfectus, ut intersint actibus theologicis, atque adeo philosophicis; et his philosophi; et professores quidem argumentando, urgendo alacriorem ac sollemniorem reddant disputationem. Adesse etiam omnes debebunt, cum magisterium erit vel doctoratus in aliquem conferendus. Quo in genere quid præfectum præstare oporteat, rectoris erit præscribere.

[124] *Qui ad argumentandum mittendi*

26. Cum nostri vocantur ad disputandum ab externis, vel ad publicas academias vel ad religiosorum conventus, ii potissimum mittendi erunt, qui biennium habent ad theologiam recolendam.

[125] *Præscribenda studendi ratio*

27. Et nostris et alumnis et externis per magistros non modo rationem studendi, repetendi, disputandi præscribat, sed etiam omne tempus ita distribuat, ut privati studii horas bene collocent.

[126] *Recognoscenda, quæ publice recitantur*

28. Nihil publice domi forisve recitari patiatur vel ab iis, qui ad gradus promoventur, vel ab iis, qui actus tum generales tum particula-

[123] *Who should attend which Acts*

25. The prefect should ensure that not only the theology students but also the theology professors attend the theological Acts and even the philosophical ones. The philosophy students should also attend these. And in fact the professors should make the disputation sharper and more serious by arguing and pressing points. Also, everyone ought to be present when the master's or doctoral degree is going to be conferred on someone. In such a case, it will be the rector's part to prescribe what the prefect ought to provide.

[124] *Who ought to be sent into debate*

26. When Jesuits are invited by non-Jesuits to dispute either at public institutions of learning or at religious communities, those in the two-year review of theology should be sent in preference to all others.

[125] *The schedule of studies should be prescribed*

27. For Jesuits and for our day students and for non-Jesuits, not only should he prescribe through the teachers the plan for studying, reviewing, and engaging in disputation, but he should also structure the whole schedule in such a way that they might arrange their hours of private study well.

[126] *What is read out in public should be inspected*

28. He should allow nothing to be read out, in the house or in public, unless he himself has inspected and approved it in due time, whether it is

res habent, vel a rhetoricis, quod non ipse tempestive recognoverit et approbaverit.

to be read out by those who are being advanced to the next grade, or by those who are taking part in the General or Special Acts, or by the rhetoricians.

[127] *Librorum delectus et copia*

29. Curet, ne scholastici libris aut utilibus careant, aut abundent inutilibus. Quare mature rectori suggerat, ne librorum, quibus in dies utimur, aut proximum in annum usuri sunt tum nostri tum externi, copia desideretur.

[127] *Selection and quantity of books*

29. He should see to it that the students do not lack useful books or have too many superfluous ones. For this reason he should give the rector timely reminders about keeping a good supply of the books that both Jesuits and non-Jesuits use every day or will use the next year.

[128] *Qui libri quibus distribuendi*

30. Theologiæ ac philosophiæ auditoribus non quoslibet, sed certos quosdam, rectore conscio, ex magistrorum consilio concedat libros; scilicet, præter Summam S. Thomæ theologis, et Aristotelem philosophis, commentarium aliquem selectum, quem privato studio consulere possint. Tridentinum Concilium omnes theologi habeant, et Bibliorum volumen; quorum lectio sit illis familiaris. An etiam aliquem ex patribus habere debeant, cum rectore consideret. Theologis præterea ac philosophis omnibus librum aliquem ad humanitatis studia pertinentem distribuat, moneatque, ut certis quibusdam temporibus legere, ubi commodum sit, non omittant.

[128] *Which books should be distributed to which people*

30. He should let the theology and philosophy students have not just any books, but certain particular ones, with the rector's knowledge and on the advice of the teachers; namely, in addition to the *Summa* of Saint Thomas for the theologians, and Aristotle for the philosophers, some carefully chosen commentary that they can consult in their private study.[55] All the theologians should have the Tridentine Council and a volume of the Bible.[56] They should become well acquainted with these texts. He should consider with the rector whether they also ought to have one of the Fathers. Moreover, he should distribute to all the theologians and philosophers some book pertaining to humanistic studies, and he should remind them not to fail to read it at certain set times when it is appropriate.

---

[55] Aristotle: Greek philosopher (384–322 B.C.), who assumed a singular importance in Scholasticism, especially with Thomas Aquinas's extensive use of his thought.

[56] Tridentine Council: the Council of Trent (1545–63); Bible: The Sacred Scriptures. For further information about the Council of Trent and the Bible, see endn. 12.

[H4] Regulæ Communes Omnibus Professoribus Superiorum Facultatum

[H4] Common Rules for All the Professors of the Higher Faculties

[129] *Finis*

1. Feratur præceptoris peculiaris intentio, tum in lectionibus, cum se occasio obtulerit, tum extra eas, ad auditores suos ad obsequium et amorem Dei ac virtutum, quibus ei placere oportet, movendos; et ut omnia sua studia ad hunc finem referant.

[129] *Final Goal*

1. Both in the classes when occasions arise, and outside of them, the special intention of the teacher should aim at moving his students to obey and love God and the virtues by which we ought to please him, and to make all their academic pursuits relate to this final goal.[57]

[130] *Orandum ante lectionem*

2. Quod ut ad memoriam eis reducatur, ante lectionis initium dicat aliquis brevem orationem ad id institutam; quam præceptor et discipuli omnes aperto capite attente audient; vel saltem ipse præceptor signo crucis se muniat aperto capite, et incipiat.

[130] *There should be prayer before the class*

2. To remind them of this, someone should say a brief prayer composed for this purpose before the beginning of the class. The teacher and all the students will listen attentively with head uncovered, or at least the teacher should bless himself with the sign of the cross, head uncovered, and begin.

[131] *Discipuli ad pietatem iuvandi*

3. Discipulos præterea iuvet crebris apud Deum precibus ac religiosis vitæ suæ exemplis. Exhortationes par erit non omittere, saltem pridie solemniorum dierum, et cum paulo longiores vacationes conceduntur. Hortetur potissimum ad orandum Deum, ad excutiendam conscientiam vesperi, ad sacramenta pænitentiæ et Eucharistiæ frequenter ac rite obeunda, ad missam quotidie, concionem singulis diebus festis audiendam, ad vitandas noxias consuetudines, ad

[131] *The students' religious devotion should be supported*

3. In addition, he should support the students with frequent prayers to God and through the holy, exemplary actions of his own life. It will be appropriate not to leave out exhortations, at least on the days preceding solemn feast days and when a little extra free time is given. Most especially, he will encourage them to pray to God, to examine their consciences in the evening, to receive the sacraments of penance and the Eucharist properly and frequently, to attend Mass daily, to hear a sermon every holy day, to avoid

---

[57] [T]he higher faculties: in Ignatius's day, this term could include philosophy, theology, law, and medicine. It stands paired with the "lower faculties" of language arts or humane letters (Ganss, *Ignatius' Idea of a Jesuit University*, 52).

vitiorum detestationem, ad virtutes colendas christiano homine dignas.

[132] *Præfecto obtemperandum*

4. Præfecto studiorum in rebus, quæ ad studia et scholarum disciplinam spectant, obtemperet; conclusiones omnes, antequam proponantur, eidem tradat recognoscendas; neque librum ullum aut scriptorem extraordinarium explicandum suscipiat; neque novam ullam docendi aut disputandi consuetudinem introducat.

[133] *In refellendo modestia*

5. In iis quæstionibus, in quibus liberum est quamcunque partem sequi, ita defendatur una pars, ut alterius etiam partis, ac multo magis prioris professoris, si contrarium docuerat, existimationi modeste ac benevole consulatur. Quin etiam, si conciliari possunt auctores, id ne negligatur, optandum est. Denique in nominandis aut confutandis auctoribus modeste se gerat.

[134] *Novitas opinionum fugienda*

6. In iis etiam, in quibus nullum fidei pietatisque periculum subest, nemo in rebus alicuius momenti novas introducat quæstiones; nec opinionem ullam, quæ idonei nullius auctoris sit, iis, qui præsunt, inconsultis; nec aliquid contra doctorum axiomata, communemque scholarum sensum doceat; sequantur potius universi probatos maxime doctores, et quæ, prout tem-

harmful habits, to hate vices, and to cultivate the virtues worthy of a Christian person.

[132] *The prefect should be obeyed*

4. He should obey the prefect of studies in matters that bear on studies and class discipline. He should hand over to him all theses for review before they are presented. Neither should he take up for comment any book or writer different from the ones usually taken, nor should he introduce any new custom in teaching or in disputation.

[133] *Moderation in rebuttal*

5. In the questions where there is the freedom to take either side, he should defend one in such a way that he calmly and respectfully gives all due credit to the other, and much more so to a previous professor, if he had taught the contrary. And in fact, if authors can be reconciled, it should be hoped that he does not neglect to do so. Finally, when he cites or refutes authors, he should conduct himself in a restrained way.

[134] *Novelty of opinions should be avoided*

6. Even in matters that present no risk to faith and religious devotion, no one should introduce new articles for discussion in matters of any significance, nor any opinion that does not belong to any suitable authority, without consulting those who are in charge, nor anything contrary to the axioms of the Doctors.[58] And he should teach the common understand-

---

[58] Doctors: seemingly, *Doctor* is used here to indicate something like "those writers who are acknowledged to be the principal teaching authorities in the disciplines." For the OED's explanation of the various meanings of the English word *axiom*, see endn. 13.

porum usus tulerit, recepta potissimum fuerint in catholicis academiis.

ing of the Schools.[59] Everybody should rather follow the most approved academic authorities and the positions that have been supported with the greatest preference in Catholic institutions, insofar as the tenor of the time allows.

[135] *Brevity in refuting others and in proving one's own positions*

7. He should not bring up opinions that are useless, out of date, absurd, or clearly false. And he should not linger too long in proposing or refuting other positions. He should not be as eager to prove the theses by the number of his arguments as by their significance. He should not digress to irrelevant material, nor should he treat some of his topics more extensively than the matter demands, or some in the wrong place. He should not pile up possible objections, but he should briefly raise the strongest of them, unless their refutation is easily apparent when the underlying principles have been mentioned.

[135] *In alienis confutandis, suisque probandis brevitas*

7. Opiniones inutiles, obsoletas, absurdas, manifesto falsas non adducat; nec in aliis referendis ac refutandis nimis immoretur. Conclusiones non tam probare studeat argumentorum numero quam pondere. Ad alienas materias non digrediatur; aut e suis alias fusius, quam res postulat, alias alieno loco pertractet. Ne coacervet quæ obiici possent; sed ex iis potissima breviter referat, nisi ex iactis fundamentis facile pateat eorum confutatio.

[136] *In auctoritatibus parcitas et fidelitas*

8. In afferendis doctorum auctoritatibus non sit nimius; si tamen habeat insigniorum auctorum testimonia ad sententiam suam confirmandam, verba ipsa, quoad fieri potest, pauca tamen et fideliter recitet; multo magis Sacrarum Scripturarum, conciliorum, sanctorum patrum. E dignitate autem ma-

[136] *Frugality and fidelity regarding authors*

8. There should not be too much citation of authoritative sources. Nevertheless, if he has testimonies of preeminent authors that confirm his own opinion, he should accurately give a precise yet brief quotation, as far as this is possible, and much more so testimonies from Scripture, the councils, and the holy Fathers.[60] But it fits a

---

[59] The Schools: medieval Scholastic philosophy had a common vocabulary and approach, although different "Schools" could be distinguished because of their support for various theses.

[60] Councils: "Councils are legally convened assemblies of ecclesiastical dignitaries and theological experts for the purpose of discussing and regulating matters of church doctrine and discipline" (*CathEncy*, s.vv. "General Councils").

[T]he holy Fathers: This phrase does not mean the popes, who have the title "Holy Father,"

gistri est nullum fere auctorem proferre, quam ipse non legerit.

[137] *De dictando*

9. Si quis citra dictationem ita
docere potest, ut quæcunque scribenda sunt, commode valeant ab
auditoribus excipi, is ne dictet,
optandum; certe ita omnino dictent, ut non verbatim interposita
mora, sed uno fere spiritu pronuncient; et, si oportuerit, repetant
totidem verbis; nec totam quæstionem dictent, mox explicent; sed
identidem dictent atque explicent
vicissim.

[138] *Discipuli quando ad auctores reiiciendi*

10. Eæ quæ in auctoribus in
promptu positis habentur, si affe-
renda sint, explicet potius, quam
dictet; quin etiam auditores ad eos
auctores, qui copiose et accurate
materiam aliquam pertractarunt,
reiiciat.

[139] *Repetitiones in schola*

11. Post lectionem in schola vel
prope scholam maneat saltem per
quadrantem, ut possint ad eum
interrogandum auditores accedere,
ut lectionum rationem interdum
exigat, utque eæ repetantur.

teacher's position to cite almost no
authority that the teacher himself has
not read.

[137] *About dictating*

9. If anyone, without going as far as
dictating, can teach in such a way that
the students can easily get whatever
ought to be written down, then it is
desirable that he not dictate. Certainly
teachers should dictate only in such a
way that they do not pause after each
word but generally in one breath. And
if there is good reason, they should
repeat in just so many words. And
they should not dictate the entire question and then explain it, but they
should repeatedly dictate and explain
in turn.

[138] *When students are to be referred
to the authors*

10. If authors have to be cited, he
should explain rather than dictate what
is contained in the ones that are readily available. In fact, he should refer the
students to those authors who treat
some matter at great length and with
precision.

[139] *Reviews in the classroom*

11. After a class, he should remain
in or near the classroom at least for a
quarter of an hour so that the students
might be able to approach him to ask
questions; so that he might, on occasion, ask them to present back to him
the gist of the classes; and so that the
classes might be reviewed.

---

but certain authoritative teachers and interpreters of Church teaching, like Augustine, Ambrose,
and Gregory the Great. The group includes some who are not bishops. The study of their writings
is called patrology or patristics. *CathEncy* provides a full development of the term "Fathers of the
Church" in endn. 14.

[140] *Repetitiones domi*

12. Domi quoque quotidie, præter sabbatha, vacationes et dies festos, hora una designanda, qua repetatur a nostris et disputetur; ut ea ratione et ingenia magis exerceantur, et difficilia, quæ occurrent, magis elucidentur. Præmoneatur itaque unus aut alter ad repetendum memoriter non plus quam per quadrantem. Postea argumentetur unus item aut alter, totidem respondentibus; si quid vero temporis supersit, dubia proponantur; ut autem supersit, magister argumentandi formam severe tueatur; et cum novi nihil affertur, præcidat argumentum

[141] *Repetitiones generales*

13. Sub finem anni ita instituendæ erunt præteritarum lectionum repetitiones, ut, nisi quid obstet, mensis integer vacuus ab illis etiam, non solum a lectionibus, relinquatur.

[142] *Disputationes hebdomadariæ*

14. In sabbatho, aliove, quem academiæ consuetudo exigit, die habeant in scholis disputationes per duas horas; longiores etiam, ubi sint magni externorum concursus. Quod si quam in hebdomadam duo festi dies, vel, cum festo uno hebdomadaria vacatio incidat, non disputetur, sed legatur sabbatho; id vero si tribus continuaretur hebdomadis, una interponatur disputatio.

[140] *Reviews at home*

12. Also every day at home except for Saturdays, vacations, and holidays, one hour should be designated for Jesuits to review and dispute. The purposes of this procedure are both to better exercise their intellectual abilities, and to better clarify the difficult points that come up. And so one or two should be reminded in advance about reviewing from memory for not more than a quarter of an hour. Later, one or two should likewise engage in argument with the same number of respondents. If any time is left, problems ought to be presented. However, in order to have some time left, the teacher should keep strictly to the formal plan for debates, and when nothing new is being raised, he should cut the argument short.

[141] *General reviews*

13. Towards the end of the year, the reviews of past classes ought to be organized in such a way that, unless something prevents it, a full month is left free of the reviews too, not just of classes.

[142] *Weekly disputations*

14. On Saturday, or on some day required by the school's custom, they should hold disputations in their classes for two hours, or even longer where there are large gatherings of non-Jesuits. But if there are two feast days in any week, or if the weekly break day occurs in conjunction with a feast day, there should be classes on Saturday, not disputations. If this goes on for three weeks, one disputation should be inserted.

[143] *Disputationes menstruæ*

15. Ubi receptus academiæ mos nihil obstat, singulis, præter tres menses æstivos ultimos, aut (si pauci sint auditores) alternis mensibus communes certo aliquo die disputationes, tum ante tum post meridiem habeantur; quot fuerint magistri, totidem auditores defendant, singuli singulorum magistrorum quæstiones.

[144] *Argumenta qui resumant*

16. Intersint disputationibus, quoad eius fieri potest, alii quoque doctores nostri professoresque, licet diversarum facultatum; qui, quo magis concertatio fervescat, argumentorum, quæ agitantur, vim urgeant; modo ne prosequendum suscipiant argumentum, cui utiliter ac strenue adhuc argumentans insistit. Id ipsum præstare liceat externis etiam doctoribus; atque adeo ad argumentandum ex instituto, nisi ea consuetudo alicubi minus probetur, invitari possunt.

[145] *Non disputent, nisi doctiores*

17. Ex auditoribus publice non disputent, nisi doctiores; ceteri privatim exerceantur, quoad ita instructi sint, ut eo loco non putentur indigni.

[146] *Disputationis cura*

18. Existimet, disputationis diem non minus esse laboriosum

[143] *Monthly disputations*

15. When the tradition of the institution does not prevent it, every month (except for the last three months in the summer), or every other month if there are not many students, there should be common disputations on some fixed day, sometimes before and sometimes after noon. There should be as many students defending as there are teachers, each one answering the questions of each teacher.

[144] *Who should take up the arguments again*

16. As far as possible, disputations also ought to be attended by other Jesuit academics and professors even though they may belong to different departments. They should forcefully press the arguments being presented to heat up the competition more, provided that they do not continue to pursue a line of reasoning on which the proponent has taken a firm stand after arguing it passionately and to good effect. Professional academics from elsewhere may also provide the same stimulus; and they may be invited even for the purpose of formally participating in the argument, unless in a given locale this custom does not meet with approval.

[145] *Only the more learned should dispute*

17. Only the more learned students should dispute publicly. The rest should practice privately until they are so well trained that they are not considered unworthy of that position.

[146] *Attending to the disputation*

18. He should be of the opinion that the day of the disputation does

fructuosumque, quam lectionis; omnemque disputationis utilitatem ac fervorem a se pendere; cui ita præsit, ut ipse videatur esse, qui in utroque concertatore concertet; collaudet, si quid afferatur boni; et attendere omnes iubeat, cum gravior aliqua proposita fuerit difficultas; suggerat subinde breve aliquid, quo vel fulciat respondentem, vel argumentantem dirigat; neque diu taceat, neque semper loquatur, ut ipsi etiam discipuli promant, quod sciunt; ipse vero, quod promptum fuerit, emendet aut expoliat; disputantem progredi iubeat, dum difficultas vim obtinet; immo augeat ipse difficultatem; nec dissimulet, si is qui argumentatur, prorepserit ad aliud argumentum; non patiatur vel argumentum pene solutum longius urgeri, vel responsionem non bene constantem diu sustineri; sed post aliquam concertationem rem totam breviter definiat et explanet; si quid denique aliud uspiam in usu est, quo disputationes reddi soleant frequentiores ac ferventiores, id sedulo retinendum.

not require less effort and produce more profit than a day of classes, and he should think that all the usefulness and zest of the disputation depends upon him. He should preside over it in such a way that he himself seems to be the one who is doing the disputing in each of the disputants. He should give ample praise if someone makes a good point. And he should tell everyone to pay attention when some rather serious difficulty has been brought up. From time to time he should suggest some concise point to support the respondent, or to guide the one making the argument. He should neither remain quiet too long nor talk all the time, so that the learners themselves bring forth what they know. But he himself should correct or refine what has been put forth. He should tell the disputant to keep moving ahead while a difficulty is gaining force; in fact, he himself should make it more of a difficulty. And he should not pretend that he does not notice if the one who is arguing has digressed into another argument. He should not allow an argument to be pressed too long when it is almost resolved or allow a response that is not really solid to be supported for a long while. But after some debate he should briefly define the whole matter and explain it. Finally, if in a given locale there is some other practice that usually causes the disputations to draw greater attendance and heightens their intensity, it should be kept and cultivated.

[147] *Cum bidello agendum*

19. Cum adiutore seu bidello a rectore constituto agat interdum, eumque de totius classis statu et de externorum etiam auditorum

[147] *Confer with the beadle*

19. He should occasionally confer with the assistant or beadle appointed by the rector and make an inquiry about how the class is doing and also

diligentia ac profectu percontetur; detque operam, ut idem suo munere fideliter et accurate fungatur.

about the diligence and progress of the non-Jesuit students.[61] And he should see to it that the beadle performs his duty faithfully and attentively.

[148] *Profectus studentium*

20. Sit denique in omnibus, divina aspirante gratia, diligens et assiduus, et profectus studentium tum in lectionibus tum in aliis literariis exercitationibus studiosus; non uni se magis, quam alteri familiarem ostendat; contemnat neminem, pauperum studiis æque ac divitum prospiciat, profectumque uniuscuiusque e suis scholasticis speciatim procuret.

[148] *Progress of the students*

20. Finally, with divine grace inspiring him, he should be diligent about everything and constantly working at it, and very concerned about the students' progress both in the class work and in the other compositional exercises. He should not be more friendly to one than to another. He should look down on no one, attending to the education of poor students just as to that of the rich, taking special care for the progress of each one of his own students.

[H5] Regulæ Professoris Sacræ Scripturæ

[149] *Præcipua sensus literalis cura*

1. Intelligat suas præcipue partes esse, divinas literas iuxta germanum literalemque sensum, qui rectam in Deum fidem bonorumque morum instituta confirmet, pie, docte, graviter explicare.

[H5] Rules for the Professor of Sacred Scripture

[149] *Concern for the literal meaning is foremost*

1. He should realize that it is especially his role to explain with devotion, learning, and seriousness the sacred texts according to their genuine and literal meaning so that this meaning might strengthen true faith in God and the principles of morality.

[150] *Et vulgatæ editionis*

2. Inter cetera, ad quæ eius intentio feratur, illud præcipuum sit, ut versionem ab Ecclesia approbatam defendat.

[150] *And for the Vulgate edition*

2. Among the other things on which he should focus his attention, defending the version approved by the Church should be foremost.[62]

---

[61] Beadle: *bidellus* is a very old academic term used for a kind of assistant who helps to take care of some of the business aspects of a university. Individual teachers sometimes had their own beadles, who might even help maintain the neatness of the classroom. See §§459–65 below.

[62] The Vulgate edition: the Latin version of the Bible made by Saint Jerome (340–420) and declared by the Council of Trent as authoritative for sermons and disputations.

[151] *Phrases Sacræ Scripturæ observandæ, et inter se conferendæ*

3. Eum sensum ut assequatur, locutiones ac figuras Sacrarum Scripturarum proprias observet; nec modo loci, quem in manibus habet, antecedentia et consequentia, sed alia quoque loca, in quibus eadem phrasis idem aut non idem valeat, solerter inter se conferat.

[151] *Sacred Scripture's expressions ought to be carefully noticed and compared with one another*

3. To arrive at the meaning he should carefully note Sacred Scripture's special ways of speaking and figures of speech. And he should also skillfully compare with each other not just the passages preceding and following the one that he is dealing with, but also other passages in which the same expression has the same or a different force.

[152] *Hebræus, græcusve textus*

4. Ex hebræis græcisque exemplaribus, quod usui fuerit, in eam rem proferat; breviter tamen; nec, nisi cum vel ipsorum latinæque editionis vulgatæ aliqua diversitas conciliationis indiget, vel aliarum linguarum idiotismi ad maiorem conferunt sive perspicuitatem sive significationem.

[152] *Hebrew or Greek text*

4. From the Hebrew and Greek originals, he should cite what might be useful for this effort, but briefly. And this should be done only when either some discrepancy that they have with the Latin version needs to be reconciled or the idiomatic expressions of the other languages contribute greater clarity or meaning.

[153] *Aliis versionibus quomodo utendum*

5. Aliarum versionum, sive latinarum recentiorum, sive Chaldaicæ, Syriacæ, Theodotionis, Aquilæ, Symmachi, nec errores, nisi et insignes et in speciem probabiles suscipiat refellendos; nec ea vicissim prætereat, quæ latinæ editioni vulgatæ fideique nostræ mysteriis valde faveant; præsertim si fuerint apud Septuaginta interpretes; de quibus honorifice semper loquendum est.

[153] *How other translations should be employed*

5. And he should not undertake to refute the errors either of the more recent Latin translations, or of the Aramaic or Syriac versions, or those belonging to Theodotion, Aquila, or Symmachus,[63] unless the errors are both famous and, on the surface, supportable. And in turn he should not leave out things that strongly favor the Latin Vulgate edition and the mysteries of our faith, especially if they are found in the Septuagint,[64] about which we always ought to speak respectfully.

---

[63] Theodotion, Aquila, Symmachus: three second-century A.D. translations of the Hebrew Bible into Greek.

[64] Septuagint: the authoritative translation of the Hebrew Scriptures into Greek, dating to the third and second centuries B.C. [M]ysteries of our faith: "revealed truths that surpass the powers of natural reason." See *CathEncy*, s.v. "Mystery."

[154] *Pontificum et conciliorum expositiones tuendæ*

6. Sic quem literalem cuiuspiam loci sensum esse significant pontificum seu conciliorum, præsertim generalium canones, eum omnino literalem esse defendat; nec alios præterea literales addat, nisi eximiis adductus coniecturis. Si quem etiam ad aliquod fidei dogma confirmandum ex instituto proferunt, eum quoque sensum, aut literalem aut mysticum, certum tamen esse doceat.

[155] *Patrum vestigiis insistendum*

7. Sanctorum patrum vestigiis reverenter insistat; inter quos si de uno aliquo sensu literali vel allegorico conveniat, præsertim dum disertis verbis loquuntur, et ex proposito de Scripturis aut de dogmatibus disputant, ab eo non recedat; si non conveniat, ex eorum variis expositionibus eam præferat, in quam a multis iam annis Ecclesia magno consensu videtur propensior.

[156] *Fidei dogmata Sacris Literis confirmanda*

8. Quin etiam, si quod est fidei dogma, quod fere quamplurimi patres aut theologi e Scripturis probare contendunt, id ipse probari inde posse non neget.

[154] *The interpretations of popes and councils ought to be protected*

6. Thus he should defend as altogether literal whatever the canons of popes or councils, especially general ones, indicate as the literal meaning of any particular passage.[65] And he should not add other literal meanings unless persuaded to do so by strikingly insightful inferences. Still, if they formally propose any meaning in order to corroborate some dogma of the faith, he should also teach that that meaning, whether literal or allegorical, is certain.[66]

[155] *Follow in the footsteps of the Fathers*

7. He should follow reverently in the footsteps of the holy Fathers. If they agree on some literal or allegorical meaning, especially in the context of formal discourse while expressly discussing the Scriptures and dogmas, he should not shy away from it.[67] But if they do not agree, then out of their various interpretations he should prefer that one toward which for many years now the Church has seemed more inclined by widespread consensus.

[156] *The dogmas of the faith that should be confirmed by Sacred Scripture*

8. In fact, if there is any dogma of the faith that most fathers or theologians usually try to prove from the Scriptures, he should not say that it can not be proved on that basis.

---

[65] Canons: authoritative decrees or directives.

[66] Allegorical: symbolic, carrying a hidden meaning. For more extensive development of the allegorical interpretation of Scripture, see endn. 15.

[67] Dogma: "A truth appertaining to faith or morals, revealed by God, transmitted from the Apostles in the Scriptures or by tradition, and proposed by the Church for the acceptance of the faithful. It might be described briefly as a revealed truth defined by the Church" (*CathEncy*, s.v. "Dogma").

[157] *Rabbinis auctoritas non concilianda*

9. Si quid sit in hebræorum rabbinis, quod vel pro latina editione vulgata, vel pro catholicis dogmatibus utiliter possit afferri, id ita afferat, ut illis propterea non conciliet auctoritatem, ne ad eos aliqui afficiantur; præsertim si fuerint ex iis, qui post Christi Domini tempora scripserunt.

[158] *In rebus aut erroribus rabbinorum non laborandum*

10. In ceteris rabbinorum rebus conquirendis aut etiam erroribus exagitandis, nisi valde celebres sint, non laboret; idemque servet in legendis quibusdam christianis interpretibus, qui plus nimio rabbinos secuti sunt.

[159] *Non admodum punctis fidendum*

11. Immo neque punctis, quod rabbinorum inventum est, confidat admodum; sed diligenter expendat, quomodo noster vel Septuaginta vel antiqui interpretes alii legerint, cum puncta non essent.

[160] *Brevitatis studium*

12. In quolibet Scripturæ loco, nisi magnum sit et moræ et operæ pretium, non hæreat nimium, ne lenti fiant progressus; quod maxime consequetur, si faciliora percurrat vel etiam omittat.

[157] *Approval should not be given to rabbinical authors*

9. If there is anything in Hebraic rabbinical writings that can be applied to good effect, either in support of the common Latin edition, or in support of Catholic dogmas, he should apply it in such a way that it does not win them authority on that account, so that no one becomes well disposed toward them. This holds especially if they are among those who wrote after the times of Christ the Lord.

[158] *The rabbis' issues or errors should not be belabored*

10. He should not expend effort in searching out the rest of the rabbis' interpretations or even in criticizing their errors, unless they are quite well known. He should follow the same approach in reading certain Christian interpreters who have followed the rabbis far more than they should have.

[159] *There should not be very much trust put in the pointing*

11. In fact, he should not put very much trust in the pointing,[68] which is a rabbinical invention, but he should carefully consider how our interpreter or the Septuagintal or other ancient interpreters read when there was no pointing.

[160] *The pursuit of brevity*

12. Unless some passage of Scripture is clearly worth the time and effort, he should not dwell on it too long, so that the forward movement is not slowed down. He will most effectively achieve this if he quickly covers the easier items or even omits them.

---

[68] Pointing: the marks used to indicate the vowel sounds in Hebrew texts.

[161] *Quæstiones scholastico more non tractandæ*

13. Quæstiones Sacrarum Scripturarum proprias scholastico more non tractet.

[162] *Chronologiæ et his simili-bus non immorandum*

14. In varia temporum ratione pervestiganda, in perscrutandis terræ sanctæ locis, aut in huius-modi aliis parum utilibus rebus (nisi locus ipse id exigat necessa-rio) non multum temporis ponat. Auctores, qui de his copiose disse-runt, satis erit indicare.

[163] *Nec allegoriis et moralibus*

15. Allegorias et moralia, si pervulgata non sint, et in sensu ipso literali quodammodo nata videantur, atque ingeniosum ac perspicax aliquid præseferant, ne prætermittat. Quæ eiusmodi non fuerint, significet tantum, quibus ex patribus depromi possint.

[164] *Nec controversiis*

16. Si quem incidat in locum, vel nobis cum hæreticis controver-sum, vel in theologicis concerta-tionibus in utramque partem iactari solitum, exponat tantum; graviter tamen et strenue, præsertim si ad-versus hæreticos agat, quantum is locus ponderis habeat ad eam quæstionem definiendam; omittat cetera, ut instituti sui memor nihil

[161] *Questions should not be treated in the Scholastic manner*

13. He should not treat questions proper to Sacred Scriptures in the Scholastic manner.

[162] *Do not linger over chronology and such*

14. He should not devote much time to tracing out the different time schemes, to carefully investigating the places of the Holy Land, or to other such things that are of little use (unless the passage itself absolutely demands it). It will be sufficient to point out the authors that treat these matters in great detail.

[163] *Nor over allegories and moral matters*

15. He should not skip over allego-ries and moral matters if they are not very widely known, and if they seem somehow embedded in the literal meaning, and if they offer something interesting and perceptive. For the matters that do not have these quali-ties, he should merely indicate where they can be found in the works of the Fathers.

[164] *Nor over controversies*

16. If he comes upon any passage over which we have a disagreement with heretics,[69] or which is usually mentioned on either side in theological debates, he should merely set it forth; but he should do this with seriousness and vigor, especially if it works against heretics, to the extent to which that passage has a relevance for settling the question. He should leave the rest out, so that he is seen to be mindful of

---

[69] Heretics: those who accept part but reject some of what is judged to be essential in the system of belief.

aliud, quam Sacras Litteras docere videatur.

what he has been commissioned to do, namely, to teach nothing other than Sacred Scripture.

[165] *Novum et vetus testamentum alternis*

17. Novum et vetus testamentum, nisi aliud interdum satius esse iudicetur, alternis annis explicet.

[165] *New and Old Testaments in turn*

17. He should teach the New and the Old Testaments in alternating years, unless occasionally some other arrangement is judged to be better.

[166] *Quotannis novus liber prælegendus*

18. Inchoatum uno anno librum non extrahat in alterum, nisi gravem ob causam; immo ad eundem librum interpretandum ne recurrat, nisi post explicatam maiorem partem præcipuorum librorum.

[166] *Every year a new book should be studied*

18. He should not extend a book begun in one year into a second, except for a serious reason. Actually, he should not return to interpret the same book unless he has already taught most of the material in the main books.

[167] *Repetitiones et lectiones domesticæ*

19. Præter repetitiones domi semel in hebdomada, lectiones etiam in refectorio interdum, ut rector præscripserit, habeantur.

[167] *Reviews and in-house classes*

19. In addition to in-house reviews once a week, classes should also sometimes be given in the dining hall, as the rector prescribes.

[168] *Prælectiones publicæ*

20. Loco ordinariæ lectionis designetur interdum ex discipulis aliquis, qui ornate et copiose locum aliquem e Sacris literis celebriorem explicet; contra quem, ubi absolverit, ex condiscipulis unus aut alter argumentetur, non aliunde tamen, quam ex variis sive Sacræ Scripturæ locis, sive linguarum idiotismis, sive Patrum interpretationibus.

[168] *Public presentations*

20. Occasionally, in place of the usual class, someone from the student body should be assigned to explicate some rather well known passage from Sacred Scripture in a polished and thorough manner. When he is finished, one or two of his fellow students should adduce proofs against him, but not on the basis of anything apart from the different passages of Sacred Scripture, or the idioms of the languages, or patristic interpretations.

[H6] Regulæ Professori Linguæ Hebrææ

[169] *Interpretandi fidelitas*

1. Nihil antiquius habeat, quam ut prima ipsa Sanctæ Scripturæ verba per quam integra fide interpretetur.

[170] *Vulgatæ defensio*

2. Inter cetera, ad quæ eius intentio feratur, illud sit, ut versionem ab Ecclesia approbatam defendat.

[171] *Grammatica sacro textui iungenda*

3. Initio anni prima grammaticæ rudimenta explicet; deinde, dum reliquas persequitur institutiones, aliquem Sacræ Scripturæ librum ex facilioribus explanet.

[172] *Præcipua cura verborum*

4. Dum sacros libros interpretatur, non tam in rebus ac sententiis expendendis laboret, quam in vi ac potestate verborum, ac propriis eius linguæ idiotismis, et in grammaticæ præceptis iuxta germanum auctorum usum observandis.

[173] *Linguæ peregrinitas industria mollienda*

5. Ita denique se gerat in docendo, ut peregrinitas et asperitas ea, qua nonnullis linguæ huius studium laborare videtur, sua industria leniatur.

[H6] Rules for the Professor of Hebrew

[169] *Fidelity in interpretation*

1. He should consider nothing more important than interpreting the original words of Holy Scripture themselves with utterly complete fidelity.

[170] *Defense of the Vulgate*

2. Among the other things on which he should focus his efforts, he should include defending the translation approved by the Church.

[171] *Points of grammar should be linked with the sacred text*

3. At the start of the year, he should explain the first rudiments of grammar; then, while he is moving on through the rest of the rules, he should explain one of the easier books of Sacred Scripture.

[172] *Chief interest in words*

4. When he is interpreting the sacred books, he should not spend as much effort on pondering the content and ideas as on taking note of the meaning and the force of the words, and the special idioms distinctive of the language, and the grammatical rules according to the actual usage of the authors.

[173] *The strangeness of the language should be mitigated by energetic activity*

5. Finally, he should conduct himself in his teaching in such a way that his energetic activity mitigates the strangeness and harshness that, in the eyes of quite a few, make this language so hard.

[H7] Regulæ Professoris Scholasticæ Theologiæ

[174] *Finis*

1. Sui muneris esse intelligat, solidam disputandi subtilitatem ita cum orthodoxa fide ac pietate coniungere, ut huic in primis illa deserviat.

[175] *S. Thomas sequendus*

2. Sequantur nostri omnino in scholastica theologia doctrinam Sancti Thomæ, eumque ut doctorem proprium habeant; ponantque in eo omnem operam, ut auditores erga illum quam optime afficiantur. Non sic tamen S. Thomæ astricti esse debere intelligantur, ut nulla prorsus in re ab ea recedere liceat; cum illi ipsi, qui se thomistas maxime profitentur, aliquando ab eo recedant; nec arctius nostros Sancto Thomæ alligari par sit, quam thomistas ipsos.

[176] *Cum qua exceptione*

3. Ergo de conceptione B. Mariæ, ac de solemnitate votorum sequantur sententiam, quæ magis hoc tempore communis est, magisque recepta apud theologos; et in quæstionibus mere philosophicis,

[H7] Rules for the Professor of Scholastic Theology

[174] *Final Goal*

1. He should realize that it is his task to combine a firmly based subtlety in disputation with an orthodox faith and religious devotion in such a way that the former, above everything else, serves the latter.

[175] *Saint Thomas should be followed*

2. Jesuits should entirely follow the teaching of Saint Thomas in Scholastic theology and they should consider him their own particular authority. And they should make every effort to ensure that the students are as well disposed toward him as possible. They should nevertheless realize that they ought not be so tied to Saint Thomas that they may not differ from that theology in any issue whatsoever, since even those very ones who most pointedly profess that they are Thomists differ from him now and then; and it is not right that Jesuits be bound more tightly to Saint Thomas than the Thomists themselves are.

[176] *With what exception*

3. Therefore, concerning the conception of Blessed Mary and the solemnity of vows,[70] they should follow the opinion that is more common at this time and more accepted among the theologians. And in purely philo-

---

[70] [C]onception of Blessed Mary: this was a controversial issue of the time, receiving an official pronouncement only in 1854. Some theologians argued that Mary, in view of her son Jesus' merits, must have been given the grace of having been conceived without any "stain of original sin." Original sin is the sin of Adam and Eve in the Garden of Eden, as recounted in the Book of Genesis, and it marks all human beings as descendants of these parents. The doctrine of the Immaculate Conception makes of Mary a special exception to this rule. See *CathEncy,* s.vv. "Immaculate Conception."

aut etiam in iis, quæ ad Scripturas et canones pertinent, licebit sequi etiam alios, qui eas facultates magis ex professo tractaverunt.

[177] *In dubiis utramvis partem sequi licet*

4. Si quando vel ambigua fuerit S. Thomæ sententia, vel in iis quæstionibus, quas S. Thomas forte non attigit, doctores catholici inter se non consenserint, licebit quamcumque partem sequi, ut dictum est in regulis communibus regula quinta.

[178] *Fidei et pietatis cura*

5. In docendo corroborandæ primum fidei alendæque pietatis cura habeatur. Quare in iis quæstionibus, quas S. Thomas ex professo non tractat, nemo quicquam doceat, quod cum Ecclesiæ sensu, receptisque traditionibus non bene conveniat, quodque aliquo modo solidæ pietatis firmitatem minuat. Quo pertinet, ut nec receptas iam, quamvis congruentes tantum rationes, quibus fidei res probari solent, refellant; nec temere novas excogitent, nisi ex constantibus solidisque principiis.

[179] *Opiniones, quæ catholicos offendunt, non asserendæ*

6. Quæ opiniones, cuiuscunque auctoris sint, in aliqua provincia

sophical questions, or even in those that pertain to the Scriptures and the canons, they will also be permitted to follow others who have treated these areas of study in a thoroughly detailed way.

[177] *In doubtful matters it is permissible to take either side*

4. If ever either the opinion of Saint Thomas is unclear or, in those questions that Saint Thomas has happened not to touch upon, Catholic teachers have not reached a consensus, it will be permissible to take either side, as has been said in rule 5 of the Common Rules.[71]

[178] *Concern for faith and religious devotion*

5. In teaching, care should be taken first for the strengthening of faith and the nourishing of religious devotion. For this reason, in the questions that Saint Thomas does not treat in a thoroughly detailed way, no one should teach anything that does not fit well with the Church's understanding and with the received traditions and that in some way diminishes the firmness of genuine religious devotion. In connection with this, they should not refute the traditional explanations used for proving matters of faith if those explanations are now accepted, even though they may be merely fitting ones. And they should not rashly devise new explanations, except on the basis of solid and lasting principles.

[179] *Opinions that offend Catholics should not be asserted*

6. He should not teach or defend opinions, from whatever authority they

---

[71] [R]ule 5 of the Common Rules: see §133 above.

aut academia catholicos graviter offendere scirentur, eas ibi non doceat aut defendat. Ubi enim nec fidei doctrina nec morum integritas in discrimen adducitur, prudens caritas exigit, ut nostri se illis accomodent, cum quibus versantur.

emanate, that are known to deeply offend Catholics in any province or institution. For where neither the teaching of the faith nor moral purity is at stake, a prudent charity demands that Jesuits accommodate themselves to those with whom they are associating.

[180] *Quadriennio cursus absolvendus*

7. Quadriennio totus theologiæ cursus absolvendus. Si ergo duo fuerint scholasticæ theologiæ professores:

[180] *The course should be finished in four years*

7. The entire course of theology ought to be finished in four years. Therefore, if there are two professors of Scholastic theology:

[181] *Quæstionum divisio*

1. Primus 43 quæstiones ex prima parte explicet primo anno; secundo anno materiam de angelis, atque unam et viginti quæstiones ex prima secundæ; tertio anno a quæstione 55 vel 71 ad finem primæ secundæ; quarto anno ex secunda secundæ materiam de fide, spe et caritate.

[181] *Division of the questions*

1. The first one should teach forty-three questions from Part I in the first year; in the second year, he should teach the material on the angels, and twenty-one questions from the first part of Part II; in the third year, from question 55 or 71 to the end of the first part of Part II; in the fourth year, the matter from the second part of Part II, concerning faith, hope, and charity.

[182] 2. Alter professor primo anno explanet ex secunda secundæ quæstiones de iustitia et iure, et præcipua quædam de religione; secundo ex tertia parte quæstiones de Incarnatione, et, si potest, graviora saltem quædam explicet de sacramentis in genere; tertio de baptismo et Eucharistia, et, si quid potest, de ordine, confirmatione, extrema unctione; quarto de pænitentia et matrimonio.

[182] 2. In the first year, the other professor should teach the questions about justice and right from the second part of Part II, and certain important points about religion; in the second year, he should teach questions about the Incarnation from Part III, and, if he can, he should explain at least certain more important points about the sacraments in general; in the third year, about baptism and the Eucharist, and, if at all possible, ordination, confirmation, and the last anointing; in the fourth year, about penance and matrimony.

[183] 3. Ubi vero tres erunt theologiæ professores, primus primo anno exponat 26 quæstiones ex prima parte; secundo reliquas eiusdem partis quæstiones, quascunque poterit; tertio ex prima secundæ quicquid poterit ante quæstionem 81; quarto anno reliquum primæ secundæ.

[183] 3. But where there are three professors of theology, in the first year, the first one should set forth twenty-six questions from Part I; in the second year, the remaining questions of the same part, whichever ones he can; in the third year, whatever he can from the first part of Part II up to question 81; in the fourth year, the rest of the first part of Part II.

[184] 4. Alter primo anno ex secunda secundæ controversias de Scriptura, de traditionibus, de Ecclesia, de concilio, de romano pontifice; secundo quæstiones de fide, spe et caritate; tertio quæstiones de iustitia et iure, de restitutione et usura, de contractibus, quantum possit; quarto si quæ de contractibus superfuerant, et quæ de religione ac statibus disputat S. Thomas.

[184] 4. In the first year, the second professor should cover from the second part of Part II the controversies about Scripture, about traditions, about the Church, about the councils, about the Roman pontiff;[72] in the second year, he should cover questions about faith, hope, and charity; in the third year, he should cover questions about justice and right, about restitution and usury,[73] and as much as he can about contracts; in the fourth year, if there is anything about contracts that is left, he should cover that and what Saint Thomas argues about religion and states of life.

[185] 5. Tertius primo anno quæstiones de Incarnatione; secundo de sacramentis in genere, de baptismo et Eucharistia; tertio de pænitentia ac matrimonio; quarto de censuris ecclesiasticis et de reliquis sacramentis.

[185] 5. In the first year, the third professor of theology should cover questions about the Incarnation; in the second year, about the sacraments in general, about baptism and the Eucharist; in the third year, about penance and matrimony; in the fourth year, about ecclesiastical censures and about the remaining sacraments.

---

[72] [T]he Roman pontiff: the pope, who inherited a title taken from the ancient Roman high priest, the *pontifex maximus*. Ancient Roman priests were called *pontifices*, or "bridge makers," for reasons that are obscure today.

[73] Usury: the lending of money at an unjust rate of interest.

[186] *Cuiusque anni quæstiones absolvenda*

8. Ex quæstionibus autem, quæ sibi explanandæ fuerint, singulas intra annum, cui adscriptæ sunt, absolvant; si quas non poterit, prætermittat omnino, nec alium in annum reiiciat, sed auditores ad certum aliquem auctorem remittat.

[187] *A quibus quæstionibus abstinendum*

9. Ut autem facilius in theologia scholastica huiusmodi progressus faciant, par est, ut a quibusdam rerum generibus abstineant, quoad eius fieri poterit. Sunt autem in primis hæc quatuor:

[188] *A Sacræ Scripturæ propriis*

1. Unum genus quæstiones aut commentationes divinarum Scripturarum proprias complectitur. Has concedant interpreti Scripturarum.

[189] *A controversiis*

2. Alterum genus in controversiis adversus hæreticos positum est; in quibus pertractandis, quoties in S. Thomæ partibus occurrerint, servent scholasticam potius, quam historicam rationem, et satis esse putent conclusionem quamlibet duobus aut tribus firmis munire fundamentis, diluere etiam totidem fere præcipuas hæreticorum calumnias. In singulis tamen indicent auctorem aliquem, ex quo cetera promere possit, qui velit.

[186] *Each year's questions ought to be finished*

8. However, of the questions that he is supposed to teach, he should finish each of them within the year to which they have been assigned. If there are any that he can not finish, he should omit them entirely and not postpone them for another year, but he should refer the students to some particular author.

[187] *From which questions they should stay away*

9. So that they might more easily make this kind of progress in Scholastic theology, it is proper that they keep away from certain kinds of matter as far as this is possible. There are mainly these four:

[188] *From matter proper to Sacred Scripture*

1. One kind includes questions or commentary proper to Sacred Scriptures. They should leave these to the scriptural exegete.[74]

[189] *From controversies*

2. The second kind comes up in the controversies against heretics. In treating these, whenever they meet them in the sections from Saint Thomas, they should keep to a Scholastic rather than a historical approach, and they should consider it sufficient to defend any thesis with two or three solid principles, and likewise, to undo the main false charges of the heretics with just about as many. Still, on particular issues, they should point out some author from whom anyone who

---

[74] [T]he scriptural exegete: the exegete investigates and determines the meaning of scriptural texts, particularly from the use of language in its original context.

wishes can produce the rest of the matter.

[190] *A philosophicis*

3. In tertio genere sunt philosophicæ res; quas haudquaquam ex instituto tractent, nec tam disputent, quam vel ab aliis vel a se explicatas promant.

[190] *From philosophical matters*

3. The third category consists of philosophical matters. They should not give them a thoroughly detailed treatment at all, and they should not subject them to disputation as much as present them as things that they or others have explained.

[191] *A casibus conscientiæ*

4. Ad quartum genus pertinent conscientiæ casus. In quo generalibus quibusdam rerum moralium principiis, de quibus disputari theologico more solet, contenti, subtiliorem illam ac minutiorem prætereant casuum explicationem.

[191] *From cases of conscience*

4. Cases of conscience fall into the fourth category. In it, they should leave out the more subtle and detailed explanation of the cases, remaining content with certain general principles of moral issues, about which there are usually disputations in the theological manner.

[192] *Eadem non iteranda*

10. Si quando S. Thomas eandem difficultatem in plures distrahit articulos, præsertim diversarum quæstionum, ne idem duobus repetatur locis, poterit vel in unam disputationem, vel etiam, si res ipsa longiorem non exigat explicationem, in compendium articulos illos redigere, ut distincte dicetur in catalogo quæstionum hisce regulis adiuncto, modo nihil prætereat, quod in articulis singulis observatione dignum sit.

[192] *The same material should not be repeated*

10. If Saint Thomas ever breaks down the same problem into several articles, especially when they belong to different questions, then, to avoid a double repetition, provided that he skip nothing noteworthy in the individual articles, he can reduce those articles into one disputation or even, if the issue itself does not call for too extended an explanation, into an abbreviated summary, as will be clearly articulated in the catalog of questions attached to these rules.

[193] *Articuli S. Thomæ quomodo explicandi*

11. Faciles percurrat articulos. Itaque prælecto titulo, mox vel indicet breviter conclusionem S. Thomæ, vel dicat, S. Thomas respondet negando vel affirmando. In difficilioribus vero progrediatur

[193] *How Saint Thomas's articles ought to be explained*

11. He should quickly run through the easy articles. And so, after the title has been read out, he should then either indicate Saint Thomas's thesis briefly or he should say that Saint Thomas answers in the negative or in

hoc fere modo atque ordine: Explicetur primum articuli titulus, si quid habet obscuritatis; tum exponatur distinctio, si qua est, ex cuius membris conclusiones nascuntur; mox conclusio primaria S. Thomæ, atque aliæ deinceps ponantur; singulisque conclusionibus, nisi perspicuæ sint, adiiciatur aliqua eiusdem ratio; quæ etiam ita explicetur, ut intelligant auditores, in distinctionibus ac rationibus S. Thomæ maiorem inesse vim, quam prima fronte aliquando videatur.

the affirmative. But in more difficult matters, he should usually proceed in this manner and in this order: First, the title of the article should be explained if it contains anything that is obscure; then he should set forth the distinction, if there is any, on the basis of whose terms the theses emerge. Next, Saint Thomas's main thesis should be presented, and then the others. Some reason for each thesis should be added to each of them, unless it is very obvious. And it should also be explained in such a way that the students understand that Saint Thomas's distinctions and reasons have more meaning than sometimes appears at first sight.

[194] *Longiores tractatus non instituendi*

12. Explicato quolibet articulo, si res exigat, quæstionem instituat; non tamen longiorem ullum tractatum, nisi in iis materiis, quæ vel in S. Thoma non habentur, vel habentur quidem, sed utilius explicantur compendio.

[194] *Lengthier treatments should not be taught*

12. If the matter calls for it, when an article has been explained, he should engage the question involved, but not any treatment that is rather lengthy, except on those topics that are not found in Saint Thomas or that are actually found there but are more usefully explained by way of an abridgment.

[195] *Aut defendendus S. Thomas, aut quæstio omittenda*

13. Non satis est doctorum sententias referre, suam reticere; sed defendat opinionem S. Thomæ, ut dictum est, vel quæstionem ipsam omittat.

[195] *Either Saint Thomas should be defended or the question omitted*

13. It is not enough that the professor cite the opinions of the academic authorities and keep quiet about his own; but he should defend the opinion of Saint Thomas, as has been said, or he should omit that particular question.

[196] *Disputationes menstruæ*

14. In disputationibus menstruis, quibus totidem defendent, quot fuerint præceptores, terni fere ante meridiem argumententur, totidem post meridiem; quilibet adversus

[196] *Monthly disputations*

14. In the monthly disputations, they will defend as many questions as there are teachers. Normally, three should debate before noon, and the same number after noon. Any person

omnes defendentes; et quidem, si nihil impediat, qui mane responderit primo loco, a prandio secundo respondeat.

can argue against all of those defending. And in fact, if nothing prevents it, the one who that morning responded in the first place, should respond after the midday meal in the second.

[H8] Catalogus Aliquot Quæstionum

[H8] Catalog of Some Questions

[H9] Ex Prima Parte Sancti Thomæ

[H9] From the First Part of Saint Thomas

[C1]   Quæstio 1 Articulus 1

[C1]   Question 1, Article 1

Nihil hic de potentia neutra. Utrum insit homini naturalis appetitus ad claram Dei visionem, differatur in I-II quæstio 3 articulus 8, vel quæstio 5 articulus 8.

Take up nothing about either potency here.[75] Postpone until I-II question 3, article 8, or question 5, article 8, whether the human person possesses a natural appetite for the clear vision of God.[76]

[C2]   Articulus 2

[C2]   Article 2

Quæ pertinent ad naturam scientiæ et ad subalternationem scientiarum, non disputentur hic, sed supponantur ex Logica.

Do not dispute here the things that pertain to the nature of science and to the subalternation of the sciences, but postulate them on the basis of logic.

[C3]   Articulus 3

[C3]   Article 3

Non tractetur hic de rationibus formalibus obiectorum scibilium; neque an scientia sit unus simplex habitus, et qualitas in genere; hæc enim philosophorum sunt; sed his

Do not treat here of the formal causes of knowable objects, nor of whether knowledge is one simple habit and a kind of quality, for this belongs to the philosophers. But,

---

[75] For background on this catalog, see endn. 16.

Potency: the ability to become or do something. This and many other such terms from Scholastic discourse have technical meanings, nuances, and varieties of usage that cannot be fully presented here. An excellent reference resource is Roy J. Deferrari, *A Latin-English Dictionary of Saint Thomas Aquinas.*

[76] [V]ision of God: the beatific vision, that is, the full enjoyment of God by those who have entered heaven.

suppositis sufficit quærere, an theologia ex aliqua ratione peculiari sit unus habitus, et una simplex qualitas.

[C4] Articulus 4

Non disputentur, sed supponantur, quæ dici solent de speculativo et practico, ut sunt differentiæ scientiarum.

[C5] Articulus 5

Non tractetur, quid sit certitudo assensus, quid firmitas, quid veritas, quid evidentia, et quotuplex; sunt enim logicorum.

[C6] Articulus 9

An decuerit Scripturam abundare metaphoris et parabolis, et an Sacræ Literæ apertæ et claræ sint, relinquantur lectori Scripturæ et controversiarum, sicut etiam tractatus de sensibus Scripturæ.

[C7] Quæstio 2

Non explicetur, sed ex Logica supponatur, quid et quotuplex sit propositio per se nota et immediata; nec rationes S. Thomæ, quibus demonstrat Deum esse, confutentur, sed potius corroborentur.

[C8] Quæstio 3 Articulus 1

An aliquod corpus moveat immotum, et an vivens nobilior sit non vivente, et an Aristoteles recte

postulating these, it suffices to ask whether in some respect theology is one habit and one simple quality.[77]

[C4] Article 4

Do not dispute but postulate what is usually said about the speculative and the practical, how they differentiate the types of sciences.

[C5] Article 5

Do not take up what certitude of assent is, or sureness, truth, evidence, or how many differentiations of these there are; this belongs to the logicians.

[C6] Article 9

Leave to the commentator on Scripture and its controversies the questions of whether it is fitting for the Scripture to be full of metaphors and parables, and whether the sacred texts are transparent and obvious. The same goes for the treatise on the senses of Scripture.[78]

[C7] Question 2

Do not explain, but postulate on the basis of logic what and how manifold an immediately self-evident proposition is. And do not refute the arguments of Saint Thomas for the existence of God but rather confirm them.

[C8] Question 3, Article 1

Leave to the philosophers whether some unmoved body might be the cause of motion and whether the

---

[77] [P]ostulating: presupposing, or taking something as a given rather than as something to be proved.

[78] [T]he senses of Scripture: the various levels of meaning that can be found in scriptural texts (literal, allegorical, moral, anagogical). See the note on §154 above.

probaverit Deum esse incorpore-
um, relinquatur philosophis.

animate is of a higher order than
the inanimate, and whether Aristotle has correctly proved that God
is incorporeal.

[C9]   Articulus 2

Nihil hic de principio indivi-
duationis.

[C9]   Article 2

Take up nothing here about the
principle of individuation.[79]

[C10]   Articulus 3

Non tractetur de distinctione
suppositi et naturæ; pertinet enim
ad III partem quæstio 3 articulus 3.
Quomodo autem distinguantur in
creaturis esse et essentia, relinquatur metaphysico.

[C10]   Article 3

Do not take up the difference between a particular substance and its
nature; for this pertains to Part III,
question 3, article 3. And leave to
the metaphysician how being and
essence should be distinguished in
creatures.

[C11]   Articulus 4

In quæstione: An Deus sit in
prædicamento, rescindantur, quæ
sunt propria philosophorum.
quæstio vero, an angeli et cæli sint
in prædicamento, tota philosopho
relinquatur.

[C11]   Article 4

In the question of whether the
Aristotelian categories apply to God,
cut out those things that specifically
belong to the philosophers.[80] But the
question of whether the categories
apply to angels and the heavens
should be left entirely to the philosopher.

[C12]   Articulus 7

An simplicitati divinæ repugnet
personarum et relationum plurali-
tas, non tractetur hic, sed infra
quæstione 28 articulo 2.

[C12]   Article 7

Do not treat here but later, in
question 28, article 2, whether the
plurality of persons and relations
contradicts divine simplicity.[81]

[C13]   Quæstio 4 Articulus 1

An reliqua perfectio, quæ for-
maliter sit in Deo, libere ei conve-

[C13]   Question 4, Article 1

Postpone until question 19, article 2, whether the rest of the perfec-

---

[79] [T]he principle of individuation: what underlies the process of the development of
a particular thing from its universal form.

[80] [T]he Aristotelian categories: Aristotle's categories lists ten possible predications,
namely, those of substance, quantity, quality, relation, place, time, position, state, action,
and affection.

[81] [W]hether the plurality of persons and relations contradicts divine simplicity: the
reference is to the Persons of the Trinity and the relationships that exist between and
among those Persons.

niat, differatur in quæstio 19 articulus 2. An autem relatio divina secundum se sit aliqua perfectio, remittatur ad materiam de Trinitate.

tion that formally belongs to God fits him unrestrictedly. Leave until the material on the Trinity whether a divine relation with respect to itself is some perfection.

[C14] Quæstio 5

Prætermittatur, et Metaphysica supponatur, quid sit bonum.

[C14] Question 5

Omit what the good is and postulate it on the basis of metaphysics.

[C15] Quæstio 7 Articulus 1

Quid Aristoteles senserit de Dei infinitate, relinquatur philosopho.

[C15] Question 7, Article 1

Leave to the philosopher what Aristotle thought about God's infinity.

[C16] Articuli 2 3 4

An creari possit aliquid infinitum in quantitate, vel in qualitatibus naturalibus, philosophi est disputare; sicut et de infinito in genere substantiæ; cum tam hoc, quam illud infinitum esse creabile, iisdem fere argumentis probari soleat, aut oppugnari. An autem possibile sit infinitum in qualitatibus supernaturalibus, a theologo disseratur, sed in II-II quæstio 24 articulus 7 tantummodo.

[C16] Articles 2, 3, and 4

It belongs to the philosopher to dispute whether anything infinite in extent or in natural qualities can be created. The same holds for an infinite thing in a type of substance, since generally the same arguments tend to be used to show or to disprove that both the latter and the former can be created. The theologian should discuss whether something infinite in supernatural qualities is possible, but only in II-II, question 24, article 7.

[C17] Quæstio 8

De ubiquitate humanitatis Christi non tractetur hic, sed in III P. quæstio 2.

[C17] Question 8

Do not treat the ubiquity of the humanity of Christ here, but in Part III, question 2.

[C18] Quæstio 9

An angeli et cœli sint entia necessaria et immutabilia, non est quæstio theologi, sed metaphysici.

[C18] Question 9

Whether angels and the heavens are necessary and immutable beings is not a question for the theologian, but for the metaphysician.

[C19] Quæstio 11

De uno, ut est passio entis, nihil dicat theologus, cum sit metaphysica res.

[C19] Question 11

About the One, as it is a property of being, the theologian should say nothing since it is a metaphysical matter.

[C20]   Articulus 3

An repugnet in subiecto quanto inhærere accidens spirituale, vel in subiecto immateriali accidens corporale, differatur in materiam de Eucharistia.

[C21]   Articulus 6

Tractare de inæqualitate præmiorum, sicut et meritorum, pertinet ad I-II quæstionem 4 articulum 2.

[C22]   Articulus 8

De cognitione beatifica animæ Christi non disputetur hic, sed in III P.

[C23]   Articulus 12

An puro viatori possit communicari evidens notitia abstractiva articulorum fidei, non hic disputandum est, sed supra quæstione I articulo 1.

[C24] Quæstio 13 Articulus 3 et 4

De distinctione attributorum et essentiæ nihil hic repetatur, si de ea supra disputatum est, quæstione 3.

[C25]   Articulus 5

Non disputetur de analogia entis, cum spectet ad metaphysicum.

[C26]   Articulus 7

Nihil hic dicatur de relationibus in genere, cum metaphysicæ speculationis sit.

[C27]   Articuli 8 9 10 11 12

Modi, quibus sumitur nomen Dei, et ea quæ dici solent de no-

[C20]   [Question 12], Article 3

Postpone until the material on the Eucharist whether it is contradictory for a spiritual accident to inhere in an extended object, or whether a corporeal accident can inhere in an immaterial one.

[C21]   Article 6

Treating the issue of the inequality of rewards, and likewise merits, pertains to I-II question 4, article 2.

[C22]   Article 8

Do not dispute here, but in Part III, about the beatific knowledge that Christ's soul had.

[C23]   Article 12

Do not dispute here, but earlier, in question 1, article 1, whether a clear abstract knowledge of the articles of faith can be communicated to a pure-hearted human being who is "on the way."

[C24]   Question 13, Articles 3 and 4

Review nothing here about the distinction between attributes and essence, if it has already been debated earlier, in question 3.

[C25]   Article 5

Do not engage in argument about the analogy of being, since it relates to the metaphysician.

[C26]   Article 7

Say nothing here about the kinds of relations since this belongs to metaphysical speculation.

[C27]   Articles 8, 9, 10, 11, and 12

Leave to the scriptural exegete the ways in which the name of God

mine Tetragrammato, relinquantur interpreti Scripturæ.

is taken, and what is usually said about the Tetragram name.[82]

[C28] Quæstiones 16 et 17

[C28] Questions 16 and 17

Disputatio de vero et falso metaphysici negotii est.

The dispute about truth and falsity is the task of the metaphysician.

[C29] Quæstio 19 articuli 9 et 12

[C29] Question 19, Articles 9 and 12

An Deus sit causa peccati, et an teneamur voluntatem nostram divinæ conformare, pertinent ad I-II. Non moretur theologus in explicanda Peripateticorum, aliorumque philosophorum sententia de providentia Dei.

Whether God is a cause of sin 1and whether we are bound to conform our will to the divine will pertains to I-II. The theologian should not delay the course's progress with an explanation of what the Peripatetics and other philosophers thought about God's providence.[83]

[C30] Quæstio 23 Articulus 1

[C30] Question 23, Article 1

Ad quem finem ordinaretur homo, si non esset finis supernaturalis, non disputetur hic, sed in I-II quæstione 2.

Do not dispute here, but rather in I-II, question 2, toward what end the human person would be ordained, if there were not a supernatural end.[84]

[C31] Articulus 3

[C31] Article 3

Quod agendum sit ei, cui sua damnatio revelaretur, non tractetur hic, sed in materia de spe.

Do not treat here what people should do if their own damnation is revealed to them.[85] Take up this idea with the material on hope.

[C32] Articulus 5

[C32] Article 5

De prædestinatione Christi, et quomodo Christus sit causa nostræ

Leave to Part III matter about the predestination of Christ, and

[82] Tetragram name: the name of God in the four consonantal Hebrew letters, YHWH.

[83] Peripatetics: ancient thinkers who followed and developed Aristotle's thinking.

"God's providence": "Providence in general, or foresight, is a function of the virtue of prudence, and may be defined as the practical reason, adapting means to an end. As applied to God, Providence is God Himself considered in that act by which in His wisdom He so orders all events within the universe that the end for which it was created may be realized" (*CathEncy*, s.vv. "Divine Providence").

[84] [T]oward what end the human person would be ordained, if there were not a supernatural end: i.e., what would be the intended fulfillment of a human person.

[85] Damnation: condemnation to hell for all eternity.

prædestinationis, relinquatur III parti.

how Christ is the cause of our predestination.[86]

[C33] Quæstio 24

Disputatio de libro vitæ, qua parte scholastica est, explicetur; cetera pertinent ad interpretem Scripturæ.

[C33] Question 24

Explain the disputation about the book of life, to the extent that it is a Scholastic matter.[87] The rest pertains to the scriptural exegete.

[C34] Quæstio 25

An actio sit in agente ut in subiecto, quæstio physicorum est, non theologorum.

[C34] Question 25

Whether an action is in the agent as in the subject is a question for the natural philosophers, not the theologians.[88]

[C35] Articulus 1

An Deus per se solum possit efficere rem, quæ est peccatum, pertinet ad I-II; sicut ad II-II: An possit per se vel per alium dicere falsum.

[C35] Article 1

Whether God, completely on his own, can bring about something that is a sin, pertains to I-II, just as it pertains to II-II whether he can say something false, on his own or through another.

[C36] Articulus 6

Nihil hic de beatitudine in genere, vel de nostra.

[C36] Article 6

Say nothing here about happiness in general, or about our particular happiness.

[C37] Quæstio 27 Articulus 1

De verbo mentis nihil aliud tractetur, quam an producatur ab intellectu nostro, ut terminus actionis, et quomodo ab ea distinguatur.

[C37] Question 27, Article 1

Do not treat the mental word at all,[89] other than whether it is produced by our intellect as the end point of an action, and how it is distinguished from it.

---

[86] Predestination: the assignment of a person to a particular eternal fate even before that person is born.

[87] [T]he book of life: a Biblical image, as in the Book of Revelation (20:12, RSV): for this text and reflections upon it, see endn. 17.

[88] For a discussion of the meaning of the expression "the natural philosophers," see endn. 18.

[89] [T]he mental word: "something conceived by the mind, by which man expresses his thoughts mentally" (*Sumtheol*, II.1.q. 93.a1).

[C38] Articulus 3

An notitia concurrat active ad actum voluntatis, ad I-II pertinet.

[C39] Quæstio 29

Quid suppositum addat supra naturam singularem, pertinet ad III partem.

[C40] Quæstio 32

An evidenter dilui possint argumenta contra mysterium Trinitatis, pertinet ad credibilitatem articulorum fidei; de qua agitur in II-II, quæstione 1 articulo 4.

[C41] Articulus 4

De varia censura et qualitate propositionum non disputetur hic, sed in materia de fide.

[C42] Quæstio 39

Non disputetur hic, quomodo persona divina distinguatur ab essentia, si quæstione 28 tractatum fuit de distinctione relationum et essentiæ.

[C43] Quæstio 43

De visibilibus signis, in quibus apparuit Spiritus Sanctus, commodius disputare potest interpres Scripturæ. Idem de apparitionibus visibilibus, quæ in veteri seu novo Testamento tribuuntur Deo, an fuerint factæ immediate per Deum, an per angelos.

[C38] Article 3

Whether knowledge actively coincides with an act of the will pertains to I-II.

[C39] Question 29

What a substance adds beyond a particular nature pertains to Part III.[90]

[C40] Question 32

Whether arguments against the mystery of the Trinity can evidently be undone pertains to the credibility of the articles of faith. This is treated in II-II, question 1, article 4.

[C41] Article 4

Do not dispute here about the issues concerning the diversity of opinion and the nature of propositions. Do this in the section on faith.

[C42] Question 39

Do not dispute here about how the divine Person is distinguished from essence if the distinction between relations and essence has been taken up in question 28.

[C43] Question 43

It is more fitting for the scriptural exegete to dispute about the visible signs in which the Holy Spirit has appeared. The same holds for visible apparitions that are attributed to God in the Old or New Testaments, and whether they were created directly by God or by angels.

---

[90] [S]ubstance: a "thing," considered apart from its non-essential properties; that which "stands under" all appearances.

[C44] Quæstio 53

An motus angelorum possit fieri in instanti, supponit multa philosophica, quæ hic non tractentur. Id quod etiam servetur in iis, quæ disputantur quæstione 54 articulis 1 et 3.

[C44]   Question 53

The question of whether the movement of angels can happen in an instant rests on many philosophical issues that should not be treated here. This should also be observed for those things that are disputed in question 54, articles 1 and 3.

[H10]   Ex Prima Secundæ

[C45] Quæstio I Articulus 1

Hic nihil, aut brevissime disserendum est de deliberata voluntate, de consensu perfecto et imperfecto, et quid sit hominem esse dominum suarum actionum; hæc enim locum suum habent inferius. Item nihil hic dicatur de causalitate finis; est enim quæstio physica.

[H10]   From the First Part of Part II

[C45]   Question 1, Article 1

Here discuss not at all or only very briefly the deliberated will, perfect and imperfect consent, and what it means that a person is the master of his or her own actions; for these things have their place later on. Likewise, say nothing here about the causality of the end; for it is a question belonging to natural philosophy.

[C46]   Articulus 2

An Deus agat propter finem, pertinet ad I partem in materia de voluntate Dei. Item, utrum natura agat propter finem, quæstio philosophica est.

[C46]   Article 2

Whether God acts for the sake of a final goal pertains to Part I in the material about the will of God. Likewise, whether nature acts for the sake of a final goal is a philosophical question.

[C47]   Articulus 3

Cavendum est, ne hic et inferius eadem quæstio disputetur; nempe: Utrum actus hominis recipiant speciem a fine. Leviter igitur hic attingatur, et plene disseratur inferius.

[C47]   Article 3

Be careful that the same question is not disputed here and later on, namely, whether a person's acts take their species from their final goal. Therefore, touch on it lightly here, and discuss it fully later on.

[C48]   Articulus 4

Quomodo bonum sit sui diffusivum, non disputetur hoc loco.

[C48]   Article 4

Do not at this point dispute about how the good is diffusive of itself.

[C49]   Quæstio 2

Vel omittatur, vel compendio exponatur, cum tota in Ethicis Aristotelis contineatur.

[C50]   Quæstio 3 Articulus 1

An Deus videatur a beatis visione Dei increata, hic explicetur, non in I parte.

[C51]   Articulus 2

An habitus sit melior suo actu, non videtur hic explicandum, cum sit quæstio philosophica, et inferius habeat suum locum.

[C52]   Articulus 3

De perfectione sensuum in corpore glorioso, eiusque dotibus, hic et quæstione 4 articulo 6 aliquid dicatur, si vacat, cum ad materiam de novissimis non perveniatur. Item, an Deus videri possit per aliquem sensum, seu sensitivam notitiam, non hic, sed in I parte disputetur.

[C53]   Articulus 4

In quo consistat summa miseria damnatorum, non explicetur hoc loco, sed inferius, ubi de pœna peccati agitur.

[C54]   Articulus 5

Nihil dicatur de intellectu practico et speculativo, nec de praxi et speculatione.

[C49]   Question 2

Either omit it or present it in an abridged form, since it is all contained in Aristotle's *Ethics.*[91]

[C50]   Question 3, Article 1

Whether God is seen by the blessed by means of an uncreated vision of God should be taught here, not in Part I.[92]

[C51]   Article 2

It does not seem good to explain here whether a habit is better than its own act, since it is a question belonging to philosophy and it has its place further on.

[C52]   Article 3

On the perfection of the senses in the resurrected body and on its endowments, something should be said here and in question 4, article 6, if there is time, since the material about the last things is yet to come. Likewise, whether God can be seen by some sense or sense knowledge should not be disputed here, but in Part I.

[C53]   Article 4

Do not explain at this point in what the worst misery of the damned consists, but do this further on, where punishment for sin is considered.

[C54]   Article 5

Nothing should be said about the practical and speculative intellect, nor about practice and contemplation.

[91] Aristotle's *Ethics:* the *Nicomachean Ethics*, a vastly influential philosophical work on happiness, the virtues, and other ethical themes.

[92] [T]he blessed: the souls who enjoy eternity in the presence of God.

[C55]   Articulus 7

De obiecto intellectus, et utrum anima naturaliter possit cognoscere substantias separatas, relinquatur philosophis.

[C56] Quæstio 4 Articulus 1

Quicquid hic disseri solet de differentia delectationis, amoris et fruitionis, differatur in quæstione de frui et uti. Item, an cum visione Dei possit aliquo modo stare tristitia, reiiciatur in III partem, ubi quæritur, an Christus secundum rationem superiorem passus sit.

[C57]   Articulus 2

An delectatio quæratur propter operationem, an contra tractetur in ethicis; hic vero nihil, vel brevissime.

[C58]   Articulus 5

An animæ sanctorum a corporibus separatæ statim Deum videant, hic tractetur, non in I parte.

[C59] [Quæstio 5] Articulus 3

Relinquatur fere I part. totus.

[C60]   Articulus 5

Nihil dicatur de merito aut de necessitate luminis gloriæ.

[C61]   Articulus 8

An vero appetitu ordinato magis appetat damnatus non esse, quam sic esse, pertinet ad quæstionem de pœna peccati.

[C55]   Article 7

Leave to the philosophers material on the object of the intellect, and whether the mind can naturally know separate substances.

[C56]   Quest1ion 4, Article 1

Whatever is usually discussed here about the difference between delight, love, and enjoyment should be postponed until the question about enjoying and using. Likewise, whether sadness can in some way coexist with the vision of God should be put off until Part III, where there arises the question about whether Christ suffered with respect to his higher reason.

[C57]   Article 2

Whether or not delight is sought on account of an activity should be treated in ethics. Here it should be taken up not at all or only very briefly.

[C58]   Article 5

Treat here, not in Part I, whether the souls of the saints, separated from their bodies, see God at once.

[C59]   [Question 5], Article 3

Leave practically the whole article to Part I.

[C60]   Article 5

Say nothing about merit or about the necessity of the light of glory.

[C61]   Article 8

But whether a damned person hungers with an ordered appetite for non-existence more than for existence in such a state pertains to the question about the punishment for sin.

[C62] Quæstio 6 Articulus 1

Non disseratur hoc loco de libero arbitrio contra hæreticos, sed in materia de gratia.

[C62] Question 6, Article 1

At this point there should not be, in opposition to the heretics, a discussion about free will. This should be done in the section on grace.

[C63] Articulus 2

Unde proveniat, quod homo sui compos sit proprie liber et dominus suorum actuum, tractetur infra in quæstione de electione.

[C63] Article 2

How it comes about that people in possession of their own faculties are free in a proper sense and the masters of their own actions should be discussed later in the section on choice.

[C64] Articulus 3

Nihil dicatur de pura omissione.

[C64] Article 3

Nothing should be said about pure omission.

[C65] Articulus 4

Disputetur hic, an voluntas possit cogi; non autem, an possit necessitari, quia de hoc inferius tractandum est.

[C65] Article 4

Here it should be disputed whether the will can be forced, but not whether it can be subjected to necessity, since this will be treated further on.

[C66] Articulus 6

Quomodo metus irritet matrimonium, votum, iuramentum et contractus, reservetur II-II et III parti.

[C66] Article 6

Reserve for II-II and Part III how fear can invalidate matrimony, vows, oaths, and contracts.

[C67] Articulus 8

Difficultates de ignorantia reserventur in quæst. 76.

[C67] Article 8

Reserve for question 76 difficulties about ignorance.

[C68] Quæstio 7

Plenior consideratio circumstantiarum non est huius loci, cum de illis sæpe inferius disserendum sit.

[C68] Question 7

A developed consideration of circumstances does not belong here, since these things will have to be discussed often later on.

[C69] Articulus 4

Nihil hic disseratur de præscientia seu prædefinitione actuum liberorum, neque de gratuita motione, qua Deus movet voluntatem humanam.

[C70] Quæstio 11

Non videtur hic quicquam disserendum de obiecto spei; neque an possit beatus frui divina essentia, non fruendo personis, vel una persona, et non aliis; hoc enim pertinet ad I partem.

[C71] Quæstio 12 Articulus 3

Non tractetur, utrum intellectus possit simul multa intelligere.

[C72] Quæstio 15

De consensu formali vel interpretativo, et an pertineat ad rationem superiorem, inferius tractandum est.

[C73] Quæstio 17

Quomodo ratio imperet membris externis; nempe despotice, an politice, disputare philosophi moralis est; breviter igitur hoc loco expediatur.

[C74] Articulus 9

Utrum in homine existente in gratia detur aliquis actus indifferens ad meritum et demeritum, disputetur in materia de merito.

[C69] Article 4

Discuss nothing here about foreknowledge or the predefinition of free acts, nor about the entirely free motion by which God moves the human will.

[C70] Question 11

It does not seem good that there should be any discussion here about the object of hope; nor about whether a person experiencing the happiness of heaven can enjoy the divine essence, without enjoying the Persons, or one Person and not the others; for this pertains to Part I.

[C71] Question 12, Article 3

Do not treat whether the intellect can know many things at the same time.

[C72] Question 15

Treat further on the formal or interpretive consent and whether it pertains to the higher reason.[93]

[C73] Question [17]

Disputing how the reason commands parts of the body, namely, whether in the manner of a despot, or in the manner of a participatory government, belongs to moral philosophy; therefore it should be handled only briefly at this point.

[C74] Article 9

Whether in a person in a state of grace there is granted any act that has nothing to do with merit or

---

[93] [T]he higher reason: "[R]eason as concerned with heavenly things." See Deferrari, *Latin-English Dictionary*, s.v. "ratio."

fault, should be debated in the material on merit.

[C75] Articulus 11

Prætereantur ea, quæ pertinent ad confessionem circumstantiarum.

[C75] Article 11

Pass over those things having to do with the confession of circumstances.

[C76] Quæstio 20 Articulus 5

Hæc difficultas repetitur in materia de peccatis; quare in eum locum reservetur. Difficultates huius articuli differantur in materiam de merito.

[C76] Question 20, Article 5

This difficulty is repeated in the material on sins; for this reason, reserve it for that place. The difficulties of this article should be postponed until the section on merit.

[C77] Quæstio 20 Articulus 4

Quæstiones quæ sunt inter 21 et 71 omitti possunt. Explicentur tamen pauca de habitibus et de virtutibus in genere.

[C77] [Question 21], Article 4

The questions between 21 and 71 can be left out. Nevertheless, a few things should be explained about habits and about virtues in general.

[C78] Quæstio 71 Articulus 4

Quomodo peccatum virtutes, præsertim infusas expellat, non hic explicetur, sed in II-II, in materia de caritate.

[C78] Question 71, Article 4

How sin casts out virtues, especially ones that are infused, should not be taught here, but in II-II, in the material on charity.

[C79] Articulus 5

Nihil hic de distinctione mortalis et venialis.

[C79] [Question 72], Article 5

Nothing should be said here about the distinction between mortal and venial.[94]

[C80] Articulus 8

Hæc difficultas satis explicata manet ex quæstione 18 articulo 5.

[C80] Article 8

This difficulty has been given sufficient explanation at question 18, article 5.

---

[94] [T]he distinction between mortal and venial: mortal sins can be related to the scriptural phrase "sins unto death" (1 John 5:16–f.). These are serious sins that are in fundamental contradiction to God's will and signify a deep separation from the divine life. Venial sins are those that do not signify such a deep break, but represent aspects of the soul that require purification before the person can participate fully in the life of the blessed. Scandal: "a word or action evil in itself, which occasions another's spiritual ruin" (*CathEncy*, s.v. "Scandal").

[C81] Quæstio 73 Articulus 8

Non descendatur ad casus particulares de scandalo vel restitutione; neque hic tractetur, utrum is, qui alium ad peccatum inducit, gravius peccet, quam qui occidit; pertinet enim ad materiam de scandalo.

[C82] Quæstio 79

Nihil dicatur de immediato Dei concursu cum secundis causis.

[C83] Quæstio 81 Articulus 3

Immaculata conceptio B. Mariæ non est huius loci, sed III partis; ubi etiam, dum de eiusdem sanctificatione agitur, tractetur quoque de fomite, et quomodo ligetur aut tollatur.

[C84] Quæstio 85

Quomodo natura lapsa differat a puris naturalibus, tractetur in materia de gratia.

[C85] Articulus 8

Quomodo Deus peccata patrum puniat in filiis, relinquatur interpreti Scripturæ.

[C81] Question 73, Article 8

Do not get into particular cases having to do with scandal or restitution;[95] and do not treat here whether the one who induces another to sin sins more gravely than one who kills: this pertains to the material on scandal.

[C82] Question 79

Nothing should be said about the immediate concursus of God with second causes.[96]

[C83] Question 81, Article 3

The Immaculate Conception of Blessed Mary does not belong here, but in Part III; when her sanctification is being taken up, "the kindling" [of sin] and how it is restricted or removed will also be discussed.[97]

[C84] Question 85

How fallen nature differs from pure natural realities, should be treated in the section on grace.[98]

[C85] [Question 87], Article 8

How God punishes the sins of the fathers in the sons should be left to the scriptural exegete.

---

[95] Restitution: "an act of commutative justice by which exact reparation as far as possible is made for an injury that has been done to another" (ibid., s.v. "Restitution").

[96] [The immediate concursus of God]: the concurrence of God, as divinely sovereign over creation, with all things.

[97] [T]he Immaculate Conception of Blessed Mary: See note on §176 above. [T]he kindling [of sin]: "those likes and dislikes that are not under full and absolute control of right reason and strong will-power" (*CathEncy*, s.v. "Incarnation").

[98] [F]allen nature: the way nature is after the fall (sin) of Adam and Eve in the Garden of Eden.

[C86]   Quæstio 89 Articulus 2

Expositio Sancti Pauli relinquatur lectori Scripturæ.

[C87]   Articulus 5

De primis motibus sensualitatis in infidelibus satis esse videntur, quæ superius de primis motibus dicta sunt. Utrum autem omnia opera infidelium sint peccata mortalia, differatur in II-II quæstione 10 articulo 4.

[C88]   Quæstio 92

Non disputetur hic, utrum peccent, qui pœnæ metu legem servant; nec utrum Deus peccata permittat, an velit. Quæstiones 101 102 104 105 et expositio S. Pauli in quæstio 89 articulus 2 prætereantur, cum Scripturarum sint.

[C89]   Articulus 5

Materia huius articuli differatur in quæstionem 114 articulum 7.

[C90]   Articulus 7

Non disputetur hic de macula peccati, nec de reatu pœnæ, nec de corruptione boni naturalis, nec de aliis huiusmodi, quæ in materia de peccatis explicata sunt.

[C86]   Question 89, Article 2

Leave the exposition of Saint Paul to the scriptural commentator.[99]

[C87]   Article 5

Concerning first movements of sensuality in those without faith, what was said earlier about first movements seems to be sufficient. However whether all the works of those without faith are mortal sins should be postponed until II-II, question 10, article 4.

[C88]   Question 92

Do not dispute here whether those people who keep the law out of a fear of punishment are committing sin, nor whether God permits sins or wishes it. Pass over questions 101, 102, 104, and 105, and the exposition of Saint Paul in question 89, article 2, since they relate closely to the Scriptures.

[C89]   [Question 109], Article 5

The matter of this article should be postponed until question 114, article 7.

[C90]   Article 7

Do not dispute here about the stain of sin, nor about the guilty state of punishment, nor about the corruption of a natural good, nor about other such things, which have been explained in the material about sins.[100]

---

[99] Saint Paul: the author of the epistles, the letters that make up a substantial part of the New Testament.

[100] The stain of sin: the effect of sin on the soul.

[C91] Quæstio 110

An gratia ponat aliquid in anima, vel hic tractetur, vel in quæstione 113, de iustificatione articulo 2.

[C91] Question 110

Whether grace puts something in the soul should either be treated here or in question 113, article 2, about justification.[101]

[C92] Quæstio 112 Articulus 1

Nihil hic dicatur de causalitate sacramentorum circa gratiam.

[C92] Question 112, Article 1

Nothing should be said here about the causality of the sacraments concerning grace.[102]

[C93] Articulus 2

Utrum gratia primi hominis et angelorum in eorum creatione data fuerit supposita ipsorum dispositione, non hic tractetur, sed in I parte.

[C93] Article 2

Whether at the creation of the first human being and of the angels their grace was given after a presupposition about their disposition had been made should not be treated here, but in Part I.[103]

[C94] Articulus 3

Non videtur hic agendum de contritione continuata Caietani, vel de intensione Scoti; pertinent enim ad materiam de pœnitentia.

[C94] Article 3

It does not seem good to consider here Cajetan's continued contrition or Scotus's *intensio*,[104] for these pertain to the matter on penance.

[C95] Quæstio 113 Articulus 4

De necessitate fidei in Christum ante vel post Evangelium promulgatum, non disputetur, nisi in II-II.

[C95] Question 113, Article 4

Dispute only in II-II about the necessity of believing in Christ before or after the Gospel was proclaimed.

---

[101] Justification: "the transforming of the sinner from the state of unrighteousness to the state of holiness" (*CathEncy*, s.v. "Justification").

[102] Sacraments: the Church has understood sacraments as "outward signs of inward grace, instituted by Christ for our sanctification" (ibid., s.v. "Sacraments). In the Catholic tradition they include baptism, confirmation, penance, Holy Communion (Eucharist), holy orders, matrimony, and the sacrament of the sick.

[103] [A]fter a presupposition about their inclination: that is, "Did the grace that they received depend on some kind of inclination that they had?"

[104] "Cajetan's continued contrition: Tommaso de Vio Gaetani Cajetan (1469–1534), a Dominican cardinal who was a Scholastic philosopher, theologian, exegete, and important commentator on Thomas Aquinas's works. Scotus's *intensio:* Duns Scotus (1270–1308), a Franciscan Scholastic thinker whose work generated a school known as Scotism.

[C96] Articulus 7

Utrum augmentum gratiæ detur in principio, an in fine actionis meritoriæ; et utrum, si operatio meritoria successiva sit, ipsa etiam gratia successive augeatur, melius reservantur in quæstionem de augmento caritatis in II-II.

[C96] Article 7

Whether the increase of grace is given at the beginning or at the end of a meritorious act; and whether, if a meritorious action follows the grace, the grace itself also increases following the action—these are questions better kept for the question about the increase of charity in II-II.

[C97] Articulus 9 [Lukács: 2]

De numero et ordine et necessitate omnium actuum, qui concurrunt ad iustificationem, hic disputetur, non in materia de pœnitentia.

[C97] Article 2

Here, not in the section on penance, dispute about the number and order and necessity of all acts that join together for justification.

[C98] [Lukács: follows C99] Articulus 3

Utrum per quælibet opera augeatur gratia et caritas, reservetur in materiam de caritate in II-II.

[C98] Question 114, Article 6

Nothing should be said here about the merit of Christ, since it pertains to Part III.

[C99] Quæstio 114 Articulus 6

Nihil hic de merito Christi dicatur, cum pertineat ad III partem.

[C99] Article 3

Reserve for the material about charity in II-II whether grace and charity increase through any works.[105]

[H11] Ex Secunda Secundæ

[C100] Quæstio 4 Articulus 3

Non tractetur hic, sed infra in materia de caritate, an caritas sit forma omnium virtutum in genere.

[H11] From the Second Part of Part II

[C100] Question 4, Article 3

Whether charity is the form of all the virtues in general should not be treated here, but later, in the section on charity.[106]

---

[105] Charity: *caritas* is free, self-giving, generous love.

[106] Form: "the intrinsic principle of existence in any determinate essence" (ibid., s.v. "Form").

[C101]   Articulus 6

Disputetur hic, an fides sit unus habitus; non tamen, an sit simplex qualitas.

[C101]   Article 6

Whether faith is a single habit should be disputed here,[107] but not whether it is a simple quality.

[C102]   Quæstio 5 Articulus 1

Nihil de fide angelorum in genere; de hac enim in materia de angelis; sed hic tantum, an fuerit fides in primo angelo si erat ei evidens Deum esse, qui loquebatur et revelabat ei mysteria.

[C102]   Question 5, Article 1

Say nothing about the faith of the angels in general, for this is taken up in the material on the angels. But here discuss only this: Was there faith in the first angel if it was evident to it that God existed, and if God spoke and revealed mysteries to it?

[C103]   Quæstio 6

Non nisi brevissime, quia difficultas in materia de gratia tractatur.

[C103]   Question 6

Treat this only in a very concise way since the difficulty is treated in the material on grace.[108]

[C104]   Quæstio 10 Articulus 2

Quæstio de baptizandis pueris infidelium reservetur in materiam de Baptismo.

[C104]   Question 10, Article 2

The question about baptizing the children of those without the faith should be kept for the material on baptism.

[C105]   Quæstio 12

Hic non fiant longi tractatus de potestate ecelesiastica et civili.

[C105]   Question 12

Here there should not be long discourses on ecclesiastical and civil power.

[C106]   Quæstio 23 Articulus 2

Materia huius articuli non hic discutienda, sed in quæstionibus de gratia; ubi etiam de distinctione caritatis et gratiæ; sed an caritas sit virtus specialis, hic in articulo 4.

[C106]   Question 23, Article 2

The material of this article should not be discussed here, but in the questions concerning grace, where there should also be something on the distinction between charity and grace; but whether charity is a special virtue should be taken up here in article 4.

---

[107] Thomas quotes Aristotle's definition of habit as "a disposition whereby that which is disposed is disposed well or ill, and this, either in regard to itself or in regard to another" (II.I, q49.a1).

[108] Question 6 concerns the cause of faith.

[C107]   Quæstio 26

Nihil hic de contritione, sed tantum, an Deus sit summe diligendus intensive, seu solum æstimative; quod in materia de pœnitentia non repetatur.

[C108]   Quæstio 61

In materia de merito non hic disputetur, utrum retributio meritorum apud Deum sit secundum iustitiam commutativam, an distributivam.

[H12]   Ex Tertia Parte

[C109]   Quæstio 1 Articulus 1

Nec de potentia obedientiali videtur hic agendum, nisi obiter, cum pertineat ad I partem in quæstione de omnipotentia Dei; nec de Incarnationis possibilitate; de qua tamen si quid hic agendum videretur, non repetatur in quæstione 2. Nec de distinctione suppositi et naturæ, sed remittatur ad quæstionem 3 articulum 3. Tandem, an sit de ratione boni se actu communicare, pertinet potius ad I partem, in quæstione de bonitate Dei, vel in quæstione de libero arbitrio Dei.

[C107]   Question 26

Take up nothing about contrition here,[109] but only whether God should be loved above all with depth of personal feeling or only in an intellectual way; this should not be repeated in the section on penance.

[C108]   Question 61

In the section on merit, do not dispute here whether God's compensation for merits follows a commutative or a distributive principle of justice.[110]

[H12]   From Part III

[C109]   Question 1, Article 14

And it does not seem good to take up obediential potency here, except in passing, since it pertains to Part I in the question about God's omnipotence.[111] Nor does it seem good to treat the possibility of the Incarnation, although if it does seem good to take anything up about it here, it should still not be repeated in question 2. The distinction between substance and nature should not be taken up either, but postponed until question 3, article 3. Finally, whether it is characteristic of the good to communicate itself in act pertains rather to Part I, in the question about God's goodness or in

---

[109] Contrition: a certain "interior repentance has been called by theologians 'contrition.' It is defined explicitly by the Council of Trent (sess. XIV, chap. iv, de Contritione): 'a sorrow of soul and a hatred of sin committed, with a firm purpose of not sinning in the future'" (ibid., s.v. "Contrition").

[110] [C]ommutative (principle of justice): one that is based on an interchangeable, equal measure ("Each gets the same"). [D]istributive principle of justice: one that is based on a proportionate measure ("The ones deserving more get more").

[111] [O]bediential potency: an ability to receive grace. [O]mnipotence: the ability to do any possible thing.

the question about God's free choice.

[C110]   Articulus 2

Quomodo nos satisfaciamus pro peccatis, et quomodo satisfactio nostra nitatur satisfactioni Christi, differatur in materiam de pœnitentia.

[C110]   Article 2

Postpone until the material on penance how we make satisfaction for sins, and how our satisfaction relies on Christ's satisfaction.[112]

[C111]   Quæstio 2

An in Deo sint tres subsistentiæ, et an essentia secundum se subsistat, an per relationes, non hic disputetur, sed supponatur ex I parte in materia de Trinitate; utrum autem possit unum essentialiter dependere a multis dependentia causali, supponatur ex philosophia.

[C111]   Question 2

Do not dispute here about whether there are three subsistent beings in God[113] or whether the essence subsists in accordance with itself, or through the relations; but this should be postulated on the basis of Part I on the material about the Trinity; however, whether it is possible for one thing to depend on many things by a causal dependency should be postulated on a philosophical basis.

[C112]   Quæstio 4 Articulus 4

Non disputetur de esse obiectivo contra Scotum, sed supponatur ex I parte in quæstione de scientia Dei.

[C112]   Question 4, Article 4

Do not dispute about objective existence in opposition to Scotus, but postulate it on the basis of Part I, in the question about God's knowledge.

[C113]   Quæstio 7

An virtus heroica differat specie a virtute communiter dicta, supponatur ex philosophia morali vel ex I-II.

[C113]   Question 7

Whether heroic virtue differs in *species* from virtue as it is commonly called should be postulated on the basis of moral philosophy or of the I-II.

[C114]   Quæstio 8 Articulus 1

An humanitas Christi active concurrat ad infusionem gratiæ, et ad opera miraculorum, cum habeat

[C114]   Question 8, Article 1

Whether the humanity of Christ actively operates concurrently with the infusion of grace and with mi-

---

[112] [S]atisfaction for sins: compensation for the damage created by sins.

[113] [T]hree subsistent beings in God: three separate Persons in one divine Being.

eandem difficultatem cum sacramentorum causalitate, ideo ne sæpe repetatur idem, possunt ista coniungi et simul tractari in materia de sacramentis in genere. Ex iis tamen si quis voluerit nonnihil in hac 8 quæstione attingere ad explicandum instrumentarium humanitatis concursum, hoc quicquid attigerit, nullo modo repetat in materia de sacramentis.

raculous works, since the same difficulty exists with the causality of the sacraments—to avoid frequent repetition, these topics can be joined and treated at the same time as the matter on the sacraments in general. Nevertheless, if anyone wishes to touch on something from these topics in this eighth question to explain the structure of human instrumentality, he should in no way repeat whatever he has touched on when he arrives at the section on the sacraments.

[C115] Articuli 2 et 3

Non videtur disputandum, qui sint, aut non sint membra Ecclesiæ, cum id pertineat ad materiam de Ecclesia.

[C115] Articles 2 and 3

It does not seem good to dispute who are or who are not members of the Church, since this pertains to material on the Church.

[C116] Quæstio 9 Articulus 1

An intelligere divinum possit communicari animæ Christi, pertinet ad I-II quæstionem 3 articulum 1.

[C116] Question 9, Article 1

Whether divine knowledge could be shared with the soul of Christ, pertains to I-II, question 3, article 1.[114]

[C117] Quæstio 10 Articulus 2

Ea, quæ ad cuiusque beati statum pertinent, quando et quomodo videantur, non tractetur hic, sed in prima parte; sicut et reliqua, quæ pertinent ad visionem Dei in communi.

[C117] Question 10, Article 2

What pertains to the state of any blessed person, when and how they seem likely to be, should not be treated here, but in the first part. The same goes for the rest of what pertains to the shared vision of God.

[C118] Quæstio 11 Articulus 1

An viator possit habere notitiam evidentem abstractivam Trinitatis, non huc pertinet, sed ad I partem.

[C118] Question 11, Article 1

Whether a person who is "on the way" can have clear abstract knowledge of the Trinity does not belong to this section, but to Part I.

[114] [D]ivine knowledge: because it is believed that in Christ, there are two natures (divine and human) in one Person, there arose the question about whether the humanity of Christ would have the same knowledge that the divine nature possesses.

[C119] Articulus 5

Quicquid de habitu hic disputari solet in communi, supponatur ex philosophia, vel ex I-II.

[C120] Quæstio 18 Articulus 4

Quæ actiones dicantur humanæ, quæ non humanæ, quæstio est I-II.

[C121] Quæstio 22

De Christi sacrificio incruento in cæna, et de ratione sacrificii et hostiæ in communi, commodius disputatur in materia de Eucharistia et missa; item de sacerdotio Melchisedech, et ut fuit figura Christi, melius est, ut disputet interpres Scripturæ.

[C122] Quæstio 24

Non repetantur hic, quæ pertinent ad prædestinationem hominum et angelorum.

[C123] Quæstio 25

Omittenda videntur, quæ hic nonnulli tractant de phantasticis imaginibus, et variis dæmonum illusionibus. Ceteræ quæstiones de Incarnatione possunt omitti, præter sex fere; quarum prima sit de officio Mediatoris; ubi etiam aliquid de invocatione sanctorum dicendum est. Secunda de con-

[C119] Article 5

Whatever is usually debated here about *habitus* in general should be postulated on the basis of philosophy or I-II.

[C120] Question 18, Article 4

Which actions should be called human and which not is a question belonging to I-II.

[C121] Question 22

It is more appropriate to discuss the bloodless sacrifice of Christ in the Supper and in general the idea of the sacrifice and victim in the material about the Eucharist and the Mass; likewise, it is better that a scriptural exegete discuss the priesthood of Melchisedech and how it was a figure of Christ.[115]

[C122] Question 24

Do not repeat here what pertains to the predestination of human beings and angels.

[C123] Question 25

It seems good to leave out what some discuss here concerning fantasy images and different illusions from the demons. The other questions about the Incarnation can be omitted, except for about six. Of these, the first is about the office of the Mediator, where something also ought to be said about the invoca-

---

[115] [T]he bloodless sacrifice of Christ in the Supper: the Eucharist, the sacrament of Holy Communion, is understood to be a non-bloody sacrifice communicating the grace of Christ's death and resurrection. [P]riesthood of Melchisedech: Melchisedech was a priest of Salem who has an favorable encounter with Abraham (Gen. 14:18–20), bringing forth bread and wine to honor him. His priesthood was theologized in the New Testament (Heb. 7). [A] figure of Christ: Christianity interpreted the Hebrew Scriptures as texts full of figures or types of the Christian account of salvation, so that there is a fundamental unity in the revelation of "Old" and "New" Testaments.

ceptione B. Mariæ. Tertia de miraculis Christi, propter quosdam
hæreticos nostri temporis, qui vim
miraculorum Christi, quantum possunt, elevare conantur. Disputare
autem de miraculis in genere, et
quæ possibilia sint Deo, pertinet
ad quæstionem de omnipotentia
Dei in I parte; nulli vero creaturæ
esse possibilia, fere disputatur in
materia de angelis. Quarta, an sint
in Christo duæ filiationes; sed non
disputetur in genere: Num una
numero relatione possit quippiam
referri ad diversos terminos. Quinta, an ratio superior sit passa in
Christo. Sexta de descensu Christi
ad inferos contra Calvinum.

tion of the saints. The second is
about the conception of Blessed
Mary. The third is about the miracles of Christ, on account of certain
heretics of our time, who are trying,
as far as they can, to make light of
the force of Christ's miracles. However to discuss miracles in general
and which are possible for God pertains to the question about the omnipotence of God in Part I; but that
such miracles are not possible for
any creature is generally discussed
in the material on angels. The
fourth is whether there are two filiations in Christ.[116] But do not discuss
in general whether by a relationship
that is one in number anything can
be related to different ends. The
fifth is whether the higher reason in
Christ suffered. The sixth is about
the descent of Christ to the underworld, over against Calvin.[117]

[H13]   De Sacramentis
in Genere

[H13]   On the Sacraments
in General

[C124]   Quæstio 60

[C124]   Question 60

Quæstio, an sacramentum sit in
aliquo prædicamento, non videtur
admodum digna theologo.

The question of whether the sacrament falls into any category does
not seem very suitable for a theologian.[118]

---

[116] Mediator: is it proper for Jesus Christ to be the mediator between God and humanity, offering recompense for the sins of Adam and Eve? Miracles: "wonders" worked by
Jesus during his earthly ministries. Filiations: The question arose whether there were two
filiations ("sonships") in Christ, since he relates to the Father as "Son" and his nativity
also seems to imply a filiation.

[117] [T]he descent of Christ to the underworld: the activity attributed to Christ during the three days (inclusive) from Good Friday to Easter Sunday, while his body lay in the
tomb after the crucifixion. Calvin: Protestant Church reformer and theologian (1509–64).

[118] [W]hether the sacrament falls into any category: the categories of Aristotle seem
to invoke a philosophical rather than a theological frame of reference.

[C125]   Quæstio 61

Utrum semper, etiam in lege naturæ, fuerit necessaria fides, non huc pertinet, sed ad II-II.

[C126]   Quæstio 62

Utrum Deus possit uti creatura tanquam instrumento ad creandum, potius est Primæ partis in materia de creatione.

[H14]   De Baptismo

[C127]   De sollemnitatibus et cæremoniis baptismi breviter. Nihil dicatur de cognatione spirituali in baptismo contrahi solita, sed ad matrimonium transmittatur. De pœna parvulorum sine baptismo decedentium non tractetur hic, sed in materia de peccato originali in I-II. Sacramenta confirmationis, ordinis, extremæ unctionis tractentur, prout vacaverit, plene vel breviter; aut etiam prætereantur, cum et faciliora sint, et habeatur in promptu, unde peti possint. Ubicunque tamen propter hæreticos ea tractatio videbitur necessaria, nequaquam omittatur.

[H15]   De Eucharistia

[C128]   An quantitas distinguatur a substantia, philosophis relinquatur; sicut et illud, de quo Scotus hic disputat, an accidens possit producere substantiam. De figuris

[C125]   Question 61

Whether faith was always necessary, even in the law of nature, does not pertain to this section, but to II-II.[119]

[C126]   Question 62

Whether God can use a creature like an instrument for creating belongs rather in Part I, in the material on creation.

[H14]   On Baptism

[C127]   Treat briefly of the solemnities and ceremonies of baptism. Nothing should be said about the spiritual relationship customarily effected in baptism, but it should be attached to the treatment of matrimony. Do not treat here the punishment of babies who die without baptism, but rather in the material on original sin in I-II. The sacraments of confirmation, orders, and the final anointing should be treated fully or briefly, as time allows; or these things might even be omitted, both because they are easier and because source materials on them are readily available. Nevertheless, wherever treating them seems called for on account of heretics, it should by no means be left out.

[H15]   On the Eucharist

[C128]   Leave to the philosophers whether quantity should be distinguished from substance, and the same goes for the point that Scotus disputes in this matter: whether an

---

[119] [E]ven in the law of nature: that is, in human beings in their natural state, even apart from the consequences of the Fall of Adam and Eve.

Eucharistiæ multiplicibus, earumque comparationibus vel nihil vel breviter.

accident can produce a substance. Say nothing about the manifold figures of the Eucharist and their comparisons, or treat them briefly.

[H16] De Pœnitentia

[H16] About Penance

[C129] An repugnet sine ulla infusione qualitatum supernaturalium, vel sine ullo pœnitentis actu iustificari peccatorem; et an pœnitere, sicut oportet, indigeat Dei auxilio gratuito, pertinent ad I-II de iustificatione. Illic etiam agendum est, non hic de ordine inter dispositionem et infusionem gratiæ. An in peccatore post peccatum transactum aliquid aliud remaneat præter obligationem ad pœnam, supponatur ex I-II in materia de peccato. Utrum pœna damni sit eadem in omnibus damnatis, pertinet potius ad materiam de peccatis et eorum effectibus. Quæstiones de restitutione, de eleemosynis [Lukács: eleemonsynas], de ieiunio, de oratione, de correptione fraterna remittantur ad II-II. Multa etiam, quæ ad casus conscientiæ spectant, relinqui possunt, ut superius annotatum est.

[C129] It pertains to I-II on justification whether it is contradictory that a sinner can be justified without any infusion of supernatural qualities or without any act of the penitent; so does the question of whether doing penance as it should be done stands in need of God's gratuitous help. There and not here is also the place to treat the relative rank of personal disposition and the infusion of grace. The question whether after the commission of sin anything remains in the sinner apart from the necessity of punishment should be assumed on the basis of I-II in the material on sin. Whether the penalty of loss is the same among all the damned pertains rather to the material on sins and their effects. Questions about restitutions, alms, fasting, prayer, and fraternal reproach should be postponed until II-II. Also many things regarding cases of conscience can be left aside, as noted earlier.

[H17] De Matrimonio

[H17] On Matrimony

[C130] Omittendum videtur, quod a quibusdam hic tractatur, an virginitas sit virtus, et qualis virtus. An maleficium maleficio possit dissolvi, pertineret sane ad II-II; sed quoniam ad eum locum raro pervenitur, et maleficium inter matrimonii impedimenta numeratur, commodius hic videtur collo-

[C130] It seems good to omit what is treated by some here, whether virginity is a virtue, and what kind of virtue it is. Whether a spell can be undone by a spell clearly would pertain to II-II; but since that place is rarely reached, and since a spell is numbered among the impediments to matrimony, it seems more fitting

candum. De substantia voti tam simplicis, quam solemnis tractandum potius videtur in II-II quam hic.

to place it here. The substance of a vow, both simple and solemn, seems better treated in II-II than here.[121]

[H18]   Regulæ Professoris Casuum Conscientiæ

[197]   *Finis*

1. Eo suam omnem operam atque industriam conferre studeat, ut peritos parochos seu sacramentorum administratores instituat.

[198]   *Quæstionum distributio*

2. Unus professorum biennio explicet sacramenta omnia et censuras, et præterea hominum status atque officia; alter biennio item decalogum; in cuius septimo præcepto aget de contractibus, semper leviter attingendo, quæ minoris momenti, aut non ita propria esse videantur, ut verbi gratia de depositione, degradatione, magia et alia huiusmodi.

[H18]   Rules for the Professor of Cases of Conscience

[197]   *Final Goal*

1. He should strive to devote all his effort and energetic activity to the training of skilled parish priests or ministers of the sacraments.

[198]   *Distribution of the questions*

2. Every two years, one of the professors should explain all the sacraments and censures, and in addition the states and duties of human beings. A second professor should explain the Ten Commandments, likewise every two years.[122] At the seventh commandment, he will discuss contracts, always touching lightly on the matters that seem less important or not so relevant, as, for example, deposition, degradation, magic, and other such things.[123]

---

[121] [V]ow, both simple and solemn: there are different views on exactly what distinguishes the vows juridically and historically, but solemn vows indicate a markedly complete surrender of the individual taking them. Simple vows, however, can be perpetual. See *Cath-Ency*, s.v. "Vows."

[122] Censures: "[m]edicinal and spiritual punishments imposed by the Church on a baptized, delinquent, and contumacious person, by which he is deprived, either wholly or in part, of the use of certain spiritual goods, until he recover from his contumacy" (ibid., s.v. "Censures"). Ten Commandments: the laws given to Moses by God on Mount Sinai. See the Bible's Book of Exodus, chap. 20, and the Book of Deuteronomy, chap. 5.

[123] Deposition *(Depositio)*: "[a] deposition is an ecclesiastical vindictive penalty by which a cleric is forever deprived of his office or benefice and of the right of exercising the functions of his orders" (ibid., s.v. "Deposition").

Degradation *(Degradatio)*: "Degadation" is "a canonical penalty by which an ecclesiastic is entirely and perpetually deprived of all office, benefice, dignity, and power conferred on

[199] *A theologicis quatenus abstinendum*

3. Etiamsi a theologicis rebus, quæ vix ullam habent cum casibus necessariam connexionem, penitus abstinere necesse sit, æquum tamen est, interdum theologica quædam, a quibus casuum doctrina pendet, brevissima definitione perstringere: ut quid character et quotuplex sit, quid peccatum mortale aut veniale, quid consensus et horum similia.

[200] *Quæstionum ratio et modus*

4. Citra scholasticum apparatum, unaquæque difficultas evolvatur per dubitationes et conclusiones; in quibus confirmandis seligantur ad summum duæ tresve rationes, nec plus æquo auctoritates coacerventur. Unicuique autem generali præcepto seu regulæ subiiciantur exempli gratia tres circiter peculiares casus.

[201] *Probabilis opinio opposita significanda*

5. Ita suas confirmet opiniones, ut, si qua alia fuerit probabilis et bonis auctoribus munita, eam etiam probabilem esse significet.

[202] *Hebdomadaria disputatio*

6. Quolibet sabbatho, prætermissa lectione, per duas horas vel

[199] *To what extent he should prescind from theological matters*

3. Even though it is utterly necessary to prescind from theological matters that have hardly any necessary connection with cases, it is nevertheless right to touch in a very delimited way upon certain theological matters on which the teaching of cases depends: for example, what is character and its varieties, what is mortal or venial sin, what is consent, and things like these.

[200] *The arrangement and method of the questions*

4. Each difficulty should be laid out through problems and theses, without going so far as a full Scholastic presentation. To confirm these, two or three reasons at the most should be selected, and an excessive number of authors should not be piled up. However, for the sake of examples, about three particular cases should be linked to each general commandment or rule.

[201] *Indicate a contrary opinion that can be approved*

5. He should confirm his own opinions in such a way that, if there is any other opinion that can be approved and that is supported by reputable authors, he should indicate that it too can be approved.

[202] *Weekly disputation*

6. On any given Saturday, the class should be cancelled, and for

him by ordination; and by a special ceremony is reduced to the state of a layman, losing the privileges of the clerical state and being given over to the secular arm. [This is the traditional definition of the word. The Church no longer can or does hand offenders "over to the secular arm.—ED.] Degradation, however, cannot deprive an ecclesiastic of the character conferred in ordination, nor does it dispense him from the law of celibacy and the recitation of the Breviary" (ibid., s.v. "Degradation").

aliquanto minus pro arbitrio provincialis et discipulorum numero, de propositis conclusionibus disputetur in schola coram magistro; in ea vero disputatione interrogationibus potissimum agatur, ut vel exigatur explanatio alicuius difficultatis, vel novus casus, mutata circumstantia aliqua, proponatur, vel alicui conclusioni opponatur canon seu doctor ex primariis, seu nonnulla brevis argumentatio, quo res plus habeat dignitatis; temperate tamen et longe infra philosophicam consuetudinem.

[203] *Domesticæ collationis forma*

7. Si ipse domesticæ casuum collationi a rectore ex provincialis præscripto præficiatur, hunc ordinem teneat: Primum materiam aliquam, de qua disserendum sit, proponat; et interdum etiam aliquid pertinens ad usum, ut de modo interrogandi poenitentem, remedia ac poenitentias imponendi, et similibus; deinde eius materiæ præcipua capita ac fundamenta ipsemet aperiat breviter, ut generalem quandam notitiam ac tamquam lucem in omnes illius tractationis partes præbeat; tum de proposita materia tres quatuorve casus seligat, quos in collationum loco iubeat affigi, notato die, quo excutiendi sint.

two hours or a little bit less, according to the judgment of the provincial and in proportion to the number of students, there should be a disputation in class in the presence of the teacher about theses that have been submitted. But in the disputation, the procedure should be conducted above all by questioning, so that either an explanation of some problematical point is demanded, or a new case is proposed with some detail altered, or a canon or a leading academic authority, or some short argumentation is raised against some thesis, to give the issue greater significance. Nevertheless, this should be done in a moderate way, and the procedure should fall well short of the customary philosophical one.

[203] *Structure of the house conference*

7. If, on a directive of the provincial, the rector puts him in charge of a house conference on cases, he should keep the following order. First, he should propose some matter that should be the subject of the discussion, and sometimes even something pertaining to practice, like the manner of questioning the penitent, of imposing remedies and penances, and similar things. Then he should himself briefly lay out the main divisions and principles of the matter, to offer a certain general idea and a kind of light on all the parts of that discourse. Then he should select from the proposed material three or four cases that he should have someone post in the conference area, along with an indication of the day when they will be examined.

[204]   *Privatum studium*

8. De his casibus propositis consulant aliqui privato studio singuli singulos auctores a præside distributos.

[205]   *Exponendæ et disputandæ sententiæ*

9. Postquam convenerint, primum utile esset, a singulis, quid suus doctor habeat, quam brevissime referri; tum qui præest, interroget fere tres (quos satius est tempestive præmoneri, et vicissim variari), quid sentiant de primo casu; postea ex his, quæ dicta sunt ab illis, colligat ipse doctrinam tutiorem et probabiliorem. Eodem deinde ordine casum secundum et reliquos deinceps eadem ratione excutiat. Illis casibus sic explicatis a præside quam brevissime et eo modo, qui servandus est in disputationibus casuum, proponantur iisdem de rebus dubitationes, respondente uno ex præmonitis; et ipso tandem, quid sentiendum sit, ad extremum edocente.

[206]   *Extraordinaria collationum materia*

10. Si quid vero alicui occurrat extra ordinariam harum collationum materiam, deferatur, si nihil obstat, ad præsidem, ut in proxime futura collatione agitetur.

[204]   *Private study*

8. Some should think over these proposed cases in private study, each one taking the particular authors assigned to him by the presider.

[205]   *The opinions to be set forth and subjected to disputation*

9. After the group has gathered, it would first be useful for each to report as briefly as possible what his own authority holds. Then the one who is presiding should usually ask three students (whom it is better to inform well in advance and to rotate in turn) what is their considered opinion about the first case. Later, he himself should glean from what they have said the safer and more approvable teaching. Then, in the same order, he should examine the second and from there the remaining cases, following the same procedure. After those cases have been explained this way by the presider as concisely as possible and in the manner that ought to be followed in disputations involving cases, problems ought to be raised about the same issues, and one of the students advised in advance should respond. And finally, at the very end, he himself should apprise them of the opinion that ought to be held.

[206]   *Special matter for the conferences*

10. But if anything outside the ordinary matter for these conferences occurs to anyone, it should be mentioned to the presider, if nothing prevents it, so that it can become a topic in the next conference.

[H19] Regulæ Professoris Philosophiæ

[207] Finis

1. Quoniam artes vel scientiæ naturales ingenia disponunt ad theologiam, et ad perfectam cognitionem et usum illius inserviunt, et per se ipsas ad eundem finem iuvant, eas, qua diligentia par est, præceptor, in omnibus sincere honorem et gloriam Dei quærendo, ita tractet, ut auditores suos, ac potissimum nostros, ad theologiam præparet, maximeque ad cognitionem excitet sui Creatoris.

[208] Sequendus Aristoteles, sed quatenus

2. In rebus alicuius momenti ab Aristotele non recedat, nisi quid incidat a doctrina, quam academiæ ubique probant, alienum; multo magis, si orthodoxæ fidei repugnet; adversus quam, si quæ sunt illius aliusve philosophi argumenta, strenue refellere studeat iuxta Lateranense Concilium.

[H19] Rules for the Professor of Philosophy

[207] Final goal

1. Since the arts and the natural sciences dispose the intellectual talents for theology and assist them in arriving at perfect knowledge and its use, and since even by themselves they help these talents toward the same final goal, the teacher should, with due diligence, honestly seeking the honor and glory of God in all things, treat them in such a way that he prepares his own students and especially Jesuits for theology and most of all rouses their desire to know their Creator.

[208] Aristotle should be followed, but to what extent

2. In matters of some importance, he should not depart from Aristotle, unless he comes across something that clashes with the teaching that educational institutions everywhere approve, and he should all the more depart from Aristotle if he contradicts orthodox belief. If there are any arguments of that philosopher or another that stand opposed to the faith, he should vigorously strive to refute them according to the Lateran Council.[124]

---

[124] Lateran Council: there were five Lateran Councils, held in the years 1123, 1139, 1179, 1215, and 1512–17. Lateran is the name for an important residence and basilica for the pope from the fourth to the fourteenth centuries. Canonically, the basilica of St. John Lateran is the cathedral church of Rome. In 1513 (session 8), the Fifth Lateran Council decreed the following: "And since truth cannot contradict truth, we define that every statement contrary to the enlightened truth of the faith is totally false and we strictly forbid teaching otherwise to be permitted." (Cf. Norman P. Tanner, ed. *Decrees of the Ecumenical Councils*, 605 f.).

[209] *Auctores male de christiana fide meriti*

3. Aristotelis interpretes, male
de christiana religione meritos,
non sine magno delectu aut legat
aut in scholam proferat; caveatque,
ne erga illos afficiantur discipuli.

[210] *Averroes*

4. Eam ob rem nec Averrois
(idem de eiusmodi aliis iudicium)
digressiones in separatum aliquem
tractatum conferat; et, si quid boni
ex ipso proferendum sit, sine
laude proferat; et, si fieri potest, id
eum aliunde sumpsisse demonstret.

[211] *Nulli sectæ adhærendum*

5. Nulli sectæ, ut averroistarum,
alexandræorum, et similium vel se
vel suos addicat; nec Averrois aut
Alexandri aut ceterorum errata
dissimulet; sed inde acrius depri-
mat eorum auctoritatem.

[212] *S. Thomas*

6. Contra vero de Sancto Thoma
nunquam non loquatur honorifice,
libentibus illum animis, quoties
oporteat, sequendo; aut reverenter

[209] *Authors who do not serve the
Christian faith well*

3. Only very selectively should he
either read or present in class interpreters of Aristotle who do not serve
Christianity well. And he should be
careful that students do not become
well disposed towards them.

[210] *Averroes*

4. For this reason, he should not
make Averroes's digressions the
subject of some separate extended
treatment[125] (and the same holds for
others of this type); and, if anything
good has to be cited from him, he
should cite it without praise; and if
it is possible, he should indicate that
he has taken it from elsewhere.

[211] *Do not adhere to any sectarian school of thought*

5. He should not commit himself
or those who are following him to
any sectarian school of thought like
that of the Averroists, of the
Alexandrians, and the like,[126] and he
should not gloss over the errors of
Averroes or Alexander or the rest,
but he should diminish their authority all the more pointedly because of
those errors.

[212] *Saint Thomas*

6. But on the other hand he
should never speak about Saint
Thomas without respect, whole-
heartedly following him as often as

---

[125] Averroes: the Latin name for Ibn Roschd, an Arabian philosopher (1126–98).

[126] Averroists: the schools of thought deriving from Averroes. Averroist thinking was
somewhat attractive to Christian thinkers in the thirteenth century. It exerted an influence
on Thomas Aquinas, but was later judged antithetical to Christian belief. Alexandrians: The
schools of thought deriving from Alexander of Hales (d. 1245), a Franciscan theologian and
philosopher who first attempted a systematic exposition of Christian teaching in light of
certain recently recovered works of Aristotle.

et gravate, si quando minus placeat, deserendo.

[213] *Philosophiæ cursus non
minor triennio*

7. Universam philosophiam non
minus, quam triennio prælegat;
idque binis quotidie horis, antemeridiana una, altera pomeridiana,
nisi aliter in aliqua universitate
constitutum sit.

[214] *Quando absolvendus*

8. Ac proinde nusquam cursus
absolvatur, antequam venerint aut
valde proximæ sint vacationes,
quæ sub anni finem dari solent.

[215] *Quæ primo anno tradenda
vel omittenda*

9. 1. Explicet primo anno Logicam, eius summa primo circiter
bimestri tradita, non tam dictando,
quam ex Toleto seu Fonsecao,
quæ magis necessaria videbuntur,
explicando.

[216] 2. In prolegomenis Logicæ
disputet tantum, an sit scientia et
de quo subiecto, et pauca quædam de secundis intentionibus;
plenam de universalibus disputationem differat in Metaphysicam;
contentus hic mediocrem quandam eorum notitiam tradere.

required, or departing from him
respectfully and reluctantly if his
position seems to have less to commend it.

[213] *The philosophical course
should be at least three years
long*

7. He should give classes on the
entire range of philosophy for not
less than three years. And this he
should do for two hours a day, one
in the morning, and a second in the
afternoon, unless in some university
there is a different arrangement.

[214] *When it should be finished*

8. And so the course should never
be finished before the free days usually given right before the end of
the year have arrived or are very
near.

[215] *What should be given or left
out in the first year*

9. 1. In the first year, after presenting its overall plan in about the
first two months, he should teach
logic, not so much dictating as explaining what seems to be more necessary from Toledo or Fonseca.[127]

[216] 2. In the preparatory sections
of logic, he should only dispute
whether it is a science, what is its
subject matter, and some few things
about second intentions. He should
put off until metaphysics a full disputation about universals.[128] At this
point he should be satisfied to give
some middling idea of them.

---

[127] For more extensive information about Aristotle, Toledo, and Fonseca, see endn. 19.

[128] Universals: a universal is a general category that embraces many particulars (for
example, "humanity" includes Ignatius).

[217] 3. De Prædicamentis etiam faciliora quædam proponat, quæ fere attinguntur ab Aristotele; cetera in postremum reiiciat annum; de analogia tamen et relatione, quoniam frequentissime in disputationes cadunt, quantum satis est, agat in Logica.

[218] 4. Librum secundum Perihermenias et ambos Priorum libros, præter octo vel novem prima capita primi, compendio percurrat; exponat tamen proprias illis quæstiones, brevissime vero eam, quæ est de contingentibus; in qua nihil de libero arbitrio.

[219] 5. Atque, ut secundus annus integer rebus physicis tribuatur, in fine primi anni plenior instituatur disputatio de scientia; in eamque coniiciantur prolegomena Physicæ maxima ex parte, ut scientiarum divisiones, abstractiones, speculativum, practicum, subalternatio, diversus quoque procedendi modus in physicis et mathematicis, de quo Aristoteles lib. 2 Physicorum; demum quicquid de definitione dicitur lib. 2 de Anima.

[217] 3. Concerning the *Categories*, he should also set forth certain easier issues to which Aristotle usually refers.[129] He should leave the rest for the very end of the year. Still, since they very often come up in disputations, he should give an adequate treatment of analogy and relation in logic.

[218] 4. He should quickly cover in a condensed form the second book of *On Interpretation* and both books of the *Prior Analytics*, except for the eight or nine chapters at the beginning of the first book.[130] He should nevertheless set out for them the questions peculiar to them, but only very briefly the one that concerns contingent things, and in this one he should take up nothing about free will.

[219] 5. And, to devote the second year entirely to topics in physics, a rather full disputation about knowledge should be set for the end of the first year. Most of the prolegomena to the *Physics* should be attached to it, namely, the divisions of the fields of knowledge, abstractions, the speculative, the practical, subalternation, and also the different manners of proceeding in physics and in mathematics, about which Aristotle comments in *Physics*, book 2; finally, whatever is said about definition in *On the Soul*, book 2.[131]

---

[129] *Categories:* see §215 above and endn. 19.

[130] *On Interpretation, Prior Analytics:* see §215 above.

[131] *Physics, On the Soul,* and the other titles that follow immediately here *(Topics, [The Sophistical] Refutations, On the Heavens, On Generation, On the Elements, Meteorologica, and Metaphysics)* are all works by Aristotle.

[220] 6. Ex Topicis vero et Elenchis, loci et fallaciæ, commodiorem in ordinem redactæ, melius explicantur initio Logicæ in summa.

[220] 6. The *loci* and fallacies from the *Topics* and *Refutations*, summarized in a more convenient arrangement, are better taught in a comprehensive overview at the beginning of logic.[132]

[221] *Quæ secundo*

10 1. Secundo anno explicet libros octo Physicorum, libros de Coelo et primum de Generatione. In octo libris Physicorum compendio tradatur textus libri sexti et septimi; etiam primi ex ea parte, quæ est de antiquorum opinionibus. In octavo libro nihil disseratur de numero intelligentiarum, nec de libertate, nec de infinitate primi motoris; sed hæc in Metaphysicis disputentur; et quidem solum ex sententia Aristotelis.

[221] *What to teach in the second year*

10. 1. In the second year he should teach the eight books of the *Physics*, the books *On the Heavens* and the first book from *On Generation*. In the eight books of the *Physics*, the text of the sixth and seventh books should be given in abridged form, as should the text of the first, from that part that concerns the opinions of the ancients. In the eighth book nothing about the number of intelligences should be discussed, nor should anything about freedom nor about the infinity of the prime mover. But these things should be subjected to disputation in metaphysics, and in fact only on an Aristotelian basis.

[222] 2. Textus secundi, tertii, quarti de Coelo breviter perstringantur, magna etiam ex parte prætereantur. In his libris non tractentur, nisi paucæ de Elementis quæstiones; de Coelo autem dumtaxat de eius substantia, et de influentiis; ceteræ mathematicæ professori relinquantur, vel conferantur in compendium.

[222] 2. The texts of the second, third, and fourth books of *On the Heavens* should be briefly skimmed, and the greater part skipped. In these books nothing should be treated, except a few questions from *On the Elements*. But from *On the Heavens*, only the questions about its substance and influences should be treated; the rest should be left to the professor of mathematics or gathered into an abridgment.

[223] 3. Meteorologica vero percurrantur æstivis mensibus ul-

[223] 3. But the *Meteorologica* should be covered in the summer

---

[132] For a discussion of the term *loci*, see endn. 20. Topics: see §215 above. Refutations: *Sophistical Refutations*. See §215 above.

tima pomeridiana scholæ hora; idque sive ab ordinario, si possit, philosophiæ professore, sive ab extraordinario, nisi aliter fieri commodius videretur.

months, in the last hour of the afternoon class. And this should be done by the regularly assigned professor of philosophy, if possible, or by one not regularly assigned, unless some other arrangement seems better.

[224] *Quæ tertio*

11. 1. Tertio anno explanabit librum secundum de Generatione, libros de Anima et Metaphysicorum. In primo libro de Anima veterum placita philosophorum summatim percurrat. In secundo, expositis sensoriis, non digrediatur in anatomiam, et cetera, quæ medicorum [Lukács: mediocrum] sunt.

[224] *What to teach in the third year*

11. 1. In the third year he will explain the second book of *On Generation,* and the books of *On the Soul* and the *Metaphysics.* In the first book of *On the Soul,* he should summarily cover the opinions of the ancient philosophers. In the second book, when the sensorial foundations have been presented, he should not digress into anatomy and the rest of the things that are the concerns of medical doctors.

[225] 2. In Metaphysica quæstiones de Deo et intelligentiis, quæ omnino aut magnopere pendent ex veritatibus divina fide traditis, prætereantur. Prooemium ac septimi et duodecimi libri textus magna ex parte diligenter explicetur. In ceteris libris seligantur ex unoquoque quidam præcipui textus, tanquam fundamenta quæstionum, quæ ad metaphysicum pertinent.

[225] 2. In the *Metaphysics,* the questions about God and intelligences that depend altogether or in greater part on truths communicated by divine faith should be skipped. The proemium and the text of the seventh and twelfth books should for the most part be carefully explained. In the rest of the books, certain leading texts from each one should be selected as the foundations of the questions that pertain to the metaphysician.

[226] *Textus Aristotelis maximi faciendus*

12. Summopere conetur aristotelicum textum bene interpretari, in eoque nihilo minus operæ, quam in quæstionibus collocet. Auditoribus etiam persuadeat, mutilam valde ac mancam futuram philoso-

[226] *Give the greatest importance to the text of Aristotle*

12. He should do his utmost to interpret the text of Aristotle well, and he should devote no less effort to it than to the questions. He should also persuade his students that their philosophy will be quite

phiam eorum, quibus id studii in pretio non sit.

[227] *Qui maxime textus, et quo modo interprætandi*

13. Quoties incidit in textus aliquos admodum celebres, et iactari sæpe solitos in disputationibus, eos accurate perpendat, illustrioribus aliquot interpretationibus inter se collatis, ut quæ quibus anteferenda sit, ex antecedentibus et consequentibus possit intelligi, vel ex vi græci sermonis, vel ex aliorum locorum observatione, vel ex insigniorum interpretum auctoritate, vel denique ex momentis rationum. Tum demum veniatur ad dubitatiunculas quasdam non nimium exquirendas quidem, sed, si cuius momenti sint, non omittendas.

[228] *Quæstionum delectus et ordo*

14. Magnum etiam quæstionum delectum habeat; et eæ quidem, quæ non ex ipsa Aristotelis disputatione nascuntur, sed ex occasione cuiuspiam axiomatis, quod is obiter inter disputandum usurpat, si aliis in libris proprium locum habent, eo reiiciantur; sin minus, continuo post textum ipsum, in quo se obtulerint, explicentur.

[229] *Quæstiones textui interserendæ*

15. Quæstiones vero, quæ per se ad materiam, de qua disputat

truncated and handicapped if they do not value this study.

[227] *What texts in particular, and how they should be interpreted*

13. Whenever he comes upon any passages that are very famous and tend to be mentioned often in the disputations, he should apply a studied attention to them, comparing several of the more famous interpretations with one another, so that it can become clear which is preferable to which, on the basis of the context, or the meaning of the Greek expression, or some observance of other passages, or the authority of famous interpreters, or, finally, from the weight of the argumentation. Then he should at last proceed to certain minor problems, which certainly should not be considered in too much depth, but which should not be left out if they have any significance.

[228] *Choice and order of questions*

14. He should draw from a large selection of questions. And if there are some that do arise not from Aristotle's actual argument but from the occurrence of some axiom that he employs in passing during a disputation, if they have a proper place in other books, then those questions should certainly be reserved for that place; if not, then they should be taught immediately after the particular text in which they occurred.

[229] *Questions that should be inserted in the text*

15. But questions that of themselves pertain to the subject matter

Aristoteles, pertinent, ne tractentur ante explicatos textus omnes ad propositam rei summam pertinentes; si quidem plures textus hi non sint, quam ut una aut altera lectione possint exponi. Sin autem excurrant longius, ut qui sunt de principiis, de causis, de motu, in his nec fusiores tractatus habeantur, nec totus Aristotelis contextus quæstionibus anteponatur, sed cum illis ita coniungatur, ut post aliquam textuum seriem, quæstiones aliquæ, quæ ex illis existant, interserantur.

about which Aristotle is disputing should not be treated before all the texts relating to the proposed overview of the matter are taught, if in fact these texts are not more than can be taught in one or two classes. However if they run on longer, as do those about first principles, causes, and motion, they should not be treated in too extensive a fashion, nor should the whole Aristotelian system be put before the questions, but it should be joined with them in such a way that some questions arising from a series of texts should be inserted right after them.

[230] *Repetitio in scholis*

16. Absolutis lectionibus, aliqui inter se audita recolant per semihoram, circiter deni uno aliquo ex condiscipulis e Societate, si fieri potest, singulis decuriis præposito.

[230] *Review in the classes*

16. When the lessons are over, some should go over them for a half hour among themselves in groups of about ten, with one of their Jesuit fellow students put in charge of each of these groups, if possible.[133]

[231] *Disputationes menstruæ*

17. Disputationes menstruæ fiant, in quibus argumententur non pauciores, quam tres mane, totidem a prandio; primus quidem per horam, ceteri vero per ternos circiter quadrantes. Et mane quidem primo loco disputet theologus aliquis (si theologorum competit copia) contra metaphysicum, contra physicum metaphysicus, physicus contra logicum; sed a prandio metaphysicus cum metaphysico, physicus cum physico, logicus cum logico. Mane item metaphysicus, a prandio physicus unam aut alteram conclusionem confirmabit breviter et philosophice.

[231] *Monthly disputations*

17. There should be monthly disputations, in which not fewer than three engage in argument in the morning, and the same number after the midday meal; the first should go for an hour, the rest for about three quarters of an hour. And in the morning in the first place, some theologian (if there are an ample number of theologians) should dispute against a metaphysician, a metaphysician against a natural philosopher, a natural philosopher against a logician; but after the midday meal, a metaphysician with a metaphysician, a natural philosopher with a natural philosopher, a logician with a logician. Likewise, in

---

[133] *Decuria:* for an explanation of this term, see endn. 21.

the morning a metaphysician, and in the afternoon a natural philosopher will confirm one or two theses, briefly and in a philosophical manner.

[232] *Summæ tempore quatenus disputandum*

18. Quo tempore summam Logicæ præceptor tradit, nec ipse, nec eius auditores ad has disputationes conveniant. Immo prima aut altera circiter hebdomada logici nihil disputent, una fere rerum explanatione contenti; ex quo tempore poterunt in sua classe defendere theses aliquas die sabbathi.

[232] *To what extent there should be disputation at the time of the general overview*

18. During the time when the teacher is giving the general overview of logic, neither he nor his students should involve themselves in these disputations. In fact, for about one or two weeks at the start, the logicians should not dispute at all, generally contenting themselves with a single explanation of the issues. After this period, they will be able to defend some theses in their own classes on Saturday.

[233] *Disputationes sollemnes*

19. Ubi non est, nisi unus philosophiæ magister, ter aut quater in anno instituat sollemniores aliquas disputationes festo aliove feriato die; idque eo splendore atque apparatu, invitatis etiam religiosis aliisque doctoribus ad argumentandum, ut ex ea re studiis nostris non infructuosus aliquis fervor accedat.

[233] *Solemn disputations*

19. Where there is only one teacher of philosophy, he should organize some disputations that are more formal three or four times a year on some feast day or on some other holiday.[134] And this he should do with impressive display and ceremonial trimmings, also inviting academics from religious orders and elsewhere to participate in the debate, so that out of the event there might arise some really productive enthusiasm for our studies.

[234] *Formæ ratio in disputando*

20. Sic ab ipso Logicæ initio iuvenes instituantur, nihil ut eos magis pudeat in disputando, quam a formæ ratione deflexisse; nihil

[234] *Procedural form in the disputations*

20. From the beginning of logic, the young men should be trained in such a way that nothing should

---

[134] [H]oliday: here used to translate "feriato die" (ferial day). In ancient Rome, a *feria* was a day on which slaves did not have to work, a "free day." In Christianity it somehow came to mean a day of the week other than Saturday or Sunday, i.e., a "weekday." In the liturgical practices of the Church, it can indicate a day on which no feast is celebrated. See *CathEncy*, s.v. "Feria."

ab illis severius exigat præceptor, quam disputandi leges ac statas vices. Itaque qui respondet, repetat primum totam argumentationem, nihil ad singulas propositiones respondendo; tum iterum propositiones, addatque: nego vel concedo maiorem, minorem, consequentiam; interdum etiam distinguat; raro autem vel declarationes vel rationes, præsertim invitis, obtrudat.

shame them more in a disputation than to deviate from the procedural form. The teacher should insist on nothing more strictly from them than the regulations and the disputation's fixed patterns of alternation. And so the one who is responding should first review the entire argument without making any response to the individual propositions. Then he should review the propositions again, adding: I deny or I concede the major proposition, the minor proposition, or the conclusion. Sometimes he should also make a distinction. However, he should rarely impose either clarifications or reasons, especially on those who do not want to accept them.

[H20] Regulæ Professoris Philosophiæ Moralis

[235] *Officium*

1. Intelligat, sui instituti nequaquam esse ad theologicas quæstiones digredi, sed progrediendo in textu breviter, docte, et graviter præcipua capita scientiæ moralis, quæ in decem libris Ethicorum Aristotelis habentur, explicare.

[236] *Tempus huius lectionis*

2. Ubi ab ipsomet philosophici cursus professore ethica prælegi non solent, exponat, qui ethica tradit, metaphysicis graviores huius scientiæ quæstiones; idque per tres quadrantes quotidie, aut semihoram.

[H20] Rules for the Professor of Moral Philosophy

[235] *Duty*

1. He should realize that it is not in any way part of his assignment to digress to theological questions, but rather to teach the main areas of moral science that are contained in the ten books of Aristotle's *Ethics*, proceeding through the text concisely, learnedly, and in a serious manner.

[236] *Time of this class*

2. Where the professor himself does not usually give classes on ethics in the philosophical course, the one who is teaching ethics should present the more important questions of this science to the students

of metaphysics.[135] And he should do this for thirty or forty-five minutes a day.

[237] *Repetitio*

3. Ethicæ repetitiones saltem decimoquinto quoque die habeantur, quo tempore rector statuerit; etiam si ob eam causam una esset metaphysica repetitio prætermittenda.

[237] *Review*

3. At least every fifteenth day there should be reviews of ethics at the time the rector sets, even if this would cause the loss of one review period of metaphysics.

[238] *Conclusiones*

4. Cum metaphysicæ auditores vel domi privatas vel in schola menstruas habent disputationes, propositionem aliquam ethicam conclusionibus semper adiungant; adversus quam per quadrantem metaphysicus disputet, qui argumentatur.

[238] *Theses*

4. When the students of metaphysics hold disputations, either private ones in house or monthly ones in class, they should always add to their theses some ethical proposition, which the metaphysician who is debating should subject to disputation for a quarter of an hour.

[H21] Regulæ Professoris Mathematicæ

[239] *Qui authores, quo tempore, quibus explicandi*

1. Physicæ auditoribus explicet in schola tribus circiter horæ quadrantibus Euclidis elementa; in quibus, postquam per duos menses aliquantisper versati fuerint, aliquid Geographiæ vel Sphæræ, vel eorum, quæ libenter audiri solent, adiungat; idque cum Euclide vel eodem die, vel alternis diebus.

[H21] Rules for the Professor of Mathematics

[239] *Which authors should be taught, when, to whom*

1. He should teach the physics students Euclid's *Elements* in class for around three quarters of an hour.[136] After they have gained some experience with the material for about two months, he should add to this something about geography or the Sphere, or about those things that are usually of interest.[137] And

---

[135] Science: *scientia* can be used to refer to any organized body of knowledge concerning a particular subject.

[136] Euclid's *Elements:* the classic work on geometry, written by Euclid, a mathematician living in Alexandria around 300 B.C.

[137] Sphere: in 1593, Christopher Clavius, a famous Jesuit mathematician and scientist, wrote *In sphaeram Ioannis de Sacro Bosco*, a commentary on Joannes de Sacrabosco's treatise on astronomy, *Sphaera*, written about 1230.

he should do this with Euclid, either on the same day or on alternate days.

[240] *Problema*

2. Singulis aut alternis saltem mensibus ab aliquo auditorum magno philosophorum theologorumque conventu illustre problema mathematicum enodandum curet; posteaque, si videbitur, argumentandum.

[241] *Repetitio*

3. Semel in mense, idque fere die sabbathi, prælectionis loco præcipua quæque per eum mensem explicata publice repetantur.

[H22] Regulæ Præfect Studiorum Inferiorum

[242] *Finis*

1. Intelligat se ad id esse delectum, ut omni ope atque opera rectorem adiuvet in scholis nostris ita regendis ac moderandis, ut, qui eas frequentant, non minus quam in bonis artibus, in vitæ probitate proficiant.

[243] *Subordinatio generali præfecto*

2. In rebus quæ ad morum disciplinam in scholis nostris pertinent, rectorem tantum, in iis vero, quæ ad studia, generalem studiorum præfectum consulat; ab eorum præscripto non recedat; nullam consuetudinem aut receptam tollat aut novam introducat.

[240] *Problem*

2. Every month, or at least every other month, he should make sure that one of the students elucidates a famous mathematical problem at a large gathering of philosophers and theologians. Afterwards, it ought to be submitted to disputation if it seems right to do so.

[241] *Review*

3. Once a month, and usually on a Saturday, in place of a lesson, all the main points taught over the course of that month should be reviewed with the whole group.

[H22] Rules for the Prefect of Lower Studies

[242] Final goal

1. He should realize that he has been chosen for this: to devote his every effort and all his attention to helping the rector direct and administer our classes so that those who are attending them progress in the moral integrity of their lives, no less than in humanistic studies.

[243] *Subordination to the general prefect*

2. He should consult only the rector in matters that pertain to moral discipline in our classes, but in those that pertain to studies, he should consult the general prefect of studies. He should not deviate from what they have prescribed. He

should neither abrogate any established custom nor introduce a new one.

[244] *Declamationes a quo probandæ*

3. Eidem præfecto quicquid ab auditoribus rhetoricæ et inferiorum facultatum publice domi forisque declamabitur, tradi curet recognoscendum. Emblemata vero et carmina, quæ celeberrimis aliquot diebus propalam collocantur, a duobus per rectorem designandis legantur omnia, atque optima seligantur.

[244] *Who should approve the declamations*

3. He should see to it that whatever will be publicly declaimed by the students of rhetoric and the lower classes, at home and elsewhere, will be turned in to the prefect for inspection.[138] But emblems and poems that are collected for public display on some of the most important days of celebration should all be read by two that the rector will appoint,[139] and the best ones should be selected.

[245] *Magistri observandi et iuvandi*

4. Regulas magistrorum inferiorum et auditorum habeat, et perinde ac suas sedulo curet observandas. Magistros ipsos iuvet ac dirigat, maximeque caveat, ne quid apud alios, præsertim vero discipulos de eorum existimatione atque auctoritate detrahatur.

[245] *Observe and help the teachers*

4. He should keep in his possession a copy of the rules for the teachers and students of the lower classes and attentively see to it that they are followed as well as his own rules are. He should help and guide the teachers themselves, and he should take special care that nothing diminishes their esteem or authority in the eyes of others, but especially in the eyes of the students.

[246] *Una docendi ratio*

5. Magnopere caveat ut novi præceptores decessorum suorum docendi morem et alias consuetudines, a nostra tamen ratione non alienas, sedulo retineant, quo minus externi frequentem magistrorum mutationem incusent.

[246] *A single approach in teaching*

5. He should give particular care to ensuring that new teachers consistently keep their predecessors' manner of teaching and other customs (though nothing foreign to our overall plan), to keep non-Jesuits

[138] Declamations: formal speeches, often displaying attention to rhetorical devices.

[139] Emblems: this use of the word emblem is now obsolete. It refers to "a drawing or picture expressing a moral fable or allegory; a fable or allegory such as might be expressed pictorially" (OED). For the early history of emblems, see Daniel Russell, "Alciati's Emblems in Renaissance France," 534 f. For the distinctive Jesuit contributions to this genre, see Peter M. Daly and G. Richard Dimler, S.J. *The Jesuit Series*.

from criticizing the frequent change of teachers.

[247] *Scholæ visendæ*

6. Quintodecimo quoque die minimum singulos docentes audiat; observet, an doctrinæ christianæ debitum tempus atque operam tribuant; an, quantum satis est, in suo penso tum persolvendo, tum recolendo progrediantur; an denique cum discipulis decore ac laudabiliter se in rebus omnibus gerant.

[247] *Visiting the classes*

6. At least every fifteen days he should attend a class given by each teacher. He should note whether they are giving due time and attention to Christian doctrine, whether they are making satisfactory progress in both finishing and reviewing their assignment, and finally whether they are conducting themselves honorably and commendably in all matters with the students.

[248] *Feriati dies et horarum mutatio*

7. Tum festos dies et vacationes, sive provinciis omnibus communes, sive suæ proprias, præsertim hebdomadarias; tum horas, quibus quoque anni tempore inchoandæ scholæ sint ac finiendæ, mature cognoscat magistrisque significet; quando item discipuli ad publicas supplicationes, aliaque id genus dimittendi, aut aliquid extra ordinem agere iubendi seu vetandi.

[248] *Feast days and changes in schedule*

7. In due time, he should notice and point out to the teachers both the feast days and the vacation days, whether common to all provinces or proper to his own, especially ones occurring during the week, and the hours at which classes have to start and end in each season of the year. The same holds for when the students have to be dismissed for public prayers and other things of that nature, or when they have to be told or forbidden to do something out of the ordinary.

[249] *Quinque scholarum gradus*

1. Caveat, ne gradus, quibus quinque scholæ inferiores, videlicet rhetorica, humanitas et tres grammaticæ constant, ulla ratione permisceantur; ut, si quando classis aliqua ob multitudinem discipulorum ex provincialis præscripto geminetur, eundem utraque gradum retineat; et si quando plures in una classe ordines statuantur, iis

[249] *Five grades of classes*

1. He should take care that the grades that make up the lower classes, namely, rhetoric, humanities, and the three grammar classes, are not in any way mixed; so that if some class, on account of a large enrollment, is ever split into two at the instruction of the provincial, each should retain the same grade. And if ever additional levels are organized in a single class, they

gradibus respondeant, qui in regu lis professorum describuntur.

[250] *Divisio grammaticæ in tres libros*

2. Quæ distinctio quo melius faciliusque servetur, omnia Emmanuelis præcepta tres in libros dividenda sunt; quorum singuli singularum scholarum sint proprii. Primus liber pro infima classe continebit primum Emmanuelis librum, et brevem introductionem syntaxeos e secundo depromptam. Secundus liber pro media classe continebit secundum librum Emmanuelis de octo partium constructione usque ad figuratam, additis facilioribus appendicibus. Tertius liber pro suprema classe continebit e secundo libro appendices secundi generis, et a figurata constructione usque ad extremum, ac librum tertium, qui est de syllabarum dimensione. Similis autem huic in tres partes, quæ tribus classibus respondeant, divisio ab iis etiam provinciis facienda esset, quæ aliam methodum, quam romanam sequuntur.

should correspond to those grades that will be described in the rules for professors.

[250] *Division of grammar into three books*

2. To better and more easily keep this distinction, all the rules of Emmanuel ought to be divided into three books; each of them should be proper to each of the classes. The first book for the lowest class will include the first book of Emmanuel, and a brief introduction to syntax drawn from the second.[140] The second book for the middle class will include the second book of Emmanuel from the syntax of the eight parts of speech up to *constructio figurata*, with the addition of the easier appendices.[141] The third book for the highest class will cover the appendices of the second kind from the second book and from the *constructio figurata* up to the end, and the third book, which is about the measurement of syllables.[142] A division similar to this one in three parts corresponding to the three classes would have to be made also

---

[140] Emmanuel: see §46 above.

The syntax of the eight parts of speech: Emmanuel gives the eight parts of speech as *nomen, pronomen, verbum, participium, praepositio, adverbium, interjectio,* and *conjunctio* (Emmanuel, *De institutione grammatica,* 104). The first page of the second book of his grammar carries the title *De octo partium orationis constructione,* and it explains that *syntax* in Greek or *constructio* in Latin means "the right arrangement of the parts of speech with one another" (ibid., 224).

[141] *[C]onstructio figurata:* this phrase denotes artful variation on the expected patterns of speech, new "twists" of phrases that may appear to be errors but should not be classified as such (ibid., 384 f.). [T]he appendices: these are short sections added at the ends of sections to expand upon the grammatical principles just given.

[142] [M]easurement of syllables: knowing the "quantity" or "length" of syllables is important for correct pronunciation and for the scansion (and hence for the composition and appreciation) of classical Latin and Greek poetry and rhythmical speech. It plays some part in distinguishing otherwise ambiguous words (e.g., *hic* means "here" if the vowel is long, "this" if short).

by those provinces that follow a method other than the Roman one.

[251] *Infimæ classis geminus ordo*

3. Cuiusque classis librum magister primo fere semestri absolvet, altero a capite repetet. Quoniam vero infimæ classis liber maior est, quam explanari uno anno ac recoli totus possit, ideo bifariam dividitur. Et expediret quidem pueros non admittere, nisi in prima parte bene instructos, ut omnibus secunda pars, sicut in ceteris classibus, uno anno explicaretur et repeteretur. Verum ubi id fieri non poterit, hæc infima classis dividenda erit in duos ordines, quorum uni prima pars libri, alteri secunda primo fere semestri prælegatur; secundo vero semestri utraque ab initio repetatur. Quæ sicubi geminetur, cum in ea duplex sit ordo, unus poterit magister inferiorem ordinem docere, alter superiorem.

[251] *The split arrangement for the lowest class*

3. The teacher will usually finish each class's book in the first semester; in the second, he will review it from the beginning. But since the lowest class's book is larger than can be completely taught and reviewed in one year, it is therefore divided into two parts. And certainly it would help not to admit boys unless they have been well instructed in the first part, so that the second part can be explained to everyone and reviewed, just as in the other classes. But where this is not possible, this lowest class ought to be divided into two levels. The book's first part should be taught to one and its second should be taught to the other, usually in the first semester. But in the second semester, each should be reviewed from the beginning. Wherever the class is split, since there are two levels in it, one teacher can teach the lower level, and a second the higher one.

[252] *Repetitionis utilitas*

4. Huius repetitionis duplex erit utilitas; prima, quod altius inhærebunt, quæ sæpius fuerint iterata; altera, ut, si qui sint præstanti ingenio, celerius quam ceteri cursum conficiant, cum singulis semestribus possint ascendere.

[252] *The usefulness of review*

4. This review is useful in two ways: First, what is more frequently repeated will be more deeply retained. Second, if any have outstanding intellectual talent, they will complete the course more quickly than the rest, since they can advance to a higher level each semester.

[253] *Collegium quinque classium*

5. Ubi igitur quinque scholæ sunt, serventur in singulis singuli gradus eo modo, quo descripti

[253] *The college of five classes*

5. So where there are five classes, each grade should be kept separate in the way in which they have been

sunt in regulis magistrorum; nec in ulla earum plus quam unus ordo, excepta infima, permittatur.

[254] *Quatuor*

6. Ubi sunt quatuor scholæ, vel, sublata rhetorica, ceteræ quatuor nihil differant ab iis, quas modo diximus; vel, quod magis placet, suprema sit rhetorica, servetque prorsus gradum in regulis professoris rhetoricæ descriptum; altera sit humanitatis, itemque servet gradum in regulis professoris expressum; tertia in duos secetur ordines, quorum superior supremæ classi grammaticæ respondeat, inferior mediæ. Quarta denique respondebit infimæ classi; duosque in ordines, ut in eius regulis dicitur, tribui poterit. Si superior tantum ordo admittatur, tertia unum tantum gradum teneat, sitque suprema grammaticæ; quarta vero duos, sitque media et infima.

[255] *Trium*

7. Ubi sunt tres scholæ, duæ inferiores retineant gradum modo præscriptum duabus ultimis in collegio quatuor classium; suprema vero vel sit pura humanitas, vel in duos dividatur ordines, quorum

described in the rules for teachers.[143] And there should never be more than one level allowed in any of them, with the exception of the lowest.

[254] *Of four*

6. Where there are four classes, either rhetoric should be removed, and the four remaining ones should differ not at all from those that we have just mentioned; or, preferably, the highest should be rhetoric, and it should decidedly keep to the grade described in the rules for the professor of rhetoric; the second should be the humanities class, and likewise, it should keep to the grade stated in the rules for the professor; the third should be divided into two levels, of which the upper should correspond to the highest grammar class, and the lower to the middle one; finally the fourth will correspond to the lowest class. It can be split into two levels, as is stated in its rules. If only the higher level is allowed, the third should contain only one grade, and it should be the highest class of grammar; but the fourth should contain two, and it should be the middle and the lowest.

[255] *Of three*

7. Where there are three classes, the two lower ones should keep the grade just prescribed for the final two in the college of four classes. But the highest should either be straight humanities, or it should be

---

[143] Grade: *gradus* (Latin for "step") indicates the stage of learning, a particular segment of the entire course of education. Many classes at the same grade level can exist in a school, but they would all be unified by a conscious adherence to an explicit statement of the grade's goal, by the particular contents presented in each class, by the particular methods and practices outlined in the *Ratio*, and by the shared schedules for the year and for the daily order.

superior rhetoricæ, inferior humanitati respondeat. Atqui ordo superior non introducetur, nisi consulto rectore, cum bonus numerus discipulorum erit, qui eius ordinis sint capaces; atque ita, ut magister studio et curæ, inferiori ordini debitæ, nullo modo desit.

divided into two levels, of which the higher corresponds to rhetoric, and the lower to humanities. But in any case the higher level should not be introduced unless the rector has been consulted, when there is a good number of students who are capable of that level. And this should be done in such a way that the teacher does not skimp on any of the attention and care that the lower level should get.

[256] *Duarum*

8. Ubi sunt duæ scholæ, inferior duos habeat ordines; quorum alter supremo ordini infimæ classis, alter mediæ classi; superior item duos, quorum alter supremæ classi grammaticæ, alter humanitati respondeat.

[256] *Of two*

8. Where there are two classes, the lower one should have two levels. Of these, one should correspond to the highest level of the lowest class, and the other to the intermediate class. Likewise, the upper one should have two, of which one should correspond to the highest grammar class, and the other to the humanities class.

[257] *Repetitio pensi in scholis duorum ordinum*

9. In his etiam scholis, ubi est ordo geminus, eadem erit pro utroque ordine, quæ dicta est 3, annui pensi repetitio. Et quidem ubi fieri posset, ut utrique sua cuique pars primo semestri explicaretur, secundo iteraretur; discipuli per biennium in eadem classe æque progrederentur atque in duabus, quæ singulis constarent ordinibus; verum, ubi id difficilius videatur, plus etiam erit temporis tribuendum.

[257] *Review of the assigned work in the classes of two levels*

9. Also in these classes where there is a splitting in the levels, there will be for each level the same review of the year's work that was mentioned in number 3. And in fact where it would be possible, each would have its own part taught in the first semester and repeated in the second. Over the course of the two years, the students in the same class would get as far as they would have gotten in two classes that consisted of one level each. But where this seems too difficult, it will require additional time.

[258] *Quæ ibidem communia, quæ propria*

10. Hoc ut obtineri possit in his scholis, in quibus ordo erit geminus, omnia præter grammaticæ prælectionem erunt omnibus communia. Ac primum quidem ciceroniana prælectio communis erit, ita ut faciliora ab inferiore, difficiliora a superiore ordine reposcantur. Deinde thema etiam unicum dari poterit, ita ut totum ordo superior excipiat, inferior primam solum, vel ultimam partem, quæ sit præceptis illi explicatis accommodata. Denique exercitationes et concertationes plerumque omnibus communes esse possunt. Sola ergo grammaticæ prælectio distincta cum sit, aut alterno quoque die singulis ordinibus, aut tempore bifariam diviso, sua utrique quotidie explicabitur recoleturve.

[258] *What is common, what is distinctive in the same situation*

10. In order for this to be achieved in these classes in which there are two levels, everything except for the grammar lesson will be common to everyone. Most important, the lesson on Cicero will be common,[144] so that easier things are demanded of the lower level, more difficult ones of the upper. Then a single theme can also be given, so that the upper level takes it all, the lower only the first or the last part, which has been modified to fit the rules that have been explained to them. Finally, everyone can usually join in the exercises and competitions. Therefore, since only the grammar lesson is distinct, either on every other day in each level, or in a period divided between the two levels, each level will have its own material presented or reviewed every day.

[259] *Novi discipuli*

9. Nullum, quoad eius fieri potest, in discipulorum numerum referat, qui non adducatur a parentibus, aliisve, quibus curæ sit; aut quem ipse non noverit; aut de quo facile non possit ab aliis sibi iam notis edoceri. Neminem vero eo quod ignobilis sit aut pauper, excludat.

[259] *New students*

9. To the extent that it is possible, he should register no one not brought in by his parents or guardians, or not known to him, or about whom he can not easily be fully informed by others that he already knows. But he should exclude no one on the grounds that he is poor or not of noble blood.

[260] *Eorum examen*

10. Eos, qui de novo adveniunt, in hunc modum examinet: roget, quænam studia coluerint, et quatenus; deinde seorsim aliquid scribe-

[260] *Their examination*

10. He should examine the new arrivals this way: He should ask what studies they have worked on, and how far they have gotten. Then

---

[144] Cicero was the most celebrated ancient Roman orator and philosophical writer (106–43 B.C.). In addition to his speeches and philosophical treatises, he left behind a substantial collection of letters and several works on rhetoric.

re, certo argumento proposito, iubeat; nonnulla item præcepta facultatum, quibus studuerint, exigat; breves aliquas sententias, sive latine convertendas, sive, si sit opus, e scriptore quopiam interpretandas proponat.

[261] *Admissio*

11. Quos probe instructos et bonorum morum aut indolis esse cognoverit, admittat; iisque regulas auditorum nostrorum ostendat, ut quales se esse oporteat, norint. Eorum nomen, cognomen, patriam, ætatem, parentes, aut eos, in quorum cura sunt, ecquis discipulorum noverit eorum domos, in libro scribat; diemque et annum, quo quisque admissus est, adnotet. Demum unumquemque in ea classe et cum eo præceptore collocet, qui ipsi conveniat, ut superiore dignus potius, quam suo indignus videri possit.

[262] *Qui non admittendi*

12. In ultimam classem fere neque admittat iuvenes ætate provectos, neque puerulos nimium teneros, nisi admodum idoneos, etiam si probæ tantum educationis gratia mitterentur.

[263] *Promotio*

13. Generalis sollemnisque promotio semel in anno post anniversarias vacationes facienda est. Si qui tamen longe excellant, atque in superiore schola magis, quam in sua profecturi videantur (quod inspiciendis catalogis rogandisque

he should propose a certain topic and tell them to write something on their own. Likewise, he should require a few rules of the subjects that they have studied. He should propose some short sentences for them to translate into Latin, or, if necessary, to interpret from some writer.

[261] *Admission*

11. He should admit those whom he finds to be properly trained and of good character and nature. He should inform them of the rules for our students, so that they might understand what is expected of them. He should register their names, surnames, countries of origin, ages, parents or guardians, and whether any student is familiar with their homes. He should mark down the day and the year in which each was admitted. Finally he should place each one in that class and with that teacher who is right for him, in such a way that he can seem worthy of a higher one rather than unworthy of his own.

[262] *Who should not be admitted*

12. He should usually not admit into the lowest class youths who are too old or, unless they are quite suitable, little boys who are too immature even if they were sent only to be properly trained.

[263] *Promotion*

13. A general and formal promotion ought to be made once a year after the annual vacations. Nevertheless, if any are far superior, and it seems that they would make more progress in a higher class than in their own (which he should realize

magistris cognoscet), nequaquam detineantur, sed quocunque anni tempore post examen ascendant; quamquam a prima classe ad humanitatem propter artem metricam, quæ secundo semestri explicatur, et ab humanitate ad rhetoricam propter Cypriani summam vix patet ascensus.

[264] *Ad examen scribendum*

14. Ad examen semel aut, si opus sit, iterum ab omnibus classibus soluta oratione, a suprema vero grammaticæ et humanitate semel etiam carmine, et, si videatur, semel græce aliquo dierum intervallo in schola scribendum est.

[265] *Examinis leges recitandæ*

15. Efficiat, ut biduo vel triduo ante examen magistri scribendum examinis causa denuncient; scribendique ad examen leges, in fine harum regularum positæ, singulis in classibus recitentur.

[266] *Præfectus præsit*

16. Scribentibus præsit ipse præfectus, aut alius, quem ipse sibi substituerit; qui, quo die scribendum est, signo dato argumentum breve potius quam longum tradat.

by examining the record book and by asking the teachers), they should not by any means be held back, but they should move to the higher class at any time of the year, after an examination. And yet, such an advancement from the first class to humanities hardly appears likely on account of the prosody that is taught in the second semester, as does an advancement from humanities to rhetoric on account of the general overview of Cyprian.[145]

[264] *There should be a written examination*

14. For the examination, all the classes should write a prose composition once, or, if it is necessary, a second time, but the highest class of grammar and the humanities class should write once also in poetry and, if it seems good, once in Greek, after an interval of some days.

[265] *The regulations for the examination should be read out*

15. About two or three days before the examination, he should have the teachers announce that there will be composition for the examination. And he should have the regulations for the examination compositions (attached to the end of these rules) read out in each of the classes.

[266] *The prefect should supervise*

16. The prefect himself, or another person whom he assigns to take his place, should supervise those who are writing. On the day set for taking the examination, after giving the signal,

---

[145] Cyprian: Cypriano Soarez or Cipriano Suarez or Cypriano Soario (1524–93), author of *De arte rhetorica libri tres* (Venice, 1569).

this person should give a theme, a brief one rather than a long one.[146]

[267] *Compositiones tribuendæ examinatoribus*

17. Compositiones in fasciculum ordine alphabeti coniectas apud se habeat; et, si nihil impediat, dividat examinatoribus, ut, si videatur, legere et errata in margine notare possint.

[267] *Compositions to be turned in to the examiners*

17. He should keep the compositions in his possession, bundled in alphabetical order. And if nothing prevents it, he should divide them up among the examiners so that, if they wish, they can read them and mark the mistakes in the margin.

[268] *Examinatores*

18. Examinatores tres esse oportet. Unus erit, ut plurimum, ipse præfectus; alios duos rerum humaniorum bene peritos, qui si fieri potest, magistri non sint, rector cum præfecto constituet. In decernendo autem plura horum trium suffragia spectabuntur. Ubi vero ingens est numerus, duo aut plura examinatorum ternaria constitui nihil vetat.

[268] *Examiners*

18. There should be three [oral] examiners. Typically, one will be the prefect himself; the rector, along with the prefect, will appoint two others, not teachers if possible, who are quite experienced in literary studies. The decision will rest on the weight of the votes made by these three. Where there is a very large number, nothing prevents the arranging of two or more three-member examination boards.

[269] *Examinandorum numerus*

19. Terni ad examen, aut etiam plures ex classibus, præsertim inferioribus, evocentur; totidemque deinceps a magistro, servato alphabeti ordine, aut alio commodiore, submittantur.

[269] *Number of those to be examined*

19. A group of three or even more should be summoned to the examination from the classes, especially the lower ones. And from then on, the same number should be sent up by the teacher, keeping alphabetical order or some order that is more convenient.

[270] *Catalogi cognoscendi*

20. Examinatores in primis perlegant magistri catalogum, et in eo recognoscant adscriptas cuique notas, dum ad examen accedit;

[270] *The record books should be examined*

20. The examiners should first of all read through the teacher's record book and review the marks noted in

---

[146] Theme: the Latin word *argumentum* means the gist or summary sketch of a composition. It can be expressed in a single phrase like "the onset of winter," but more frequently, in the *Ratio* it seems to refer to a short, prepared paragraph dictated to students who will creatively elaborate the topic. Sometimes *argumentum* is translated as "summary of the content" or as "subject."

conferendo, si opus sit, cum superioribus eiusdem anni catalogis, ut quid quisque profecerit aut profecturus sit, facilius appareat.

it for each one, when the student is coming to take the examination. They should compare them, if necessary, with earlier record books from the same year, so that the progress that each one has made or is going to make might be more readily apparent.

[271] *Examinis ratio*

21. Examinis ratio hæc erit: primum, suæ quisque compositionis partem, si videatur, recitet; deinde errata corrigere, et eorum rationem reddere iubeatur, præcepto contra quod peccatum sit, indicato. Postea grammaticis vernaculum aliquid statim latine vertendum proponatur; omnesque de præceptis et rebus, quæ in quaque schola tradita sunt, interrogentur. Denique brevis, si sit opus, loci cuiuspiam ex libris in schola explicatis interpretatio exigatur.

[271] *The structure of the examination*

21. This will be the structure of the examination: First, each should read out, if it seems good, part of his own composition. Then he should be told to correct his errors, and to give an account of them, indicating the rule that was broken. Later, something in the vernacular should be proposed to the grammar students for translation into Latin on the spot;[147] and everyone should be asked about the rules and the material taught in each class. Finally, the examiners should require a brief commentary, if necessary, on some passage from the books taught in class.

[272] *Quando ferenda sententia*

22. Post cuiusque ternarii examen, recentibus adhuc examinatorum iudiciis, sententiæ de interrogatis ferantur, habita compositionis, notæ a magistro additæ, et interrogationis ratio.

[272] *When they should vote*

22. After the examination of each set of three, when the examiners' judgments are still fresh, there should be a vote on the examinees, taking into account the composition, the grade submitted by the teacher, and the way the examination went.

[273] *De dubiis*

23. Ad constituendum de dubiis præfectus quotidianas eorum scriptiones per intervalla exigat; cum iisdem iudicibus conferat, ut eos, si videatur, rursus scribere iubeant

[273] *About doubtful cases*

23. To settle doubtful cases, the prefect should call for their daily work at intervals. He should have a discussion with those examiners so that, if it seems right, they should

---

[147] [S]omething in the vernacular: *vernaculum aliquid.* The vernacular language is sometimes also called the *patrius sermo* or the *sermo vulgi.*

et examinent. Porro in dubiis ratio ætatis, temporis in eadem classe positi, ingenii ac diligentiæ habenda erit.

[274] *Silentio sententiæ suppri-mendæ*

24. Peracto demum examine, quid de unoquoque statuendum sit, silentio supprimatur, nisi quod, antequam publice recitetur, suus cuique magistro catalogus ostendendus erit.

[275] *Inepti*

25. Si quis sit plane ineptus ad gradum faciendum, nullus deprecatori sit locus. Si quis ægre quidem aptus, sed tamen propter ætatem, tempus in eadem classe positum, aut aliam rationem promovendus videatur, id ea conditione, nisi quid obstiterit, fiat, ut, si minus suam magistro probarit industriam, ad inferiorem scholam remittatur; nec in catalogo eius ratio habeatur. Si qui denique ita sint inutiles, ut nec eos promoveri deceat, nec ullus in propria classe fructus speretur, agatur cum rectore, ut, eorum parentibus aut curatoribus perhumaniter admonitis, locum non occupent.

[276] *Promulgatio*

26. Publice promovendorum catalogus vel ad singulas seorsim classes, vel in aula simul ad omnes

have them take another written and oral examination. Moreover, in cases of doubt, they ought to take account of their age, the time they have spent in that particular class, their talent, and their diligence.

[274] *The judgments ought to be kept quite confidential*

24. When an examination is over at last, the decision on each person should be kept quite confidential, except that each teacher will have to be shown his own record book before it is publicly announced.

[275] *The incompetent*

25. If anyone is plainly incompetent to advance to the next level, there should be no place for an intercessor. If anyone is just barely competent but nevertheless, on account of his age, the time spent in the same class, or another reason, it seems right to advance him, then, unless something prevents it, this should happen on the condition that if his effort fails to satisfy the teacher, he will be sent back to a lower class and an account of his performance not kept in the record book. Finally, if any are so ineffective that it is not fitting that they be advanced, and no good result would be expected in their own classes, it should be arranged with the rector that they do not keep their place in the school, after their parents or guardians have very courteously been given notice.

[276] *Public announcement*

26. The list of those who are to be advanced should be publicly read out, either to each of the classes

recitetur. Si qui longe inter cæte-
ros emineant, primi honoris causa
nominentur; in cæteris alphabeti
vel doctrinæ ordo servabitur.

separately or in the hall at the same
time to everyone. If any stand out
far beyond the rest, they should be
named first, to honor them. For the
rest, the order of the alphabet or the
level of learning will be followed.

[277] *Librorum catalogus*

27. Ante instaurationem studiorum de catalogo librorum, qui eo
anno explicandi sunt in scholis
nostris, conficiendo, mature referat
ad rectorem, ut res cum præfecto
generali et cum magistris commu-
nicetur; eodemque modo statuatur,
si qui forte in anno libri sive scriptores commutandi sint.

[277] *List of books*

27. Before the formal reopening
of studies, he should in good time
bring to the rector's attention the
matter of drawing up the list of
books that are going to be taught
that year in our classes, so that the
general prefect and the teachers
might participate in this matter. In
the same way, there should be a
decision on whether perhaps any
books or authors should be changed
that year.

[278] *Librorum copia*

28. Efficiat, ut tempestive cum
publicis bibliopolis agatur, ne librorum, quibus aut in dies utimur,
aut sequentem in annum usuri
sumus tum nos, tum externi, copia
desideretur.

[278] *Supply of books*

28. He should ensure that the
public booksellers are engaged early
on so there is no shortfall in the
supply of books that we (both the
Jesuits and non-Jesuits) either use
from day to day, or are going to use
in the coming year.

[279] *Locorum assignatio*

29. Cuiuslibet anni initio sua
singulis auditoribus scamna et con-
sessores vel per se, vel per magistros, alumnis etiam et convictoribus per eorum moderatores assig-
net (nisi forte alicubi ex doctrinæ
ordine sedendi ordo statuatur);
nobilibus quidem commodiora,
nostris vero [Lukács: veros] et aliis
item religiosis, si adsint, ab externis separata subsellia [Lukács: sub-
sellias]; neque committat, ut
magna aliqua commutatio, se ins-
cio, fiat.

[279] *Assignment of places*

29. At the beginning of any year
he should assign each of the students his own bench and bench
partner, either directly or through
the teachers. He should do this both
for the day students and for the
boarders through their directors
(unless perhaps somewhere the order of seating is determined by the
level of instruction). Of course, he
should assign the better seats to
those of noble families; but to Jesuits and to other religious likewise, if
they are present, he should assign

seating separate from that of the non-Jesuits. And he should fully expect that no great change will be made without his knowledge.

[280] *Privati studii tempus*

30. Permagni interest, ut auditoribus non modo nostris, sed alumnis etiam vel convictoribus, et, si nihil obstiterit, externis quoque præfectus per magistros vel per alios illorum collegiorum præfectos tempus ita distribuat, ut privati studii horas bene collocent.

[280] *Time for private study*

30. It is a matter of very great importance that the prefect, through the teachers or through other prefects of those colleges, so structure the schedule not only for Jesuit students but also for the day students and boarders, and if nothing prevents it for outsiders as well, that they might manage their private study time well.

[281] *Immunitas nulla*

31. Nullam det cuipiam, præsertim diuturnam, nisi gravi de causa, a versibus et græcis discendis immunitatem.

[281] *No exemption*

31. Except for a serious reason, he should give no one an exemption, especially an extended one, from learning poetry, even Greek poetry.

[282] *Declamationes menstruæ*

32. Curet, ut declamationes menstruæ, quæ publice in aula a rhetoribus habentur, superiorum etiam classium frequentia, non modo rhetorum et humanistarum cohonestentur. Ideoque magistri admoneantur, ut suos quisque auditores invitent. Ex nostris vero nemini abesse liceat, nisi a rectore potestatem impetrari.

[282] *Monthly declamations*

32. He should see to it that the monthly declamations that are held by the rhetoricians publicly in the hall are graced not only by the assembly of rhetoricians and humanities students but also by that of the upper grammar classes. And therefore the teachers should be reminded that each should invite his own students. No Jesuits should be allowed to be absent without obtaining permission from the rector.

[283] *Scholarum disputationes*

33. Consideret, quando, qua ratione et quo convenire debeant scholæ ad disputandum inter se; nec solum disputandi rationem ante præscribat, sed etiam, dum certatur, præsens ipse sedulo curet, ut fructuose, modeste, pacate gerantur omnia. Eodemque modo

[283] *Class disputations*

33. He should consider when, according to what form, and where the classes ought to convene to dispute among themselves. And he should not only prescribe ahead of time the structure of the disputation, but also, while the debate is going on, he himself should be pres-

rhetorum et humanistarum decla-
mationibus seu prælectionibus,
quas in gymnasio habere solent,
intersit.

[284] *Academiæ*

34. Ad literarias exercitationes
altius imprimendas det operam, ut,
si rectori videbitur, in classibus
non modo rhetoricæ et humanitatis, sed etiam grammaticæ academiæ instituantur; in quibus statis
diebus, certisque legibus, quæ in
fine libri habentur, vicissim prælegatur, disputetur, aliæque boni
auditoris partes agantur.

[285] *Præmia publica*

35. De præmiis distribuendis ac
declamatione, dialogove tum fortasse habendo, tempestive superiori in memoriam revocet. In qua
distributione leges, quæ in fine
harum regularum collocantur, ser-
vandæ erunt, et in singulis classibus ante scriptionem promulgandæ.

[286] *Privata*

36. Det quoque operam, ut,
præter publica præmia, privatis
etiam, quæ rector collegii suppedi-
tabit, præmiolis, vel signo aliquo
victoriæ magistri in sua quisque
schola discipulos excitent, cum vel
adversarium vincendo, vel totum

ent and take constant care that all
things are managed productively,
temperately, and peacefully. In the
same way, he should attend the declamations or classes of the rhetoricians and humanities students that
are usually held in the school.

[284] *Academies*

34. He should make an effort to
have the literary exercises take a
firm hold. If the rector approves,
academies should be organized, not
only for the classes in rhetoric and
the humanities, but also for those in
grammar. In these academies, on set
days and according to the particular
regulations that are included at the
end of this book, there should be a
rotating presentation of lessons,
disputations, and other activities
that are characteristic of a good student.[148]

[285] *Public prizes*

35. Early on, he should remind
the superior about giving out
awards and about holding a declamation or perhaps a dialog on that
occasion. In the distribution of the
awards, the regulations that are
placed at the end of these rules
must be followed, and they ought to
be formally read out in each of the
classes before the writing.

[286] *Private ones*

36. He should also see to it that,
in addition to the public prizes, the
teachers, each in his own class, also
spur the students on with private
little prizes or some sign of victory,
which the rector of the college will
supply. This should happen when,

---

[148] [I]ncluded at the end of this book: see §§481– 527 below.

aliquem librum repetendo, memoriterve reddendo, vel illustre aliquid eiusmodi agendo in dies commeruisse videbuntur.

from time to time, they seem to have merited them either by overcoming an opponent, or by reviewing all of some book, or by reciting it by heart, or by doing some such noteworthy thing.

[287] *Censor seu prætor*

37. Suum in unaquaque classe, pro regionum consuetudine, publicum censorem, vel, si censoris nomen minus placeat, decurionem maximum, aut prætorem constituat; qui, ut in honore sit apud condiscipulos, privilegio aliquo cohonestandus erit; iusque habebit, magistro approbante, leviores poenas a condiscipulis deprecandi. Is observet, si quis aut ante signum datum ex condiscipulis vagetur in atrio, aut scholam alienam ingrediatur, aut a propria, seu a suo loco discedat; deferat etiam ad præfectum, quinam quotidie desiderentur; si quis non discipulus scholam intrarit; demum si quid, absente seu præsente magistro, peccetur in schola.

[287] *Censor or praetor*

37. He should appoint in each class his own public censor, according to local custom, or if the name of censor is not so appealing, a chief decurion, or a praetor.[149] This person should be honored with some privilege, so that he is respected among his fellow students. With the teacher's approval, he will have the right to release his classmates from lighter punishments. He should notice if anyone is either wandering away from his classmates in the courtyard before the signal is given or going into classes that are not his own, or leaving his own class, or his own place. He should also report to the prefect the ones absent each day; if anyone who is not a student has come into the class; and finally, if any mischief occurs in class, whether the teacher is present or not.

[288] *Corrector*

38. Propter eos, qui tum in diligentia, tum in iis, quæ ad bonos mores pertinent, peccaverint, et cum quibus sola verba bona et exhortationes non sufficiunt, corrector, qui de Societate non sit, constituatur. Ubi haberi non poterit, excogitetur modus, quo castigentur, vel per aliquem ex ipsis scholasticis, vel alia convenienti

[288] *Disciplinarian*

38. On account of those who fall short sometimes in their diligence and sometimes in those things that pertain to good character, and with whom kind words and exhortations alone are not enough, a disciplinarian who does not belong to the Society should be appointed. When one is not available, a way to punish them should be devised, administered ei-

---

[149] *Censor, praetor, decurion:* terms taken from ancient Roman civil and military administration.

ratione. Propter domestica vero delicta non plectantur in schola, nisi raro et magna de causa.

ther through one of the students themselves or by some suitable method. But they should not be whipped in class for some transgression having to do with their home life, except rarely and for a substantial reason.

[289] *Correctionem recusantes*

39. Qui autem plagas recusant, aut cogantur, si tuto possint; aut, si quando id indecore fiat, cum grandioribus videlicet, iis gymnasium nostrum interdicatur, conscio tamen rectore; sicut et iis, qui frequenter absunt a schola.

[289] *Those who refuse correction*

39. The ones who refuse to take a whipping either should be compelled, if this can be done safely, or if it ever becomes unseemly, as it certainly does with the bigger students, forbidden to enter our school. But still the rector must be apprised of the matter. The same should also be the case with those who are frequently absent from class.

[290] *A schola removendi*

40. Cum nec verba, nec correctoris officium satis esset, et in aliquo emendatio non speraretur, aliisque esse offendiculo videretur, præstat a scholis eum removere, quam, ubi parum ipse proficit et aliis nocet, retinere. Hoc autem iudicium rectori, ut omnia ad gloriam et servitium Dei, ut par est, procedant, relinquetur.

[290] *Those who should be removed from class*

40. When neither words nor the disciplinarian's office is sufficient, and someone is not expected to improve, and he seems to be a hindrance to the others, it is better to remove him from classes than to keep him where he himself is getting little help and harming others. But this judgment will be left to the rector, so that everything might proceed, as it should, for the glory and the service of God.

[291] *Coercendi*

41. Si casus aliquis acciderit, ubi in remedium offendiculi præstiti satis non esset a scholis expellere, ad rectorem referat, ut is videat, quid præterea conveniat providere. Quamvis, quoad eius fieri poterit, in spiritu lenitatis, pace et caritate cum omnibus conservata, sit agendum.

[291] *Those that must be punished more severely*

41. If some incident occurs where expulsion would not be a sufficient remedy for an offense committed, he should report it to the rector, so that he might see what might be a fitting alternative arrangement. And yet, as far as it can be, the matter ought to be handled in a spirit of

gentleness, preserving peace and charity with everyone.

[292] *Reditus ad scholas nemini pateat*

42. Reditus ad scholas nostras nemini pateat eorum, qui vel semel eiecti sunt, vel ultro sine legitima causa discesserunt, quin prius rector admoneatur; cuius erit, quid expediat, iudicare.

[292] *Easy readmission to classes should be available to no one*

42. Without the rector being advised beforehand, readmission to our classes should be unavailable to any of those who have either been expelled once or have left on their own initiative without a good reason. It will be up to the rector to decide what solution is the best.

[293] *Atrii quies*

43. Nihil in atrio, nec in scholis, etiam superioribus patiatur armorum, nihil ociosorum, nihil concursationum atque clamorum; nec iuramenta, nec iniurias verbo aut facto illatas, nec inhonestum aut dissolutum quid in eis permittat. Si quid acciderit, componat statim; et cum rectore agat, si quid est, quod atrii quietem ullo modo perturbet.

[293] *The quiet of the courtyard*

43. He should tolerate no weapons, no idle pursuits, no shoving or shouting in the courtyard or in the classes, even the higher ones. He should allow no swearing in them, or verbal or physical injuries, or anything vile or licentious. If any such thing occurs, he should restore order immediately. And he should take it up with the rector, if there is anything that in any way disturbs the quiet of the courtyard.

[294] *Atrium et scholæ lustrandæ*

44. Non modo toto scholarum tempore in atrio, sive in conclavi, unde atrii prospectus pateat, sit assiduus, verum etiam scholas ante datum signum ad ingrediendum interdum lustret; semperque ad atrii ianuam cunctis exeuntibus præsto sit.

[294] *Make rounds of the courtyard and the classes*

44. Not only should he constantly be present in the courtyard, or in a room that looks out onto the courtyard, during the entire time for classes, but he should also occasionally make rounds of the classes before the signal to enter has been given. And he should always be on hand at the door of the courtyard when everyone is leaving.

[295] *Templum et missæ*

45. Curet, ut scholarum ingressus in templum egressusve strepitu careat; et nunquam, nisi præsente aliquo magistrorum, aut etiam plu-

[295] *Church and Masses*

45. He should make sure that the classes enter and leave the church without noise. And they should never attend Mass unless there is

ribus, missam audiant; cui non modo omnes quotidie religiose intersint, sed etiam recte atque ordine distributi.

some teacher present, or even several of them. They should all attend every day not only devoutly but also seated in good order and by their rank in class.

[296] *Confessio*

46. Diebus et horis ad excipiendas discipulorum confessiones constitutis, videat, ut confessarii tempestive adsint; templum ipse per id tempus ingrediatur identidem; curetque, ut modeste ac pie se pueri gerant.

[296] *Confession*

46. On the days and hours set for hearing students' confessions, he should see that the confessors are there on time. He himself should repeatedly enter the church during that time. And he should see to it that the boys are behaving calmly and devoutly.

[297] *Schola non evocandi*

47. Ne ipse quidem præfectus, nisi parce, præsertim prælectionum tempore, e scholis discipulos evocet; si quid in ea re peccetur ab aliis, rectorem edoceat.

[297] *Students not to be called out of class*

47. Especially when lessons are underway, not even the prefect himself should call students from their classes, except sparingly. If any others fail to follow this policy, he should fully inform the rector.

[298] *Discipulorum opera non utendum*

48. Nullo autem tempore discipulorum opera aut ad scribendum, aut ad ullam rem aliam utatur, aut alios uti sinat.

[298] *Do not make use of student labor*

48. At no time should he make use of student labor, either for writing or for any other thing, or allow others to make use of it.

[299] *Regulæ palam collocandæ*

49. Regulæ omnium externorum discipulorum communes in loco, ubi publice legi possint, et in quavis præterea classe, propalam sunt affigendæ, et cuiusque fere mensis initio in rhetorica, cæterisque inferioribus recitandæ.

[299] *Make a set of the rules available*

49. The common rules for all non-Jesuit students ought to be openly posted in a place where they can be read publicly, and in every class besides. And usually at the beginning of each month they ought to be read out in the rhetoric classes and in the other lower ones.

[300] *Vices præfecti generalis*

50. Ubi non erit præfectus studiorum superiorum, curam subeat ipse, rectore probante, recognoscendi ea, quæ publice declamantur, et libros nostris scholasticis, eodem conscio rectore, distribuendi.

[300] *Assuming the role of the general prefect*

50. Where there is not going to be a prefect for higher studies, he himself, with the approval of the rector, should take charge of reviewing those things that are openly declaimed and of distributing books to Jesuit students, with the rector's full awareness.

[H23] Scribendi ad Examen Leges

[H23] Regulations for Taking Examinations

[301] Scriptioni intersint

1. Intelligant omnes, ipso scriptionis die si qui, nisi gravibus distenti causis, desiderentur, eorum in examine nullam habitum iri rationem.

[301] *They should be present for the examination*

1. Everyone should realize that if any are missing on the examination day, then, unless they have been detained for serious reasons, they will get no grade for it.

[302] *Scribendi tempus*

2. Mature veniendum ad scholam, ut scribendi argumentum, et ea, quæ tum præfectus per se vel per alium traditurus est, fideliter excipiant, absolvantque omnia intra finem scholarum. Nam post indictum silentium, nemini cum aliis, ne cum præfecto quidem ipso, sive cum eo, quem ipse sibi substituerit, loqui licitum fore.

[302] *Time for writing*

2. They should come to class on time to accurately take down the subject for the composition and whatever the prefect is going to give them at that time directly or through another person, and to finish everything before the end of classes. For after silence has been declared, no one will have permission to speak with others, not even with the prefect himself or with the one whom he himself has put in his own place as a substitute.

[303] *Apparatus*

3. Accedere oportet instructos libris, ceterisque rebus ad scribendum necessariis, ne ab ullo quidquam petere inter scribendum necesse sit.

[303] *Materials*

3. They should arrive equipped with books and writing materials so that it will not be necessary for them to request anything from anyone during the time for composition.

[304] *Forma*

4. Apposite ad uniuscuiusque classis gradum, dilucideque scribendum, et ex thematis verbis modisque præscriptis. Ambigue scripta in deteriorem partem acceptum iri; verba etiam omissa vel temere immutata, difficultatis evitandæ causa, pro erratis fore.

[305] *Cavendum a consessoribus*

5. Cavendum a consessoribus; nam si duæ forte compositiones similes ac geminæ reperiantur, utramque habitum iri pro suspecta, cum uter ab utro furatus sit, exploratum esse non possit.

[306] *Egressus e schola*

6. Ad fraudes evitandas, si cui forte potestatem exeundi, postquam scribi coeptum sit, dare necessitas cogat, is et argumentum scriptionis et quicquid scripserit, apud præfectum relinquat, sive apud eum, qui tum scholæ præest.

[307] *Scriptionis traditio*

7. Compositione absoluta, suo quisque loco, quæ scripsit, diligenter recolat, castiget, expoliat, quantum velit; nam simul atque compositio tradita præfecto sit, si quid deinde correctum oporteat, haud quaquam redditum iri.

[308] *Adscribendum nomen*

8. Rite complicanda, ut præfectus iusserit, sua unicuique compo-

[304] *Form*

4. Examinations should be written clearly and in a manner appropriate to the grade of each group, using the subjects, words, and styles prescribed. What has been written unclearly will be taken for the worse. Also, words omitted or rashly changed to dodge a difficulty will be counted as wrong.

[305] *Students sitting together must be careful*

5. Students sitting together must be careful; for if two compositions happen to be found to be similar or identical, each of the two will be considered suspect when it is not be possible to ascertain which one has been stolen from the other.

[306] *Leaving class*

6. If necessity happens to force anyone to get permission to leave after the examination has started, then, in order to avoid cheating, he should leave both the summary of the topic and his composition with the prefect or with the one who is in charge of the class.

[307] *Turning in the composition*

7. When the composition is finished, each one at his own place should carefully go over what he has written, correct it, and refine it as much as he wishes. For as soon as the composition has been turned in to the prefect, if anything then needs to be corrected, it will not be given back to him under any circumstances.

[308] *Name to be written down*

8. Each one should fold his own composition in the proper manner,

sitio, atque in tergo nomen tantum scriptoris cum cognomine latine adscribendum, quo facilius compositiones omnium in alphabeti, si libeat, ordinem redigi possint.

as the prefect has instructed, and only the name with the surname of the writer ought to be written on the back in Latin, so that everyone's papers can be more easily put into alphabetical order, if desired.

[309] *Scriptionis absolutio*

9. Cum suam quisque compositionem redditurus accedit ad præfectum, secum suos habeat libros, ut ea tradita, statim silentio exeat e schola; ceteri vero, aliis discedentibus, loca non mutent, sed compositionem, quo coeperint loco, perficient.

[309] *Finishing the writing*

9. When each one who is about to turn in his composition goes up to the prefect, he should have his own books with him, so that when he has turned it in, he might leave the class immediately in silence. The rest, however, should not change places as the others leave, but they will finish their compositions in the places where they started them.

[310] *Tempus*

10. Si quis tempore ad scribendum attributo non absolverit, eam ipsam partem, quam scripserit, tradet. Idcirco probe intelligi ab omnibus oportebit, quantum temporis ad scribendum concedatur, quantum ad describendum et recognoscendum.

[310] *Time*

10. If anyone does not finish in the time allotted for writing, he will turn in the part that he has written. Therefore, everyone ought to know exactly how much time is allowed for writing, how much for copying it out, and how much for checking it.

[311] *Accessus ad examen*

11. Denique cum ad examen accedunt, libros, qui explicati sint eo anno, de quibus interrogandi sunt, afferant; dumque unus interrogatur, ceteri qui adsunt, diligenter attendant. Verum neque annuant aliis, neque corrigant nisi rogati.

[311] *Coming in to the [oral] examination*

11. Finally when they come in to the examination, they should be carrying along the books that have been taught that year, on which they will be asked questions. While one is being asked questions, the rest who are present should pay careful attention. But they should not nod to the others, and they should not correct them unless asked.

[H24] Leges Præmiorum

[312] *Præmiorum numerus*

1. Rhetoricæ octo præmia proponentur: duo solutæ orationis latinæ, duo carminis; duo solutæ orationis græcæ, totidem græci carminis. Sex item, sed eodem plane ordine in humanitate et in prima classe grammaticæ, relicto scilicet græco carmine, cuius infra rhetoricam fere non est usus. Quatuor deinceps in omnibus aliis inferioribus, relicto etiam latino carmine. Unus præterea aut alter in singulis classibus, qui optime omnium christianam doctrinam recitaverit, præmio donetur. Poterunt tamen, ubi ingens aut parvus est numerus discipulorum, plura vel pauciora dari, dummodo potior semper solutæ orationis latinæ ratio habeatur.

[313] *Scriptionum dies*

2. Scribendi certamen in distinctos dies dividatur, ita ut alius dies orationi latinæ, alius scribendis versibus, alii item duo dies græcæ orationi ac versibus tribuantur.

[314] *Constitutæ horæ*

3. Omnes, in suam quisque scholam diebus et horis ad scribendum constitutis, conveniant.

[315] *Egressus et colloquium interdicitur*

4. Accepto scribendi argumento, ante absolutam scriptionem ac traditam, nemo e sua schola egrediatur; neque cum alio intra sive extra

[H24] Regulations for Prizes

[312] *The number of awards*

1. Eight awards should be offered in rhetoric: two for Latin prose, two for poetry; two for Greek prose, the same number for Greek poetry. In the humanities class and in the first grammar class, six should be offered in like manner but keeping to the same arrangement, leaving aside, of course, Greek poetry, which is generally not practiced before rhetoric. Next, four awards should be offered in all the other lower classes, also leaving aside Latin poetry. In addition, in each of the classes, one or two who recite Christian doctrine best of all should be given an award. Still, where the number of students is very high or low, more or fewer awards can be given, provided that the place of Latin prose is always given the greater emphasis.

[313] *Days for writing*

2. The writing competition should be divided up into separate days in such a way that one day is given to Latin prose and another to the writing of verses, and likewise two other days to Greek prose and poetry.

[314] *Set hours*

3. Everybody should assemble, each in his own class, on the days and at the hours assigned for writing.

[315] *Leaving and talking is forbidden*

4. After the summary of the composition's content has been given, no one should leave his class before the writing is finished and turned

gymnasium colloquatur. Si egredi, facta tamen potestate, necesse sit, argumentum et quicquid scripserit, apud eum, qui tum scholæ præest, relinquatur.

in; and no one should speak with anyone else, inside or outside the school. If, however, someone has to leave, then after permission has been granted, the topic and whatever he has written should be left with the one who is in charge of the class at that time.

[316] *Tempus ut prorogandum*

5. Si quis longius spatium ad rem accuratius perficiendam expetit, is, modo ne pedem e schola efferat, neque ultra occasum solis tempus proroget, quamdiu voluerit, maneat.

[316] *How the time should be extended*

5. If anyone requests a longer period to complete the assignment more carefully, he should stay as long as he wishes, provided that he does not set foot outside the class, or extend the time beyond sunset.

[317] *Scriptiones obsignandæ*

6. Suam quisque scriptionem accurate descriptam, aliquo addito, quo maluerit, signo, sine nomine tamen, cum discedere volet, gymnasii præfecto, vel alteri, quem ipse sibi substituerit, reddat; aliam item chartam, in qua cum nomine et cognomine sit idem signum expressum, diligenter obseratum, ne nomen inspici possit, eidem tradat.

[317] *The composition should be marked with a sign*

6. When he wishes to leave, each one should turn in his own composition, carefully written out, to the school prefect, or to another person whom the prefect has put in his place, adding some sign that he prefers, but without a name; likewise, he should turn in to the same person another page on which the same sign has been set, along with his name and surname, carefully folded so that the name can not be seen.

[318] *Tuto asservandæ*

7. Gymnasii cuiusque præfectus omnia sedulo et fideliter asservet; neque chartas nomina continentes, priusquam factum sit iudicium, resignet.

[318] *They should be kept safe*

7. The prefect of each school should keep constant and faithful guard over all of these papers, and he should not unfold the papers containing the names before the decision has been made.

[319] *Iudices*

8. Iudices tres et docti et graves, quorum aliquis externus esse poterit, si loci postulet consuetudo, qui nesciant, cuius quæque sit scriptio,

[319] *Judges*

8. Three judges who are both learned and respected should be chosen. One of them can be from outside if local custom requires it.

deligantur. Hi, perlectis omnibus scriptis et re diligenter inspecta, plurium suffragio omnes ordine victores, et eorum quoque, qui ad victores proxime accesserunt, unum aut alterum in unoquoque genere declarent.

They should not know to which person each of the compositions belongs. When they have read through all the compositions and carefully examined the contents, these judges should declare by a plurality of votes all the winners by level, and also one or two in each category out of those who came very close to the winners.

[320] *Iudicii forma*

9. In iudicio, cuius melior erit orationis forma, is ceteris omnibus, licet plurima scripserint, anteferatur. Si qui genere ipso et stylo pares in scribendo erunt, plura paucioribus anteponantur. Si in hoc etiam sint pares, qui orthographia præstiterit, victor sit. Si orthographia et ceteris rebus pares fuerint, ei, qui elegantius expresserit literarum notas, præmium adiudicetur. Si pares omnino sint, vel dividatur præmium, vel geminetur, vel sorte ducatur. Si quis in omnibus generibus scribendi ceteros vicerit, is etiam omnium generum præmia consequatur.

[320] *The criteria for the decision*

9. In the decision, the composition that has the better structure should be preferred over all the rest, even though they have written the most. If there are any whose writing is equally good in that particular genre and style, then the longer composition should be preferred to the shorter one. If in this respect they are equal as well, the winner should be the one whose spelling is better. If they tie in spelling and in the other categories, the prize should be awarded to the one whose penmanship is more elegant. If they tie in all respects, then the prize should be divided or doubled, or taken by lot. If anyone does better than the rest in all the writing categories, he should also get the awards in all the categories.

[321] *Nomina resignanda*

10. Iudicio perfecto, præfectus cum rectore et præfecto generali chartas, in quibus nomina certantium cum signis adscripta erunt, resignet; nomina victorum e signis diligenter, ne erret, investiget; cognita nemini, præterquam magistris enunciet.

[321] *The names to be disclosed*

10. After arriving at a decision, the prefect, together with the rector and the general prefect, should open up the papers on which the names of the competitors have been written in connection with their signs. He should carefully examine the names of the winners on the basis of the signs so that he does not make a mistake. And he should an-

nounce what he has learned to no one except for the teachers.

[322] *Præmiorum apparatus*

11. Constituto deinde die, quanto maximo fieri poterit apparatu et hominum frequentia, nomina victorum publice pronuncientur, et in medium procedentibus præmia cuique sua honorifice dividantur. Si quis non aderit, nisi potestatem iustis de causis, quæ rectori probentur, acceperit a præfecto, præmium, vel optimo iure sibi debitum, amittat.

[322] *Ceremonies for awarding the prizes*

11. Then on the appointed day, with as much ceremony and in the presence of as large an assembly as possible, the names of the winners should be announced publicly, and their prizes should be given out in a dignified way to each of them as they proceed to center stage. If anyone is not present, he should lose his prize, even if he has every right to it, unless he has gotten permission from the prefect for good reasons that are approved by the rector.

[323] *Distributio*

12. Unumquemque victorem præco evocabit hoc fere modo: Quod felix faustumque sit rei literariæ, omnibusque nostri gymnasii alumnis primum, secundum, tertium etc. præmium solutæ orationis latinæ, græcæ, carminis latini, græci etc. meritus et consecutus est N. Tum victori tradat præmium, nec fere sine aliquo ad rem maxime apposito carmine brevissimo; quod statim, si commode fieri possit, a cantoribus repetatur. Ad extremum addat idem præco, si qui proxime accesserint, quibus aliquid etiam præmii loco dari licebit.

[323] *Distribution*

12. The announcer will call each winner forward usually in this way: "What a happy and favorable occasion it is for Literature, and for all the students of our school, that (NAME) has merited and won the first, second, third, etc. prize for Latin prose composition, for Greek composition, for Latin poetry, for Greek, etc." Then he should hand the prize to the winner, usually with some very short poem especially appropriate to the achievement, which if it can be conveniently managed, should be repeated at that very moment by singers. At the end, the announcer should add any who came very close, and to these something can also be given as a prize.

[324] *Fraudum poena*

13. Contra has leges si quis peccaverit, aut fraudem ullam commiserit, eius scriptionis nulla ratio habeatur.

[324] *Penalty for cheating*

13. If anyone is guilty of an infraction of these regulations or engages in any cheating, no account should be taken of his composition.

[H25] Regulæ Communes Professoribus Classium Inferiorum

[325] *Finis*

1. Adolescentes, qui in Societatis disciplinam traditi sunt, sic magister instituat, ut una cum literis mores etiam christianis dignos in primis hauriant. Feratur autem eius peculiaris intentio tam in lectionibus, cum se occasio obtulerit, quam extra eas, ad teneras adolescentium mentes obsequio et amori Dei, ac virtutum, quibus ei placere oportet, præparandas; sed præcipue ea, quæ sequuntur, observet.

[326] *Oratio ante lectionem*

2. Orationem brevem ante scholæ initium dicat aliquis ad id institutam; quam præceptor et discipuli omnes aperto capite et flexis genibus attente audient. Ante lectionis vero initium ipse præceptor signo crucis se muniat aperto capite, et incipiat.

[327] *Missa et concio*

3. Missæ et concioni curet ut intersint omnes; missæ quidem quotidie, concioni vero diebus festis; ad quam præterea bis saltem singulis hebdomadis eos in Quadragesima mittat, aut etiam pro regionis consuetudine ducat.

[H25] Rules Common to All the Professors of the Lower Classes

[325] *Final goal*

1. The teacher should train the youths who are entrusted to the Society's education in such a way that, along with letters, they also and above all interiorize the moral behavior worthy of a Christian. However, his special attention, both in the lessons whenever the occasion arises and apart from them, should be directed at preparing their impressionable young minds for the devoted service and love of God and the virtues by which we ought to please him. But he should take special note of those things that follow.

[326] *Prayer before the lesson*

2. Before the beginning of class, someone should say a brief prayer composed for this purpose. The teacher and all the students will listen attentively, kneeling down with their heads uncovered. Before the beginning of the lesson, the teacher should bless himself with the sign of the cross, head uncovered, and begin.

[327] *Mass and sermon*

3. He should see to it that they are all present at the Mass and at the sermon—at Mass every day, but at the sermon on feast days. Beyond this, he should send them to the sermon at least twice a week in Lent or even take them, according to the local custom.

[328] *Doctrina christiana*

4. Doctrina christiana in classibus præsertim grammaticæ, vel etiam in aliis, si opus sit, feria sexta aut sabbatho ediscatur ac memoriter recitetur, nisi forte alicubi, et a novis discipulis etiam sæpius recitanda videretur.

[329] *Adhortatio*

5. Piam cohortationem vel doctrinæ explicationem feria item sexta aut sabbatho habeat per semihoram. Hortetur autem potissimum ad orandum Deum quotidie, præcipue vero ad coronam B. Virginis, aut officium quotidie recitandum, ad excutiendam conscientiam vesperi, ad sacramenta poenitentiæ et Eucharistiæ frequenter ac rite obeunda, ad vitandas noxias consuetudines, ad vitiorum detestationem, ad virtutes denique colendas christiano homine dignas.

[330] *Colloquia spiritualia*

6. Privatis etiam colloquiis eadem ad pietatem pertinentia inculcabit; ita tamen, ut nullum ad religionem nostram videatur allicere; sed si quid huiusmodi cognoverit, ad confessarium reiiciat.

[328] *Christian doctrine*

4. Especially in grammar classes, or in others as well if necessary, Christian doctrine should be learned by heart and recited from memory on Friday or Saturday, unless perhaps in some places it would seem good for it to be recited even more frequently, by new students as well.

[329] *Exhortation*

5. On Friday or Saturday, for half an hour, he should give a devout exhortation or a doctrinal lesson. However, he should most especially exhort them to pray to God every day, and particularly to pray daily the rosary or the office of the Blessed Virgin,[150] to make an examination of conscience at evening, to receive the sacraments of penance and Communion frequently and properly, to avoid bad habits, to hate vices, and finally to cultivate the habits worthy of a Christian person.

[330] *Spiritual conversations*

6. In private conversations as well, he will impress on them the same things pertaining to devotion, but he will do this in such a way that he does not appear to be enticing anyone to our form of religious life. But if he does notice anything along this line, he should send the person off to his confessor.

---

[150] Rosary: a structured set of prayers said while the person praying meditates on particular events of the Christian story of salvation, often measured off by the use of a string of beads, under the spiritual patronage of Mary. The Latin word for rosary here is *corona*. For further background on the rosary, see endn. 22.

[D]evotion to the Virgin: for example, the Office of the Blessed Virgin, which is "A liturgical devotion to the Blessed Virgin, in imitation of, and in addition to, the Divine Office." See *CathEncy*, s.vv. "Little Office of Our Lady." For additional information about the Divine Office, see endn. 23.

[331] *Litaniæ et devotio B. Virginis*

7. Litanias Beatissimæ Virginis sabbatho sub vesperum in sua classe recitari iubeat, vel, si moris sit, in templum ad easdem cum ceteris audiendas ducat. Pietatem vero in eandem Virginem et angelum etiam custodem discipulis diligenter suadeat.

[331] *Litanies and devotion to the Blessed Virgin*

7. He should have the litanies of the Blessed Virgin recited in his class on Saturday around evening,[151] or if it is in keeping with the custom, he should take them into the church to hear them with the rest. And he should diligently encourage his students to cultivate a devotion to the Virgin and also to their guardian angels.[152]

[332] *Lectio spiritualis*

8. Lectionem spiritualem, præsertim de sanctorum vitis, vehementer commendet; contra vero non solum ipse ab impuris scriptoribus, et omnino in quibus sit aliquid, quod bonis moribus nocere queat, iuventuti prælegendis abstineat, sed ab iisdem etiam extra scholam legendis discipulos, quam maxime potest, deterreat.

[332] *Spiritual reading*

8. He should enthusiastically recommend spiritual reading, especially about the lives of the saints. And on the other hand, he should not only for his own part refrain from teaching to the young those writers that are not wholesome and avoid altogether those in whom there is anything that can be damaging to good morals, but he should also discourage students as much as he possibly can from reading them even outside of class.

[333] *Confessio*

9. Confessiones singulis mensibus ut a nemine omittantur, efficiat. Iubebit autem eos tradere suum in schedula descriptum nomen, cognomen et classem confessariis, ut schedulas postea recognoscens, quinam defuerint, intelligat.

[333] *Confession*

9. He should make sure that no one misses confession each month. However he will tell them to turn in to the confessors their own names, surnames, and classes, written down on a piece of paper, so that when later reviewing the slips he might know which ones have missed it.

---

[151] Litanies: "[a] litany is a well-known and much-appreciated form of responsive petition, used in public liturgical services, and in private devotions, for common necessities of the Church, or in calamities—to implore God's aid or to appease His just wrath" (*Cath-Ency*, s.v. "Litany"). For an example of a litany, see endn. 24.

[152] Guardian angels: the spiritual beings who are given the special care of individuals.

[334] *Orandum pro discipulis*

10. Oret Deum sæpe pro suis discipulis, eosque religiosæ vitæ suæ exemplis ædificet.

[334] *He ought to pray for the students*

10. He should pray often to God for his own students, and he should edify them by the examples of his own religious life.

[335] *Præfecto obtemperandum*

11. Præfecto horum studiorum obtemperabit in iis, quæ ad hæc studia et scholæ disciplinam pertinent; quo inconsulto, neque ullum in scholam admittet aut dimittet, nec librum ullum suscipiet explicandum, nec ullam cuivis a communibus scholæ exercitationibus immunitatem dabit.

[335] *Obey the prefect*

11. He will obey the prefect of these studies in what pertains to the academic work and to class discipline. Without consulting with the prefect, he will not admit any student into class or dismiss him, nor will he take up any book to teach, nor will he give anyone an exemption from the common class exercises.

[336] *Gradus cuiusque scholæ*

12. Scholæ omnes in suo se gradu contineant; et de rhetorica quidem et humanitate dicetur seorsim, grammaticæ vero tres scholæ esse debent, quibus eiusdem quidam quasi cursus absolvatur. Omnia proinde Emmanuelis præcepta tres in partes dividenda sunt; quarum singulæ singularum scholarum sint propriæ; ita tamen, ut in unaquaque classe ea semper, quæ in schola proxime inferiore tradita sunt, recurrantur, prout in cuiusque magistri regulis indicabitur.

[336] *The grade of each class*

12. Every class should keep to its own particular grade.[153] Both rhetoric and humanities will be treated separately, but there ought to be three grammar classes, which should bring to completion a certain kind of course of study in this subject. Accordingly, all the rules of Emmanuel should be divided into three parts. Of these, each part should be proper to each of the classes, but in such a way that each class reviews what was taught in the class immediately preceding it, just as the rules for each teacher will indicate.

[337] *Græcæ grammaticæ divisio*

13. In græca etiam grammatica hæc fere divisio erit: Prima pars a primis elementis ordiendo simplicia nomina, verbum substantivum et verba item simplicia complectitur; secunda nomina contracta,

[337] *The division of Greek grammar*

13. In Greek grammar there will also usually be this division: The first part, starting from the first elements, includes the simple nouns, the verb to be and likewise simple verbs. The second part includes con-

---

[153] See §253n for an explanation of "grade."

verba circumflexa, verba in Mi, et faciliores formationes pro media classe; tertia reliquas partes orationis, seu quæcumque Rudimentorum nomine continentur, exceptis dialectis ac difficilioribus annotationibus pro suprema classe; quarta, quæ humanitati tribuitur, omnem syntaxim; quinta denique pars, quæ est rhetoricæ, artem metricam.

tracted nouns, circumflex verbs, verbs in -mi, and the easier expressions for the middle class.[154] The third part includes the remaining parts of speech, or whatever falls under the heading of rudiments, except the dialects and the more difficult annotations, for the highest class. The fourth part includes what is given to the humanities year, all the syntax; finally, the fifth includes prosody,[155] which belongs to rhetoric.

[338] *Divisio temporis*

14. Divisio temporis, quod in rhetorica binis minimum horis, in humanitate vero et ceteris scholis duabus et dimidiata mane, totidemque a prandio, binis item minimum die vacationis definitur, eadem semper esse debebit, ut certum sit, quæ horæ quibus exercitationibus impendantur.

[338] *The schedule*

14. The schedule, which in rhetoric is set at two hours at least, but in humanities and in the other classes at two and a half hours in the morning, and the same after the midday meal, and likewise at a couple of hours as a minimum on a break day, always ought to be the same, so that it is clear what hours are spent on what exercises.

[339] *Quatenus commutanda*

15. Harum tamen exercitationum ordo ad provincialis præscriptum pro loci consuetudine immutari potest; dummodo eædem omnino, eademque spatia temporis illis in cuiusque magistri regulis assignata retineantur, et in semel coepto constantia servetur.

[339] *To what extent the schedule ought to be changed*

15. Still, the order of these exercises can be changed in accordance with local custom at the instruction of the provincial, provided that all the same matter and the same time periods assigned for them in the rules for each teacher are kept, and provided that constancy is kept in the order once it has been initiated.

---

[154] [C]ontracted nouns, circumflex verbs: in Greek, some words change a vowel sound or add a certain pitch accent on account of the addition of certain endings. [V]erbs in -mi: there is in Greek a class of verbs ending in *-mi* that takes a special set of endings.

[155] Prosody *(ars metrica):* linguists today use the word *prosody* to cover things like rhythm, speed, stress, volume, word groupings, and so on, in ordinary speech. In the study of classical languages, the term has been applied to the study of poetic meters, which requires the "art of measuring long and short syllables" and various set patterns of those syllables.

[340] *Dies festus in sabbathum incidens*

16. Si festus dies inciderit in sabbathum, eius diei exercitationes in antecedentem diem revocentur vel omittantur.

[341] *Die vacationis quæ divisio*

17. Eadem divisio die vacationis erit, ubi non assignantur propriæ exercitationes; singulæ enim, quæ aliis diebus fiunt, pro portione contrahendæ, aut earum aliqua in orbem prætermittenda, tempusque aliquod concertationi relinquendum.

[342] *Latine loquendi usus*

18. Latine loquendi usus severe in primis custodiatur, iis scholis exceptis, in quibus discipuli latine nesciunt; ita ut in omnibus, quæ ad scholam pertinent, nunquam liceat uti patrio sermone; notis etiam adscriptis, si qui neglexerint; eamque ob rem latine perpetuo magister loquatur.

[343] *Memoriæ exercitatio*

19. Memoriæ traditas prælectiones discipuli decurionibus recitent; de quorum officio infra regula dicetur; nisi forte alius placeat mos in rhetorica. Ipsi vero decuriones decurioni maximo vel magistro persolvent. Qui magister aliquot quotidie ex desidiosis fere, quique serius ad ludum venerint, recitare iubet ad explorandam decurionum fidem, omnesque in officio continendos. Sabbatho audita per unam vel etiam plures hebdomadas pub-

[340] *Holiday falling on Saturday*

16. If a holiday falls on a Saturday, the exercises for that day should be moved up to the previous day or left out.

[341] *Schedule for a break day*

17. The same schedule holds for a break day that does not have its own exercises assigned. For everything done on the other days ought to be abbreviated proportionately, or some of it should be left out in rotation, and some time left for the competition.

[342] *The practice of speaking Latin*

18. Above all, the practice of speaking Latin should be rigorously observed, except in those classes in which the students do not know Latin. It should be maintained in such a way that it is never permissible to make use of the vernacular in anything pertaining to class, and lapses should even be recorded. For this reason, the teacher should speak Latin all the time.

[343] *Exercise of memory*

19. Unless perhaps another custom is preferred in rhetoric, the students should recite the memorized lessons to the decurions, the rule about whose office will be stated below. The decurions themselves will deliver their recitations to the chief decurion or to the teacher. Every day the teacher usually calls upon several of the students who are lazy and who have been tardy and tells them to recite, in order to ascertain the trustworthiness of the

lice memoriter reddantur. Libro autem absoluto, deligi poterunt interdum, qui illum e suggestu ab initio pronuncient non sine præmio.

decurions, and to keep them all on task. On Saturday, the lessons of one or even more weeks should be performed from memory in front of the whole group. When the book is finished, sometimes students can be selected to deliver it aloud from the beginning, speaking from the platform and getting some prize.

[344] *Scriptiones afferendæ*

20. Scriptiones afferendæ in classibus grammaticæ quotidie præter diem sabbathi; in ceteris solutæ quidem orationis quotidie, præter diem vacationi et sabbathi; carminis vero bis tantum, proximo scilicet post dominicum et vacationis diem; græci demum thematis saltem semel, quo die magistro libuerit, a prandio.

[344] *Written work should be brought in*

20. In the grammar classes, written work should be brought in every day except for Saturdays. On the other days, there should certainly be prose compositions, except for break days and Saturdays. But poetic compositions should be brought in only twice, namely on the days following Sundays and break days. Finally, a Greek theme ought to be brought in at least once, after the midday meal on a day fitting the teacher's preference.

[345] *Corrigendæ*

21. Scriptiones corrigendæ ferme privatim et submissa voce cum unoquoque discipulorum, ut iis interim stylum exercendi tempus detur. Expedit tamen quotidie aliquot exempla, modo ex optimis, modo ex deterrimis, tum initio, tum in fine publice recitare atque perpendere.

[345] *Written work should be corrected*

21. Written work should usually be corrected privately and in a low voice with each of the students, so that occasionally time for practicing their style may be given to them. Nevertheless, it helps to recite in front of the group and to evaluate several samples every day, now from the best, now from the worst, sometimes at the beginning, and sometimes at the end of class.

[346] *Corrigendi ratio*

22. Modus corrigendæ scriptionis in universum est indicare, si quid contra præcepta peccatum sit; interrogare, quomodo emendari possit; iubere, ut æmuli, statim

[346] *The way to correct*

22. Generally, the way to correct the written work is to indicate if any rule has been broken; to ask how it can be corrected; to tell them, as rivals, to correct something

ut aliquid deprehenderint, publice corrigant, præceptumque, contra quod peccatum est, proferant; laudare denique, si quid apte perfectum sit. Hoc autem dum publice peragitur, primum discipuli scriptionis exemplum (quod semper, præter id, quod magistro describitur, afferendum est) secum ipsi legant et emendent.

aloud and outright as soon as they catch it,[156] and to cite the rule that has been broken; finally to offer praise if anything has been done right. However, while this is being carried out in front of everyone, the students should read to themselves and correct the first copy of their written work (which always ought to be brought to class, in addition to what is copied out for the teacher).

[347] *Corrigendæ quamplurimæ*
23. Quotidie scriptiones singulorum a magistro corrigi oporteret, cum præcipuus et maximus inde fructus existat. Si tamen multitudo non patitur, corrigat quamplurimas potest, ita ut quos uno die discipulos præterit, altero vocet. Eam ob causam diebus præsertim, quibus carmina afferuntur, scriptiones aliquas æmulis emendandas dispertiat (quod quo commodius fiat, unusquisque non suum tantum, sed etiam æmuli nomen a tergo scriptionis inscribat) aliquas ipse magister pomeridiano tempore, dum memoriter recitatur, aliquas, si libuerit, domi corrigat.

[347] *Correct as many as possible*
23. Every day everyone's written work ought to be corrected by the teacher, since that is the source of the greatest and most substantial benefit. Nevertheless, if the large number does not allow it, he should correct as many as he can, in such a way that the students he misses one day he calls on the next. For this reason, especially on the days on which poems are being brought in, he should distribute some written works to be corrected by the rivals (facilitating this by having each one write on the back of the assignment not only his own name but the name of his rival as well), and the teacher himself should correct some assignments in the afternoon while the recitation from memory is going on, and others, if he would like, at home.

[348] *Exercitationes inter corrigendum*
24. Exercitationes varias, dum scripta corrigit, pro scholæ gradu, modo hanc, modo illam imperet. Nulla enim re magis adolescentium industria, quam satietate languescit.

[348] *Exercises during the correction*
24. He should require a variety of exercises appropriate for the grade level of the class, now one type, now another, while he corrects the written material. For nothing dampens the industry of adolescents more than feeling that they have had

---

[156] Rivals: friendly competitors, partners in the "game" of learning.

enough of something and are finished.

[349] *Repetitio*

25. Repetitio prælectionis tum hesternæ, tum præsentis eodem se habeat modo; fiatque vel ab uno tota, vel potius a pluribus per partes, ut omnes exerceantur. Repetantur autem præcipua et utilissima, primum fere a provectioribus, deinde etiam ab aliis; idque vel continenti oratione, vel ad singulas magistri interrogationes interrupta, æmulo inter repetendum corrigente, si alter erret, vel si cunctetur, antevertente.

[349] *Review*

25. A review of the lesson should be held in the same manner both for the previous day and for the current one. And it should all be done in its entirety by one person, or, even better, in sections by several so that everyone practices. What is most important and useful should be reviewed, usually by the more advanced first, and then also by the others. And it should be done either in a continuous address, or in one that is interrupted by the teacher's particular questions, while one rival makes corrections during the review if the other makes a mistake, or anticipates him if he delays.

[350] *Repetitio die sabbathi*

26. Die sabbathi omnia, quæ per hebdomadam prælecta sunt, recolantur. Quod si qui interdum profiteantur, de iis omnibus, vel de toto libro se responsuros, ex iis aliquot delectos reliqui binis ternisve lacessant interrogationibus non sine præmio.

[350] *Review on Saturday*

26. On Saturday, they should go over again everything that was taught during the week. But if on occasion any claim that they are ready to be examined on all of the material or on the entire book, then the rest should quiz several students selected from them two or three at a time; finally, some prize should be awarded.

[351] *Prælectio*

27. In prælectionibus veteres solum auctores, nullo modo recentiores explicentur. Multum autem proderit, si magister non tumultuario ac subito dicat, sed quæ domi cogitate scripserit, totumque librum vel orationem, quam præ manibus habet, ante perlegerit. Forma autem prælectionis hæc ferme erit: Primum, totam conti-

[351] *Lesson*

27. In the lessons, only the old authors should be taught, and by no means the more recent ones. It will be very profitable if the teacher does not give scattered reflections improvised on the spot, but rather what he has thoughtfully written out at home, and if he has read ahead of time the entire book or speech that he has in hand. This will be the

nenter pronunciet, nisi aliquando in rhetorica et humanitate longior esse debeat. Secundo, brevissime argumentum exponat, et connexionem, ubi erit opus, cum iis, quæ antecesserant. Tertio, unamquamque periodum prælegens, si quidem latine interpretetur, obscuriores explanet, unam alteri nectat, ac sententiam non quidem inepta metaphrasi unicuique verbo latino alterum verbum latinum reddendo, sed eandem sententiam apertioribus phrasibus declarando aperiat; si vero vulgi sermone, servet, quoad fieri potest, collocationem verborum. Sic enim numero assuescunt aures. Quod si sermo patrius non patitur, prius ad verbum fere omnia, postea ad vulgi consuetudinem explicet. Quarto, a capite recurrens, nisi malit ipsi explicationi inserere, observationes tradat cuique scholæ accommodatas. Quas vero excipiendas censuerit, quæ multæ esse non deberent, vel interrupte inter explicandum, vel seorsim, prælectione iam habita, dictet. Utile autem solet esse, ut grammatici nihil scribant, nisi iussi.

usual structure of the lesson: First, he should read the whole passage straight through, unless sometimes in rhetoric or in the humanities classes that would have to take too long. Second, he should, in a very concise way, summarize the content and, where this is necessary, its connection with what had gone before. Third, reading out each sentence, if he interprets it in Latin, he should explain what tends to be unclear; he should connect one idea with another; and he should make the idea plain not by clumsily substituting each Latin word with another Latin word, but rather by stating that idea in more accessible expressions. But if he uses the vernacular, he should preserve the word order as far as is possible, for this way the ear grows accustomed to the order. And if the vernacular does not allow it, he should teach almost everything first word by word and later according to the vernacular idiom. Fourth, he should make comments suitably fashioned for each class, starting again from the top, unless he prefers to insert them in the explanation itself. But either intermittently during the explanation, or separately after the lesson has been finished, he should dictate what he thinks should be gotten from the passage. Such items should not be numerous. But remember: it is usually effective to have the grammar students write nothing unless told to do so.

[352] *Prælectio historici et poetæ*

28. Historici et poetæ prælectio illud habet peculiare, quod historicus celerius fere excurrendus; in

[352] *The lesson on the historian and poet*

28. The lessons on historians and on poets are different insofar as the

poeta sæpe oratoria paraphrasis accurate facta plurimum decet; faciendumque, ut discipuli poetæ oratorisque stylum internoscere consuescant.

[353] *Prælectio præceptorum*

29. In prælegenda tum Cypriani rhetorica, tum arte metrica, tum latina græcave grammatica, et horum similibus ad præcepta spectantibus, res ipsæ potius, quam verba perpendenda sunt. In grammaticæ vero præsertim inferioribus classibus, cum incidit aliquid difficilius, illud ipsum uno aut pluribus diebus recolatur, aut faciliora quædam ex aliis grammaticæ partibus interponantur repetanturve.

[354] *Scribendi argumentum*

30. Scribendi argumentum non dictandum ex tempore, sed meditato et fere descripto, quod ad imitationem Ciceronis, quantum fieri potest, et ad normam cuiusdam narrationis, suasionis, gratulationis, admonitionis, aliarumque id genus rerum dirigatur; et quidem tum latina lingua, tum patria scribendum esset, ubi dictatur ad verbum. Dictatum porro statim magister iubeat recitari; explicet, si quid forte difficilius; phrases aliaque præsidia subministret; semperque, excepto rhetore, inter dictandum admoneat, quo modo quævis pars conscribenda sit et interpungenda. Aliquid vero extraordinarium solito

historian's work ought to be covered rather quickly most of the time, whereas the poet's work often calls for a carefully constructed prose paraphrase. The teacher should see to it that the students get accustomed to distinguishing what stylistically belongs to a poet and what to a prose writer.

[353] *The lesson on the rules*

29. In giving lessons on Cyprian's rhetoric, whether on prosody, or on Latin or Greek grammar, or on things similar to these that have to do with the rules, he should give careful consideration to the actual content rather than to the words. But especially in the lower grammar classes, when something difficult comes up, it should be worked on for one or more days, or certain easier things from the other parts of grammar should be mixed in or reviewed.

[354] *Summary of the composition's content*

30. The subject for a composition should not be dictated spontaneously, but with careful forethought and usually from written notes. The theme should aim at an imitation of Cicero, as much as possible, and it should aim at the pattern of a certain narration, persuasion, congratulation, warning, and other such forms. And when it is dictated word for word, it should have to be written both in the Latin and in the native language. Next the teacher should have the dictation recited right away. He should explain anything that happens to be a bit difficult. He should supply

amplius præscribendum est, cum plures dies festi incidunt, vel cum vacationes, tum maiores tum minores, indicuntur.

[355] *Concertatio*

31. Concertatio, quæ vel magistro interrogante, æmulisque corrigentibus, vel ipsis invicem æmulis percontantibus fieri solet, magnifacienda; et quoties tempus permittit, usurpanda, ut honesta æmulatio, quæ magnum ad studia incitamentum est, foveatur. Poterunt autem vel singuli, vel plures ex utraque parte committi, præcipue ex magistratibus; vel unus etiam plures lacessere. Privatus fere privatum petet, magistratus magistratum; privatus etiam interdum magistratum, eiusque dignitatem, si vicerit, sive aliud præmium aut victoriæ signum consequi poterit, prout scholæ dignitas et locorum ratio postulabit.

[356] *Extraordinariæ exercitationes*

32. Extraordinariæ exercitationes utilitatem magnam habent; in quibus illud universe dicendum est, ea quæ publice pronunciabuntur, ut non memoria solum discipulorum, sed ingenium etiam excolatur, a magistro expolienda quidem diligenter, nunquam tamen de in-

phrases and other helps. And during his dictation, except in the rhetoric class, he should always remind them how each part ought to be written down and punctuated. When several feast days occur or when vacations are declared, whether longer or shorter, something special should be written out more fully than usual.

[355] *Competitions*

31. Much should be made of competitions, which tend to occur either with the teacher asking questions and the rivals correcting, or with the rivals doing the quizzing among themselves. And as often as the time allows it, competitions ought to be employed in order to feed an honorable rivalry, which is a great spur to studies. They can be set to a competition of one side against another, made up of individuals or small groups drawn especially from the officers; or one student can also quiz several. Usually a private will question a private, an officer will question another officer. Also from time to time, a private will question an officer and, if he wins, he can attain his rank or some other award or sign of victory, just as the rank of the class and the scheme of the positions require.

[356] *Special exercises*

32. Special exercises are very useful. In general, we ought to mention the following about them: to cultivate not only the students' memories but also their intellectual talents, the teacher must attentively refine, but never fashion from scratch, those things that will be delivered in front of the group. And

tegro facienda; eademque de versibus, qui in publico proponuntur,
ratio est. Laborandum etiam, ut
vocem, gestus et actionem omnem
discipuli cum dignitate moderentur.

[357] *Prælectio seu declamatio
in schola*

33. Prælectio vel græca latinave
oratio aut carmen in rhetorica quidem et humanitate alternis fere
sabbathis, una schola alteram invi-
tante, habeatur; in reliquis sola
prælectio non tam habeatur, quam
audita ex cathedra repetatur, nullis
fere invitatis; nec nisi singulis mensibus.

[358] *Concertatio cum proxima
classe*

34. Concertatio cum proxima
classe erit aliquoties in anno, quo
die præfecto studiorum inferiorum
visum fuerit, per horam fere de iis
tantum rebus, quæ utrique classi
communes sunt, utroque moderan-
te præceptore. Bini ternive, aut
plures disputabunt ex optimis utriusque classis discipulis; vel ex
condiclu ad singulas interrogationes responsionesque antea instructi; vel ex ingenio, quicquid libeat,
percontantes; vel dubitationes ab
uno propositas, præsertim de rhetorica, impugnantes.

the same approach holds for the
verses that are presented before the
group. Also there should be a real
effort made to get the students to
control in a dignified way their
voice, their gestures, and every feature of their delivery.

[357] *Lesson or declamation in
class*

33. Usually on every other Saturday, there should be a lesson, or a
Greek or Latin speech or a poem (in
the rhetoric and the humanities
classes); and on these occasions, one
class should invite another. On the
other Saturdays, there should not be
a lesson so much as a review of
what the teacher had formally
taught; generally on these occasions,
no one should be invited. This
should happen only once a month.

[358] *Competition with the closest
class*

34. Several times a year, there
will be a competition with the closest class, on a day that seems good
to the prefect of lower studies, usually for an hour, only on those
things that are common to both
classes, with each of the teachers
moderating. Groups of two or three
or more of the best students of each
class will debate. Earlier they will
have been prepared for individual
questions and answers on the basis
of what has been agreed upon, or
they will use their wits to ask whatever they like; or they will take a
position to counter the problems
that someone raises, especially concerning rhetoric.

[359] *Magistratus*

35. Magistratus eligendi præmiisque etiam, si videbitur, afficiendi, nisi id alicubi in rhetorica minus necessarium videretur, singulis fere aut alternis mensibus. Ad eam rem semel soluta oratione, semel etiam, si videatur, in superioribus classibus carmine græceve scribant in schola toto scholæ tempore, nisi in inferioribus melius videatur semihoram concertationi relinquere. Qui omnium optime scripserint, summo magistratu, qui proxime accesserint, aliis honorum gradibus potientur; quorum nomina, quo plus eruditionis res habeat, ex græca romanave republica militiave sumantur. Duas autem fere in partes ad æmulationem fovendam schola dividi poterit, quarum utraque suos habeat magistratus, alteri parti adversarios, unicuique discipulorum suo attributo æmulo. Summi autem utriusque partis magistratus primum in sedendo locum obtineant.

[360] *Decuriones*

36. Decuriones etiam a præceptore statuantur, qui memoriter recitantes audiant, scripta præceptori colligant et in libello punctis notent, quoties memoria quemque fefellerit, qui scriptionem omiserint, aut duplex exemplum non tulerint, aliaque, si iusserit præceptor, observent.

[359] *Officers*

35. Usually every month or every other month, officers should be chosen and even honored with awards, if it seems good, unless somewhere this seems less necessary in rhetoric. To this end, they should write in class once in prose, and once also, if it seems good, in the higher classes in verse or in Greek, for an entire class period, unless it seems better in the lower classes to leave a half hour for a competition. Those who have written best of all should assume the highest office. Those who have come closest to the best should take the other honorary ranks. The names of these ranks should be taken from the Greek or Roman republic or military service, to give the practice a more scholarly dimension. The class can be divided, usually into two parts, to foster rivalry. Each should have its own officers corresponding to those on the other side, and each of the students should have his own designated rival. The highest officials of each side should get the first place in the seating arrangement.

[360] *Decurions*

36. The teacher should also appoint decurions to hear the students' memory recitations, collect written work for the teacher, and tally up in a notebook how many times each fell short in the memorization, who did not do their written work or bring in a second copy. They should also take note of other things, if the teacher tells them to.

[361] *Ad examen præparatio*

37. Ad promotionem generalem uno ferme ante examen mense strenue discipuli in præcipuis quibusque rebus in omnibus classibus, excepta fortasse rhetorica, exerceantur. Quod si quis longe intra annum excelleret, de eo magister referat ad præfectum, ut privatim examinatus, gradum ad superiorem scholam facere possit.

[362] *Catalogus*

38. Catalogum discipulorum alphabeti ordine conscriptum præfecto tradat. Quem catalogum interdum in anno recognoscat, ut, si quid sit opus, immutari queat; accuratissime vero, cum generale discipulorum examen impendet. In eo autem catalogo quamplurimos potest, discipulorum gradus distinguat; videlicet, optimos, bonos, mediocres, dubios, retinendos, reiiciendos; quæ notæ numeris significari possent 1 2 3 4 5 6.

[363] *Disciplinæ cura*

39. Disciplinam omnem nihil æque continet atque observatio regularum. Hæc igitur præcipua sit magistri cura, ut discipuli tum ea, quæ in eorum regulis habentur, observent; tum ea, quæ de studiis dicta sunt, exequantur. Quod spe honoris ac præmii metuque dedecoris facilius, quam verberibus consequetur.

[361] *Preparation for the examination*

37. For the general advancement to the next grade, just about one month before the examination, the students in all classes except perhaps rhetoric should vigorously practice all the essential material. But if in the course of the year anyone excels notably, the teacher should inform the prefect of this, so that after he has been privately examined, he might be able to advance to a higher class.

[362] *Register*

38. He should turn in to the prefect a register of students, written in alphabetical order. From time to time during the year, he should review it, so that it can be changed if there is any need; but he should do this very carefully when the general examination of the students is near. And in the register he should distinguish the levels of as many students as he can; namely, the best, the good, the average, the doubtful, those to be kept, those to be expelled. These marks can be signified with the numbers 1, 2, 3, 4, 5, and 6.

[363] *Concern for discipline*

39. Nothing preserves the entire effort of well-ordered learning as effectively as the observance of the rules. This should be the teacher's leading concern: that the students both observe what is contained in their rules and carry out what has been said about their studies. This will be achieved more easily by the hope of honor and award and by the fear of shame than it will by corporal punishment.

[364] *Puniendi ratio*

40. Nec in puniendo sit præ-
ceps, nec in inquirendo nimius;
dissimulet potius, cum potest sine
cuiusque damno; neque solum
nullum ipse plectat (id enim per
correctorem præstandum), sed omnino a contumelia dicto factove
inferenda abstineat; nec alio quempiam, quam suo nomine vel cognomine appellet; poenæ etiam loco
aliquid literarium addere ultra quo-
tidianum pensum, utile interdum
erit. Inusitatas autem et maiores
poenas ob ea præsertim, quæ extra scholam deliquerint, sicut eos,
qui plagas recusant, præsertim si
grandiores sint, ad præfectum reiiciat.

[364] *Method of punishment*

40. He should not be quick to
punish, nor overly eager about finding things out. Rather he should
look the other way when he can do
so without harm to anyone. And not
only should he whip no one himself
(for the disciplinarian ought to take
care of that) but he should abstain
altogether from insulting treatment
in word or in deed. And he should
not call anyone by a name other
than the person's own name or surname. And by way of a punishment
it will occasionally be useful to add
some kind of written work beyond
the daily assignment. However, he
should leave to the prefect unusual
and more severe penalties, especially
for those misdeeds that they have
committed outside of class, just as
he should pass on to the prefect
those who refuse to take a whipping, especially if they are rather
fully grown.

[365] *Assiduitas*

41. Assiduitatem maxime a discipulis requirat; nec proinde ad
publica spectacula sive ludos eos
dimittat; si quis abfuerit, aliquem
ex condiscipulis, vel alium ad eius
domum mittat; et, nisi idoneæ affe-
rantur excusationes absentiæ, poe-
nam sumat. Qui plures dies sine
causa abfuerint, ad præfectum re-
mitti, nec sine eius consensu recipi
debent.

[365] *Constant attendance*

41. He should especially demand
constant attendance from the students. And so he should not send
them off to public performances or
entertainments. If anyone is absent,
he should send one of his fellow
students or someone else to his
home. And unless suitable excuses
for the absence are presented, he
should impose a punishment. Anyone who is absent for several days
without good cause ought to be sent
on to the prefect and not taken back
without his agreement.

[366] *Confessionum dies*

42. Ne confessionum causa
quicquam remittatur ex iis, quæ

[366] *Confession days*

42. So that no special class work
is lost on account of confessions, he

scholarum propria sunt, terni vel plures, ubi sit opus, initio mittantur ad confitendum; deinde, ut singuli redeunt, ita ex ceteris singuli binive submittantur; nisi forte alicubi ad confessionem simul omnes ire consueverint.

should, at the beginning of class, send groups of three at a time, or more where necessary, to confess. Then as they return one by one, others from the ones that are left should be sent down individually or in pairs, unless perhaps in some places they have gotten used to going to confession all at the same time.

[367]   *Silentium et modestia*

43. Silentium et modestiam servandam in primis curet, ut nemo per scholam vagetur, nemo locum mutet, nemo ultro citroque munera schedasque mittat; ut a schola non egrediantur, præsertim duo vel plures simul.

[367]   *Silence and modesty*

43. He should take special care to ensure that silence and modesty are preserved, so that no one wanders around in class, no one changes place, and no one sends gifts and notes back and forth. He should make sure that they do not leave class, especially two or more at the same time.

[368]   *Egressu a schola*

44. Cavendum est, ne facile, præsertim prælectionis tempore, a quopiam discipuli evocentur; ut confusio etiam et clamor in egressu præcipue vitetur, magistro sive e suggestu sive ad ianuam spectante, proximi quique valvis primi exeant; vel alia ratione curetur, ut modeste omnes et silentio egrediantur.

[368]   *Leaving school*

44. Precautions should be taken so that the students are not easily called out of class by anyone, particularly during a lesson. Also, in order to avoid confusion and noise at dismissal, all those nearest the doors should leave first, while the teacher looks on, either from the platform or at the door. Or some other way should be found to ensure that all the students leave in silence and in a well-behaved manner.

[369]   *Academiæ*

45. Academias instituat, si rectori videbitur, ex regulis, quæ propterea seorsim conscriptæ sunt; ad quas discipuli maxime festis diebus vitandi otii et malarum consuetudinum causa conveniant.

[369]   *Academies*

45. If it seems good to the rector, he should establish academies on the basis of the rules that have been written down separately for this purpose. These academies should meet, especially on feast days, in order to avoid idleness and bad habits.

[370] *Agere cum discipulorum parentibus*

46. Si necesse videretur discipulorum causa cum eorum parentibus interdum loqui, rectori proponat, an ii per præfectum vel alium accersendi sint, vel etiam, si personæ dignitas postulet, conveniendi.

[371] *Familiaritas et colloquia*

47. Familiarem non se uni magis, quam alteri ostendat; cum iisque extra scholæ tempus non nisi breviter, ac de rebus seriis, loco etiam patenti, hoc est non intra scholam, sed pro scholæ foribus, aut in atrio, aut ad ianuam collegii, quo magis ædificationi consulat, colloquatur.

[372] *Pædagogi*

48. Nemini pædagogum inconsulto rectore proponat, nec a pædagogis permittat aliis domi prælectionibus onerari discipulos, sed tantum auditas exigi.

[373] *Nullus pro schola sumptus*

49. Nullius opera utatur in describendo, aut in aliquo, quod ad usitatas scholæ exercitationes non pertineat; nullaque in re illos pro schola sumptum facere patiatur.

[374] *Profectus studentium*

50. Sit denique in omnibus divina aspirante gratia diligens et assiduus et profectus studentium tum

[370] *Meeting with the parents of students*

46. If it sometimes seems necessary for the sake of the students to speak with their parents, he should ask the rector whether they should be summoned by the prefect or by someone else, or even met by such a person, if their social position calls for it.

[371] *Familiarity and conversations*

47. He should not show himself to be more familiar with one student than with another. He should speak with students outside of school time only briefly, and about serious matters. Also, he should do this in an open place, that is, not inside a classroom, but in front of the classroom's door, or in the courtyard, or at the school's main door, so that he might take better thought for edification.

[372] *Tutors*

48. He should suggest a tutor for no one without consulting the rector, and he should not allow students to be burdened by the tutors with other lessons at home. They should be responsible only for the ones they have had in class.

[373] *No expense for class*

49. He should use no one's labor to write things out, or to do anything that does not pertain to the customary class exercises. And in no matter should he allow them to bear an expense on behalf of the class.

[374] *Progress of the students*

50. Finally, with the assistance of divine grace in everything, he should be diligent and persistent

in lectionibus, tum in aliis literariis exercitationibus studiosus. Contemnat neminem, pauperum studiis, æque ad divitum bene prospiciat, profectumque uniuscuiusque e suis scholasticis speciatim procuret.

and deeply interested in the progress of the students, both in the lessons and in the other literary exercises. He should not look down on anyone, attending just as well to the studies of the poor as to those of the wealthy. And he should take good care of the progress of each one of his own students in particular.

[H26] Regulæ Professoris Rhetoricæ

[375] *Gradus*

1. Gradus huius scholæ non facile certis quibusdam terminis definiri potest; ad perfectam enim eloquentiam informat, quæ duas facultates maximas, oratoriam et pæticam comprehendit (ex his autem duabus primæ semper partes oratoriæ tribuantur), nec utilitati solum servit, sed etiam ornatui indulget. Illud tamen in universum dici potest, tribus maxime rebus, præceptis dicendi, stylo et eruditione contineri. Præcepta, etsi undique peti et observari possunt, explicandi tamen non sunt in quotidiana prælectione, nisi rhetorici Ciceronis libri, et Aristotelis tum Rhetorica, si videbitur, tum Pætica. Stylus (quamquam probatissimi etiam historici et pætæ delibantur) ex uno fere Cicerone sumendus est; et omnes quidem eius libri ad stylum aptissimi, orationes tamen solæ prælegendæ, ut artis præcepta in orationibus expressa cernantur. Eruditio denique ex historia et moribus gentium, ex auctoritate scriptorum et ex omni doctrina, sed parcius ad captum discipulorum accersenda. Ex græcis ad rhe-

[H26] Rules for the Professor of Rhetoric

[375] *Grade*

1. The grade of this class can not easily be defined by certain set terms, for it aims at an education in perfect eloquence, which includes two most important subjects, oratory and poetics (out of these two, however, the leading emphasis should always be given to oratory) and it does not only serve what is useful but also indulges in what is ornamental. Still, by and large, it can be said to consist in three things especially: rules for speaking, for style, and for scholarly learning. Even though the rules can be found and studied in a very wide range of sources, only Cicero's books on rhetoric and Aristotle's, both the *Rhetoric*, if it seems good, and the *Poetics* should be taught in the daily lesson. Style should be taken almost exclusively from Cicero (although the most approved historians and poets are sampled also). And of course all his books are most suitable for style, but only the speeches should be covered in the lessons, so that the rules of the art might be perceived as they are expressed in the speeches. Finally, scholarly learning should come

toricam pertinet syllabarum maxime dimensio, et plenior auctorum et dialectorum cognitio. Summam logicæ in fine anni rhetoricæ magister non explicet.

from cultural history based on authoritative writers and on every kind of learning, but these things should be brought in rather sketchily, in proportion to the students' capacity. From Greek, prosody especially pertains to rhetoric, as does a deeper knowledge of authors and dialects. The teacher should not present a general overview of logic at the end of the year of rhetoric.

[376] *Divisio temporis*

2. Divisio temporis hæc erit: Prima hora antemeridiana memoria exerceatur, scripta a decurionibus collectas præceptor corrigat, varias interim, de quibus infra regula quinta, discipulis exercitationes iniungens; denique hæsterna prælectio recolatur. Secunda hora antemeridiana prælectioni detur, vel præceptorum, si a prandio explicetur oratio, vel orationis, si præcepta; dummodo in eo, quod anni initio cæptum est, constantia servetur. Succedat repetitio, et quando opus est, argumentum detur scribendæ orationis vel carminis; reliquum, si quid est temporis, vel concertationi, vel iis, quæ prima hora scripserint, recognoscendis tribuatur. Prima hora pomeridiana habeatur, post repetitionem postremæ, nova prælectio vel orationis, si mane præcepta exposita, vel præceptorum, si oratio. Huic repetitio de more succedat. Secunda hora pomeridiana græci auctoris postrema prælectione repetita, nova explicetur atque exigatur. Reliquum tempus modo corrigendis græcis scriptionibus, modo græcæ syntaxi et arti metricæ, modo græcæ concertationi reser-

[376] *Schedule*

2. This will be the schedule: In the first morning hour, the memory should be exercised. The teacher should correct the written work that has been collected by the decurions, in the meantime assigning various exercises to the students (about which see the fifth rule below). Finally, the previous day's lesson should be reviewed. The second hour of the morning should be given to the lesson, either on the rules if a prose passage is being taught after the midday meal, or on a prose passage if rules are being taught then, provided that there is a continuation of what was started at the beginning of the year. A review should follow, and, when needed, a subject for a prose composition or a poem should be given. The rest of whatever time remains should be given either to a competition, or to an examination of what they wrote in the first hour. In the first afternoon hour, a fresh lesson should be undertaken after the review of the last one, either of a prose passage if rules were taught in the morning, or of rules if a prose passage was taught then. A review should typically follow this activity. In the second afternoon hour, after

vetur. Die vacationis explicetur historicus vel poeta, vel aliquid ad eruditionem pertinens; et recolatur. Die sabbathi, post brevem totius hebdomadæ repetitionem, mane prima hora explanetur historicus vel poeta. Ultima hora aut habeatur ab aliquo discipulorum declamatio vel prælectio, aut ad humanistas audiendos eatur, aut concertetur. A prandio explicetur poeta vel historicus; græca recolantur. Sicubi vero, præter duas horas tum mane tum vesperi, semihora additur, ea historico vel pætæ tribuenda; quod si fiat, sabbathi prælectiones vel non differant ab aliis diebus, vel, iis omissis, repetitio plenior instituatur et concertatio.

the last lesson on the Greek author has been reviewed, a new one should be taught and required back from the students. The remaining time should be kept sometimes for correcting Greek compositions, sometimes for Greek syntax and prosody, sometimes for competitions in Greek. On a break day, a historian or a poet should be taught, or something pertaining to scholarly learning; and this should be reviewed. On Saturday, after a brief review of the entire week, a historian or poet should be taught in the first morning hour. In the final hour, either a declamation or a lesson should be given by one of the students, or they should go to hear the humanities students, or there should be a competition. After the midday meal, a poet or a historian should be taught; Greek should be reviewed. But wherever a half hour is added beyond the two hours both in the morning and in the afternoon, it should be devoted to the study of a historian or a poet. But if this happens, Saturday's lessons either should not differ from those of the other days, or, when they are omitted, there should be a more thorough review and a competition.

[377] *Memoriæ exercitatio*

3. Quoniam memoriæ quotidiana exercitatio rhetori necessaria est, atque in hac classe sæpe longius prælectiones excurrunt, quam ut tradi commode memoriæ possint, præceptor statuet ipse, quid quantumque ediscendum, et quomodo, si exigere velit, recitandum. Immo ex usu esset, ut subinde aliquis e suggestu recitaret, quæ ex optimis auctoribus didicisset, ad

[377] *Memory exercise*

3. Since daily exercise of the memory is necessary for the rhetorician, and lessons in this class often run on for a longer time than can be conveniently committed to memory, the teacher himself will set what and how much is to be learned by heart, and how it should be recited, if he wishes to require this. And in fact it should be a matter of standing practice that from time to time someone

memoriæ exercitationem simul cum actione iungendam.

[378] *Scriptionis corrigendæ ratio*

4. In scriptione corrigenda indicet, si quid in artificio oratorio aut pætico, in elegantia cultuque sermonis, in connectenda oratione, in numeris concinnandis, in orthographia, aut aliter peccatum fuerit; si quis locus perperam, si obscure, si humiliter tractatus, si decorum minime servatum, si qua digressio longior fuerit, et alia generis eiusdem. Denique, oratione absoluta, suam quisque, quam ante per partes attulerat, totam simul descriptam aut saltem correctam præceptori offerat, ut eas esse ab omnibus perfectas appareat.

[379] *Exercitationes inter corrigendum*

5. Exercitationes discipulorum, dum scripta magister corrigit, erunt exempli gratia locum aliquem pætæ vel oratoris imitari, descriptionem aliquam, ut hortorum, templorum, tempestatis, et similium efficere phrasim eandem modis pluribus variare, græcam orationem latine vertere, aut contra; pætæ versus tum latine, tum græce soluto stylo complecti; carminis genus aliud in aliud commutare; epigrammata, inscriptiones, epitaphia condere; phrases ex bonis

should recite from the platform what he has learned from the best authors, for the sake of combining memory exercise with delivery.

[378] *Method of correcting the composition*

4. In the correction of the composition he should point out if there was any fault in the artistry of the prose or poetry, in the elegance and adornment of speech, in the compositional unity, in the patterning of the verse rhythms, in spelling, or in anything else. Also he should note if any passage reads incorrectly, or unclearly, or is handled too informally, or if decorum has not been kept very well, or if there is too long a digression, or if there is anything like these things. Finally, when the prose compositions are completed, so that it might be clear that everyone has done them, each one should hand in to the teacher what he had earlier brought in by section, the whole thing written out at one time or at least corrected.

[379] *Exercises during correction*

5. While the teacher corrects the written work, the students' exercises will include things like imitating some passage of a poet or prose writer; some description (for instance, of gardens, of churches, of a storm) and varying the same expression of similar things in several ways; translating Greek speech into Latin, or the reverse; expressing the meaning of a poet's verses both in Latin prose and in Greek; changing one type of poem into another; composing epigrams, inscriptions, epitaphs; selecting expressions, Greek or Latin, from good

oratoribus et poetis, seu græcas seu latinas excerpere, figuras rhetoricas ad certas materias accommodare; ex locis rhetoricis et topicis plurima ad rem quampiam argumenta depromere, et alia generis eiusdem.

[380] *Prælectio*

6. Prælectio duplex est. Altera ad artem pertinet, in qua præcepta; altera ad stylum, in qua orationes explicantur. In utraque autem duo animadvertenda. Primum, qui auctores ad prælegendum suscipiantur, deinde quis modus interpretandi teneri possit. De primo satis dictum est regula prima; unus enim Cicero ad orationes, ad præcepta præter Ciceronem Aristoteles adhibendus est. Oratio nunquam prætermittenda. Præceptorum etiam explicatio toto fere anno continuanda esset. Ingens enim est vis oratoriorum præceptorum; huius tamen loco, ubi mos ferat, inclinante iam anno, alicuius auctoris usus, qui maiorem eruditionem aut varietatem contineat, non interdicitur. Pætæ vero aliqua prælectio poterit interdum vel præceptorum vel orationis prælectionibus interponi.

[381] *Præceptorum interpretatio*

7. Quod autem ad interpretandi rationem attinet, si explicentur præcepta: Primo, præcepti sensus aperiendus, interpretum collatis sententiis, si obscurior sit, nec inter eos conveniat. Secundo, alii rhetores, qui idem præcipiant, vel

prose writers and poets, fitting rhetorical figures to given topics; furnishing several arguments for some issue or other from the rhetorical *loci* and *topoi;* and other activities of this type.[157]

[380] *Lesson*

6. The lesson is twofold. One part pertains to the art, in which rules are taught; the other to style, in which compositions are. In each however, two things should be given attention: first, which authors are chosen for presentation in the lesson, then what type of interpretation can be followed. About the first, enough has been said in the first rule. For Cicero alone should be used for prose; Aristotle should be used for rules beyond those of Cicero. Prose composition should never be left out. Also, the explanation of the rules should usually be continued for the entire year. For the supply of rules for prose composition is vast. Still, in place of this where the custom supports it, while the year is coming to an end, the reading of some author who offers greater scholarly learning or variety is not forbidden. But from time to time some lesson on a poet or on prose composition can be inserted into the lessons on rules.

[381] *Interpretation of the rules*

7. The following bears on the method of interpretation, if the rules are being taught: First, the meaning of the rule should be made plain; the opinions of the interpreters should be assembled if the rule is rather obscure and they do not agree. Second,

---

[157] [T]he rhetorical *loci* and *topoi:* see the note on §220 above.

idem auctor, si alibi idem præcipit, afferendus. Tertio, ipsius præcepti ratio aliqua excogitanda. Quarto, oratorum ac poetarum loci aliquot similes, maxime illustres, in quibus eo præcepto usi sint, adducendi. Quinto, si quid ex varia eruditione et historia ad rem facit, addendum. Ad extremum, quo modo ad res nostras accommodari possit, indicandum; idque quanto maximo fieri potest delectu ornatuque verborum.

other rhetoricians who teach the same thing, or that very author, if he teaches the same thing elsewhere, should be cited. Third, some reason for that particular rule should be thought out. Fourth, several similar passages in prose writers and poets, especially well-known ones, where they employ that rule should be quoted. Fifth, if different kinds of learning and history contribute anything to the matter, it should be added. At the very end, it should be indicated how it can be accommodated to our interests. And this can be done with the most impressive diction and verbal artistry possible.

[382]   *Oratoris interpretatio*

8. Si vero explicetur oratio vel poema: Primo, exponenda sententia, si obscura sit, et variæ interpretationes diiudicandæ. Secundo, tota artificii ratio, inventionis scilicet, dispositionis et elocutionis exploranda, quam apte se orator insinuet, quam apposite dicat; vel quibus ex locis argumenta sumat ad persuadendum, ad ornandum, ad movendum; quam multa sæpe præcepta uno eodemque loco permisceat; quo pacto rationem ad faciendam fidem figuris sententiarum includat, rursusque figuras sententiarum figuris verborum intexat. Tertio, loci aliquot tum re, tum verbis similes afferendi, aliique oratores vel pætæ, qui eodem præcepto ad aliquid simile persuadendum vel narrandum usi sint, producendi. Quarto, res ipsæ sapi-

[382]   *Interpretation of a composition*

8. But if a discourse or a poem is being taught:[158] First, the idea should be explained if it is obscure, and the different interpretations should be distinguished. Second, the whole plan of the construction (namely, of the invention, arrangement, and expression) should be examined— how skillfully the orator works himself into our good graces, how appropriately he speaks; or from what *loci* he takes his arguments for persuading, for embellishing, for moving; how many rules he often mixes in one and the same *locus*; how he incorporates a means for creating trust through his figures of thought, and again weaves those figures of thought with the figures of speech. Third, some passages similar both in matter and in words ought to be cited, and other orators or poets who

---

[158] Discourse: *oratio* can mean a speech or discourse or prose composition. Later in this section we find invention: in rhetoric, the "finding" of the arguments or topics that should be used; arrangement: structure of the argument; expression: the particular words chosen to communicate the argument.

entum sententiis, si res ferat, confirmandæ. Quinto, ex historia, ex fabulis, ex omni eruditione, quæ ad locum exornandum faciant, conquirenda. Ad extremum, verba perpendenda, eorum proprietas, ornatus, copia, numerus observandus. Hæc autem non ideo allata sunt, ut semper omnia consectetur magister, sed ut ex iis seligat, quæ opportuniora videbuntur.

made use of the same rule to persuade or narrate something similar should be presented. Fourth, the issues themselves should be confirmed by the sayings of the wise, if the matter supports this. Fifth, things that contribute to the enhancement of the passage should be sought out from history, from narratives, and from the entire range of scholarly learning. Toward the end, the words should be weighed; their appropriateness, their charm, their possible variety, their rhythm should be noted. However these things are brought up not with the intention that the teacher should always pursue all of them, but rather that he might select from them the things that seem more serviceable.

[383] *Argumentum scribendæ orationis*

9. Dictandum argumentum orationis vel initio cuiusque mensis totum, vel singulis hebdomadis per partes (singulis enim mensibus ad summum singulæ absolvendæ orationes); sit autem breve, quod per omnes eat orationis partes; locos confirmationis et amplificationis, figuras præcipuas, quæ adhiberi possent, locos etiam aliquos bonorum auctorum ad imitandum, si videbitur, indicet. Interdum, demonstrato scriptore aliquo, ad cuius imitationem orationem informent, verbo tenus res proponatur.

[383] *Summary of the prose composition's content*

9. The summary of the prose composition's content should be dictated either all at the beginning of each month, or every week by divisions (for one composition at most should be finished every month). It should be short, but it should go through all the parts of a prose composition. And if it seems good, he should indicate *loci* for confirmation and amplification, the main figures of speech that can be applied, and also some other *loci* of good authors for imitation. Sometimes, when he has pointed out some writer in imitation of whom they are shaping their composition, he should simply suggest the topic.

[384] *Carminis*

10. Carminis etiam argumentum aut scripto aut verbo, vel solam

[384] *For poetry*

10. The subject for a poem can also be given in writing or orally,

significando rem vel certa adiecta sententia tradi potest; idque aut breve, ut epigrammatis, odæ, elegiæ, epistolæ, quod singulis vicibus expediatur; aut longius, ut pluribus vicibus, quemadmodum orationem, sic poema contexant.

either by signifying only the theme or with the addition of a given saying. And either it can be brief, like an epigram, ode, elegy, or letter, which might be best done in individual sessions; or it can be rather long, so that they construct the poem over several sessions just like a prose composition.

[385] *Græci thematis ratio*

11. Græci thematis eadem fere ratio erit, nisi per aliquod tempus verbatim omnia dictanda semel saltem in singulas hebdomadas, vel soluta oratione vel carmine censeantur.

[385] *The plan of the Greek theme*

11. The same plan will generally hold for the Greek theme, unless it is decided that for a time everything should be dictated word by word at least once a week, whether in prose or in verse.

[386] *Concertatio*

12. Concertatio seu exercitatio sita erit tum in corrigendis iis, quæ alter æmulus in alterius oratione deprehenderit; tum in iis, in quibus prima hora se exercuerint, invicem proponendis; tum in figuris dignoscendis aut conficiendis; tum in rhetoricæ aut epistolarum aut carminum aut historiæ præceptis reddendis applicandisve; tum in exponendis auctorum locis difficilioribus et difficultatibus explanandis; tum in moribus antiquorum rebusque ad eruditionem pertinentibus, exquirendis; tum in hieroglyphicis, symbolis, pythagoreis, apophtegmatis, adagiis, emblematis, ænigmatisque interpretandis; tum in declamando, et similibus ad præceptoris arbitrium.

[386] *Competition*

12. Competition or exercise will find a place sometimes in the correction of errors that one rival has caught in the other's speech; sometimes presenting in turn whatever they practiced in the first hour; sometimes in distinguishing and fashioning figures of speech; sometimes in stating and applying the rules of rhetoric or letters or poems or history; sometimes in presenting the more difficult passages of authors and explaining the difficulties; sometimes in investigating issues in ancient culture and matters that belong to the field of scholarly learning; sometimes in interpreting hieroglyphics, symbols, Pythagorean doctrines, apothegms, adages, emblems, and riddles;[159] sometimes in declaiming, and in similar activities, at the teacher's discretion.

---

[159] Apothegm: "a terse, pointed saying, embodying an important truth in few words; a pithy or sententious maxim" (OED). Adage: "a maxim handed down from antiquity; a proverb" (ibid.).

[387] *Græca prælectio*

13. Græca prælectio, sive oratorum sive historicorum sive poetarum, non nisi antiquorum sit et classicorum, Demosthenis, Platonis, Thucydidis, Homeri, Hesiodi, Pindari et aliorum huiusmodi (modo sint expurgati); inter quos iure optimo SS. Nazianzenus, Basilius et Chrysostomus reponendi. Ac priore quidem semestri oratores aut historici interpretandi; interponi autem poterunt semel in hebdomada aliqua epigrammata, vel brevia poemata; posteriore vicissim explicetur poeta, interiecto semel oratore aut historico. Interpretandi ratio, quamquam quæ eruditionis artisque sunt, respuere omnino non debet; proprietatem tamen potius usumque linguæ spectabit. Quamobrem locutiones aliquæ singulis prælectionibus dictandæ.

[388] *Græca grammatica*

14. Græca syntaxis et syllabarum dimensio ineunte anno alternis diebus, si sit opus, explicanda; syntaxis quidem breviter, præcipua quædam capita recolendo.

[389] *Prælectio die vacationis*

15. Eruditionis causa die vacationis pro historico et poeta liceat interdum alia magis recondita proferre, ut hieroglyphica, ut emblemata, ut quæstiones ad artificium pæticum spectantes, de epigrammate, epithaphio, ode, elegia, epopæia, tragædia; ut de senatu ro-

[387] *Greek lesson*

13. The Greek lesson, whether on orators or on historians or on poets, should only be on the ancient classical authors: Demosthenes, Plato, Thucydides, Homer, Hesiod, Pindar, and others like this (provided they are expurgated). Saints Gregory Nazianzen, Basil, and Chrysostom should quite rightly be included with them.[160] And in the first semester, orators or historians should be interpreted; some epigrams or brief poems can be inserted once a week. In the second semester in turn, a poet should be taught, with an orator or a historian inserted once a week. Although the method of interpretation should not at all disdain matters of scholarly learning and art, it will nevertheless focus more on the propriety and the use of language. And for this reason, some expressions should be dictated in the individual lessons.

[388] *Greek grammar*

14. Greek syntax and prosody should be taught, if there is a need, from the beginning of the year on alternate days. But the syntax should be taught concisely, by working through the most important sections.

[389] *Lesson on the break day*

15. For the sake of scholarly learning, on the break day, in place of reading a historian and poet, occasionally some other, more esoteric material can be presented, such as hieroglyphics, emblems, questions bearing on poetic construction, concerning epigrams, epitaphs, odes,

---

[160] For information on Demosthenes and the other eight authors just mentioned, see endn. 25.

mano, de atheniensi, de utriusque gentis militia; ut de re hortensi, vestiaria, de triclinio, de triumpho, de sibyllis, et aliis generis eiusdem; modice tamen.

[390] *Privata declamatio*

16. Declamatio, vel prælectio, vel carmen, vel græca oratio, vel carmen simul et oratio, humanistis convenientibus postrema semihora antemeridiana ab uno aut altero discipulorum e suggestu alternis sabbathis habeatur.

[391] *Publica declamatio*

17. In aula templove gravior oratio aut carmen vel utrumque nunc latine, nunc græce vel declamatoria actio, expositis utrinque rationibus, lataque sententia, singulis fere mensibus habeatur; non tamen, nisi recognita et approbata a præfecto studiorum superiorum.

[392] *Carmina affigenda*

18. Affigantur carmina scholæ parietibus alternis fere mensibus ad aliquem celebriorem diem exornandum, vel magistratus promulgandos, vel alia quapiam occasione, selectissima quæque a discipulis descripta. Immo etiam pro regionum more aliquid prosæ brevioris; quales sunt inscriptiones, ut clypeorum, templorum, sepulcrorum, hortorum, statuarum; quales

elegies, epic, tragedy;[161] or such as items about the Roman or Athenian senate, or about Greek or Roman military service; or such as items relating to gardening, clothing, dining, or the triumphal procession, the sibyls, and other similar subjects. But this should be done in moderation.

[390] *Private declamation*

16. A declamation, or a lesson, or a poem, or a Greek speech, or a poem and a speech together, should be presented from the platform by one or two students every other Saturday, at an assembly where all humanities students have gathered, in the last half hour before noon.

[391] *Public declamation*

17. Usually every month, in the hall or church, there should be a presentation of either a somewhat serious speech or poem or both, sometimes in Latin, sometimes in Greek, or there should be the delivery of a declamation, including the exposition of two sides and a judgment rendered, but not unless it is reviewed and approved by the prefect of higher studies.

[392] *Poems should be posted*

18. Poems should be posted on the classroom walls, usually every other month, to enhance some particularly special day or to announce the officers formally, or on some other occasion. They should be the choicest ones written out by the students. In fact there should also be, in accordance with the local custom, some short prose compositions, such as inscriptions for shields, churches,

---

[161] For information on these literary references, see endn. 26.

descriptiones, ut urbis, portus, exercitus; quales narrationes, ut rei gestæ ab aliquo divorum; qualia denique paradoxa, additis interdum, non tamen sine rectoris permissu, picturis, quæ emblemati vel argumento proposito respondeant.

[393] *Privatæ scenæ*

19. Poterit interdum magister brevem aliquam actionem, eclogæ scilicet, scenæ, dialogive discipulis argumenti loco proponere, ut illa deinde in schola distributis inter ipsos partibus, sine ullo tamen scenico ornatu exhibeatur, quæ omnium optime conscripta sit.

[394] *Nostrorum exercitatio*

20. Nostris exercendis sicut omnia, quæ de ratione docendi diximus, communia sunt, ita illa peculiaria, ut domi ter aut quater in hebdomada per horam, quo tempore commodissimum rectori videbitur, repetitiones coram magistro, aut alio quem rector ipse statuerit, habeant; in quibus prælectiones latine, græceve recolantur, solutaque oratio et carmen latine, græceve corrigantur; iubeanturque quotidie aliquid ediscendo, memoriam excolere, multumque et attente legere; nihil enim æque fæcundat ingenium, quam ut ad aulæ, templi, scholæque suggestum, quod illis cum externis condiscipulis commune est, addito etiam refectorio, frequentius singuli se dicendo exerceant; ut denique publice semper in loco quopiam idoneo

tombs, gardens, statues; such as descriptions of a city, a port, an army; such as narrations, as of a deed performed by some saint; finally, such as paradoxes, with the occasional addition of pictures that correspond to an emblem or to a proposed subject, but not without the rector's permission.

[393] *Private performances*

19. From time to time, the teacher can propose as a subject to the students some brief dramatic action, namely, one belonging to an eclogue, or a scene, or a dialog, so that then in class, with the parts divided up among them, the best of all the compositions might be acted out, but without any stage props.

[394] *Training for Jesuits*

20. Just as whatever we have said about the educational scheme is shared by everyone, so some things are special to the training of Jesuits. For example, three or four times a week in their residence for an hour, at a time when the rector thinks best, they should hold reviews in the presence of their teacher or someone else whom the rector himself has appointed. In these reviews, they should go over their Latin or Greek lessons, and correct their Latin prose or poetry, or Greek. They should be told to cultivate their memory by learning something by heart every day, and to do a good bit of careful reading aloud. For nothing sparks the wit as well as the practice of rather frequent solo delivery from a podium in the auditorium, the church, and the classroom (all of which they share with their non-

sua carmina præceptori probata, suo adscripto nomine, proponant.

Jesuit fellow students), and in the dining hall as well. Lastly, they should post their own signed poetic compositions publicly, always in some appropriate place, after they have been approved by the teacher.

[H27] Regulæ Professoris Humanitatis

[H27] Rules for the Professor of Humanities

[395] *Gradus*

1. Gradus huius scholæ est, postquam ex grammaticis excesserint, præparare veluti solum eloquentiæ; quod tripliciter accidit: cognitione linguæ, aliqua eruditione, et brevi informatione præceptorum ad rhetoricam spectantium. Ad cognitionem linguæ, quæ in proprietate maxime et copia consistit, in quotidianis prælectionibus explicetur; ex oratoribus unus Cicero iis fere libris, qui philosophiam de moribus continent; ex historicis Cæsar, Salustius, Livius, Curtius, et si qui sunt similes; ex poetis præcipue Virgilius, exceptis Eclogis et quarto Aeneidos; præterea odæ Horatii selectæ, item elegiæ, epigrammata et alia poemata illustrium poetarum antiquorum, modo sint ab omni obscænitate expurgati. Eruditio modice usurpetur, ut ingenium excitet interdum ac recreet, non ut linguæ observationem impediat. Præceptorum rhetoricæ brevis summa ex Cypriano, secundo scilicet semestri, tradetur; quo tempore, omissa philosophia Ciceronis, faciliores aliquæ eiusdem orationes, ut pro lege Manilia, pro Archia, pro Marcello, ce-

[395] *Grade*

1. The grade of this class consists in the preparing of the ground, as it were, for eloquence, after the students have passed beyond the stage of grammatical study. This preparation happens in a threefold way: by an understanding of the language, by some scholarly learning, and by getting a summary notion of the rules pertaining to rhetoric. For the knowledge of the language, which consists especially in propriety and abundance of expression, the daily lessons should be devoted to teaching Cicero alone of the orators, usually through those books that contain his moral philosophy; Caesar, Sallust, Livy, Curtius, from the historians, and any others like these;[162] from the poets, especially Vergil, setting aside the *Eclogues* and the fourth book of the *Aeneid*; in addition, select odes of Horace, and likewise, elegies, epigrams, and other poems of famous ancient poets, provided that they have been expurgated of everything indecent and offensive. Scholarly learning should be employed moderately, so that now and then it stimulates the mental powers and refreshes them without impeding the

---

[162] For information on Caesar and the other five authors mentioned in this section, see endn. 27.

teræque ad Cæsarem habitæ sumi poterunt. Græcæ linguæ pars illa pertinet ad hanc scholam, quæ syntaxis proprie dicitur. Curandum præterea, ut mediocriter scriptores intelligant et scribere aliquid græce norint.

learning of the language. The brief summary overview of the rules of rhetoric from Cyprian will of course be given in the second semester. At that time, Cicero's philosophy being set aside, some of the easier speeches, like the *Pro lege Manilia, Pro Archia, Pro Marcello,* and the others delivered to Caesar can be taken. The part of the Greek language that is properly called syntax pertains to this class. In addition, care should be taken that the students attain a passable understanding of the writers and an ability to write something in Greek.

[396] *Divisio temporis*

2. Divisio temporis hæc erit: Prima hora matutina memoriter recitetur M. Tullius et ars metrica apud decurione. Scripta a decurionibus accepta præceptor corrigat, varias interim, de quibus infra regula Quarta, discipulis exercitationes iniungens. Ad extremum publice nonnulli recitent, et decurionum notæ a magistro cognoscantur. Secunda hora matutina repetatur postrema breviter prælectio; novaque per semihoram, vel paulo amplius explicetur; mox exigatur, et, si quid supersit temporis, in mutua discipulorum concertatione ponatur. Ultima semihora initio primi semestris historicus et ars metrica alternis diebus; arte vero metrica absoluta, historicus quotidie percurratur; altero deinde semestri Cypriani rhetorica quotidie modo explicetur, modo recolatur, aut disputetur. Prima hora pomeridiana memoriter poeta græcusque

[396] *Schedule*

2. This will be the schedule: In the first hour in the morning, Marcus Tullius and prosody should be recited from memory to the decurion.[163] The teacher should correct the written work that has been picked up by the decurions, meanwhile giving the students various exercises to do (on this, see rule 4 below). At the very end of the hour, several students should recite in front of the class, and the teacher should review the decurions' marks. In the second hour of the morning, the last lesson should be reviewed briefly, and a new one should be taught for half an hour or for a little more. Right away the students should be asked to repeat it, and, if there is any time left, they should compete with each other on it. In the final half hour, at the beginning of the first semester, a historian and prosody should be taken on alternate days; but when prosody is finished,

---

[163] Marcus Tullius: Cicero. See the note on §258 above.

auctor recitetur, recognoscente magistro decurionum notas; scriptaque, vel quæ mane imperata sunt, vel quæ ex domo allatis superfuerint, corrigente. Ad extremum thema dictetur. Sesquihora consequens pætæ, tum recolendo tum explicando, et græcæ, tum prælectioni tum scriptioni, ex æquo dividatur. Die vacationis prima hora recitetur memoriter, quod proxima vacatione prælectum est; et scriptiones, quæ supersunt, de more corrigantur. Secunda hora aliquid epigrammatum aut odarum aut elegiarum, sive aliquid ex libro tertio Cypriani de tropis, de figuris, et præcipue de numero ac pedibus oratoriis, ut iis initio anni assuescant; sive chria aliqua aut progymnasma explicetur recolaturque; sive denique concertetur. Die sabbathi mane prima hora publice recitentur memoriter totius hebdomadæ prælectiones; hora secunda recolantur. Ultima semihora aut habeatur ab aliquo discipulorum declamatio vel prælectio, aut ad rhetores audiendos eatur, aut concertetur. A prandio prima semihora reddatur memoriter poeta et catechismus, magistro scripta, si quæ per hebdomadam superfuerint, et decurionum notas recognoscente. Sesqui hora consequens poetæ recolendo, vel alicui brevi poemati explicando exigendoque, et græcis eodem modo ex æquo dividatur. Ultima semihora in explicatione catechismi, vel pia cohortatione, nisi feria sexta habita sit, ponetur;sin autem, in ea re ferme, in

a historian should be covered every day. Then in the second semester, Cyprian's *Rhetoric* should be taken every day, sometimes taught, sometimes reviewed, or there should be a disputation. In the first afternoon hour, a poet and a Greek author should be recited from memory, while the teacher checks over the marks of the decurions and corrects the written work, either what was assigned in the morning, or what is left of the homework. At the very end, a theme should be dictated. The following hour and a half should be split equally between a poet, sometimes in review, sometimes in explanatory presentation, and Greek, sometimes a lesson and sometimes a composition. On the break day, in the first hour, what was taught on the preceding break day should be recited from memory, and the remaining compositions should be corrected as usual. In the second hour, there should be something from the epigrams or odes or elegies or something from Cyprian's third book on tropes, on figures, and especially on oratorical rhythm and measures, so that they get accustomed to them at the beginning of the year; or some *chria* or preparatory exercise should be taught and gone over again;[164] or lastly there should be a competition. On Saturday, in the first hour of the morning, the lessons of the entire week should be recited from memory in front of the group, and they should be gone over again in the second hour. In the final half-hour, either a declamation or a lesson

---

[164] *Chria:* a little story ending with a point or a witty saying. Preparatory exercise: *progymnasma* in Greek (plural: *progymnasmata*).

cuius locum tum catechismus successerat.

should be given by one of the students, or they should go to hear the rhetoricians, or there should be a competition. After the midday meal, in the first half hour, a poet and the catechism lesson should be given back from memory,[165] while the teacher reviews the marks of the decurions and the written assignments, if there are any left over from the week. The following hour and a half should be split equally in the same manner between reviewing a poet or in the explanation of some short poem and the testing of students on it, and Greek. The last half hour will be given to teaching catechism to the students or giving them a devout exhortation, unless this was done Friday. If it was, then the half hour will usually be given to whatever had been displaced by the catechism study at that time.

[397] *Scriptionis corrigendæ ratio*
3. In scriptione corrigenda indicet, si quid minus proprium aut elegans aut numerosum sit; si minus recte locus ad imitandum propositus expressus; si quid in orthographia aliterve peccatum sit; variis modis idem efferri iubeat, ut dicendi copiam ex hac exercitatione condiscant.

[397] *Method of correcting the composition*
3. In the correction of the composition, he should point out if anything is lacking in propriety or elegance or measure; if a literary passage assigned for imitation is not quite correctly expressed; if there is any mistake in spelling or anything else. He should tell them to express the same thing in different ways, so that they might acquire a great abundance of expressions from this exercise.

[398] *Exercitationes inter corrigendum*
4. Exercitationes, dum scripta corrigit, erunt exempli gratia ex

[398] *Exercises during the correction*
4. There will be exercises while he is correcting the written work, for example, selecting phrases from the

[165] Catechism lesson: catechisms are "summaries of Christian doctrine for the instruction of the people" (*CathEncy*, s.vv. "Roman Catechism"). They are frequently structured in question-and-answer form.

prælectionibus phrases excerpere, easque pluribus modis variare, Ciceronis periodum dissolutam componere, versus condere, carmen unius generis alio permutare, locum aliquem imitari, græce scribere, et alia generis eiusdem.

[399] *Prælectio*

5. Prælectio eruditionis ornamentis leviter interdum aspersa sit, quantum loci explicatio postulat; se totum potius magister effundat in latinæ linguæ observationes, in vim etymologiamque verborum, quam ex probatis petet auctoribus, maxime ex antiquis; in locutionum usum ac varietatem, in auctoris imitatione; nec alienum putet aliquid patrio interdum sermone efferre, si vel ad interpretandum in primis valeat, vel aliquid habeat eximii. Quando autem orationem explicat, præcepta artis exploret. Ad extremum licebit, si videatur, omnia patrio sermone, sed quam elegantissimo vertere.

[400] *Argumentum scribendi*

6. Dictandum argumentum scribendi. Primo quidem semestri ad epistolæ fere formam vulgi sermone ad verbum; quod sæpe proderit ita componere, ut totum ex prælectionibus iam explicatis hinc inde decerptum sit. Semel autem fere in hebdomada suo marte conscribant, aliquo prius epistolarum

lessons, varying them in several ways, putting in order a scrambled sentence from Cicero, composing verses, transposing a poem from one genre into another, imitating some literary passage, writing Greek, and other things of the same kind.

[399] *Lesson*

5. To the extent that the teaching of the passage demands it, the lesson should sometimes be sprinkled lightly with ornaments of scholarly learning. The teacher should put the whole focus of his efforts on making comments on the Latin language and on the sense and the root meanings of words, which he should glean from approved authors, especially from the ancients; on the use and variety of expressions, and on the imitation of the author. And he should not think it out of place that from time to time he cite some expression in the vernacular, either if it is especially helpful for getting the meaning or if it has some other noteworthy feature. However, when he teaches a prose composition, he should examine the rules of the art. At the very end he can, if it seems good, translate everything into the vernacular, but as elegantly as possible.

[400] *Summary of the composition's content*

6. The summary of the composition's content should be dictated. Of course, in the first semester, it should be done word for word, usually in the form of a letter, and in the vernacular. Often it will help to compose it in such a way that the whole thing is taken here and there from the lessons already taught. Usually

genere explicato, indicatisque Ciceronis aut Plinii epistolis ad illud pertinentibus. Altero deinde semestri excitetur ingenium; et chriæ primo, tum proæmia, narrationes et exornationes, facili ac fuso argumento proposito, conficiantur. Carminis argumentum latine dictet multa locutionum varietate. Græci thematis eadem ac latinæ prosæ ratio erit, nisi quod fere ex ipso auctore depromendum, et ratio syntaxeos præmonstranda.

once a week they should write their compositions without any outside help, after some type of letter has been taught, and after the relevant letters of Cicero or Pliny have been referenced.[166] Then in the second semester, their wit should be sparked: after the proposal of an easy and broad subject, they should compose *chriae* at first, then *procmia*, narratives, and embellishments.[167] The teacher should dictate the subject of a poem in Latin with a considerable variety of expression. The same method will be used for the Greek theme as for the Latin prose, except that it is usually to be taken right from the author, and the way the syntax works should be pointed out in advance.

[401] *Concertatio*

7. Concertatio seu exercitatio sita erit tum in iis, quæ alter æmulus in alterius scriptione deprehenderit; tum in iis, in quibus prima hora se exercuerint, proponendis; tum in phrasibus a præceptore habitis memoriter dicendis aut variandis; tum in epistolarum ac rhetoricæ præceptis reddendis aut applicandis; tum in exquirenda quantitate syllabarum, allata memoriter regula vel pætæ exemplo; tum in proprietate aut etymologia aliqua investiganda; tum in aliquo græci latinive auctoris loco interpretando; tum in græcis difficilioribus et anomalis verbis inflectendis formandisque; et aliis generis eiusdem ad præceptoris arbitrium.

[401] *Competition*

7. Competition or exercise will find a place sometimes in the correction of errors that one rival has caught in the other's composition; sometimes in presenting what they practiced in the first hour; sometimes in reciting from memory or varying phrases given by the teacher; sometimes in giving back or applying the rules for letter writing and rhetoric; sometimes in determining the quantity of syllables, citing from memory a rule or example from a poet; and in searching out some particular quality or root meaning of a word; sometimes in explaining the meaning of some passage of a Greek or Latin author; sometimes in conjugating the more difficult and irregular Greek

---

[166] Pliny: Pliny the Younger (Gaius Plinius Caecilius Secundus, A.D. 61/62–113?) held a number of political offices under Domitian, Nerva, and Trajan and was the author of letters (*Epistulæ*), published in ten books.

[167] *Prœmia*: introductions.

[402] *Ars metrica et rhetorica*

8. Ars metrica celeriter recurretur, in iis solum inhærendo, quibus magis egere videbuntur, et exercendo potius, quam explicando. Rhetoricæ item Cypriani non tam verba, quam præcepta breviter illustrentur, additis ex eodem libello exemplis et, si res ferat, ex quotidianis prælectionibus.

[403] *Græca prælectio*

9. Græca prælectione alternis diebus grammatica et auctor explanabitur; grammaticæ quidem, breviter decursis iis, quæ in prima classe tradita fuerant, syntaxim, et rationem accentuum persequatur. Auctor vero primo semestri solutæ orationis sumetur ex facilioribus, ut aliquæ orationes Isocratis et sanctorum Chrysostomi et Basilii, ut ex epistolis Platonis et Synesii, ut aliquid selectum ex Plutarcho; altero semestri carmen aliquod explicabitur, exempli gratia ex Phocylide, Theognide, sancto Gregorio Nazianzeno, Synesio, et horum similibus. Explicatio autem, ut huius scholæ fert gradus, linguæ potius cognitioni, quam eruditioni serviat. Inclinante autem anno græcarum syllabarum ratio tradi poterit cum auctore alternis diebus. Poterunt etiam interdum dissoluta carmina concinnari.

verbs; and in other activities of this kind, at the teacher's discretion.

[402] *Prosody and rhetoric*

8. Prosody will be covered quickly, by sticking only to those things that the students seem to need more, and by practice more than by explanation. Likewise, it is not so much the words of Cyprian's Rhetoric as his rules that should be concisely clarified, with examples added from the same book and, if the material supports it, from the daily lessons.

[403] *Greek lesson*

9. In the Greek lesson, the grammar and an author will be taught on alternate days. After briefly running through the grammatical material that had been covered in the first class, he should treat the syntax and the way the accents are used. In the first semester, one of the easier prose writers will be chosen, like some speeches of Isocrates and of Saints Chrysostom and Basil, or selections from the letters of Plato and Synesius, or something chosen from Plutarch.[168] In the second semester, some poem will be taught, for example, from Phocylides, Theognis, Saint Gregory Nazianzen, Synesius, and the like. The teaching, in accordance with this class's grade, should promote language comprehension rather than scholarly learning. However, as the year comes to an end, the system of Greek syllables can be given together with an author, on alternating days. From time to time, they can also rearrange scrambled poems into poetic meters.

---

[168] For information on Isocrates and the other Greek authors and scholars mentioned in this section, see endn. 28.

[404] *Carmina affigenda*

10. Affigantur carmina scholæ parietibus alternis fere mensibus ad aliquem celebriorem diem exornandum, vel magistratus promulgandos, vel alia quapiam occasione, selectissima quæque a discipulis descripta; immo etiam pro regionum more aliquid prosæ breviores, quales sunt inscriptiones, ut clypeorum, templorum, sepulchrorum, hortorum, statuarum; quales descriptiones, ut urbis, portus, exercitus; quales narrationes, ut rei gestæ ab aliquo divorum; qualia denique paradoxa; additis interdum, non tamen sine rectoris permissu, picturis, quæ emblemati vel argumento proposito respondeant.

[404] *Poems should be posted*

10. The choicest poems composed by the students should be posted on the walls of the class, usually every other month, to enhance some particularly special day, or to announce the officers formally, or on some other occasion. And certainly, in accordance with local custom, there should also be some briefer bits of prose, like inscriptions, such as for shields, churches, tombs, gardens, statues; like descriptions, such as for a city, a port, an army; like narratives, such as deeds performed by some saint; finally like paradoxes. Pictures should sometimes be added, only with the rector's permission, ones that correspond to an emblem or to a subject that has been proposed.

[H28] Regulæ Professoris Supremæ Classis Grammaticæ

[H28] Rules for the Professor of the Highest Grammar Class

[405] *Gradus*

1. Gradus huius scholæ est absoluta grammaticæ cognitio; ita enim recolit ab initio syntaxim, ut addat omnes appendices; deinde explicet constructionem figuratam, et de arte metrica. In græcis autem octo partes orationis, seu quæcunque rudimentorum nomine continentur, dialectis ac difficilioribus annotationibus exceptis. Quod ad lectiones pertinet, ex oratoribus quidem explicari poterunt primo semestri gravissimæ quæque Ciceronis *ad Familiares, ad Atticum, ad Quintum fratrem* epistolæ; altero vero liber *de Amicitia, de Senectute, Paradoxa,* et alia huiusmodi; ex poetis vero primo semestri selectæ

[405] *Grade*

1. The grade of this class consists in a thorough knowledge of grammar. For the teacher repeats syntax from the beginning in such a way that he adds all the appendices; then he should teach *constructio figurata* and prosody. And in Greek he should teach the eight parts of speech, or whatever things are included under the heading of rudiments, leaving aside dialects and the more difficult annotations. As for what pertains to texts: in the first semester, from the orators, certain very important letters of Cicero to his friends and family, to Atticus, and to Quintus his brother can be taught; in the second, the books *On*

aliquæ ac purgatæ Ovidii, tum elegiæ tum epistolæ; altero quædam item selecta et purgata ex Catullo, Tibullo, Propertio, et Virgilii *Eclogis;* vel etiam libri eiusdem Virgilii faciliores, ut quartus *Georgicorum,* quintus et septimus *Aeneidos;* ex græcis S. Chrysostomus, Aesopus, Agapetus, et horum similes.

Friendship, On Old Age, the *Paradoxes,* and things like this.[169] From the poets, in the first semester, some selected and expurgated elegies and letters of Ovid can be taught;[170] in the second, likewise some selected and expurgated pieces from Catullus, Tibullus, Propertius, and the *Eclogues* of Vergil; or even Vergil's easier books, such as the fourth book of the *Georgics,* the fifth and seventh of the *Aeneid;* from the Greek, Saint Chrysostom, Aesop, Agapetus, and authors like these.

[406] *Divisio temporis*

2. Divisio temporis hæc erit: Prima hora matutina memoriter recitetur M. Tullius et grammatica decurionibus; scripta a decurionibus collecta præceptor corrigat; varias interim, de quibus infra regula quarta, discipulis exercitationes iniungens. Secunda hora matutina repetatur postrema breviter Ciceronis prælectio, novaque per semihoram explicetur atque exigatur; postremo thema dictetur. Ultima semihora matutinæ, grammaticæ prælectione repetita, nova explicetur et exigatur, admista interdum concertatione. Ac primo quidem semestri præcepta constructionis in inferiore scholæ tradita decurrantur; propria deinceps ex professo explicentur; alternis vero diebus artis metricæ præcepta generalia, omissis exceptionibus; posteriore autem semestri recolatur per duos minimum menses pars illa grammaticæ, quæ est propria

[406] *Schedule*

2. The schedule will be as follows: In the first morning hour, Marcus Tullius and grammar will be recited to the decurions from memory. The teacher should correct the written work collected by the decurions, giving the students various exercises to do in the meanwhile (about which, see the fourth rule below). In the second morning hour, the last lesson on Cicero should be briefly reviewed, and a new one taught and demanded back for a half hour; finally, a theme should be dictated. The last half hour of the morning, after the grammar lesson has been reviewed, a new one should be added and demanded back, with a competition occasionally being added in. And of course in the first semester the rules for construction given in the lower class should be gone over quickly; next, the items belonging to this grade should be taught in thorough detail. On alternate days, the general

---

[169] *On Friendship, On Old Age:* two philosophical dialogs on the stated topics. *Paradoxes: Paradoxes of the Stoics,* Cicero's first philosophical work, dating to 46 B.C.

[170] For information on Ovid and the other authors mentioned in this section, see endn. 29.

primæ classis, et alternis diebus ars metrica, regulas iam explicatas breviter percurrendo, in aliis, quantum necesse est, hærendo; absoluta vero repetitione grammaticæ quotidie deinceps ars metrica explicetur, adiectis exceptionibus, carminum generibus, et quæ de patronymicis atque accentu traduntur. Prima semihora pomeridiana memoriter poeta græcusque auctor recitetur, recognoscente magistro decurionum nota scriptaque, vel quæ mane imperata sunt, vel quæ ex domo allatis superfuerint, corrigente. Sesquihora consequens pætæ, tum recolendo tum explicando, et græcæ, tum prælectioni tum scriptioni, ita dividatur, ut græcis paulo plus detur quam semihora. Ultima semihora, vel quod illius reliquum fuerit, in concertationibus collocandum. Die sabbathi mane publice recitentur memoriter totius hebdomadæ, vel totius libri prælectiones. Secunda hora recolantur. Ultima semihora concertetur. Idem fiat a prandio, nisi quod prima hora etiam memoriter recitatur catechismus. Ultima semihora in explicatione catechismi vel pia cohortatione, nisi feria sexta habita sit, ponetur; sin autem in ea re ferme, in cuius locum tum catechismus successerat.

precepts of prosody should be taught, with the exceptions set aside. In the second semester, for at least two months, there should be a review of that part of grammar that belongs to the first class, and on alternate days, there should be a review of prosody that proceeds by briefly skimming through the rules already taught and by dwelling on others as much as is necessary. But when the review of grammar is over, prosody should be taught every day from then on, adding exceptions, poetic genres, and the usual material on patronymics and accent.[171] In the first half hour of the afternoon, a poet or a Greek author should be recited from memory, while the teacher reviews the decurions' marks or corrects what was assigned in the morning or what is left from the homework. The following hour and a half should be divided between the review or explication of a poet and Greek, sometimes a lesson and sometimes a composition. A little more than a half an hour should be given to Greek. The last half hour, or for what is left of it, should be devoted to competition. On Saturday morning, the lessons of the entire book or of the entire week should be recited from memory in front of the group. In the second hour they should be reviewed. In the final half hour, there should be competition. The same thing should be done after the midday meal, except that catechism

[171] Patronymics: names derived from the names of the fathers; for example, the patronymic of Achilles was Peliades or "son of Peleus."

Accent: the accent marks (acute, grave, circumflex) originally indicated pitch (that is, tones rising, falling, or mixed) rather than stress. The system of accents was invented in Alexandria in the Hellenistic era and kept as part of the study of ancient Greek even long after pitch was no longer practiced or remembered.

is also recited from memory in the first hour. The last half hour will be devoted to teaching catechism or giving a devout exhortation, unless this was done Friday. If it was, then the half hour will usually be given to whatever had been displaced by the catechism study at that time.

[407] *Scriptionis corrigendæ ratio*

3. In scriptione corrigenda indicet, si quid contra præcepta grammaticæ, orthographiæ, interpunctionis peccatum sit; si declinatæ difficultates, si non habita elegantiæ aut imitationis ratio.

[407] *Method for correcting a composition*

3. In correcting a composition he should point out whether the student broke any rules of grammar, spelling, or punctuation; whether he dodged any difficulties; and whether he failed to take aspects of elegance or imitation into account.

[408] *Exercitationes inter corrigendum*

4. Exercitationes tradendæ discipulis, dum scripta corrigit, erunt exempli gratia vernacula dictata, tum ad auctoris imitationem, tum ad syntaxis præcepta, latina facere, lectionem ciceronianam ex latino in patrium sermonem transferre, eandem latine transcribere, inde phrases elegantiores excerpere, ex grammaticæ præceptis recens explicatis dubitationes æmulis et locutiones proponendas depromere, dissolutos versus concinnare aut conficere, græca describere, et alia generis eiusdem.

[408] *Exercises during correction*

4. Exercises should be given the students while [the professor] corrects the written work. There will be, for example, putting vernacular dictations into Latin, sometimes in imitation of an author and sometimes in accord with the rules of syntax; translating a Ciceronian reading from Latin into the vernacular; writing out that translation in Latin, excerpting the more elegant phrases from it; coming up with questions for the rivals and proposing expressions to them from the grammatical rules recently taught; rearranging scrambled verses into the proper order or composing them; writing in Greek; and other activities of this kind.

[409] *Prælectio*

5. Prælectionis forma hæc erit: Primo, argumentum, tum latino tum patrio sermone, perstringat. Deinde, unamquamque periodum ita interpretetur, ut vernacula expositio latinæ subinde subiiciatur.

[409] *Lesson*

5. The lesson will take the following shape: First, he should lightly touch upon the summary of the content, both in Latin and in the native tongue. Then, he should interpret each full sentence in such a way that

Tertio, a capite recurrens (nisi malit ipsi explicationi inserere) binas aut ternas seligat voces, quarum vim aut originem expendat, unoque aut altero eiusdem præsertim auctoris exemplo confirmet. Translationes etiam evolvat ac demonstret, fabulas cum historiis, et quæ ad eruditionem pertinent, si quæ incidant, brevi expediat; binas etiam ternasve phrases elegantiores excerpat. Postremo, scriptoris verba vulgi sermone decurrat. Licebit autem latinum argumentum, observationes, proprietates et phrases quam brevissime dictare.

the vernacular explanation is constantly joined to the Latin. Third, starting again from the top (unless he prefers to insert it in the explanation itself), he should choose two or three expressions, whose meaning or origin he should examine carefully, and he should confirm it with one or two examples, especially from the same author. Also he should explain and illustrate the metaphors, and he should briefly clarify the stories along with histories and what pertains to scholarly learning, if any such things come up. He should also pick out two or three of the more elegant expressions. Finally, he should run through the writer's words in the vernacular. He can dictate as briefly as possible the Latin summary, comments, special features of the diction, and expressions.

[410] *Argumentum scribendi*

6. Dictandum argumentum scribendi ad epistolæ fere formam vulgi sermone ad verbum, quod ad præcepta syntaxeos, et ad Ciceronis imitationem referatur. Semel autem fere singulis mensibus, aut domi loco quotidianæ scriptionis, aut in schola ad magistratus creandos, postquam aliquantum profecerint, suo marte conscribant, aliquo prius epistolarum genere explicato, indictisque Ciceronis epistolis ad illud pertinentibus, et aliquot ab ipso præceptore eiusdem generis dictatis exemplis.

[410] *Subject matter for writing*

6. The subject matter of the composition should be dictated, usually in the form of a letter, word for word, and in the vernacular. It should be related to the rules of syntax and to the imitation of Cicero. Usually once every month, however, either at home as the daily composition, or in class for the purpose of appointing the officers, when they have made a little progress, they should write it out without any assistance, after some type of letter has been explained, and after the relevant letters of Cicero have been pointed out, and after several examples of the same type have been dictated by the teacher himself.

[411] *Carmina*

7. Carmina poterunt initio quidem soluto solum verborum ordine, mox etiam verbis aliquibus immutatis, ad extremum facillimo argumento cum multa locutionum varietate dictari.

[412] *Græcum thema*

8. Græci thematis eadem ac latinæ prosæ ratio erit, nisi quod fere ex ipso auctore depromendum, et ratio syntaxeos præmonstranda.

[413] *Græca prælectio*

9. Græcæ prælectionis, quæ quadrantem horæ vix excedet, eadem ratio sit, nisi quod cum græcus auctor sumitur (sumi autem poterit, quando præfectus censuerit, alternis cum grammatica diebus) verba singula tractanda sunt facillimis etiam in universum, si videatur, syntaxeos regulis indicatis.

[414] *Concertatio*

10. Concertatio seu exercitatio sita erit tum in iis, quæ alter æmulus in alterius scriptione deprehenderit, tum in iis, in quibus prima hora se exercuerint, proponendis, tum in phrasibus a præceptore habitis memoriter dicendis, tum in vernaculis locutionibus mutuo ex præscripto syntaxeos, aut ad Ciceronis imitationem exigendis, aut variandis (faciendumque, ut locutionem propositam statim, qui interrogatur, iisdem reddat verbis, eamque paulisper meditatus non verbatim, sed totam simul latine

[411] *Poems*

7. Poems can be dictated, at first only in a prose form, soon also with some of the words changed, and at the end with a very easy summary of the content, with a considerable variety of expressions.

[412] *Greek theme*

8. The method for the Greek theme will be the same as for the Latin one, except that it is usually to be taken right from the author, and the way the syntax works should be pointed out in advance.

[413] *Greek lesson*

9. The same plan should hold for the Greek lesson, which will barely extend beyond a quarter of an hour, except that when a Greek author is taken (which can happen on days alternating with those given to grammar, when the prefect has thought it good), the words should be treated one by one, and generally even the easiest rules of syntax should be noted, if it seems desirable to do this.

[414] *Competition*

10. Competition or exercise will find a place sometimes in the correction of errors that one rival has caught in the other's composition; sometimes in presenting what they practiced in the first hour; sometimes in reciting from memory phrases given by the teacher; sometimes in their asking one another for vernacular expressions in their regular forms or in imitation of Cicero, or in varying such expressions (this should be done in such a way that the one asked immediately gives back the proposed expression in the same

efferat) tum in epistolarum præceptis reddendis, tum in exquirenda quantitate syllabarum, allata memoriter regula, vel poetæ exemplo, tum in proprietate aut etymologia aliqua investiganda, tum in aliquo græci latinive auctoris loco interpretando, tum in græcis nominibus aut verbis inflectendis formandisque, et aliis id genus ad præceptoris arbitrium.

words, and after thinking about it for a little while, produces all at once, not word for word, the entire expression in Latin); sometimes in giving back the rules for letter writing; sometimes in determining syllable quantities, citing from memory some rule or poetic example; sometimes in finding some special aspect or some root meaning of a word; sometimes in interpreting some passage of a Greek or Latin author; sometimes in giving the cases and inflections of nouns or verbs;[172] and in other similar activities, at the teacher's discretion.

[H29] Regulæ Professoris Mediæ Classis Grammaticæ

[415] *Gradus*

1. Gradus huius scholæ est, totius quidem grammaticæ, minus tamen plena cognitio; explicat enim ab initio libri secundi usque ad figuratam constructionem, facillimis solum adiunctis appendicibus; seu iuxta romanam methodum a communi verborum constructione usque ad figuratam, additis facilioribus appendicibus. Ex græcis ad hanc scholam pertinent nomina contracta, verba circumflexa, verba in Mi et faciliores formationes. Ad prælectiones vero non nisi familiares Ciceronis epistolæ, et facillima quæque Ovidii carmina; et secundo semestri, si

[H29] Rules for the Professor of the Middle Grammar Class

[415] *Grade*

1. The grade of this class consists in a comprehensive, though less than complete, knowledge of grammar. For he teaches from the beginning of the second book up to *constructio figurata*, with the addition of only the easiest appendices; or, according to the Roman method, he teaches from the typical paradigms of verbs up to the *constructio figurata*, adding the easier appendices.[173] From Greek, contract nouns and circumflex verbs in -mi and the easier forms pertain to this class. For the lessons, included are only the letters of Cicero to family and friends, and some of Ovid's easiest poems, and in the second semes-

---

[172] [I]nflections of nouns or verbs: i.e., all the possible forms of these parts of speech, sometimes according to a special category like "present tense, indicative mood."

[173] [R]oman method]: because of the opinions of some of the Jesuit teachers in Rome, a revised and simplified version of Alvarez's grammar was published by Father Horace Torsellini in 1584. See Farrell, *Jesuit Code*, 446–48.

præfectus censeat, græcus cate-chismus aut Cebetis tabula.

[416]   *Divisio temporis*

2. Divisio temporis hæc erit: Prima hora matutina memoriter recitetur M. Tullius et grammatica apud decuriones; scripta a decurio-nibus collecta præceptor corrigat, varias interim, de quibus infra re-gula quarta, discipulis exercitatio-nes iniungens. Secunda hora matu-tina repetatur postrema breviter Ciceronis prælectio, novaque per semihoram explicetur atque exiga-tur; postremo thema dictetur. Ul-tima semihora matutina aliquid ex primo grammaticæ libro, et de declinatione nominum, ac dein-ceps de præteritis ac supinis, quod concertando exerceatur, recolen-dum. Prima hora pomeridiana me-moriter grammatica, tum latina tum græca, et suis diebus poeta recitetur, recognoscente magistro decurionum notas scriptaque, vel quæ mane imperata sunt, vel quæ ex domo allatis superfuerint, corri-gente; ad extremum grammaticæ, et alternis diebus pætæ postrema prælectio recolatur. Secunda hora pomeridiana per semihoram syn-taxis explicetur et repetatur; poste-riore tamen semestri syntaxis item, et alternis diebus poeta explicetur. Per alteram semihoram græca tra-

ter, if the prefect thinks it proper, the Greek catechism or the *Table of Cebes*.[174]

[416]   *Schedule*

2. The schedule will be as follows: In the first morning hour, Marcus Tullius and grammar should be re-cited to the decurions from memory; the teacher should correct the writ-ten work collected by the decurions, assigning the students various exer-cises to do in the meantime (about which see the fourth rule below). In the second morning hour the last lesson of Cicero should be briefly reviewed, and a new one should be taught and demanded back for a half hour; finally a theme should be dic-tated. In the last half hour of the morning, there should be a review of something from the first book of grammar, and about the declension of nouns, and next about the past tenses and the verbals, which should be practiced in competition.[175] In the first afternoon hour, grammar, some-times Latin and sometimes Greek, and, on the proper days, a poet should be recited from memory, while the teacher checks the marks of the decurions and corrects the written work, either what was as-signed that morning, or what is left from the homework. At the very end, there should be a review of the last lesson on grammar, and of a

---

[174] [G]reek catechism: see ibid., 257n55. Father George Mayer (1564–1623) had trans-lated a catechism by Peter Canisius into Greek in 1595: *Petri Canisii Societatis Iesu theologi cate-chismus Graecolatinus.*

Table of Cebes: The *Pinax Cebetis* or *Tabula Cebetis* is a Greek work, perhaps from the first century B.C., in which a teacher or sage explains to a student the meaning of an allegorical picture showing the paths of virtue and vice.

[175] Declensions: sets of endings that are regularly used for various types of nouns. Verbals: verb-related forms like gerunds (verbal nouns), participles (verbal adjectives), infini-tives, and supines.

dantur. Ultima semihora concertationi seu exercitationi tribuatur. Die sabbathi mane prima hora publice recitentur memoriter totius hebdomadæ vel totius libri prælectiones. Secunda hora recolantur. Ultima semihora concertetur. Idem fiat a prandio, nisi quod prima hora cum grammatica et poeta recitatur etiam catechismus. Ultima semihora in explicatione catechismi, vel nonnunquam pia cohortatione, nisi feria sexta habita fuerit, ponetur; sin autem, in ea re ferme, in cuius locum tum catechismus successerat.

poet on alternate days. In the second afternoon hour, for a half-hour, syntax should be taught and reviewed. In the second semester, however, syntax should be taught the same way every other day, in alternation with a poet. For the second half hour, Greek should be taught. The last half hour should be devoted to competition or practice. On Saturday, the first hour in the morning, the lessons of the whole week, or of the whole book, should be recited from memory in front of the group. In the second hour, they should be reviewed. In the last half hour, there should be a competition. The same thing should happen after the midday meal, except that catechism is recited along with grammar and poetry in the first hour. The last half hour should be used for the teaching of the catechism, or sometimes for a pious exhortation, unless this was done Friday. If it was, then the half hour will usually be given to whatever had been displaced by the catechism study at that time.

[417] *Scriptionis corrigendæ ratio*

3. In scriptione corrigenda indicet, si quid contra præcepta grammaticæ, orthographiæ, interpunctionis peccatum sit, si declinatæ difficultates; omnia ad grammaticarum præceptionum normam expendat; coniugationesque ipsas et rudimenta, sumpta occasione, in memoriam revocet.

[417] *Method of correcting the composition*

3. In the correction of the composition, he should point out whether anything is wrong in grammar, spelling, or punctuation, or whether the student dodged any difficulties. He should evaluate everything according to the standard of the rules of grammar. And he should recall to their minds even the conjugations and the rudiments, as the opportunity arises.

[418] *Exercitationes inter corrigendum*

4. Exercitationes, dum scripta

[418] *Exercises during the correction*

4. While he corrects the papers, there will be exercises, for example:

corrigit, erunt exempli gratia vernacula dictata tum ad auctoris imitationem, tum præcipue ad syntaxis
præcepta latina facere; lectionem
Ciceronis vulgi sermone convertere, eandem latine transcribere, ex
grammaticæ præceptis, recens
præsertim explicatis, dubia æmulis
et locutiones proponendas depromere, græca describere, et alia
generis eiusdem.

[419]   *Grammatica exigenda*

5. In repetitione prælectionis
capiat interdum occasionem difficiliora declinandi, coniugandi, et
grammaticæ quomodocunque exigendæ.

[420]   *Prælectio Ciceronis*

6. Prælectionis ciceronianæ,
quæ septenos fere versus non excedet, hæc forma sit: Primo, totam
continenter pronunciet, eiusque
argumentum brevissime patrio sermone perstringat. Secundo, periodum ad verbum vulgi sermone
interpretetur. Tertio, a capite recurrens structuram indicet, et periodum retexens, quæ verba, quos
casus regant, ostendat; pleraque ad
explicatas grammaticæ leges perpendat, latinæ linguæ observationem unam aut alteram, sed quam
facillimam, afferat; metaphoras
exemplis rerum notissimarum demonstret; unam denique aut alteram phrasim excerpat, quas solas
cum argumento dictabit. Quarto,

turning vernacular dictations into
Latin, sometimes in imitation of an
author, sometimes especially according to rules of syntax; translating a
passage of Cicero into the vernacular; writing out the same in Latin;
providing questions and phrases to
be proposed to the rivals about the
rules of grammar, especially the ones
recently taught; writing out Greek
passages, and other things like these.

[419]   *Requiring students to give the
grammatical material*

5. In the review of the lesson, he
should sometimes take the opportunity to decline and conjugate the
more difficult words, and require
them to give the grammatical material in any way whatsoever.[176]

[420]   *Lesson on Cicero*

6. The lesson on Cicero, which
usually should not exceed seven
lines each, should take this form:
First, he should deliver the whole
passage straight through, and summarize its content very briefly in the
native tongue. Second, he should
interpret the complete sentence word
for word in the vernacular. Third,
running through it from the beginning, he should point out its structure, and breaking down the whole
sentence, he should show what verbs
govern which cases. And he should
carefully consider most of it according to the grammatical laws that
have been taught, and he should
make one or two observations about
the Latin language, but ones that are
as easy as possible. He should illus-

---

[176] [T]o give the grammatical material in any way whatsoever": for example, they can
be asked to produce any "row" or "column" of a table of forms. They are not simply quizzed
on the forms in the order in which they were written down.

scriptoris iterum verba vernaculo sermone decurrat.

trate the metaphors with examples from what is very well known. Finally, he should select one or two phrases, which he will dictate by themselves, along with the summary of the content. Fourth, he should again run through the words of the writer in the vernacular.

[421] *Argumentum scribendi*

7. Dictandum argumentum scribendi vulgi sermone ad verbum perspicuum, nec fere versibus septenis longius, quod ad præcepta syntaxis et Ciceronis imitationem referatur. Interdum discipuli aliquam Ciceronis brevem versionem, aut aliquod græcum tempus seu nomen subscribere iubeantur.

[421] *Theme for the composition*

7. The theme for the composition should be dictated in the vernacular word for word in clear language, and usually not with more than seven lines at a time. It should relate to the rules of syntax and the imitation of Cicero. Sometimes the students should be told to write down below it some short version of a Ciceronian passage or some Greek tense or noun.

[422] *Grammaticæ prælectio*

8. Grammaticæ prælectio non nisi singula præcepta, ad summum cum brevi aliqua appendice aut exceptione, contineat.

[422] *Grammar Lesson*

8. The grammar lesson should include only individual rules with, at the most, some brief appendix or an exception.

[423] *Græca prælectio*

9. In græcis tradendis eadem proportione serventur, et fere ex usu videtur esse vernaculas voces casibus ac personis addere, omniaque plerumque voce patria declarare.

[423] *Greek lesson*

9. In teaching Greek, the same guidelines should be followed proportionally. Generally, experience seems to indicate that it is good to add vernacular expressions to the cases and persons, and for the most part to say everything in the native tongue.

[424] *Concertatio*

10. Concertatio seu exercitatio sita erit tum in iis, quæ alter æmulus in alterius scriptione deprehenderit; tum in iis, in quibus prima hora se exercuerint, proponendis; tum in phrasibus a præceptore habitis memoriter dicendis; tum in

[424] *Competition*

10. Competition or exercise will find a place sometimes in the correction of errors that one rival has caught in the other's composition; sometimes in presenting what they practiced in the first hour; sometimes in reciting from memory phrases got-

vernaculis locutionibus mutuo ex præscripto syntaxeos, aut ad Ciceronis imitationem exigendis (faciendumque, ut locutionem propositam statim, qui interrogatur, iisdem repetat verbis; eamque paulisper meditatus non verbatim, sed totam simul latine efferat); tum in difficilioribus nominibus ac verbis, quæ præsertim in prælectione occurrerint, vel continenti vel interrupto casuum ac temporum ordine, vel singulis per se, vel coniuncto simul adiectivo substantivoque et pronomine inflectendis; tum in præteritis et supinis quam celerrime reddendis, et aliis id genus, arbitrio præceptoris.

ten from the teacher; sometimes in their asking one another for vernacular expressions in their regular forms or in imitation of Cicero (this should be done in such a way that the one asked immediately gives back the proposed expression in the same words, and after thinking about it for a little while, produces all at once, not word for word, the entire expression in Latin); sometimes in inflecting the more difficult nouns and verbs, especially those that have come up in the lesson, either in continuous sequence or with a break in the order of cases and tenses,[177] either each one individually, or with a substantive joined with an adjective and a verb joined with a pronoun; sometimes in giving the past tenses and verbals as quickly as possible, and in other similar activities, at the teacher's discretion.

[H30] Regulæ Professoris Infimæ Classis Grammaticæ

[H30] Rules for the Professor of the Lowest Grammar Class

[425] *Gradus*

1. Gradus huius scholæ est rudimentorum perfecta, syntaxis inchoata cognitio. Incipit enim a declinationibus usque ad communem verborum constructionem. Et quidem ubi duo erunt ordines, inferiori ex primo libro nomina, verba, rudimenta, præcepta quatuordecim de constructione, genera nominum tribuentur; superiori vero ex primo libro de nominum declinatione

[425] *Grade*

1. The grade of this class consists in a perfect knowledge of the rudiments and a beginner's knowledge of syntax. For it starts from the declensions and goes up to the regular syntax of verbs. And where there are two tracks, the lower will take from the first book the material on the nouns, the verbs, the rudiments, the fourteen rules of syntax, and the types of nouns.[178] The upper will

---

[177] [E]ither in continuous sequence or with a break in the order of cases and tenses: see the note on §419 above.

[178] [T]the fourteen rules of syntax: Emmanuel's grammar gives fourteen rules on syntax to guide beginners, entitled "Praecepta aliquot de constructione" (*De institutione grammati-*

sine appendicibus, et de præteritis ac supinis; e secundo autem introductio syntaxis sine appendicibus usque ad impersonalia.

take from the first book the material on the declensions of nouns without the appendices, and the material on the past tenses and verbals. From the second book, the upper level will take the introduction to syntax without the appendices, up to the impersonal verbs.[179]

[426] *Divisio temporis*

2. ' Divisio temporis hæc erit: Prima hora matutina memoriter Marc. Tullius et grammatica apud decuriones recitetur; scripta a decurionibus collecta præceptor corrigat, varias interim, de quibus infra regula quarta, discipulis exercitationes iniungens. Secunda hora matutina repetatur postrema breviter Ciceronis prælectio, novaque per semihoram explicetur atque exigatur; postremo thema dictetur. Ultima semihora matutina utrique ordini aliquid ex primo grammaticæ libro iuxta partem cuique descriptam explicetur aut recolatur, vel alterno quoque die singulis ordinibus, vel quotidie utrique; postea vero omnia vel a magistro vel invicem per concertationem reposcantur. Quibus autem diebus novum a prandio præceptum constructionis non erit proponendum (pluribus enim diebus fere singula inculcanda sunt), tum prælectio hæc matutina in locum pomeridianæ succedat; ultima autem semihora matutina tota concertationi, seu exercitationi concedatur. Prima hora pomeridiana memoriter grammatica tum latina tum græca reci-

[426] *Schedule*

2. The schedule will be as follows: In the first morning hour, Marcus Tullius and the grammar should be recited to the decurions from memory. The teacher should correct the written work collected by the decurions, assigning to the students various exercises to do in the meantime (about which, see the fourth rule below). In the second morning hour, the last lesson on Cicero should be briefly repeated and a new one taught and heard back for a half hour; finally a theme should be dictated. The last half hour of the morning, for each track, something from the first book of the grammar should be taught or reviewed according to the part assigned to each, either every other day for each track, or daily for each one. Later everything should be demanded back either by the teacher or by turns in a competition. On the days on which a new rule of construction does not have to be presented after the midday meal (for individual ones should usually be impressed on the students' minds for several days), then this morning lesson should be continued in the afternoon lesson. The final half hour

ca, 134 f.).

[179] The impersonal verbs: verbs of the third person that do not take a personal subject; e.g., *licet* (it is allowed) or *placet* (it pleases).

tetur, recognoscente magistro de-curionum notas scriptaque, vel quæ mane imperata sunt, vel quæ ex domo allatis superfuerint, ad summum per semihoram corrigente. Ad extremum postrema grammaticæ prælectio recolatur. Secunda hora pomeridiana superi-ori quidem ordini syntaxis, inferio-ri vero quatuordecim præcepta ex-planentur; græcis vero paulo plus quadrante tribuatur. Ultima semi-hora concertetur, vel aliquod dicta-tum ex grammaticæ legibus expen-datur. Die sabbathi mane prima hora publice recitentur memoriter totius hebdomadæ prælectiones; secunda hora recolantur; ultima semihora concertetur. Idem fiat a prandio, nisi quod prima hora simul cum grammatica recitatur etiam catechismus. Ultima semi-hora in explicatione catechismi, vel pia cohortatione, nisi feria sexta habita fuerit, ponetur; sin autem, in ea re ferme, in cuius locum tum catechismus successerat.

of the morning should all be given to competition or to exercise. In the first hour of the afternoon, grammar should be recited, both Latin and Greek, while the teacher checks over the marks of the decurions and cor-rects the written work for at most a half hour, either what was assigned in the morning, or what remains from the homework. Toward the very end, the last grammar lesson should be reviewed. In the second afternoon hour, syntax should be taught to the upper track, but the fourteen rules should be taught to the lower one; a little more than a quarter of an hour should be given to Greek. In the last half hour, there should be competitions, or some-thing dictated from the rules of grammar should be carefully consid-ered in light of the grammatical rules. On Saturday, in the first hour of the morning, there should be a recitation of all the lessons of the week from memory in front of the class; in the second hour they should be reviewed; in the last half hour there should be competitions. The same thing should happen after the midday meal, except that catechism is also recited in the first hour to-gether with the grammar. The last half hour should be devoted to teaching catechism, or to a devout exhortation, unless this was done Friday. If it was, then the half hour will usually be given to whatever had been displaced by the catechism study at that time.

[427] *Scriptionis corrigendæ ratio*

3. In scriptione corrigenda indi-cet, si quid contra præcepta gram-maticæ, orthographiæ, interpunc-

[427] *The method of correcting the composition*

3. In correcting the composition, he should point out whether the stu-

tionis peccatum, si declinatæ difficultates; omnia ad grammaticarum præceptionum normam expendat; coniugationes et declinationes ex occasione repetere non omittat.

[428] *Exercitationes inter corrigendum*

4. Exercitationes discipulorum, dum scripta magister corrigit, erunt exempli gratia vernacula dictata e syntaxis præscripto latina facere, lectionem ciceronianam ex latino in vulgi sermonem transferre, eandem latine transcribere; ex grammaticæ præceptis, recens præsertim explicatis, dubia æmulis et locutiones proponendas deprómere, concordantias concinnare, aut componere, græca describere, et alia generis eiusdem.

[429] *Grammatica exigenda*

5. In repetitione prælectionis capiat interdum occasionem declinandi, coniugandi, et grammaticæ quomodocunque exigendæ.

[430] *Prælectio Ciceronis*

6. Prælectionis ciceronianæ, quæ quaternos fere versus non excedet, hæc forma sit: Primo, totam continenter pronunciet, eiusque argumentum brevissime vulgi sermone perstringat. Secundo, periodum ad verbum vulgari ser

dent broke any rules of grammar, spelling, or punctuation or whether he dodged any difficulties. He should evaluate everything according to the standard of the grammatical rules. He should not omit reviewing the conjugations and declensions as the opportunity arises.

[428] *Exercises during the correction*

4. While the teacher is correcting the written work, there will be exercises for the students, for example, turning something dictated in the vernacular into Latin on the basis of a syntactical rule; translating a passage from Cicero from Latin into the vernacular; and writing that same passage out in Latin; coming up with questions and expressions based on grammatical rules, especially the ones recently taught, to be put to their rivals; fashioning expressions that are in agreement or putting them in proper word order; writing out some Greek material; and other similar activities.

[429] *Calling for the grammatical material*

5. In the review of the lesson, he should sometimes take the opportunity to decline nouns, to conjugate verbs, and to require the students to give back the grammatical material in any manner whatsoever.

[430] *Lesson on Cicero*

6. The Ciceronian lesson, which usually should not exceed four lines at a time, should be structured as follows: First, he should deliver the whole passage without interruption, and he should very briefly summarize its subject in the vernacular. Sec

mone interpretetur. Tertio, a capite recurrens structuram indicet, et periodum retexens, quæ verba quos casus regant, ostendat, pleraque ad explicatas grammaticæ leges perpendat, latinæ linguæ ob servationem unam aut alteram, sed quam facillimam afferat; metaphoras exemplis rerum notissimarum demonstret; nec quicquam, nisi forte argumentum, dictet. Quarto, scriptoris iterum verba vulgi sermone decurrat.

ond, he should interpret the entire sentence literally in the vernacular. Third, running through it again from the beginning, he should point out its structure, and, breaking down the whole sentence, he should show which words govern which cases, and he should consider most of it in light of the rules of grammar that have been taught. He should make one or two observations on the Latin language—but they should be as easy as possible. He should illustrate the metaphors with very familiar examples. And he should dictate nothing, except perhaps the summary of the content. Fourth, he should again run through the words of the writer in the vernacular.

[431] *Argumentum scribendi*

7. Dictandum argumentum scribendi vulgi sermone ad verbum perspicuum, nec fere versibus quaternis longius; quod ad præcepta grammaticæ potissimum referatur; eique interdum discipuli aliquem Ciceronis brevem versionem aut locutionem ex præscripto syntaxis, aut ea ipsa, quæ sunt ex græcis rudimentis ediscenda, aut alia id genus subscribere iubeantur.

[431] *Summary of the composition's content*

7. The summary of the composition's content should be dictated in the vernacular, word for word, in clear language, and usually not more than four lines at a time. It should relate especially to the grammatical rules. Sometimes the students should be told to write down below it some short translation of Cicero or an expression based on a rule of syntax, or what has to be learned by heart from the Greek rudiments, or other things of this type.

[432] *Grammaticæ prælectio*

8. Grammaticæ prælectio non nisi singula ad summum præcepta contineat; quæ nisi bene percepta sint, ad alia non veniatur.

[432] *Grammar lesson*

8. The grammar lesson should contain only single rules at the most. If these are not grasped well, do not go on to others.

[433] *Concertatio*

9. Concertatio seu exercitatio sita erit tum in iis, quæ alter æmu-

[433] *Competition*

9. Competition or exercise will find a place sometimes in the correction

lus in alterius scriptione deprehenderit; tum in iis, in quibus prima hora se exercuerint, proponendis; tum in vulgaribus locutionibus invicem ad syntaxis præscriptum exigendis (faciendumque, ut locutionem propositam statim, qui interrogatur, iisdem reddat verbis, eamque, paulisper meditatus, non verbatim, sed quantum fieri potest, totam simul latine efferat); tum in difficilioribus nominibus ac verbis, quæ præsertim in prælectione occurrerint, vel continenti, vel interrupto casuum ac temporum ordine, vel singulis per se, vel coniuncto simul adiectivo substantivoque et pronomine inflectendis; tum in rudimentorum definitionibus et exemplis proferendis; tum in verborum flexionibus ex latino in vulgarem, ex vulgari sermone in latinum celeriter vertendis; tum in iis, quæ activa voce dicta sunt, passive efferendis; tum in præteritis et supinis; tum in nominum generibus et casibus quæcunque proposita fuerunt, indicandis; et horum similibus ad præceptoris arbitrium.

of errors that one rival has caught in the other's composition; sometimes in presenting those things that they practiced in the first hour; sometimes in their asking one another for vernacular expressions, according to a syntactical rule (this should be done in such a way that the one asked immediately gives back the proposed expression in the same words, and after thinking about it for a little while, produces all at once, not word for word, the entire expression in Latin); sometimes in inflecting the more difficult nouns and verbs, especially those that have come up in the lesson, either in continuous sequence or with a break in the order of cases and tenses, either each one individually, or with a substantive joined with an adjective and a verb joined with a pronoun; sometimes in producing examples and definitions from the rudiments; sometimes in quickly turning various forms of verbs from Latin into the vernacular, and from the vernacular into Latin; sometimes in transforming active expressions into passive ones; sometimes in producing verbs' past tenses and verbals; sometimes in identifying the genders and cases of whichever nouns have been proposed, and in similar activities, at the teacher's discretion.

[H31] Regulæ Scholasticorum Nostræ Societatis

[434] *Animi puritas et intentio*

1. In primis animi puritatem custodire, et rectam in studiis intentionem habere scholastici nostri

[H31] Rules for Jesuit Students

[434] *Purity of heart and intention*

1. Jesuit students should try above all to guard their purity of heart and to keep a right intention in studies, seeking in them nothing other than

conentur; nihil aliud in his, nisi divinam gloriam et animarum fructum quærentes; et in suis orationibus gratiam, ut in doctrina proficiant, crebro petant, ut tandem idonei, sicut ab iis sperat Societas, ad vineam Christi Domini Nostri exemplo ac doctrina excolendam evadant.

God's glory and people's spiritual benefit; and in their own prayers, they should frequently ask for the grace to progress in learning so that, one day, finally prepared, they may go to cultivate the vineyard of Christ our Lord by their example and learning in just the way that the Society hopes they will.

[435] *Solidarum virtutum cum studiis coniunctio*

2. Serio et constanter ad studia animum applicare deliberent; utque cavendum sibi putent, ne fervore studiorum intepescat solidarum virtutum ac religiosæ vitæ amor; ita sibi vicissim persuadeant, nihil gratius se Deo facturos in collegiis, quam si ea intentione, de qua dictum est, studiis se diligenter impendant; et licet nunquam ad exercenda ea, quæ didicerint, perveniant, illum tamen studendi laborem ex obedientia et caritate, ut par est, susceptum, opus esse magni meriti in conspectu divinæ et summæ Maiestatis apud se statuant.

[435] *Combining the essential virtues with studies*

2. They should resolve to apply their minds earnestly and steadily to their studies. And as they should think that they ought to be taking care not to let the fervor of studies dampen their love of the essential virtues and religious life, so they should persuade one another in turn that they are going to do nothing more pleasing to God in the colleges than if they apply themselves diligently to their studies with that intention about which we have spoken. And even if they never come to employ those things that they have learned, they should fix firmly in their hearts the conviction that the very labor of their study, undertaken out of due obedience and charity, must be of great merit in the sight of the divine and supreme Majesty.

[436] *Ex superioris præscripto studendum*

3. Iis facultatibus singuli operam dabunt, eosque audient præceptores, quos superior assignabit; præscriptam vero a præfecto vel a magistro divisionem temporis ac rationem studendi servent diligenter universi; nec aliis, quam ab eodem præfecto sibi traditis, utantur libris.

[436] *Study ought to be undertaken at the instruction of the superior*

3. Each individual will focus his efforts on those areas of study, and he will have classes with those teachers that the superior will assign. They all should carefully keep the schedule and the study plan prescribed either by the prefect or by the teacher, and they should not

make use of books other than those given to them by that prefect.

[437] *Diligentia*

4. In audiendis lectionibus sint assidui, et in eis prævidendis diligentes; et postquam eas audierint, repetendis; iis, quæ non intellexerint, interrogandis; aliis vero, quæ oportuerit, adnotandis, quo in posterum memoriæ defectui consulatur.

[437] *Diligence*

4. They should faithfully attend classes, being diligent about looking ahead to them, reviewing them afterwards, and asking about whatever they have not understood, while noting down other things that they really ought to know, in order to provide for what their memories will probably not retain at a later date.

[438] *Disputationes publicæ*

5. Intersint ordinariis scholarum, ad quas accedunt, disputationibus; et singulare sui specimen in doctrina præbere, modeste tamen, curent.

[438] *Public disputations*

5. In addition, they should be present at the regularly scheduled disputations of the classes that they attend; and they should make sure that they show themselves at their exemplary best as students, but still in a modest way.

[439] *Privatæ*

6. Privatis præterea et quotidianis disputationibus ac repetitionibus omnes intersint; et qui disputant, ei qui præest, religiose obediant.

[439] *Private disputations*

6. In addition, they should all be present at the daily private disputations and reviews, and the disputants should give religious obedience to the one who is in charge.

[440] *Modestia*

7. Cum ad publicas scholas eundum erit, eant et redeant invicem associati cum ea modestia interiore et exteriore, quæ ad sui et aliorum ædificationem conveniat.

[440] *Modesty*

7. When they have to go to classes outside the house, they should both go and return in each other's company with that interior and exterior modesty that is suited to their own edification and to that of others.

[441] *Colloquia cum externis*

8. Eorum colloquia, qui cum scholasticis externis loquendi habuerint facultatem, sint solum de rebus ad literas vel ad profectum spiritus pertinentibus, prout ad maiorem Dei gloriam omnibus utilius fore iudicabitur.

[441] *Conversations with non-Jesuits*

8. The conversations of those who have the opportunity to speak with non-Jesuit students should be only about matters pertaining to academics or to spiritual progress, just as it is judged more helpful for everyone, for the greater glory of God.

[442] *Latinæ linguæ usus*

9. Omnes quidem, sed præcipue humaniorum literarum studiosi, latine loquantur; atque hi memoriæ, quod a suis magistris præscriptum fuerit, commendent; ac stylum in compositionibus diligenter exerceant.

[443] *Studii tempus*

10. Ultra duas horas nemo aut legendo aut scribendo ad laborem incumbat, quin studium intermittat aliquantulo temporis intervallo.

[444] *Privati studii ratio*

11. Horis privato studio attributis, qui superioribus facultatibus dant operam, domi relegant, quæ scripserunt in scholis, eaque curent intelligere; et intellecta sic examinent, ut ipsi sibi obiiciant, et quæ obiecerint, solvant; quæ nequeunt, adnotent ad interrogandum vel disputandum.

[H32] Institutio Eorum Qui per Biennium Privato Studio Theologiam Repetunt

[445] *Quæ scholasticorum regulæ illis communes*

1. Scholasticorum regulas, præter eas, quæ ad lectiones in scholis audiendas, earumque repetitiones pertinent, non secus ac ceteri discipuli observent; præsertim vero ne studiorum fervore solidarum

[442] *Use of the Latin language*

9. Of course, everyone, but especially those pursuing the humanities, should speak in Latin. They should commit to memory what their teachers tell them to, and they should diligently practice their style in their compositions.

[443] *Time for study*

10. No one should devote more than two hours to work, either in reading or in writing, without interrupting this study for some small interval of time.

[444] *Plan for private study*

11. During the hours set aside for private study, those working at the more advanced subjects should read over at home what they have written in their classes, and they should make sure that they understand it. And what they understand they should probe in such a way that they even raise objections to themselves and resolve them. What they can not resolve they should note down for questioning or disputation.

[H32] The Training of Those Who Are Reviewing Theology in Private Study for Two Years

[445] *What rules they share with the students*

1. They should observe the rules for students no differently than the others receiving training, except for those rules that pertain to attending and reviewing classes. And they should especially make sure with all

virtutum amor intepescat, omni diligentia curent.

due diligence that their love of the essential virtues does not grow tepid from their intense interest in their academic pursuits.

[446] *Collationi casuum et disputationibus intersint*

2. Similiter, ut alii theologiæ auditores, collationi casuum, omnibus actibus et menstruis etiam eorum disputationibus intersint.

[446] *They should be present at the conference on cases and at the disputations*

2. In the same way, like the other students of theology, they should be present at the conference on cases, at all Acts, and also at their monthly disputations.

[447] *Argumenta quando resument*

3. In philosophorum autem disputationibus menstruis non solum interesse debebunt, sed poterunt etiam argumenta resumere; itemque in hebdomadariis theologorum, si magistri non adsint.

[447] *When they will enter into the discussions*

3. However, in the matter of the monthly disputations of the philosophers, not only should they be present, but they can even enter into the discussion. And the same goes for the weekly disputations of the theologians, if the teachers are not present.

[448] *Quæstiones omissæ vel compendio tractatæ*

4. Pro ratione studendi et distributione horarum a præfecto præscripta diligens et accuratum studium instituant earum materiarum, quas vel nullo modo, vel compendio audierunt, adhibitis commentariis eorum, qui eas diligentius pertractarunt.

[448] *Questions left out or treated in an abridgment*

4. In keeping with the plan of study and the schedule prescribed by the prefect, they should arrange a diligent and careful study of those matters that they have taken in class in an abridgment or not at all, employing the commentaries of those who have treated them in considerable detail.

[449] *Studium præcipuarum quæstionum*

5. Deinde studeant præcipuis disputationibus totius theologiæ, verbi gratia ex prima parte de visione, de scientia, de prædestinatione, de Trinitate, itemque ex aliis partibus, tum ea quæ ab aliis scripta sunt, diligenter perpendendo, tum proprio etiam ingenio ca-

[449] *Study of the main questions*

5. Then they should study the chief disputations of all of theology (for example, from Part I, about the Beatific Vision, about God's knowledge, about predestination, about Trinity, and likewise from the other parts), sometimes by studying the writings of others with attentive consideration, and sometimes by arrang-

pita quædam et principia theologiæ, unde præcipuarum quæstionum series pendeat, disponendo, servatis tamen quam diligentissime iis, quæ de doctrina Sancti Thomæ sequenda a Societate constituta sunt.

ing, even through the use of their own creative intelligence, certain headings and the chief points of theology on which the series of the main questions depends. They should accomplish this while still preserving as scrupulously as possible whatever has been formally established as what the Society ought to follow with respect to the teaching of Saint Thomas.

[450] *Scribendæ ex professo quæstiones*

6. Scribant ex instituto quæstiones aliquas cum suis fundamentis et conclusionibus, et obiectorum solutionibus more scholastico, perinde ac si ea prælegere in schola deberent, easque singulis vel alternis saltem mensibus præfecto studiorum ostendant, ut ab eo dirigantur.

[450] *Questions to be written in thorough detail*

6. Following a formally prescribed procedure, they should write some questions along with their essential principles and theses and some solutions to objections in the Scholastic manner, just as if they had to teach them in class, and every month, or at least every other month, they should show them to the prefect of studies, so that he might give them some direction.

[451] *Privatæ lectiones*

7. Habere etiam interdum poterunt eiusmodi lectiones vel privatim coram nostris doctoribus, vel in ipsis repetitionibus theologorum per tres circiter horæ quadrantes, ut ad extremum patres, qui adsunt, argumentari possint; vel denique, si videatur, in refectorio.

[451] *Private classes*

7. Sometimes, for about three-quarters of an hour, they can also give such classes either privately, in the presence of our academics, or in the theologians' reviews, so that at the very end the fathers who are present can engage in the argument; or finally, if it seems good, they can hold them in the dining hall.

[452] *Publicæ*

8. Consimiles quæstiones habere etiam poterunt de præclara aliqua materia, quæ denis ad summum prælectionibus absolvatur, in ea schola eoque tempore, ut qui voluerint theologi, convenire possint.

[452] *Public classes*

8. They can also give classes on the same type of questions about some well-known subject matter, which should be finished in ten classes at the most, in a class and at a time that will allow the theologians

who want to do so to gather to gether.

[453] *The Acts*

9. The time should be allotted for them to participate in four Special Acts and one General one. And certainly the first Special Act should usually take place near the beginning of the first semester, the second at the end; and from then on, the rest should be formally held this way every semester so that the General Act closes the final semester.

[454] *By what method they may defend their own opinions*

10. In the Acts, they should be free to depart from the opinions of their teachers, and to defend their own, if they would like, provided that they are in no way out of keeping with the teaching of Saint Thomas, in accordance with the decree of the Fifth Congregation. They should nevertheless do this in such a way that they come to a timely agreement with the prefect, and with the one who has to preside, concerning not only the opinions themselves, but also the foundations and the principles by which they want to defend them. In fact, so that they might give a better sample of their own intellectual powers, the presider should allow them to answer freely and not interrupt them, except for just when it is necessary.

[455] *Scholarly learning*

11. In sum, they should understand that in this two-year period they ought to make sure that they become thoroughly competent, not only in theology, but in all the

[453] *Actus*

9. Distribuatur illis tempus ad quatuor actus particulares et unum generalem habendum; et primus quidem particularis sub initium fere primi semestris, alter in fine; et sic deinceps singulis semestribus reliqui celebrentur, ita ut generalis ultimum semestre claudat.

[454] *Suas opiniones qua ratione licet defendere*

10. Liberum eis sit in actibus a magistrorum suorum sententiis discedere, suasque, si libeat, tueri, dummodo nulla ratione alienæ sint a S. Thomæ doctrina ex quintæ congregationis decreto; ita tamen, ut non solum de sententiis ipsis, sed etiam de fundamentis ac principiis, quibus eas tueri volunt, tempestive cum præfecto, eoque, qui præsidere debet, consentiant. Immo, quo melius sui ingenii specimen dent, sinet præses eos libere respondere, nec, nisi cum maxime necesse sit, interpellabit.

[455] *Eruditio*

11. Intelligant denique biennio hoc curandum sibi esse, ut non solum in theologia docti ac prompti, sed in omni etiam eccle-

siastica eruditione, quæ theologum maxime decet, evadant.

[456] *Concilia, controversiæ, canones*

12. Itaque singulis diebus certum tempus habeant ad accuratam Sacræ Scripturæ, conciliorum, controversiarum et canonum lectionem; et semper aliquo ordine notent, quæ notatu digna videbuntur; nihil tamen parent ad conciones ex professo; et ex hoc studio aliquid interdum prælegant vel in triclinio, vel alibi, prout superiori videbitur.

[457] *Canonum studium*

13. In canonum studio partem iudiciariam omittant, in ecclesiastica toti versentur.

[458] *Naturæ propensio attendenda*

14. Speciatim in id maxime studium incumbant, ad quod se magis propensos senserint, re diligenter cum superiore communicata; ita tamen, ut ex aliis, quæ præscribuntur, nullum omittant.

[H33] Regulæ Adiutoris Magistri sive Bidelli

[459] *Magistro obtemperet*

1. Huius munus erit omnia, quæ a magistro de scholarum potissimum exercitationibus iniuncta fuerint, diligenter exequi.

Church-related learning that theologians especially ought to have.

[456] *Councils, controversies, canons*

12. And so they should have a set time every day for a careful reading of Sacred Scripture, of the councils, of controversies, and of canons; and they should always take orderly notes on whatever seems worthy of this. Nevertheless, they should prepare nothing in detail for sermons; and from time to time they should give classes on something from this study either in the dining hall or elsewhere, as the superior thinks good.

[457] *Study of the canons*

13. In their study of the canons, they should leave out the judicial section, and concentrate entirely on the ecclesiastical material.

[458] *Natural inclination ought to be considered*

14. They should devote their study most particularly to that toward which they feel themselves more inclined, after carefully consulting with their superior on this matter. But they should still do this in such a way that they leave out none of the other things that are prescribed.

[H33] Rules for the Teacher's Assistant, or the Beadle

[459] *He should obey the teacher*

1. His task will be to diligently carry out whatever the teacher assigns, especially for the class exercises.

[460]   *Agenda circa scholam*

2. Curet, ut et classis et cathedra munda sit, ut in ea pie depicta aliqua tabella pendeat, ut subselliorum sit satis, ut munda eadem sint ac recte disposita, ut quassata vel fracta reficiantur, ut certa nostris scamna itemque aliis religiosis separata ab externis assignentur, ut scholæ tempestive aperiantur.

[461]   *Discipuli opportune monendi*

3. Eos opportune moneat, ad quos deinceps per vices disputare, repetere, theses defendere, aliaque huiusmodi præstare, ut constitutum a magistro fuerit, pertinebit.

[462]   *De conclusionibus*

4. Præmoneat septem fere ante diebus eos, qui hebdomadarias theses sunt defensuri. Curabit autem, ut eæ propositiones in tempore conscriptæ sint; eas vero primum ad magistrum perferet corrigendas, tum ad præfectum recognoscendas; quibus denique correctis atque recognitis, eum, qui defensurus est, admonebit, ut quot erunt opus exempla, descripta afferat; eorum autem unum bene descriptum pridie quam sit disputandum, mane publice affiget, reliqua disceptantibus deinde distribuet.

[460]   *Things to be done around the classroom*

2. He should see to it that the classroom and the teacher's chair are clean, that some holy picture hangs in the room, that there are enough seats, that these are clean and well arranged, that the ones that are shaky or broken are repaired, that particular benches set apart from non-Jesuits are assigned for Jesuits and likewise for other religious, and that the classrooms are opened on time.

[461]   *Students are to be reminded at the right time*

3. At the right time, he should remind those whose turn is coming up for disputing, reviewing, defending theses, and making other such presentations, as the teacher has decided.

[462]   *About the theses*

4. Usually about seven days in advance, he should remind those who are going to defend the weekly theses. He will make sure that the propositions have been written down for the occasion. First he should take them to the teacher for correction, and then to the prefect for review. When they have finally been corrected and reviewed, he will remind the one who is going to defend to bring along as many copies as are needed. On the morning of the day before the disputation, he will openly post one of them that has been nicely written out, and he will then distribute the rest to the disputants.

[463]   *Horologium*

5. Horologium tum in lectionibus, tum in disputationibus semper
habeat; ac tum præfectum tum
præceptorem tempestive temporis
elapsi admoneat, quo spatia ad
disputandum singulis præstituta
serventur; et ex præscripto præfecti signum det disputantibus tum
inchoandi, tum finiendi.

[463]   *Timepiece*

5. He should always have a timepiece, both in the classes and at the
disputations. And at a good moment,
he should bring to the attention of
the prefect and the teacher how
much time has passed, to ensure that
each person gets the formally allotted amount of time for his part of
the disputation. At the prefect's instruction, he should give the disputants the starting and ending signals.

[464]   *Publici actus*

Classem vel aulam ad publicos
actus iuxta academiarum consuetudinem ornandam curet; iisque, qui
ad huiusmodi actus aut ad quascunque disputationes invitati fuerint, sive argumentandi, sive eas
cohonestandi causa, loca distribuat.

[464]   *Public Acts*

6. He should take care to prepare
the classroom or the hall for the public Acts according to the academic
custom. He should arrange the places for those who have been invited
to such Acts or to disputations of any
sort, either to take part in the argument or to honor them with their
presence.

[465]   *Quod ad Superiorem
deferendum*

7. Si quem nostrorum abesse a
prælectionibus, repetitionibus, disputationibus, aut aliquid eorum
omittere, quæ ad studiorum rationem, vel morum disciplinam pertinent, notaverit, ad superiorem de-
feret.

[465]   *What should be reported to the
superior*

7. If he notices that any Jesuit has
missed lessons, reviews, disputations,
or left out anything pertaining to the
plan of studies or to moral behavior,
he should report this to the superior.

[H34] Regulæ Externorum Auditorum Societatis

[H34] Rules for Non-Jesuit Students

[466]   *Doctrina pietati iungenda*

1. Qui discendi causa Societatis
Iesu gymnasia frequentant, intelligant, Deo iuvante non minus cura-
tum iri pro viribus, ut pietate ceterisque virtutibus, quam ut ingenuis
artibus imbuantur.

[466]   *Learning should be joined with
devotion*

1. Those who attend Jesuit academic institutions to get an education should realize that, with God's
help, there will be no less intense an
effort to steep them in devotion and

the other virtues than there will be to steep them in the liberal arts.

[467] *Quæ cuiusque schola*

2. Eam quisque classem frequentabit, quæ illi post examen a præfecto fuerit assignata.

[467] *Which class for each one*

2. Each person will attend that class to which he has been assigned by the prefect after the examination.

[468] *Confessio et missa*

3. Singulis saltem mensibus omnes peccata confiteantur; ac missæ sacrificio quotidie constituta hora, concioni vero diebus festis decenter intersint.

[468] *Confession and Mass*

3. At least once a month, everyone should confess his sins. At the appointed time and in an appropriate manner, they should attend the sacrifice of the Mass every day, and the sermon on feast days.

[469] *Doctrina christiana*

4. Explicationi catechismi singulis hebdomadis omnes intersint, eiusque compendium ediscant, ut a magistris fuerit constitutum.

[469] *Christian teaching*

4. Each week everyone should attend the catechism instruction and learn by heart the abridgment that the teachers have drawn up for it.

[470] *Arma in scholam non inferenda*

5. Nemo ex nostris discipulis gymnasium cum armis, gladiolis, cultris, aut aliis eiusmodi, quæ pro locis aut temporibus interdicta fuerint, ingrediatur.

[470] *Weapons should not be brought into the classroom*

5. No student of ours should set foot in the school with weapons, swords, knives, or other things like this, which have been forbidden for the places or times involved.

[471] *A quibus, abstinendum*

6. Abstineant omnino a iureiurando, a contumeliis, iniuriis, detractionibus, mendaciis, a ludis vetitis, a locis etiam noxiis, vel a præfecto scholarum interdictis; denique a rebus omnibus, quæ morum honestati adversentur.

[471] *From what they ought to abstain*

6. They should abstain altogether from swearing, and from verbal abuse, violent behavior, speaking badly of others, and lying; and from forbidden games; and also from places that are harmful or forbidden by the class prefect; and finally, from whatever conflicts with moral integrity.

[472] *Corrector ut adhibendus*

7. Intelligant, in iis, quæ ad mores ac studia bonarum artium spectant, cum præcepta sive admonitiones minus proderunt, magistros correctoris opera in ipsis puniendis

[472] *How a disciplinarian should be employed*

7. They should realize that their teachers are going to employ the service of a disciplinarian to punish them in those matters that bear on

usuros; qui aut pænas recusarint, aut spem emendationis non ostenderint, aut ceteris molesti, sive exemplo suo perniciosi fuerint, sciant se ex nostris scholis esse dimittendos.

morals and the study of the liberal arts, when rules or warnings have not done very much good. The ones who either refuse punishment, or do not show hope of correction, or harass the others, or exert a harmful influence by their example should realize that they are going to be dismissed from our schools.

[473] *Obedientia*

8. Omnes suis quisque magistris obtemperent; rationem vero studendi ab illis præscriptam, tum in scholis tum domi quam diligentissime servent.

[473] *Obedience*

8. Everyone should be obedient, each to his own teacher. Everyone should follow the study plan prescribed by his teacher both in classes and at home as diligently as possible.

[474] *Diligentia et assiduitas*

9. Serio animum ad studia et constanter adiiciant; sint in scholis mature frequentandis assidui, in audiendis et recolendis prælectionibus, ceterisque obeundis exercitationibus diligentes. Quod si quid minus assequantur, aut si quid dubitent, magistrum consulant.

[474] *Diligence and regular attendance*

9. They should earnestly and steadily apply their minds to their studies. They should attend school regularly and on time, diligently taking and reviewing the classes and engaging in all the other exercises as well. But if they do not quite get something or if they have any questions, they should go to the teacher for help.

[475] *Quies et silentium*

10. In scholis ne hac illa divagentur, sed in suis quisque subselliis locisque modeste ac silentio sibi ac suis rebus intenti sint; neque schola egrediantur, nisi facta a magistro exeundi potestate. Ne scamna, cathedram, sellas, parietes, ianuas, fenestras, neque aliud quidpiam pingendo, scribendo, scalpello, aliave ratione deturpent seu notent.

[475] *Quiet and silence*

10. They should not move around here and there in class, but they should stay in their own seats and places, focused calmly and silently on themselves and their own work. And they should not leave school unless permission to leave has been given by the teacher. They should not deface or mark benches, the chair, seats, walls, doors, windows, or anything else with drawing, with writing, with a pen knife, or in any other way.

[476] *Quæ fugiendæ consuetudines*

11. Pravas aut etiam suspectas aliorum consuetudines fugiant; cum iis tantummodo versentur, quorum exemplo et consuetudine in literarum studio virtutumque proficiant.

[477] *A quibus libris abstinendum*

12. A libris perniciosis et inutilibus legendis prorsus abstineant.

[478] *Spectacula et scenæ interdicantur*

13. Neque ad publica spectacula, comædias, ludos, neque ad supplicia reorum, nisi forte hæreticorum, eant; neque personam ullam in externorum scenis agant, nisi data prius a magistris vel a præfecto gymnasii potestas.

[479] *Pietas*

14. Sincerum animum purumque conservare, ac divinis legibus summa diligentia obtemperare nitantur; Deo vero ac sanctissimæ Virgini Deiparæ, ceterisque sanctis persæpe atque ex animo se commendant. Angelorum opem assidue, præcipue vero angeli custodis, implorent. Modestiam tum alibi semper, tum in templo atque in schola potissimum servent.

[480] *Vitæ exemplum*

15. In rebus denique atque actionibus omnibus ita se gerant, ut facile quivis intelligat, eos non minus virtutum vitæque integritatis esse, quam literarum doctrinæque studiosos.

[476] *What company they should avoid*

11. They should avoid bad or even suspect company. They should spend time only with those whose example and companionship help them make progress in their academics and in their pursuit of the virtues.

[477] *From what books to abstain*

12. They should altogether abstain from reading harmful and useless books.

[478] *Shows and plays forbidden*

13. They should not go to public shows, comedies, or plays, or to the punishments of criminals, except perhaps heretics. And they should not play any role in the stage productions of non-Jesuits, unless permission has first been given by their teachers or by the school's prefect.

[479] *Religious devotion*

14. They should strive to keep their minds pure and spotless and to obey God's laws with the utmost diligence. They should very frequently and with complete sincerity commend themselves to God and to the most holy Virgin mother of God, and to the other saints. They should continually beg the help of the angels, especially of their guardian angels. They should observe modesty always when they are elsewhere, and especially when they are in church and in class.

[480] *The example of their lives*

15. In sum, they should behave in all matters and undertakings in such a way that anyone might easily perceive that they are no less passionately concerned about the virtues

and about the integrity of their lives than about academics and learning.

[H35] Regulæ Academiæ

[481] *Academia quid*

1. Academiæ nomine intelligimus cætum studiosorum, ex omnibus scholasticis delectum, qui aliquo ex nostris præfecto conveniunt, ut peculiares quasdam habeant exercitationes ad studia pertinentes.

[482] *Qui admittendi*

2. Hoc ex numero omnes censentur, qui sunt ex congregatione B. Virginis eo ipso, quod in illam recipiuntur; et religiosi, si qui nostras scholas frequentant. Ceterum, ubi mos tulerit, et rectori videatur, alii etiam admitti poterunt, qui ex congregatione, atque adeo qui ex nostris scholasticis non sint.

[483] *Academici quales*

3. Academicos christiana virtute ac pietate, diligentia in studiis et scholarum legibus servandis ceteris omnibus discipulis præstare et exemplo esse oportet.

[484] *Academiæ moderatores*

4. Collegii rector moderatorem vel ex ipsis magistris, vel ex aliis nostris idoneum aliquem unicuique academiæ præficiet.

[485] *Quotuplex academiæ*

5. In unam academiam theologi et philosophi fere convenire poterunt; in alteram rhetores et humanistæ; in tertiam omnes grammati-

[H35] Rules for Academies

[481] *What an academy is*

1. By the term academy, we understand a group of committed students, chosen from the entire student body, who join together under the charge of a Jesuit to hold certain special exercises pertaining to studies.

[482] *Who should be admitted*

2. Included in this group are all those who are members of the Sodality of the Blessed Virgin, by virtue of their acceptance into it, and also religious, if any attend our classes. But, where the custom supports it and it seems good to the rector, others can also be admitted—those who do not belong to the Sodality and even those who are not students of ours.

[483] *The qualities that the members of an academy should have*

3. Members of an academy ought to serve as good examples and lead all the other students in Christian virtue and religious devotion, in diligence in their studies, and in keeping the class rules.

[484] *Moderators of the academy*

4. The rector of the college should put some suitable person, either one of the teachers or one of the other Jesuits, in charge of each academy.

[485] *How many kinds of academies*

5. The theologians and the philosophers can usually be grouped into one academy; into a second, the rhetoricians and humanities students;

ci, si nec nimis multi sint, nec ita doctrina inæquales, ut eædem exercitationes omnibus fructuosæ esse non possint; alioquin singulis scholis suas academias habere liceat.

into a third, all the grammar students, if they are neither so overly numerous nor so disparate in learning that the same exercises can not be profitable for all of them; otherwise, each class may have its own academy.

[486] *Assiduitas et exercitatio*

6. Assiduitate academicorum et exercitationum fervore academiæ fructus maxime continetur. Quare, si qui sæpius abessent, aut exercitationes per vices obire recusarent, præsertim vero, qui propter immodestiam perturbationi aliis aut offensioni essent, dimittendi erunt.

[486] *Constant attendance and exercise*

6. The profit of an academy derives especially from the regular attendance of the members and from the vitality of their exercises. For this reason, if any are too often absent or refuse to take their turns in the exercises, or especially if any bother or offend others on account of a lack of self-control, they ought to be dismissed.

[487] *Magistratus*

7. Magistratus, qui in unaquaque academia tertio quartove quoque mense pluribus academicorum, secretisque suffragiis eligentur, hi ferme erunt: academiæ rector, duo consiliarii et unus secretarius; quibus alii etiam addi poterunt, muneraque distribui pro academicorum frequentia, loci consuetudine et rectoris collegii iudicio.

[487] *Officers*

7. Officers will be chosen by secret ballot in each academy every three or four months by a plurality of the members. They will usually include the rector of the academy, two counselors and one secretary.[180] Others can also be added to these, and their duties distributed in proportion to the size of the group, the local custom, and the judgment of the rector of the college.

[488] *Rector*

8. Rector in academia theologorum plerumque sıt theologus; quod si interdum ex philosophis eligendus videretur, sit saltem metaphysicus. In academia item rhetorum et grammaticorum, quando ex diversis classibus constant, vel plerumque eligatur ex classe superiore, vel alternis, ut collegii

[488] *Rector*

8. For the most part, the rector in the academy of theologians should be a theologian; but if it sometimes seems good to pick one of the philosophers, he should be at least a metaphysician. Likewise in the academy of rhetoricians and grammar students, when they come from different classes, the rector should be

---

[180] The rector of the study circle would probably be called its "president" in contemporary organizations.

rector censuerit. Is autem eligendus, qui virtute, ingenio et doctrina præstet; cuius erit academiam
promovere, præire ceteris virtute
ac diligentia, et actum aliquem ex
præcipuis academiæ vel initio vel
in fine rectoratus habere. Poterit
autem rector academiæ theologorum interdum, si sit theologus,
absente magistro, philosophos defendentes dirigere, et argumentan-
tium argumenta resumere et urgere.

chosen either from the higher class
for the most part, or in alternation,
as the rector of the college has decided. That one who is preeminent
in virtue, intellectual talent, and
learning ought to be selected. It is up
to him to motivate the academy, to
lead the others in virtue and diligence, and to participate in some Act
based on the principal activities of
the academy either at the beginning
or at the end of his period as rector.
The rector of the academy of theologians can sometimes, if he is a theologian, direct the philosophers who
are defending theses when the teacher is absent, and take up and press
the arguments of those who are
making them.

[489] *Consiliarii*

9. Consiliarii erunt rectori loco
et honore proximi, eiusque absen-
tis vices primus consiliarius tene-
bit, priore etiam absente secundus;
eaque munera obibunt, quæ moderator academiæ per se aut per
rectorem imponet.

[489] *Counselors*

9. The counselors will have a position and status next to the rector's.
The first counselor will take his place
when he is absent, and the second
will do so when the first is also absent. They will undertake the duties
that the moderator of the academy
imposes, either on his own or
through the rector.

[490] *Secretarius*

10. Secretarius libros omnes
academiæ diligenter servabit. Nomina academicorum eo ordine,
quo in academiam recipiuntur, in
libro scribet; in quem etiam seorsim nomina magistratuum, cum
eliguntur, et omnia academiæ acta,
non tacitis academicorum, qui aliquid præstiterint, nominibus, refe-
ret; rhetorum etiam orationes, poemata et carmina, quæ affiguntur, a
moderatore selecta. Idem tempestive eos, ut se comparent, admone-

[490] *Secretary*

10. The secretary will carefully
keep all the books of the academy.
He will register in a book the names
of the members in the order in
which they are received into the
academy. He will also separately register in it the names of the officers,
when they are chosen, and all the
Acts of the academy, including the
names of the members who have
distinguished themselves in some
way. He will also list the rhetoricians' compositions, poems, and lyr-

bit, quos a moderatore cognoverit academiæ exercitationes obituros, nisi in academia theologorum necesse videatur id fieri per bidellum. In fine cuiusque academiæ publice pronunciabit, quænam exercitationes et a quibus habendæ sint. Publice theses et in rhetorica etiam problemata, vel ænigmata dissolvenda mature proponet.

ics chosen by the moderator and posted. Likewise, he will remind in good time those that he learns from the moderator are going to engage in the exercises of the academy to get ready, unless it seems necessary in the theologians' academy for this to be done through the beadle. At the end of each group meeting he will publicly announce what exercises are to be held and by whom. Also, allowing sufficient advance time, he will present the group with the theses and rhetorical problems and any riddles to be solved.

[491] *Consultationes*

11. Ter aut quater in anno, videlicet post creationem rectoris, consultationes, vel omnium academicorum, vel saltem magistratuum simul cum moderatore habebuntur ad academiam promovendam, eaque tollenda, quæ eius progressum impedire videantur.

[491] *Consultations*

11. Three or four times a year, certainly after the appointment of the rector, there shall be consultations, either of all the members of the academy, or at least of the officials together with the moderator, to move the academy forward, and to eliminate whatever seems to be impeding its progress.

[492] *Regularum lectio*

12. Vel in his consultationibus, vel ante creationem rectoris, academiæ regulæ legantur; quæ vel in tabella scriptæ sint, vel in libro academiæ, in quo etiam omnia deinceps academicorum nomina scribenda erunt.

[492] *The reading of the rules*

12. Either in these consultations or before the appointment of the rector, the rules of the academy should be read. These should be written on a placard or in the academy's record book, which also is to contain all the names of the members in sequence.

[H36] Regulæ Præfecti Academiæ

[493] *Ad pietatem promovendi*

1. Ad pietatem academicos, non solum ad studia promoveat; quod virtutum exemplo et privatis, cum tulerit occasio, colloquiis præstare poterit.

[H36] Rules for the Prefect of an Academy

[493] *Their religious devotion ought to be encouraged*

1. He should urge the members forward in religious devotion, not just in studies. He will be able to achieve this by his example and by

private conversations when the occasion arises.

[494] *Regularum observatio*

2. Academiæ regulas diligenter servari curet, imprimisque academicorum quotidianis exercitationibus assiduitatem ac diligentiam exigat.

[495] *Exercitatio*

3. Efficiat, ut omnes academici variis exercitationum generibus, quantum fieri potest, per vices exerceantur.

[496] *Nil sine superiore innovandum*

4. Nec receptas consuetudines tollat, nec novas introducat sine facultate rectoris; nec quicquam faciat, quod alicuius momenti sit, quod non cum ipso communicet; et quæ præscripta fuerint, diligenter exequetur.

[497] *Academiæ tempus*

5. Horas academiæ, repetitionum scilicet, disputationum et similium ita dispenset, ut horas congregationis non impediant, quo academici commode possint utrisque exercitationibus interesse; quam etiam ob rem nullus erit sine magna causa congregationis tempore privatis colloquiis detinendus.

[494] *Keeping the rules*

2. He should carefully see to it that the rules of the academy are followed, and above all, he should demand regular attendance and diligence in the daily exercises of the members.

[495] *Exercise*

3. He should have all the members of the academy practice the different kinds of exercises in turn, as far as this is possible.

[496] *No innovations should be introduced without the superior*

4. He should not suspend the traditional customs, nor should he introduce new ones without permission from the rector; nor should he do anything that is of any importance without consulting him about it. He should diligently carry out what has been prescribed.

[497] *Time for the academy*

5. He should so arrange the academy's hours, namely, the reviews, disputations, and the like, that they do not conflict with the times for assemblies, so that the members can conveniently attend both exercises. For this same reason, no one should be held back for private conferences at an assembly time without a very good reason.

[H37] Regulæ Academiæ Theologorum et Philosophorum

[498] *Quæ exercitationes*

1. Huius academiæ exercitationes quatuor fere generum esse solent: quotidianæ prælectionum repetitiones, disputationes, prælectiones seu problemata, solemniores actus, quibus conclusiones publice defendantur.

[499] *Repetitiones*

2. Repetitiones per horam circiter singulis fient, quibus scholæ habentur, diebus; iis exceptis, qui menstrua disputatione impediuntur; ea vero fient hora, quæ commodissima videbitur, modo in Quadragesima liberum concionis tempus saltem bis in hebdomada relinquatur.

[500] *Repetitionum forma*

3. Repetent seorsim singulæ classes, una theologiæ et tres philosophiæ, si totidem sint præceptores, uno aut altero academicorum audita recolente, uno etiam aut altero argumentantibus. Ac theologiæ quidem repetitionibus præerit ipse præfectus academiæ, aut eius socius, aut certe alius ex provectioribus quarti fere anni theologus, a rectore collegii constitutus; philosophiæ vero repetitionibus in singulis classibus aliquis item præerit ex nostris fere theologus; quem idem rector designaverit.

[H37] Rules for the Academy of Theologians and Philosophers

[498] *What exercises*

1. The exercises of this academy generally ought to belong to four categories: daily reviews of the lessons; disputations; lessons or problems; and Acts that are more formal than usual, at which theses are publicly defended.

[499] *Reviews*

2. Except for those that conflict with the monthly disputation, reviews will take place for about an hour on each school day. They will be held at the time that seems most convenient, but in Lent the time should be left free for a sermon at least twice a week.

[500] *The structure of the reviews*

3. The individual classes, one of theology and three of philosophy, should review separately, if there are the same number of teachers, having one or two of the members going over what was given in class, and one or two engaging in argumentation. And the prefect of the academy himself or his assistant or one of the more advanced theologians, usually from the fourth year, appointed by the rector of the college, will be in charge of the theology reviews. But usually a Jesuit theologian whom the rector has designated will likewise be in charge of the philosophy reviews in the individual classes.

[501]   *Disputationum forma*

4. Disputationes erunt aut semel, ubi pauci sunt academici, aut, ubi sunt multi, bis in hebdomada, scilicet die vacationis aut etiam dominico. Ac die quidem dominico a prandio per horam unus, ut plurimum, ex philosophis defendet duobus argumentantibus; die vero vacationis per duas horas duo tresve defendent, unus theologus, alii philosophi, totidem similiter aut pluribus argumentantibus.

[502]   *Conclusiones*

5. Theologus si solus defendat, conclusiones semper aliquas philosophicas proponet, metaphysicus physicas et logicas, physicus etiam logicas. Argumentabuntur contra theologos theologi, contra philosophos primo loco semper aliquis ex classe proxime superiore, secundo unus ex condiscipulis.

[503]   *Disputationibus quis præsideat*

6. Disputationibus tam philosophicis quam theologicis, si intersit proprius defendentis magister, ipsius erit præsidere; sin minus, præsidebit præfectus academiæ aut eius socius.

[504]   *Prælectiones*

7. Prælectiones etiam interdum haberi poterunt, quibus quæstionem aliquam suo marte perfectam, vel ingeniosum problema, expositis in utramque partem confirmatisque rationibus, aliquis academico-

[501]   *The structure of the disputations*

4. The disputations will be held either once a week, where there are few members, or twice where there are many, namely, on the break day or also on Sunday. And on Sunday after the midday meal, typically one of the philosophers will defend for an hour, with two raising objections. But on the break day, two or three will defend for two hours, one a theologian, the others philosophers, with the same number or more raising objections.

[502]   *Theses*

5. If a theologian defends alone, he will always propose some philosophical theses, a metaphysician will propose some from physics and logic, and a natural philosopher will also propose some from logic. Theologians will bring objections against theologians. Someone from the group just above his own will always raise objections against the philosophers in the first place, and in the second, one of his classmates will.

[503]   *Who should preside over the disputations*

6. If the teacher of the one defending is in attendance, it will be his part to preside over the disputations, both for philosophical and for theological ones; if not, the prefect of the academy or his assistant will preside.

[504]   *Lessons*

7. Sometimes lessons can also be given for which a member occupying the teacher's chair should treat in a scholarly manner some question or a clever problem that he has fully prepared without any assistance, the

rum ex cathedra erudite pertractet, uno aut altero argumentante. Huiusmodi autem prælectiones necesse erit præfecto academiæ, priusquam habeantur, ostendi ac probari.

[505] *Actus*

8. Solemniores actus ipse academiæ rector, nisi quid obstet, aut alius a præfecto delectus, interdum habere poterit; Natalis videlicet, Paschatis, Pentecostes aut alio opportuno tempore; quibus actibus certam aliquam theologiæ aut philosophiæ materiam, aliquibus conclusionibus comprehensam, defendent, magistro præsidente.

[506] *Actuum celebritas*

9. Hi actus, ut cum aliquo apparatu fiant, curandum; adhibeatur autem a defendente præfatio aliqua et epilogus, quæ prius sint (ut cetera, quæ publice recitantur) a generali studiorum præfecto recognita et approbata. Externi etiam ad argumentandum, aliique poterunt ad audiendum, quo disputatio celebrior sit, invitari.

[507] *Introductio*

10. Uno circiter ante studiorum renovationem mense, si rectori videatur, per quindecim minimum dies iis, qui philosophiam audituri sunt, introductio vel summa ab aliquo ex nostris, quem rector, vel

arguments being laid out and supported on both sides, with one or two members raising objections. It will be necessary, however, that lessons like this be shown to the prefect of the academy and approved before they are given.

[505] *Acts*

8. Unless something prevents it, the rector of the academy himself, or another person chosen by the prefect, can hold more formal Acts from time to time, namely, at Christmas, at Easter, at Pentecost, or at some other suitable time. For these Acts, they shall defend some set theological or philosophical subject matter, expressed in thesis form, with the teacher presiding.

[506] *The Acts as grand events*

9. Care should be taken that these Acts are put on with some formal display. The one defending should present some preface and final summary that have first been reviewed and approved by the general prefect of studies (like other material that is read out publicly). Outsiders can also be invited to participate in the argumentation, and others can be invited to hear it, in order to increase the attendance at the disputation and to make it a more important event.

[507] *Introduction*

10. About one month before the formal reopening of studies, if it seems good to the rector, a Jesuit picked by the rector or perhaps a member picked by the prefect should present an introduction or general overview for at least fifteen days to

forte ex academicis, quem præfectus statuerit, explicetur.

[508] *Conclusiones recognoscendæ*

11. Conclusiones omnes tam solemniorum actuum, quam etiam hebdomadariæ priusquam defendantur aut affigantur, erunt et a præfecto academiæ et a proprio defendentis magistro recognoscendæ.

[H38] Regulæ Præfecti Academiæ Theologorum et Philosophorum

[509] *Exercitationum forma*

1. Præter communia, quæ de præfecto in universum dicta sunt in regulis academiæ, illud etiam animadvertat, ut in quotidianis repetitionibus eadem repetendi et argumentandi, eadem disputandi forma modusque servetur, quem nostri in domesticis repetitionibus tenent; in actibus vero et aliis conclusionibus defendendis consueta ratio teneatur.

[510] *Visitandæ repetitiones*

2. Visitet proinde sæpe repetitiones, nunc has nunc illas; videatque, ut diligenter ac modeste fiant, et ut repetitores recte suo officio fungantur; quos etiam, ut oportuerit, diriget.

[511] *Qui magis exercendi*

3. Non erit ab re eos exerceri sæpius quam alios, qui proxime sunt cursum philosophiæ vel theo-

those who are going to study philosophy.

[508] *Theses to be reviewed*

11. Before they are defended or posted, all the theses of both the more formal Acts and the weekly ones ought to be examined by the prefect of the academy and by the teacher of the one defending.

[H38] Rules for the Prefect of the Academy of Theologians and Philosophers

[509] *Structure of the exercises*

1. In addition to the common points that were stated generally in the rules for the academy, he should also see to it that in the daily reviews, the same structure and manner of reviewing, of raising objections, and of holding disputations that Jesuits keep in their in-house reviews should be maintained. In the Acts and in the defense of other theses, the customary procedure should be kept.

[510] *The review sessions should be visited*

2. Accordingly, he should often visit the reviews, sometimes these, sometimes those. And he should see that they are being conducted with diligence and restraint, and that the reviewers are performing their task correctly. He should also give them direction, as need be.

[511] *Who should get more practice*

3. There will be a point to having some members practice more frequently than the others: namely,

logiæ defensuri, vel aliquem academiæ actum habituri; quos etiam ad hunc finem, ut instructiores sint, monebit et diriget.

those who are coming up next to defend the philosophical or theological course, or who are going to participate in some Act for the academy. He will also advise and guide these members for the purpose of getting them better prepared.

[512] *De socio*

4. Cum socio, si a rectore dabitur, ita poterit curam laboremque partiri, ut ei, nisi quid obstet, theologiæ repetitiones committat; et cum eo, si videbitur, alternis diebus præsertim vacationis disputationibus præsideat; ceteraque per eum ad quotidianas conclusiones et extraordinarios actus spectantia, prout necesse iudicaverit, exequatur.

[512] *About the assistant*

4. He can share the responsibility and work with an assistant, if the rector gives him one, in such a way that he entrusts him with the reviews of theology, unless anything prevents this. And if it seems good, the assistant should preside with him on alternate days, especially at the disputations on the break day. Just as the academy prefect judges necessary, he should carry out through the assistant whatever has to do with the daily theses and the Acts not regularly scheduled.

[H39] Regulæ Academiæ Rhetorum et Humanistarum

[513] *Academiæ dies*

1. Diebus dominicis, vel ubi commodius erit, die vacationis convenient loco a rectore collegii designato.

[514] *Quæ exercitationes moderatori habendæ*

2. Exercitationes huius academiæ hæ fere erunt: moderator, prout opportunum iudicaverit, nunc lectiones seu quæstiones habebit de selecta aliqua materia vel auctore; nunc præcepta aliqua dicendi magis recondita ex Aristo-

[H39] Rules for the Academies of Rhetoricians and Humanities Students

[513] *Day for the academy*

1. On Sundays, or on the break day where it is more convenient, they will meet in a place designated by the rector of the college.

[514] *What exercises are to be held by the moderator*

2. The exercises of this academy will generally include the following: Just as he judges the time to be right, the moderator will at some times give lessons or present questions on some chosen material or author; or at other times, he will give some rather

tele, Cicerone aliisve rhetoribus tradet; nunc aliquem auctorem percurret et ab academicis exiget; nunc iisdem problemata solvenda proponet, et alia huiusmodi.

unfamiliar rules for speaking taken from Aristotle, Cicero, or other rhetoricians; or again at other times, he will quickly cover some author and ask the members of the academy questions about that material; and at other times, he will set them problems to be solved, and the like.

[515]   *Quæ academicis*

3. Sæpe etiam, his omissis, academici ipsi nunc orationes, nunc carmina, nunc declamationes habeant vel memoriter vel ex tempore; nunc invicem accusationes et defensiones ipso probante instituant; nunc lectiones habeant, duobus minimum adversus lectorem disputantibus; nunc theses defendant oppugnentque oratorio magis more, quam dialectico; nunc emblemata et insignia de certa aliqua materia componant; nunc inscriptiones aut descriptiones; nunc ænigmata faciant aut dissolvant; nunc in inventione se exerceant singuli, ad propositam materiam confirmationis locos excogitantes, sive improviso seu meditato; nunc in elocutione figuras verborum ac sententiarum inventæ rei accommodantes; nunc dialogorum, poematum, tragædiarum argumenta conscribant; nunc integram præclari oratoris orationem aut pætæ carmen imitentur; nunc symbola quædam faciant, ut scilicet de una re proposita singulis suam sententiam afferant; nunc distributis alicuius auctoris libris singuli ex eo sententias vel phrases decerptas proferant. Denique in iis

[515]   *What exercises should be held by the members of the academy*

3. The members of the academy themselves should also often skip such exercises and sometimes deliver speeches, sometimes poems, sometimes declamations either from memory or spontaneously; sometimes they should engage in speeches for the prosecution and for the defense in turn, with the moderator's approval; sometimes they should present classes, with at least two in disputation against the presenter; sometimes they should defend theses, arguing in a manner that is more oratorical than dialectical; sometimes they should fashion emblems and insignia on some designated subject matter; sometimes inscriptions or descriptions; sometimes they should contrive riddles or solve them; sometimes they should practice invention one at a time, coming up with *loci* to support a proposed theme, whether on the spot or after some study time; sometimes they should practice elocution by suiting figures of language or thought to the material that has been found;[181] sometimes they should sketch dialogs, poems, or tragedies; sometimes they should imitate a whole oration by an illustri-

---

[181] [T]he material that has been found: see the note on §382 above. Invention is "finding out what one could or should say." "The material found" is what results from this process.

se exerceant, quæ eloquentiam gignere, et ab ea enasci solent.

ous orator, or a poem by a famous poet; sometimes they should construct certain symbols, in such a way that they produce their own sayings about a single topic that has been proposed for everyone individually; sometimes, after the books of some author have been distributed, they should each produce sayings or phrases gleaned from it. Finally they should practice whatever usually gives rise to eloquence and is produced by it.

[516] *Publicæ exercitationes*

4. Harum exercitationum aliquæ splendidiores, ut prælectiones, declamationes, thesium defensiones operæ pretium est, præsertim a rectore academiæ, fieri cum apparatu interdum aliquo et corona.

[516] *Public exercises*

4. It is worthwhile to have some of the more impressive of these exercises (such as the lessons, declamations, and defenses of theses) presented especially by the rector of the academy, occasionally [this being done] with some formal ceremony and [before] a circle of guests.

[517] *Præmia privata*

5. Privata interdum præmia melius aliquid scribentibus aut recitantibus, aut ænigmata problemataque solventibus dari poterunt.

[517] *Private awards*

5. Sometimes private awards can be given to those distinguishing themselves in composition or recitation or in solving riddles and problems.

[518] *Præmia publica*

6. Præmia item solemniora omnibus simul academicis semel in anno distribui poterunt, sive ex contributione, sive qua magis ratione rectori collegii placebit.

[518] *Public awards*

6. Likewise, the more formal awards can be distributed to all the members together once a year, whether on the basis of a grant, or according to whatever scheme the rector of the college likes.

[519] *Festum B. Virginis dies*

7. Semel saltem in anno festus aliquis Beatæ Virginis dies, quem collegii rector determinabit, celebri pompa orationis, poematis, versuum ad parietes affixorum, emblematum item et insignium variorum exornabitur.

[519] *Feast day of the Blessed Virgin*

7. At least once a year, some feast day of the Blessed Virgin to be determined by the rector of the college will be celebrated with a full and formal ceremony consisting of a speech, a poem, and verses posted on the walls, and likewise emblems and various insignia.

[H40] Regulæ Academiæ Grammaticorum

[520] *Grammaticæ exercitatio*

1. Plerumque moderator aliquid selectum ex grammatica, quasi præcurrens, quod in schola sunt habituri, vel ex auctore eleganti et iucundo præleget, vel etiam repetitionem instituet, exercitationemque eorum, quæ in schola exposita sunt.

[521] *Repetitio*

2. Initio academiæ semper unus paratus veniet ad respondendum de iis, quæ proxima academia dicta fuerint; adversus quem terni aut plures dubitationes aut vernaculas locutiones latine vertendas proponere poterunt, eodemque modo prælectionem a moderatore habitam statim recolent.

[522] *Disputatio*

3. Frequenter et acriter disputabitur, exercebitur interdum stylus, interdum memoria; variabuntur phrases, aliquid etiam ex versibus et græca grammatica proponetur et alia fient huiusmodi, ex præscripto moderatoris.

[523] *Memoria*

4. Aliqui interdum, aut etiam omnes, parati venient ad aliquod apophthegma breve, vel factum aliquod memoriter enarrandum.

[H40] Rules for the Academy of Grammar Students

[520] *Grammar practice*

1. Usually the moderator should give a lesson on something chosen from the grammar, or something from an elegant and pleasant author, in a way previewing what they are going to have in class, or he should organize a review of and an exercise on what has been presented in class.

[521] *Review*

2. At the beginning of the meeting, one member will always come prepared to answer questions about what was said at the previous meeting. Against him, three or more can pose questions or suggest vernacular expressions to be translated into Latin, and in the same manner they will immediately go over the lesson given by the moderator.

[522] *Disputation*

3. There should be keen and frequent disputations. Sometimes there will be exercises in style, sometimes in memory; expressions will be varied, and also something will be proposed from verse and from Greek grammar. And other similar activities will take place, at the moderator's instruction.

[523] *Memory*

4. Occasionally, some members or even all of them will come prepared to recount some short apothegm or some deed from memory.

[524] *Prælectiones privatæ*

5. Prælectiones ipsas in schola habitas a præceptore, addita præfatiuncula, et aliqua, si videbitur, annotatione, e suggestu interdum dicent.

[525] *Publicæ*

6. Operæ pretium erit haberi interdum aliquas prælectiones ab academicis, præsertim a rectore apparatu invitatuque maiore, addita concertatione duorum aut trium, privatis etiam præmiis, si libeat, distributis.

[526] *Pœnæ literariæ*

7. Poterit a moderatore pœnæ loco aliquid literarium exigi, iuberique, ut eorum nomina, qui minus bene aut diligenter se gesserint, publice recitentur.

[527] *Exercitationum varietas*

8. Eæ denique exercitationes proponi et variari debent, quæ ita utilitatem habeant adiunctam, ut gratæ etiam et decoræ sint, quo magis ea voluptate academicorum animi ad studia incitentur.

[524] *Private lessons*

5. They will sometimes deliver from the platform the same lessons given by the teacher in class, with the addition of a short preface and some comment, if it seems proper.

[525] *Public lessons*

6. It will be worthwhile for members, especially the rector, to give some lessons occasionally, with more of a show and a bigger audience,[182] with the addition of a competition between two or three members, and even the distribution of private awards, if desired.

[526] *Literary punishments*

7. Some literary work can be required by the moderator as a punishment, and he can tell someone to read out for everyone to hear the names of those who have not conducted themselves as well or diligently as they should have.

[527] *The variety of exercises*

8. In sum, the exercises that are proposed and varied ought to be ones that are not only useful but also pleasant and attractive, so that the enjoyment that they bring might more deeply inspire the members' interest in their studies.

---

[182] [E]specially by the rector: that is, by the leader of the group.

Appendix 1

RATIO STUDIORUM TIMELINE

1491   Ignatius is born to a noble Basque family in Guipúzcoa, Spain.

1521   Ignatius is seriously wounded in battle at Pamplona. During his recovery he reads from Ludoph the Carthusian's *Life of Christ* and from the *Flos sanctorum* (which recounts the lives of the saints). He undergoes a conversion that leads him away from the courtly life toward that of an itinerant holy man dedicated to God. He soon composes a book of spiritual exercises (the forerunner of the *Spiritual Exercises*) to help himself and others to achieve spiritual fulfillment.

1523   Ignatius goes to the Holy Land with the intention of helping souls and spreading the Gospel, but he is compelled to leave because of the dangers of the time.

1524   Realizing that he could help souls more effectively if he had an education, Ignatius goes to Barcelona and at the age of thirty-three begins to learn Latin in a class with very young boys.

1526   Ignatius studies at the University of Alcalá, Spain.

1527   Ignatius studies at the University of Salamanca, Spain.

1528–35   Ignatius studies at the University of Paris, eventually earning a master's degree.

1534   Ignatius and his early companions take vows at a chapel in Montmartre.

1540   The Society of Jesus receives official approval as a religious order.

1541   *Fundación de collegio:* directives for those entering the Society with a need for academic training (Lukács: 2–3). This document already shows the sequential structure of Letters first, Philosophy second, and Theology third.

1543–56   Ignatius drafts, revises *Constitutions,* which expresses the need for a document like the *Ratio studiorum,* which would provide a detailed treatment of (1) the lecture times, their order, their method; (2) exercises in compositions and in disputations; and (3) methods of delivering orations and reading verses publicly (*ConsCN* 455 [p. 180]).

1545   *Constitutiones collegii Patavini:* The first part outlines the structure of the academic training as imparted in Padua; it includes a "Parisian" kind of emphasis on academic exercises.

1546   College of Gandía. Non-Jesuit students are being taught.

1547   Polanco's *Industriæ.* Ignatius's secretary, drawing up this guide for the spiritual and academic formation of Jesuits at Ignatius's request, foresees that some will be *litterati* and have a more intense academic training than others. This document is not issued, but its content informs the *Constitutions.*

1548   Opening of the College of Messina. According to Coudret, it was here that the Society "first undertook the task of educating youth, and initiated its system of dividing the pupils into distinct classes with lessons accommodated to their individual capacities. From here the first *Ratio studiorum,* written for the Roman College, was sent to the other colleges which had been instituted according to its norm" (cited in Farrell, *Jesuit Code,* 48).

1550   The first full draft of the Society's general *Constitutions* appears.

1551   Fr. Jean Pelletier and fourteen Jesuits open the Roman College, which Ignatius wanted to make "the center and model of the Society's educational work" (Farrell, *Jesuit Code,* 69). The tablet on the front door read: "SCUOLA DI GRAMMATICA, D'HUMANITÀ E DI DOTTRINA CRISTIANA, GRATIS."

1551   Fr. Hannibal Coudret's plan for the school at Messina, followed by Nadal's *De studiis Societatis.* Ignatius states to various college rectors that "no rule of studies was to be considered fixed or final until a program applicable to all the schools could be drafted and approved."

1553–56   The schools at Gandía and Messina become universities, provoking a better working-out of the entire academic plan, with study of some academic constitutions that are already in use at other universities. The Society's universities are first mentioned in 1553 or 1554.

1558   *Ratio studiorum* for the Roman College This document included rules for the prefect of studies, the teachers, and the students.

1562–75   "[P]ainstaking examination and revision of every element contained in [the early formulas used for school organization]" (Farrell, *Jesuit Code,* 153). Ledesma put together the *Ratio Borgiana* (the name being derived from the general at the time, Francis Borgia). This is the first "common and universal *Ratio,*" promulgated in 1569 and used until the 1591 *Ratio* was sent out as a universal norm for studies on a trial basis.

1564   Distribution of prizes at Rome: not the first, but a trend-setting occasion. The rules for the distribution of prizes were written by an outstanding teacher of rhetoric, Fr. Peter John Perpinian. These appear in the *Ratio* of 1591.

ca. 1565   **Jerome Nadal** (1507–80) finishes his *Ordo studiorum* (Farrell, *Jesuit Code,* 76ff.).

1565   Earliest reference to the *Summa Sapientia,* in the documents of the Second General Congregation. The *Summa* was a collection of regulations drafted by Nadal and others to govern the administration of colleges. It was a forerunner of the *Ratio.*

1573   Third General Congregation proposes that the *Summa Sapientia* be examined, revised, and made normative for the entire Society.

1575 James Ledesma (1519–75) fashions blueprint for the Roman College: *De ratione et ordine studiorum Collegii Romani*, "perhaps the most substantial contribution to the development of the Jesuit code of education" (Farrell, ibid., 169).

1577 Fr. General Everard Mercurian, fourth general of the Society, codifies instructions and rules for particular officials involved in running schools.

1581 Fr. Claudio Aquaviva elected fifth general of the Society; immediately he appoints a committee of twelve to compose "a formula of studies."

1584 Aquaviva appoints an entirely new committee of six to carry on this work: John Azor (Spain); Gaspar González (Portugual); Jame Tyrie (Scotland); Peter Busée (Holland); Anthony Ghuse (Flanders); Stephen Tucci (Sicily). These work from December 8, 1584, until the summer of 1585, meeting three hours a day, spending the rest of the time "examining correspondence and ordinances from various Provinces, the statutes of noted universities, the Fourth Part of the *Constitutions*, and other documents relating to studies, local customs, and discipline" (Farrell, ibid., 225).

1586 First *Ratio* issued, explicitly not a definitive document and never tried in schools. The committee requested a written critique from committees of at least five fathers in each province.

1586–91 Responses from the provincial committees are examined and work on a new edition is begun. Tucci, Azor, González continue to work on it, aided by professors from the Roman College: Robert Bellarmine, Francis Suarez, Benedict Sardi, Benedict Giustiniani, Peter de Parra, Bento Pereira, Francis Benci, Horace Torsellini, and (probably) Fulvius Cardulo.

1591 Second *Ratio* issued, binding but not final. Three years of testing were to be followed by written criticisms of it, which would prepare for a definitive version.

1599 Promulgation of the "definitive" *Ratio studiorum*, on January 8.

1773–1814 Suppression of the Society.

1832 Trial version of a revised *Ratio studiorum*, with contemporary adaptations. This document was never officially established as the norm in the way that the 1599 text had been.

Appendix 2
THOMISTIC QUESTIONS IN THE CATALOG

Taken from *The Summa Theologica of St. Thomas Aquinas,* literally translated by Fathers of the English Dominican Province, 2nd ed. rev., 1920. Consulted in the preparation of this book was the Online Edition, 2003, by Kevin Knight, http://www.newadvent.org/summa/. The numbering has been corrected according to Bianchi, *Ratio atque institutio* (2002).

[H9] From the First Part

[C1]	Question 1, Article 1	Whether, besides philosophy, any further doctrine is required
[C2]	Art. 2	Whether sacred doctrine is a science
[C3]	Art. 3	Whether sacred doctrine is one science
[C4]	Art. 4	Whether sacred doctrine is a practical science
[C5]	Art. 5	Whether sacred doctrine is nobler than other sciences
[C6]	Art. 9	Whether Holy Scripture should use metaphors
[C7]	Ques. 2	The existence of God
[C8]	Ques. 3, Art. 1	Whether God is a body
[C9]	Art. 2	Whether God is composed of matter and form
[C10]	Art. 3	Whether God is the same as His essence or nature
[C11]	Art. 4	Whether essence and existence are the same in God
[C12]	Art. 7	Whether God is altogether simple
[C13]	Ques. 4, Art. 1	Whether God is perfect
[C14]	Ques. 5	Goodness in general
[C15]	Ques. 7, Art. 1	Whether God is infinite
[C16]	Arts. 2, 3, 4	Whether anything but God can be essentially infinite / Whether an actually infinite magnitude can exist / Whether an infinite multitude can exist
[C17]	Ques. 8	The existence of God in things
[C18]	Ques. 9	The immutability of God
[C19]	Ques. 11	The unity of God
[C20]	[Ques. 12], Art. 3	Whether the essence of God can be seen with the bodily eye
[C21]	Art. 6	Whether of those who see the essence of God, one sees more perfectly than another
[C22]	Art. 8	Whether those who see the essence of God see all in God
[C23]	Art. 12	Whether God can be known in this life by natural reason

[C24] Ques. 13, Arts. 3 and 4   Whether any name can be applied to God in its literal sense / Whether names applied to God are synonymous

[C25]   Art. 5   Whether what is said of God and of creatures is univocally predicated of them

[C26]   Art. 7   Whether names which imply relation to creatures are predicated of God temporally

[C27]   Arts. 8, 9, 10, 11, 12   Is this name "God" a name of nature, or of the operation / Is this name "God" a communicable name / Is it taken univocally or equivocally as signifying God, by nature, by participation, and by opinion / Is this name, "Who is," the supremely appropriate name of God / Can affirmative propositions be formed about God

[C28] Qq. 16 and 17   Truth / Falsity

[C29] Ques. 19, Arts. 9 and 12   Whether God wills evils / Whether five expressions of will are rightly assigned to the divine will

[C30] Ques. 23, Art. 1   Whether men are predestined by God

[C31]   Art. 3   Whether God reprobates any man

[C32]   Art. 5   Whether the foreknowledge of merits is the cause of predestination

[C33] Ques. 24   The book of life

[C34] Ques. 25   The power of God

[C35]   Art. 1   Whether there is power in God

[C36]   Art. 6   Whether God can do better than what He does

[C37] Ques. 27, Art. 1   Whether there is procession in God

[C38]   Art. 3   Whether any other procession exists in God besides that of the Word

[C39] Ques. 29   The divine Persons

[C40] Ques. 32   The knowledge of the divine Persons

[C41]   Art. 4   Whether it is lawful to have various contrary opinions of notions

[C42] Ques. 39   The Persons in relation to the essence

[C43] Ques. 43   The mission of the divine Persons

[C44] Ques. 53   The local movement of the angels

[H10] From the First Part of Part II

[C45] Ques. 1, Art. 1   Whether it belongs to man to act for an end

[C46]   Art. 2   Whether it is proper to the rational nature to act for an end

[C76] Ques. 20, Art. 5	Whether the consequences of the external action increase its goodness or malice
[C77] [Ques. 21], Art. 4	Whether a human action is meritorious or demeritorious before God, according as it is good or evil
[C78] Ques. 71, Art. 4	Whether sin is compatible with virtue
[C79] [Ques. 72], Art. 5	Whether the division of sins according to their debt of punishment diversifies their species
[C80] Art. 8	Whether excess and deficiency diversify the species of sins
[C81] Ques. 73, Art. 8	Whether sin is aggravated by reason of its causing more harm
[C82] Ques. 79	The external causes of sin
[C83] Ques. 81, Art. 3	Whether the sin of the first parent is transmitted, by the way of origin, to all men
[C84] Ques. 85	Whether the sin of the first parent is transmitted, by the way of origin, to all men
[C85] [Ques. 85], Art. 8	Whether anyone is punished for another's sin
[C86] Ques. 89, Art. 2	Whether venial sins are suitably designated as "wood, hay, and stubble"
[C87] Art. 5	Whether the first movements of sensuality in unbelievers are mortal sin
[C88] Ques. 92	The effects of law
[C89] [Ques. 109], Art. 5	Whether man can merit everlasting life without grace
[C90] Art. 7	Whether man can rise from sin without the help of grace
[C91] Ques. 110	The grace of God as regards its essence
[C92] Ques. 112	The cause of grace
[C93] Art. 2	Whether any preparation and disposition for grace is required on man's part
[C94] Art. 3	Whether grace is necessarily given to whoever prepares himself for it, or to whoever does what he can
[C95] Ques. 113, Art. 4	Whether a movement of faith is required for the justification of the ungodly
[C96] Art. 7	Whether the justification of the ungodly takes place in an instant or successively
[C97] Art. 9	Whether the justification of the ungodly is God's greatest work
[C98] Ques. 114, Art. 6	Whether a man can merit the first grace for another
[C99] Art. 3	Whether a man in grace can merit eternal life condignly

[H11] From the Second Part of Part II

[C100]	Ques. 4, Art. 3	Whether charity is the form of faith
[C101]	Art. 6	Whether faith is one virtue
[C102]	Ques. 5, Art. 1	Whether there was faith in the angels, or in man, in their original state
[C103]	Ques. 6	The cause of faith
[C104]	Ques. 10, Art. 2	Whether unbelief is in the intellect as its subject
[C105]	Ques. 12	Whether the children of Jews and other unbelievers ought to be baptized against their parents' will
[C106]	Ques. 23, Art. 2	Whether charity is something created in the soul
[C107]	Ques. 26	The order of charity
[C108]	Ques. 61	The parts of justice

[H12] From Part III

[C109]	Ques. 1, Art. 1	Whether it was fitting that God should become incarnate
[C110]	Art. 2	Whether it was necessary for the restoration of the human race that the Word of God should become incarnate
[C111]	Ques. 2	The mode of union of the Word incarnate
[C112]	Ques. 4, Art. 4	Whether the Son of God ought to have assumed human nature abstracted from all individuals
[C113]	Ques. 7	The grace of Christ as an individual man
[C114]	Ques. 8, Art. 1	Whether Christ is the Head of the Church
[C115]	Arts. 2 and 3	Whether Christ is the Head of men as to their bodies or only as to their souls / Whether Christ is the Head of all men
[C116]	Ques. 9, Art. 1	Whether Christ had any knowledge besides the divine
[C117]	Ques. 10, Art. 2	Whether the Son of God knew all things in the Word
[C118]	Ques. 11, Art. 1	Whether by this imprinted or infused knowledge Christ knew all things
[C119]	Art. 5	Whether this knowledge was habitual
[C120]	Ques. 18, Art. 4	Whether there was free will in Christ
[C121]	Ques. 22	The priesthood of Christ
[C122]	Ques. 24	The predestination of Christ
[C123]	Ques. 25	The adoration of Christ

[H13] On the Sacraments in General

[H14] On Baptism
[H15] On the Eucharist
[H16] On Penance
[H17] On Matrimony

Appendix 3

GOALS AND CONTENTS OF THE LITERARY GRADES

Lowest Grammar [425]

perfect knowledge of rudiments and a beginning knowledge of syntax

LATIN: only the easiest letters of Cicero

LATIN GRAMMAR: lower track takes nouns, verbs, rudiments, fourteen rules of construction, genders and nouns from the grammar's first book; the higher track takes the matter on the declensions, past tenses, verbals, from the introduction to syntax up to the impersonal verbs

Greek Grammar: rudiments, single rules at the most [431–32]

Middle Grammar [415]

a complete though not exhaustive knowledge of grammar

LATIN: Only **Cicero's letters** *Ad familiares* and the **simplest poems of Ovid.**

LATIN GRAMMAR: **Alvarez's** *Grammar* or the **Roman Method**, Book 2 to *constructio figurata* (plus the easy exceptions)

GREEK: **Greek catechism** or the *Tabula of Cebes*

GREEK GRAMMAR: Contract nouns, circumflex verbs, -*mi* verbs, easier verb formations

Highest Grammar [405]

a complete and perfect knowledge of grammar

LATIN: Semester 1: **Cicero's more important letters from** *Ad familiares, Ad Atticum, Ad Quintum*; Semester 2: *De amicitia, De senectute, Paradoxa,* **and the like.** Poets: Semester 1: some selected and expurgated **elegies and epistles of Ovid;** Semester 2: selections from **Catullus, Tibullus, Propertius, Vergil's** *Eclogues* or also some of the **easier books of Vergil (e.g.,** *Georgics* **4) and** *Aeneid* **5, 7**

LATIN GRAMMAR: Review syntax from beginning (including all the exceptions); figures of speech, rules of prosody.

GREEK: St. John Chrysostom, Aesop, Agapetus, and such authors.

GREEK GRAMMAR: can alternate day by day with lessons on an author.

Humanities [395]

the foundations for the course in eloquence, after grammar has been completed

LATIN: Daily readings in the works of Cicero, esp. the ethical ones. History: **Caesar, Sallust, Livy, Curtius,** others like them. Poetry: **Vergil** (except the *Eclogues* and *Aeneid* 4); **Horace's Odes;** also possible: elegies, epi-

GREEK: Syntax. Greek reading and composition. **Easier authors: Orations of Isocrates** or **St. Chrysostom** or **St. Basil; some letters of Plato** and **Synesius** or a

grams, other poems of recognized poets (expurgated); "erudition" or "scholarly learning" introduced, but the focus on language is maintained. 2nd Semester: Rules of rhetoric from *De arte rhetorica* of **Cyprian Soarez**; some of **Cicero's simpler speeches**, e.g., **Pro lege Manilia, Pro Archia, Pro Marcello, and the Caesarian orations** (instead of the philosophical works).

LATIN GRAMMAR: Prosody covered rapidly.

selection from **Plutarch**; 2nd Semester: poem explained, e.g., from **Phocylides, Theognis, St. Gregory Nazianzen, Synesius**, and the like. Greek prelection: grammar and author on alternate days.

GREEK GRAMMAR: The Greek lesson alternates between grammar and an author day by day [403].

Rhetoric [375]

"ad perfectam eloquentiam informat," through oratory first and then *poetica*, using precepts of rhetoric, stylistics, and erudition

LATIN: Daily prelection is confined to the **oratorical works of Cicero, to Aristotle's** *Rhetoric,* **and if desired, his** *Poetics.* **Cicero** is the one model of style, though the **best historians and poets** are to be sampled. All of Cicero's works are appropriate models of style, but only the prose works are matter for prelection. Erudition is to be sought in the study of historical events, ethnology, authoritative views of scholars, and various sources of knowledge, but rather sparingly.

GREEK: Rules of prosody, general acquaintance with the **various authors and the various dialects**: Demosthenes, Plato, Thucydides, Homer, Hesiod, Pindar, and the like; SS. Gregory Nazianzen, Basil, and Chrysostom

GREEK GRAMMAR: syntax and prosody, alternating day by day with an author

Appendix 4

DAILY SCHEDULE FOR THE LOWER CLASSES

Lowest Grammar Class: Daily Schedule [426]

First morning hour

(1)   Recitation of Cicero and grammar from memory to the decurions

(2)   Decurions collect the written work

(3)   Teacher corrects the written work while students do various exercises

Types of exercises [428]

- turning something dictated in the vernacular into Latin on the basis of a syntactical rule
- translating a passage from Cicero from Latin into the vernacular
- and writing that same passage out in Latin
- coming up with questions and expressions based on grammatical rules, especially the ones recently taught, to be put to their rivals
- fashioning expressions that are in agreement, or putting them in proper word order
- writing out some Greek material
- other similar activities

Second morning period

(1)   Brief review of the last lesson of Cicero

(2)   New lesson on Cicero

(3)   Students repeat the lesson (totaling thirty minutes for this new lesson and the repetition)

(4)   Dictation of a theme

(5)   Final half-hour: review or presentation of something from the first book of grammar, for each track every day or every other day. Later, this material is given back by the students to the teacher or in competition. On days when no new construction is given after lunch, the morning lessons continues into the afternoon, with the final half-hour of the morning all given to competition or to exercise.

First afternoon hour

(1)   Half an hour of recitation of grammar (sometimes Latin and sometimes Greek) while the teacher checks the decurions' marks and the written work (from the morning or what is left from the homework)

(2)   Review of the last grammar lesson

Second afternoon period: an hour and a half

(1)   Upper track: syntax lesson; lower track: the fourteen rules of syntax

(2)   A little more than fifteen minutes for Greek

(3) The last half-hour: competitions or careful consideration of a dictation in light of the grammatical rules

On Saturday

First morning hour

Recitation from memory of the lessons of the entire week, performed in front of the class

Second morning period: one and a half hours

(1) Review these lessons again

(2) In the final half-hour, competitions

After lunch

(1) The same thing, except that catechism is also recited from memory in the first hour

(2) The last half-hour: catechism teaching or a devotional exhortation, unless this was done Friday. If so, take what catechism study had displaced.

Middle Grammar Class: Daily Schedule [416]

First morning hour

(1) Recitation of Cicero and grammar from memory to the decurions

(2) Decurions collect the written work

(3) Teacher corrects the written work while students do various exercises

Types of exercises [418]

- turning vernacular dictations into Latin, sometimes in imitation of an author, sometimes especially according to rules of syntax
- translating a passage of Cicero into the vernacular
- writing out the same in Latin
- providing questions and phrases to be proposed to the rivals about the rules of grammar, especially the ones recently taught
- writing out Greek passages, and other things like these

Second morning period

(1) Brief review of the last lesson of Cicero

(2) New lesson on Cicero

(3) Students repeat the lesson (totaling thirty minutes for this new lesson and the repetition)

(4) Dictation of a theme

(5) Final half-hour: review of something from the first book of grammar and about the declension of nouns, and next about the past tenses and the verbals, practiced in competition

First afternoon hour

(1)   Grammar (sometimes Latin and sometimes Greek)

(2)   On the proper days, the recitation of a poet while the teacher checks the decurions' marks and the written work (from the morning or what is left from the homework)

(3)   On alternating days, a review of the last grammar lesson or a review of a poet

Second afternoon period: an hour and a half

(1)   First half-hour: on alternate days, a syntax lesson, or a lesson on a poet

(2)   Second half-hour: a Greek lesson

(3)   The last half-hour: competition or practice

On Saturday

First morning hour

Recitation from memory of the lessons of the entire book or of the entire week, performed in front of the class

Second morning period: one and a half hours

(1)   Review these lessons again

(2)   In the final half-hour, a competition

After lunch

(1)   The same thing, except that catechism is also recited from memory in the first hour

(2)   The last half-hour: catechism teaching or a devotional exhortation, unless this was done Friday. If so, take what catechism study had displaced.

Highest (First) Grammar Class: Daily Schedule [406]

First morning hour

(1)   Recitation of Cicero and grammar from memory to the decurions

(2)   Decurions collect the written work

(3)   Teacher corrects the written work while students do various exercises

Types of exercises [408]

- putting vernacular dictations into Latin, sometimes in imitation of an author and sometimes according to the rules of syntax
- translating a Ciceronian reading from Latin into the vernacular
- writing out that translation in Latin, excerpting the more elegant phrases from it
- coming up with questions for the rivals and proposing expressions to them from the grammatical rules recently taught

- rearranging scrambled verses into the proper order or composing them
- writing in Greek
- and other activities of this kind

Second morning hour

(1) Brief review of the last lesson of Cicero

(2) New lesson on Cicero taught for thirty minutes

(3) Students repeat the lesson (totaling thirty minutes for this new lesson and the repetition)

(4) Dictation of a theme

(5) Final half-hour

  (a) Review of the grammar lesson

  (b) New grammar lesson

  (c) Repetition of that lesson, occasionally including a competition

Content

First semester: quickly review the rules for construction given in the lower class; then teach the matter for this grade in detail. On alternate days, teach the general precepts of prosody, but not the exceptions.

Second semester: at least two months of a review of the grammar that belongs to this level. On alternate days, a review of prosody that skims through rules already taught and dwells on the others as needed. When grammar is finished, prosody should be taught every day, with the exceptions, poetic genres, and the material on patronymics and accent.

First afternoon hour

(1) Recitation of a poet or a Greek author from memory while the teacher checks the marks of the decurions and corrects the written work (either the morning's work, or what remains from the homework)

Second afternoon period: an hour and a half

(1) Half of the time: review of a poet or a lesson on a poet

(2) The other half: sometimes a Greek lesson and sometimes a Greek composition

(3) During the last half-hour, or what remains: a competition

On Saturday

First morning hour

Recitation from memory of the lessons of the entire book or of the entire week, performed in front of the class

Second morning period: one and a half hours

(1) Review these lessons again

(2) In the final half-hour, a competition

After lunch

(1) The same thing, except that catechism is also recited from memory in the first hour

(2) The last half-hour: catechism teaching or a devotional exhortation, unless this was done Friday. If so, take what catechism study had displaced.

Humanities: Daily Schedule [396]

First morning hour

(1) Recitation of Cicero and prosody from memory to the decurions

(2) Decurions collect the written work

(3) Teacher corrects the written work while students do various exercises

Types of exercises [398]

selecting phrases from the lessons

· varying them in several ways

· putting in order a scrambled sentence from Cicero

· composing verses

· transposing a poem from one genre into another

· imitating some literary passage

· writing Greek

· other things of the same kind

(4) Several students' recitations in front of the class while the teacher reviews the decurions' marks

Second morning hour

(1) Review of the last lesson

(2) New lesson for thirty minutes or a little more

(3) Students repeat the lesson

(4) If time allows, student competion on the lesson

(5) Final half-hour

At the beginning of the first semester: study of a historian and of prosody on alternating days. When prosody is finished: study of a historian every day.

Second semester: Cyprian's *Rhetoric* every day, either taught or reviewed, or a disputation.

First afternoon hour

(1) Recitation of a poet and a Greek author from memory while the teacher checks the marks of the decurions and corrects the written work (either the morning's work, or what remains from the homework)

(2) Dictate a theme

Second afternoon period: an hour and a half

(1) Half of the time should be spent on a review of a poet or a lesson on a poet

(2) The other half should be given to a Greek lesson or a Greek composition

On a break day

First morning hour

Recitation from memory of what was taught on the preceding break day, during the correction of the remaining compositions

Second morning hour

One of the following

- something from the epigrams or odes or elegies
- something from Cyprian's third book on tropes, on figures, and especially on oratorical rhythm and measures, so that they get accustomed to them at the beginning of the year
- some *chria* or preparatory exercise should be taught and gone over again
- a competition

On Saturday

First morning hour

Recitation from memory of the lessons of the entire week, performed in front of the class

Second morning period: one and a half hours

(1) Review these lessons again

(2) In the final half-hour, a student should give a declamation or present a lesson, or the class should go to hear the rhetoricians, or there should be a competition.

After lunch

(1) First half-hour: students should give back a poet and the catechism lesson, while the teacher reviews the marks made by the decurions and the written assignments

(2) The following ninety minutes:

    (a) Half of the time period: review of a poet or explanation of some short poem and the testing of the students on it

    (b) The other half: Greek

    (c) The last half-hour: catechism teaching or a devotional exhortation, unless this was done Friday. If so, the material that the catechism study had displaced.

Rhetoric: Daily Schedule [376]

First morning hour

(1) Exercise of the memory

(2) Decurions collect the written work

(3) Teacher corrects the written work while students do various exercises

    Types of exercises [379]

- imitating some passage of a poet or prose writer
- some description (for instance, of gardens, of churches, of a storm) and varying the same expression of similar things in several ways
- translating Greek prose passage into Latin, or the reverse
- expressing the meaning of a poet's verses both in Latin prose and in Greek
- changing one type of poem into another
- composing epigrams, inscriptions, epitaphs
- selecting expressions, Greek or Latin, from good prose writers and poets, fitting rhetorical figures to given topics
- furnishing several arguments for some issue or other from the rhetorical *loci* and *topoi*
- and other activities of this type

(4) Review of the previous day's lesson

Second morning hour

(1) The lesson: rules if a prose passage is being taught after lunch or a prose passage if rules are being taught then, continuing what was started at the beginning of the year

(2) Competition or an examination of what the students wrote in the first hour

(3) Review

(4) Subject for a prose composition or a poem

(5) Remaining time: either a competition or an examination of what students wrote in the first hour

First afternoon hour

(1) Review of the last lesson

(2) New lesson, a prose passage if rules were taught in the morning, or rules if a prose passage was given then

(3) Review this lesson

Second afternoon hour

(1) Review of the last lesson on the Greek author

(2) New lesson on Greek author

(3) The hearing of this lesson back from the students

(4) Remaining time: correction of Greek compositions, or Greek syntax and prosody, or competitions in Greek

On a break day

Teach a historian or poet or present some relevant scholarly background

On Saturday

First morning hour

Brief review of the entire week

Lesson on a historian or a poet

Second morning hour

A lesson or a declamation given by a student, or the class goes to hear the humanities students or a competition is held

After lunch

Lesson on a poet or a historian

Review of Greek

If a half-hour is added to the two morning and two afternoon hours

A historian or a poet should be studied during that time, and the Saturday lessons should be like those of the other days. If lessons are not presented on Saturday, there should be a more thorough review and competition.

ENDNOTES

1. The title helps to indicate that the *Ratio studiorum* was written, approved, and promulgated in a manner that attributed great authority to the code of education that it carried, even while that code allowed for considerable flexibility. The formula *Ratio atque institutio* suggests a system that has been deliberately and formally established as normative, covering both the idea of the education's structure *(ratio)* and the normative quality of the intended customary manner *(institutio)* of delivering that education. The word *institutio* by itself can mean "arrangement," "system," "establishment," or "custom." But it can also mean "training" or "education," being famously used in a first-century A.D. Latin text much celebrated in the Renaissance, Quintilian's treatise on education, the *Institutio oratoria* (Oratorical Training). Cicero uses the phrase *ratio atque institutio* in *De officiis,* II.xi.39: "Ac mea quidem sententia omnis ratio atque institutio vitæ adiumenta hominum desiderat" (Certainly in my view every structured plan for life requires help from other people). In its Jesuit usage, the title fits the work that aims to be the comprehensive official guiding document for Jesuit education and a part of the Society's Institute (see the note on §7 above and endn. 3 below.).

2. The *Ratstud* is composed to fulfill the mandate given in the *Constitutions,* Part IV, chap. 13, no. 2. For a modern translation of the *Constitutions* containing the *General Norms* published according to the directives of General Congregation 33, see *The Constitutions of the Society of Jesus and Their Complementary Norms (ConsCN),* marginal number C455[vv.1-3] (p. 180). The italic capital *C* indicates that the section (marginal) number given refers to the *Constitutions* and not the *General Norms.* The superscript [vv.] indicates the "verse numbers" provided in this and other modern editions of the *Constitutions.* Here follows a translation of this passage:

> [1]Concerning the hours of the lectures, their order, and their method, and concerning the exercises both in compositions (which ought to be corrected by the teachers) and in disputations within all the faculties, and in delivering orations and reading verses in public—[2]all this will be treated in detail in a separate treatise [approved by the general]. This present constitution refers the reader to it, [3]with the remark that it ought to be adapted to places, times, and persons, even though it would be desirable to reach that order as far as this is possible.

The original Latin for this passage reads as follows:

> De statutis lectionum horis, ordine ac modo, et de exercitationibus tam compositionum (quas a Magistris emendari oportet) quam disputationum in omnibus Facultatibus, et pronuntiandi publice orationes et carmina, speciatim in quodam tractatu, per Generalem Præpositum approbato, agetur seorsum, ad quem hæc Constitutio nos remittit; id dumtaxat monendo, illa locis, temporibus et personis accommodari oportere; quamvis ad illum ordinem accedere, quoad fieri potest, conveniat.

3. The *Formula* states that the order was "founded chiefly for this purpose: to strive especially for the defense and propagation of the faith and for the progress of souls in Christian life and doctrine, by means of public preaching, lectures, and any other ministration whatsoever of the word of God, and further by means of the Spiritual Exercises, the education of children and unlettered persons in Christianity, and the spiritual consolation of Christ's faithful through the hearing of confessions and administering the other sacraments" (*ConsCN*, 1550 *Formula*, no. 1[vv.1,2] [pp. 2f.]). For further background on the *Formula*, see Ganss, *Cons.* 36.

4. Farrell writes as follows:

Ignatius made provision for two types of schools for externs, which he distinguished by the names of college and university. The former embraced classes in grammar, the *litteræ humaniores*, and Rhetoric; but sometimes also courses in arts (philosophy, science, and mathematics) and even in theology were added if a sufficient number of students called for them. Ordinarily, however, courses in the arts and in theology were reserved to the universities, and students who wished to pursue them were to be sent from a town where they had completed the Humanities in a Jesuit college to another town where there was a Jesuit university. In Ignatius' conception the university included the "college" with its teaching of language and literature, and added the faculties of arts and theology. The faculties of law and medicine, if admitted into the university, were not to be administered by the Society "since they are more remote from its Institute." In practice the Society opened few universities [in this early period], and so it became the custom in after years to distinguish three types of educational institutions, the gymnasium which restricted its teaching to language and literature, the college which added the course of arts, and sometimes a course in theology, and finally the university." (Farrell, *Jesuit Code*, 144f.)

5. The *CathEncy* explains "doctores" thus:

(Lat. *Doctores Ecclesiæ*)—Certain ecclesiastical writers have received this title on account of the great advantage the whole Church has derived from their doctrine. In the Western church four eminent Fathers of the Church attained this honour in the early Middle Ages: St. Gregory the Great, St. Ambrose, St. Augustine, and St. Jerome. . . . In the Eastern Church three Doctors were pre-eminent: St. John Chrysostom, St. Basil, and St. Gregory Nazianzen. [And St. Athanasius was later added as a fourth.]. . . . To these great names others have subsequently been added. The requisite conditions are enumerated as three: *eminens doctrina, insignis vitæ sanctitas, Ecclesiæ declaratio* (i.e., eminent learning, a high degree of sanctity, and proclamation by the Church). (*CathEncy*, s.vv. "Doctors of the Church")

6. In 1954 the distinction between various forms *Acta* took was presented thus:

Præter disputationes supra commemoratas, interdum aliæ quædam maiore apparatu externo instituantur, qui actus publici appellari solent. Eorum duo sunt genera: Actus generales, in quibus de universa Philosophia scholastica sive de universa sacra Theologia scholastica, et Actus peculiares, in quibus de quadam parte longiore earundem disciplinarum disputatur. (*Ratio studio-*

rum superiorum Societatis Iesu ad normam Congregationum Generalium XXVIII et XXIX exarata, 48, no. 103.1 [Rome, 1954])

(In my translation this reads: Beyond the disputations mentioned above, from time to time certain other ones should be given that make more use of outward display, the ones that are usually called "public acts." There are two varieties of these acts: General Acts, in which the entirety of Scholastic philosophy or sacred theology is subjected to disputation, and Special Acts, in which certain major areas of these disciplines are so subjected.)

Into the twentieth century there are records of the occurrence of Grand Acts (covering both philosophy and theology). One was given by a Spanish Jesuit, Father Joachim Vilallonga, at Saint Louis University in 1903, before an audience that included the United States President Theodore Roosevelt (See Nugent, 1903).

7. The distinction between the rank of Doctor or Master has been explained thus:

[The master of arts degree was] an academic degree higher than that of Bachelor. The conferring of the degree of Master of Arts, as a title invested with certain specific academic privileges, is closely connected in origin with the early history of the University of Paris, which was the mother-university in arts as Bologna was in law. Originally, the degree meant simply the right to teach, the Licentia docendi, and this right could be granted, in Paris, only by the Chancellor of the Cathedral of Notre Dame, or the Chancellor of St. Geneviève. . . . In medieval times, the title of Master was practically synonymous with that of Doctor, the former being more in favour at Paris and the universities modelled after it, and the latter at Bologna and its derivative universities. At Oxford and Cambridge a distinction came to be drawn between the Faculties of Law, Medicine, and Theology and the Faculty of Arts in this respect, the title of Doctor being used for the former, and that of Master for the latter. In Germany, "Doctor" is exclusively used, but the German university diploma still frequently evidences the original equivalence of the two titles, the recipient being styled Magister Artium et Doctor Philosophiæ. In France the original practical equivalence of the Licentiate and the Mastership, or the Doctorate, developed into a distinction amounting to separate degrees." (*CathEncy,* s.vv. "Master of Arts")

8. The OED explains *collatio* thus:

II. Conference, discourse, refection, light repast. 5. A personal conferring together; consultation, conference, esp. of a private or informal sort. b. A discourse, sermon, or homily; a treatise, exposition. Obs. 6. The title of the celebrated work of John Cassian, A.D. 410–420 *Collationes patrum in scetica eremo commorantium,* i.e., Conferences of (and with) the Egyptian Hermits. In OE., *collationes* [meant] relations, narratives, discourses, and in ME. collation had the sense: Relation, account. Obs. 7. "The reading from the *Collationes* or lives of the Fathers, which St. Benedict (*Regula* xlii, see 6b.) instituted in his monasteries before compline"*(Dict. Chr. Antiq.).* Whether the name actually originated in the *Collationes patrum* read on these occasions does not appear certain. Already in Isidore, a 640, the name is simply *collatio* (*Regula S. Isidori* c. viii, "ad audiendum in Collatione Patrem . . . ad collectam conveniant. . . .

Sedentes autem omnes in Collatione tacebunt nisi," etc. Du Cange). By Sma-
ragdus a 850, and Honorius of Autun (c 1300), the *collatio* is explained as
being itself a conference of the monks upon the passage read, "aliis confe-
rentibus interrogationes, conferunt alii congruas responsiones." (See Du
Cange).

9. In the original Latin rule 49 reads: "In singulis Domibus clausuræ fines accurate præscribat, curetque ut partes huic legi obnoxiæ patenter indicentur et ipsa lex
servetur diligenter. Curet quoque ut cetera castitatis præsidia sedulo adhibeantur,
ita ut in re quæ summi est momenti præcaveantur omnia pericula." Rule 56 reads,
"Si cui ob peculiaria studia peculiares libros concesserit, curet ut iam ab initio deter-
minatæ bibliothecæ addicantur."

10. The *CathEncy* has this to say regarding the "Rogation Days":

The Major Rogation, which has no connexion with the feast of St. Mark
(fixed for this date much later) seems to be of very early date and to have
been introduced to counteract the ancient Robigalia, on which the heathens
held processions and supplications to their gods. St. Gregory the Great (d.
604) regulated the already existing custom. The Minor Rogations were introduced by St. Mamertus, Bishop of Vienne, and were afterwards ordered by
the Fifth Council of Orleans, which was held in 511, and then approved by
Leo III (795–816). (*CathEncy*, s.vv. "Rogation Days")

11. The meaning of the term "rector" can be phrased thus:

Priests who preside over missions or quasi-parishes are called rectors: in
England and the United States they are removable and irremovable, or per-
manent. These latter are known also as missionary rectors (M.R.). The term
rector is applied likewise to the heads of universities, seminaries, and colleges; to the local superiors of religious houses of men; to the pope, as rector of the world, in the conferring of the tiara. In some universities, e.g.
Louvain, the actual president is known as *rector magnificus*. (*CathEncy*, s.v.
"Rector")

"What is prescribed for the rector in the twenty-fifth rule of his office": rule
25 for rectors reads, "Consultores aliosque omnes, cum ei aliquid proponunt, libenter et benigne excipiat, et eum præcipue cui Admonitoris officium commissum est"
(*Regulæ Societatis Iesu*, p. 154). (Or, in English, He should gladly and kindly receive
his consultors and all others, particularly the one appointed to be his admonitor,
when they present something to him.)

12. The Council of Trent was a major council reforming the Catholic Church
and stating its self-understanding in contrast to alternative views that were being
followed by Protestants and others in the wake of the activities of reformers like
Martin Luther (1483–1546). It was not, however, as comprehensive in its scope as is
sometimes claimed, but focused on the pope, the bishops, and pastors. See John W.
O'Malley, S.J., "The Council of Trent: Myths, Misunderstandings, and Misinformation," 205–23.

The multicultural, non-European closed set of texts that we know as the
Bible has long been a basic text informing Western civilization. Considered by be-

lievers to be Revelation (i.e., the Word of God), it contains Christianity's foundational sacred narratives, laws, truths, and wisdom in two major parts: the "Old Testament," which contains the Hebrew Scriptures, and the "New Testament." The latter consists of Greek texts including the Gospels, which narrate the deeds and words of Jesus Christ; the Acts of the Apostles (history of the early Church); letters or epistles by early Church leaders, like Paul, James, John, and Peter; and apocalyptic prophecy (the Book of Revelation).

13. According to the *Oxford English Dictionary* (OED), the word *axiom* has these meanings:

> 1. A proposition that commends itself to general acceptance; a well-established or universally conceded principle; a maxim, rule, law. b. Specially restricted by Bacon to: An empirical law, a generalization from experience. Obs. 2. Logic. A proposition (whether true or false). 3. Logic and Math. "A self-evident proposition, requiring no formal demonstration to prove its truth, but received and assented to as soon as mentioned" (Hutton).

14. The term Fathers of the Church includes this chronological consideration:

> It follows that, as our own Fathers are the predecessors who have taught us, so the Fathers of the whole Church are especially the earlier teachers, who instructed her in the teaching of the Apostles, during her infancy and first growth. It is difficult to define the first age of the Church, or the age of the Fathers. It is a common habit to stop the study of the early Church at the Council of Chalcedon in 451.
>
> "The Fathers" must undoubtedly include, in the West, St. Gregory the Great (d. 604), and in the East, St. John Damascene (d. about 754). It is frequently said that St. Bernard (d. 1153) was the last of the Fathers, and Migne's "Patrologia Latina" extends to Innocent III, halting only on the verge of the thirteenth century, while his "Patrologia Græca" goes as far as the Council of Florence (1438–9). These limits are evidently too wide. It will be best to consider that the great merit of St. Bernard as a writer lies in his resemblance in style and matter to the greatest among the Fathers, in spite of the difference of period. St. Isidore of Seville (d. 636) and the Venerable Bede (d. 735) are to be classed among the Fathers, but they may be said to have been born out of due time, as St. Theodore the Studite was in the East. (CathEncy, s.vv. "Fathers of the Church")

15. An instance of the use of allegory in Paul's Letter to the Galatians (4:22–24a, Revised Standard Version) follows:

> For it is written that Abraham had two sons, one by a slave and one by a free woman. But the son of the slave was born according to the flesh, the son of the free woman through promise. Now this is an allegory: these women are two covenants. One is from Mount Sinai, bearing children for slavery; she is Hagar.

Allegorical interpretation of Scripture was strongly promoted in Alexandria through figures like Philo (ca. 20 B.C.–ca. A.D. 50), Clement (ca. A.D. 150–215), and Origen (A.D. 185–232), while literal approaches were favored in Antioch. Augustine of Hippo (A.D. 354–430) explains the idea of the various senses (levels of meaning) of Scripture in his *De doctrina Christiana*.

16. Other translators of the *Ratstud* have usually chosen either to leave this catalog untranslated or to place it in an appendix because of the technicality of the theological material that it contains. It is included here to give a full and accurate rendition of the original. The authors considered this technical material important enough to put into the main body of the text. In fact, the matter could be quite controversial, and it was of supreme interest, given the religious crises of that day. The handling of the Thomistic theses underwent a change over the course of the earlier *Ratio* documents of 1586 and 1591. (For a narrative summary of the changes, see John W. Padberg, S.J., "Development of the *Ratio studiorum*," 80–100). The catalog also reveals a conscientious concern for the economy and structure of course content for the sake of a more effective pedagogy.

17. "And I saw the dead, great and small, standing before the throne, and books were opened. Also another book was opened, which is the book of life. And the dead were judged by what was written in the books, by what they had done." The image evokes the idea of the community of those blessed souls who have been chosen by—and have chosen—God. Aquinas seeks to define what is meant by this phrase and whether it has something to do with predestination. He argues that it is the knowledge of God firmly remembering that he has predestined some to eternal life.

18. Thomas Aquinas writes as follows:

> To natural philosophy pertains the consideration of the order of things which human reason considers but does not create—so that we put metaphysics also under natural philosophy. But the order which reason creates of its own act by consideration pertains to rational philosophy, the office of which is to consider the order of the parts of speech with reference to one another and the order of the principles with reference to one another and to the conclusions. The order of voluntary actions pertains to the consideration of moral philosophy, while the order which the reason creates in external things through the human reason pertains to the mechanical arts.

This translation is slightly adapted from the citation given in *CathEncy*, s.v. "Philosophy." Natural philosophy, whose usage later made it synonymous with physics, covered much material that would now be taken up in the sciences.

19. Logic: Aristotle's logical thought is found in a collection of works sometimes called the *Organon: Categories, On Interpretation, Prior Analytics, Posterior Analytics, Topics, On Sophistical Refutations*. In the Aristotelian tradition, logic stands at the introduction to the philosophical course because it involves the art of drawing correct conclusions and therefore underlies many types of knowledge.

Toledo: Francisco Toledo (1534–96): Spanish Jesuit philosopher, theologian, educator, and the first Jesuit to be made a cardinal. He is the author of *Introductio in dialecticam Aristotelis* (Rome, 1561) and *Commentaria una cum quæstionibus in universam Aristotelis logicam* (Rome, 1572).

Fonseca: Pedro da Fonseca (1526–99): Portuguese Jesuit philosopher, theologian, and educator. He wrote the *Institutionum dialecticarum libri octo* (Lisbon, 1564).

20. In the history of rhetoric there has been a confusion between *loci communes* (commonplaces) and *topoi* (topics). (*Topoi* means "places" in Greek, and the Latin *loci* could be used to translate that Greek term.) Here, *loci* refers to the Aristotelian *topics*, which are essentially categories that can be used to shape an argument. In addition to the special topics used in a single area, like physics, there are general topics, like "definition" or "conflicting facts," which can be used in many different kinds of discourse. Commonplaces, or *loci communes,* also help to shape an argument and they can also be used in various arguments, but they are not categories. Rather, they are typical themes or subjects or treatments of an idea, and they can be effective, memorable passages intentionally collected for use in other contexts.

21. The device known as *decuria* is mentioned by the rhetorician Cypriano Soarez in 1553: "Each of these classes is divided into certain orders, which we call *decuriæ* because they contain ten pupils in each. In the class itself one of the students has control of all the *decuriæ,* though the single groups of ten also have their leader, called the *decurio* or captain of the body of ten" (Farrell, *Jesuit Code,* 119 f.): On Soarez, see the note to §263 in the text above.

For more on the history of *decuriæ,* see Aldo Scaglione, *The Liberal Arts and the Jesuit College System.* 12 f., 72–74. He finds them in evidence "in Paris only at the College of Montaigu . . . mentioned in 1503, though not again until after 1550," with other examples occurring "at Deventer and at Strasbourg under Sturm, and then again among both the Jesuits and the Reformed" (Scaglione, *Liberal Arts,* 13).

22. According to *CathEncy,* s.v. "Rosary,"

As regards the origin of the name, the word *rosarius* means a "garland or bouquet of roses," and it was not infrequently used in a figurative sense; e.g., as the title of a book, to denote an anthology or collection of extracts. An early legend which after travelling all over Europe penetrated even to Abyssinia connected this name with a story of Our Lady, who was seen to take rosebuds from the lips of a young monk when he was reciting Hail Marys and to weave them into a garland which she placed upon her head. A German metrical version of this story is still extant dating from the thirteenth century. The name "Our Lady's Psalter" can also be traced back to the same period. *Corona* or *chaplet* suggests the same idea as *rosarium.*

23. According to *CathEncy,* s.vv. "Divine Office,"

"Divine Office" signifies etymologically a duty accomplished for God; in virtue of a Divine precept it means, in ecclesiastical language, certain prayers to be recited at fixed hours of the day or night by priests, religious, or clerics, and, in general, by all those obliged by their vocation to fulfil this duty. The Divine Office comprises only the recitation of certain prayers in the Breviary, and does not include the Mass and other liturgical ceremonies.

The Breviary is "a book containing the entire canonical office" (see ibid., s.v., "Breviary").

24. The Loreto Litany of the Blessed Virgin Mary, approved in 1587, starts this way, with the congregation giving the appropriate responses:

Lord, have mercy. *[Response:]* Christ, have mercy.

Lord, have mercy. Christ, hear us. Christ, graciously hear us.

God, the Father of heaven, have mercy on us.

God the Son, Redeemer of the world, have mercy on us.

God the Holy Spirit, have mercy on us.

Holy Trinity, one God, have mercy on us.

Holy Mary, *[Response, repeated after each invocation below:]* pray for us.

Holy Mother of God,

Holy Virgin of virgins,

Mother of Christ,

Mother of the Church,

Mother of divine grace,

Mother most pure,

Mother most chaste,

Mother inviolate,

Mother undefiled,

Mother most amiable,

Mother most admirable,

Mother of good counsel,

Mother of our Creator,

Mother of our Savior,

Virgin most prudent,

Virgin most venerable,

There are thirty-three more such lines and then a few closing prayers, ending as follows:

Let us pray. Grant, we beg you, O Lord God, that we your servants may enjoy lasting health of mind and body, and by the glorious intercession of the Blessed Mary, ever Virgin, be delivered from present sorrow and enter into the joy of eternal happiness. Through Christ our Lord. *[Response:]* Amen.

25. Demosthenes: the most famous and exemplary ancient Greek orator (383–322 B.C.).

Plato: leading ancient Greek philosopher (428–347 B.C.).

Thucydides: ancient Greek historian (460–398 B.C.), who wrote of the conflicts between Athens and Sparta in the Peloponnesian Wars.

Homer: ancient Greek epic poet (mid-eighth to mid-seventh century B.C.), author of the *Iliad* and the *Odyssey.*

Hesiod: ancient Greek didactic and mythological poet (mid-seventh century B.C.), author of the *Works and Days* and the *Theogony.*

Pindar: ancient Greek lyric poet (518–438 B.C.), some of whose poems celebrating athletic champions survive *(Odes).*

Gregory Nazianzen: bishop and Doctor of the Church (A.D. 325–89), author of poetry, epistles, and orations.

Basil: bishop and Doctor of the Church (329–79), author of letters and many theological, scriptural, spiritual, and homiletic works.

Chrysostom: bishop and Doctor of the Church (347–407), famous orator and author of many theological and scriptural works.

26. Epigram: "A short poem ending in a witty or ingenious turn of thought, to which the rest of the composition is intended to lead up" (OED).

Epitaph: "An inscription upon a tomb. Hence, occasionally, a brief composition characterizing a deceased person, and expressed as if intended to be inscribed on his tombstone" (OED).

Ode: in antiquity, an ode is "a poem intended or adapted to be sung," but later it was a "lyric, often in the form of an address; generally dignified or exalted in subject, feeling, and style, but sometimes (in earlier use) simple and familiar (though less so than a song)" (OED).

Elegy: originally, an elegy was "a song of lamentation, esp. a funeral song or lament for the dead" (OED). Later, it meant any poem written in the meter typically used by the ancients for elegiac poems.

Epic: classically, a narrative poem in a particular kind of meter (dactylic hexameter) recounting great deeds of heroes.

Tragedy: dramatic enactment of a serious and important event.

Sibyls: prophetic women in ancient Mediterranean cultures.

27. Caesar: Gaius Julius Caesar (100?-34 B.C.), the famous Roman military and political figure who wrote commentaries describing his military campaigns, notably the *Gallic Wars* and the *Civil Wars.*

Sallust: Gaius Sallustius Crispus (86–34 B.C.), one of the first to write historical monographs *(Catiline's War; the Jugurthine War).*

Livy: Titus Livius (59 B.C.?–A.D. 17), the author of a monumental and comprehensive history of Rome *(Ab urbe condita)* from its foundations to his own days.

Curtius: Quintus Curtius Rufus (first century A.D.?), author of *The Story of Alexander the Great.*

Vergil: Publius Vergilius Maro (70 B.C.–A.D. 19), generally considered the greatest Latin poet, is the author of the *Eclogues* (or *Bucolics*), brief pastoral dialogs; the *Georgics,* a didactic poem on the agricultural life; and the *Aeneid,* an epic recounting the prehistory of Rome's foundation in the life of the Trojan war hero Aeneas.

Horace: Quintus Horatius Flaccus (65–8B.C.), Roman lyric poet famous for his *Odes, Epodes, Satires, Letters,* and the *Ars poetica.*

Pro Lege Manilia, Pro Archia, Pro Marcello: speeches delivered by Cicero.

The others delivered to Caesar: *Pro Marcello, Pro Ligario,* and *Pro Rege Deiotaro,* given in 46 and 45 B.C. after Caesar's victory over Pompey.

Cyprian: See §263 above.

28. Isocrates (436–338 B.C.): one of the greatest ancient Greek rhetoricians.

Synesius (died A.D. 414): bishop of Ptolemais (in what is now Libya). He was a disciple of the Alexandrian non-Christian astronomer, mathematician, and philosopher Hypatia (d. A.D. 415) and the author of letters, orations, and neo-Platonic philosophical tracts.

Plutarch (A.D. 46–120): influential Greek biographer and moral essayist.

Phocylides (sixth-century B.C.): Greek poet to whom was ascribed a long didactic poem that was probably written by a Jew or a Jewish-Christian in the first century B.C. or in the first century A.D.

Theognis (sixth century B.C.): didactic and elegiac Greek poet.

29. Ovid: Publius Ovidius Naso (43B.C.–A.D. 17/18), a leading love poet and author of elegies; his masterpiece was the long-influential *Metamorphoses*, a connected narrative of many mythological stories.

Catullus: Gaius Valerius Catullus (84?–54? B.C.), along with Tibullus and Propertius, a leading love poet of the late Roman Republic, known for his expressive intensity.

Tibullus (55/50 B.C.–A.D. 18/19): author of elegiac love poems.

Propertius Sextus Propertius (49/47–16/15 B.C.): author of elegiac love poems.

Aesop: (sixth century B.C.), the freed Greek slave who stands at the beginning of a long tradition of fables.

Agapetus: a deacon at Constantinople in the early sixth A.D., author of a series of exhortations to Justinian on the duties befitting his role as emperor.

For the *Georgics:* see the note on §395 above.

Bibliography

Abbreviations Used in This Book

ConsCN   *See* Constitutions of the Society of Jesus and Their Complementary Norms.

Ganss, *Cons.*   *See* Ganss, *The Constitutions of the Society of Jesus.*

MattGM   *See For Matters of Greater Moment*

Ratio   *See Ratio atque institutio studiorum Societatis Iesu* and the *Ratio studiorum* itself, as translated in this book.

Works Consulted and Cited

Alvarez, Emmanuel (Alvarus, Manoel). *De institutione grammatica libri tres juxta editionem Venetam anni 1575.* Paris: Adrianus le Clere et Soc., 1859.

Aquinas, St. Thomas. *"Summa theologica": Literally Translated by Fathers of the English Dominican Province.* 2nd ed. rev., 1920.

    There is also an on-line edition, 2002, edited for the Web by Kevin Knight: http://www.newadvent.org/summa

Atteberry, John, and John Russell, eds. *"Ratio Studiorum": Jesuit Education, 1540–1773.* Chestnut Hill, Mass.: Boston College, 1999.

Bartlett, Dennis Alan. *The Evolution of the Philosophical and Theological Elements of the Jesuit "Ratio Studiorum": An Historical Study, 1540–1599.* Ann Arbor, Mich.: University Microfilms International, 1985.

Bertrán Quera, Miguel. *La pedagogía de los Jesuitas en la "Ratio studiorum": La fundación de colegios, orígenes, autores y evolución histórica de la "Ratio," análisis de la educación religiosa, caracterológica e intelectual.* San Cristóbal, Caracas : Universidad Católica del Táchira, Centro de Estudios Interdisciplinarios; Universidad Católica Andrés Bello, Instituto de Investigaciones Históricas, 1984.

Bianchi, Angelo. *"Ratio atque institutio studiorum Societatis Iesus": Ordinamento degli studi della Compagnia di Gesù.* Milan: Biblioteca Universale Rizzoli, 2002.

Bonachea, Rolando E., ed. *Jesuit Higher Education: Essays on an American Tradition of Excellence.* Pittsburgh: Duquesne University Press, 1989.

Brizzi, Gian Paolo, ed. *La "Ratio studiorum": Modelli culturali e pratiche educative dei Gesuiti in Italia tra cinque e seicento.* Rome: Bulzoni, 1981.

Brown, Stephen F. "Theology and Philosophy." In *Medieval Latin: An Introduction and Bibliographic Guide,* edited by F. A. C. Mantello and A. G. Rigg, 267–87. Washington, D.C.: Catholic University of America Press, 1996 .

Buckley, Michael J., S.J. *The Catholic University as Promise and Project: Reflections in a Jesuit Idiom.* Washington, D.C.: Georgetown University Press, 1998.

Cabral Texo, Jorge. *El "Ratio Studiorum de la Compañía de Jesús": Su influencia en el primer plan de estudios de la Universidad de Córdoba.* Buenos Aires: Impr. y Casa Editora de Coni Hnos., 1912.

Cacho Vázquez, Xavier. *La "Ratio studiorum de la Compañía de Jesús" y los valores.* México, D.F.: Universidad Iberoamericana, Centro de Integración Universitaria, 1994.

Catholic Encyclopedia, The. New York: Robert Appleton Company, 1909. Consulted in the preparation of this book was the on-line edition, prepared for the Web in 2002 by Kevin Knight. http://newadvent.org/cathen

Codina Mir, Gabriel, S.J. *Aux sources de la pédagogie des Jésuites: Le "modus parisiensis."* Rome : Historical Institute of the Society of Jesus, 1968.

Colombat, Bernard. *La grammaire latine en Frane à la Renaissance et à l'Âge classique: Théories et pédagogie.* Grenoble: Ellug, Université Stendahl, 1999.

Constitutions of the Society of Jesus and Their Complementary Norms: A Complete English Translation of the Official Latin Texts. Saint Louis: The Institute of Jesuit Sources, 1996.

Dainville, François de. *L'éducation des Jésuites (XVIe-XVIIIe siècles).* Paris: Les Éditions de Minuit, 1978.

Daly, Peter M., and Richard Dimler, G., S.J. *The Jesuit Series.* From the series Corpus librorum emblematum. Montreal: McGill-Queen's University Press, 1997.

Deferrari, Roy J. *A Latin-English Dictionary of Saint Thomas Aquinas.* Boston: Daughters of St. Paul, 1960.

Donohue, John W., S.J. *Jesuit Education: An Essay on the Foundation of Its Idea.* New York: Fordham University Press, 1963.

Duminuco, Vincent J., S.J., ed. *The Jesuit "Ratio studiorum": 400th Anniversary Perspectives.* New York: Fordam University Press, 2000.

Farrell, Allan Peter, S.J. *The Jesuit Code of Liberal Education: Development and Scope of the "Ratio studiorum."* Milwaukee: Bruce Publishing Company, 1938.

———. *The Jesuit "Ratio studiorum" of 1599.* Washington, D.C.: Conference of Major Superiors of Jesuits 1970.

Fitzpatrick, Edward A., ed. *St. Ignatius and the "Ratio studiorum."* Translation of the *Ratio studiorum,* by A. R. Ball; translation of the *Constitutions,* Part IV, by Mary Helen Mayer. New York: McGraw-Hill, 1933.

For Matters of Greater Moment: The First Thirty Jesuit General Congregations. Edited by John W. Padberg, S.J., S.J., Martin O'Keefe, S.J., and John McCarthy, S.J. Saint Louis: Institute of Jesuit Sources, 1994.

Franca, Leonel. *O método pedagógico dos jesuitas: O "Ratio Studiorum," introdução e tradução.* Rio de Janeiro : Agir, 1952.

Ganss, George, S.J. *Saint Ignatius' Idea of a Jesuit University.* 2nd ed. Milwaukee: Marquette University Press, 1956.

———, trans. and ed. *The Constitutions of the Society of Jesus.* St. Louis: Institute of Jesuit Sources, 1970.

Gehl, Paul F. *A Moral Art: Grammar, Society, and Culture in Trecento Florence.* Ithaca and London: Cornell University Press, 1993.

Gil, Eusebio, and Carmen Labrador. *La pedagogía de los jesuitas, ayer y hoy.* Madrid: Universidad Pontificia de Comillas, 1999.

Gil, Eusebio, ed., with Carmen Labrador, A. Diez Escanciano, and J. Martinez de la Escalera. *El sistema educativo de la Compañía de Jesús: La "Ratio studiorum."* Edición bilingüe, estudio histórico-pedagógico, bibliografía. Madrid : Universidad Pontificia Comillas, 1992.

Grendler, Paul F. *Schooling in Renaissance Italy: Literacy and Learning, 1300–1600.* Baltimore and London: Johns Hopkins University Press, 1989.

Homann, Frederick A., and Ladislaus Lukács. *Church, Culture, and Curriculum: Theology and Mathematics in the Jesuit "Ratio studiorum."* Philadelphia : Saint Joseph's University Press, 1999.

Instituto Ignacio de Loyola. *Anuario del Instituto Ignacio de Loyola (Loiolako Inazio Institutuen Urekaria: Cuarto Centenario de la "Ratio Studiorum").* San Sebastian: Universidad de Deusto, 1999.

Jaeger, C. Stephen. *The Envy of Angels: Cathedral Schools and Social Ideals in Medieval Europe, 950–1200.* Philadelphia: University of Pennsylvania Press, 1994.

Luce, Giard, et al. *Les Jésuites à la Renaissance: Système éducatif et production du savoir.* Paris: Presses universitaires de France, 1995.

Martinez Marquez, Eduardo. *Vigencia del "Ratio studiorum de la Compañia de Jesus."* Habana, Colegio de Belen, 1957.

McCabe, William H., S.J. *An Introduction to the Jesuit Theater.* Edited by Louis J. Oldani, S.J. Saint Louis: The Institute of Jesuit Sources, 1983.

McGucken, William J., S.J. *The Jesuits and Education: The Society's Teaching Principles and Practice, Especially in Secondary Education in the United States.* New York: The Bruce Publishing Company, 1932.

Mestre, Antonio, and Itzíar Vilar Rey. *"Ratio studiorum": Una llibreria jesuïta a la Universitat de València.* València : Universitat de València, 2001.

Nugent, Daniel C. "The Grand Act at St. Louis University." *The Woodstock Letters* 32 (1903): 82–93.

O'Malley, John W., S.J. "The Council of Trent: Myths, Misunderstandings, and Misinformation." In *Spirit, Style, Story: Essays Honoring John W. Padberg, S.J.,* edited by Thomas M. Lucas, S.J., 205–23. Chicago: Loyola Press, 2002.

———. *The First Jesuits.* Cambridge: Harvard University Press, 1993.

———. "The Jesuit Educational Enterprise in Historical Perspective." In *Jesuit Higher Education: Essays on an American Tradition of Excellence,* edited by Rolando Bonachea, 10–25. Pittsburgh: Duquesne University Press, 1989.

Ong, Walter J., S.J. *Ramus: Method, and the Decay of Dialogue: From the Art of Discourse to the Art of Reason.* Cambridge, Massachusetts: Harvard University Press, 1983.

Oxford English Dictionary. Used in the preparation of this present volume was the on-line edition: http://dictionary.oed.com/entrance.dtl

Padberg, John W., S.J. "Development of the *Ratio studiorum.*" In *The Jesuit "Ratio studiorum": 400th Anniversary Perspectives,* Edited by Vincent J. Duminuco, S.J., 80–100. New York: Fordham University Press, 2000.

Pâquet, André. *"Ratio studiorum": Code pédagogique de la Compagnie de Jésus.* Montréal: Aux Éditions de l'Entr'aide, 1940, 1940.

Pedersen, Olaf. *The First Universities: Studium Generale and the Origins of University Education in Europe.* Cambridge: Cambridge University Press, 1998.

Rashdall, Hastings. *The Universities of Europe in the Middle Ages.* Edited by F. M. Powicke and A. B. Emden. 3 vols. Sandpiper Edition. London: Oxford University Press, 1997; originally published in 1895.

Ratio atque institutio studiorum Societatis Iesu. Vol. 5 of the *Monumenta Paedagogica Societatis Iesu,* edited by Ladislaus Lukàcs. Vol. 129 of the series Monumenta Historica Societatis Iesu, 357–454. Rome: Historical Institute of the Society of Jesus, 1986.

"Ratio studiorum": Plan raisonné et institution des études dans la Compagnie de Jésus. Edition bilingue latin-français. Presented by Adrien Demoustier and Dominique Julia. Translated by Léone Albrieus and Dolorès Pralon-Julia. Annotations and commentary by Marie-Madeleine Compère. Paris: Belin, 1997.

This bilingual edition makes use of the same marginal section numbers as does this present English edition.

Ratio studiorum superiorum Societatis Iesu: Ad normam Congregationum Generalium XXVIII et XXIX exarata. Rome: General Curia of the Society of Jesus, 1954.

Regulæ Societatis Iesu. Rome: General Curia of the Society of Jesus, 1932.

Rubio i Goday, Àngel, and Miquel Batllori. *"Ratio studiorum": L'ordenació dels estudis dels jesuïtes.* Vic: Eumo, 1999.

Russell, Daniel. "Alciati's Emblems in Renaissance France." *Renaissance Quarterly,* 34, no. 4 (1981): 534–54.

Salomone, Mario. *Ratio atque institutio studiorum Societatis Jesu: L'ordinamento scolastico dei collegi dei gesuiti.* Milan: Feltrinelli economica, 1979.

Scaglione, Aldo. *The Liberal Arts and the Jesuit College System.* Philadelphia: John Benjamins Publishing Company, 1986.

Schafly, Daniel L., Jr. "The *Ratio Studiorum* on Alien Shores: Jesuit Colleges in St. Petersburg and Georgetown." *Revista Portuguesa de Filosofia* 55 (1999): 253–74.

———. "True to the *Ratio Studiorum?* Jesuit Colleges in St. Petersburg." *History of Education Quarterly* 37 (1997): 421–34.

Schwickerath, Robert, S.J. *Jesuit Education: Its History and Principles Viewed in the Light of Modern Educational Problems.* Saint Louis: B. Herder, 1903.

Sirignano, Fabrizio Manuel. *L'itinerario pedagogico della "Ratio studiorum."* Naples: Luciano, 2001.

Tanner, Norman P., ed. *Decrees of the Ecumenical Councils.* 2 vols. New York: Sheed and Ward, 1990.

Tinsley, Barbara Sher. "Johann's Sturm's Method for Humanistic Pedagogy." *Sixteenth Century Journal* 20 (1989): 10, 23–40.

Tripole, Martin, S.J., ed. *Jesuit Education 21: Conference Proceedings on the Future of Jesuit Higher Education.* Philadelphia: St. Joseph's University Press, 2000.

———. *Promise Renewed: Jesuit Higher Education for a New Millenium.* Chicago: Jesuit Way, 1999.

Note: Many other relevant items can be found in the bibliographies of Ganss *Ignatius' Idea,* Gehl, Grendler, McCabe, and Scaglione, all listed above.

INDEX

NOTE: The numbers below indicate the bracketed paragraph numbers in the text of the *Ratio*

Urbe Condita, 395

ability, in arts of written communication, 8; scholarly, 35; average, 74; outstanding, 105; exercising, 140; to write in Greek, 395

Abraham, 154, C121

abridgment, of topics not found in Aquinas, 194; *Physics,* 221; *On the Heavens,* 222; review of material for biennium students, 448; memory of catechetical material, 469, C49

absence, from case conferences, 21; from disputations and review sessions, 78; from monthly declamations, 282; report by censor, chief decurion or praetor, 287; from class 289; class, 365; academies, 486; teacher's, 488; rector's and first counselor's, 489

abstaining, from insulting treatment, 364; from bad behavior, 471; from harmless and useless books, 477

academics, learned persons, 2, 5, 106, 110, 111, 122, 144, 233, 451

academics, 8; units, 10; positions, 15, 22; exercises, 16n, 72; ceremony, 88; order, 99; pursuits, 129, 445; approved authorities, 134, 195, 202; term *bidellus,* 147n; work, 335; conversations, 441; custom, 464; institutions, 466; studies, 476, 480

academy, [H35–H40]; private, 14; defined, 14n 30, 481; for training teachers, 53; for language study, 81; prerequisite for sodality membership, 97; for literary exercises, 284; establishing, 369; meaning, members' qualities, 483; moderators, 484; different kinds, 485; attendance and exercises, 486; officers, 487; rector of an academy, 488; counselors, 489; secretary, 490; regular consultation about, 491; reading of rules, 492; keeping of the rules, 494; encouragement of exercises, 495; times to meet, 497; types of exercises, 498; management of the reviews, 500; presiding over disputations, 503; lessons, 504; formal acts held by academy's rector, 505; review of theses, 508; structure of the academy's exercises, 509; frequent practice in, 511; academy prefect and the assistant, 512; day to meet, 513; what exercises held by moderator, 514; what exercises held by the members, 515; public exercises, 516

accent, pitch accents in Greek, 337; in schedule of highest grammar class, 406; acute, 406

Achilles, 406

Acquaviva, Claudio, 1n

act, of submission to God, 47

Act, academic 16; academic act defined, 16n; theological, 105; special, 106; general, 107; theses published, 108; schedule for, 109, 122; those given by non-Jesuits, 110; who presides over, 111; number of theses, 112; philosophical, 117, 122; for day students and boarders, 119; who attends, 123; inspection of material for, 126; biennial students, 446, 453, 454; beadle's part in, 464; and academies, 488, 490, 498, 505, 506, 508, 509, 510, 512

activity, classroom, 58n; interfering with studies, 78; of reformers 128n; energetic, 173, 197; of a good student, 284; in rhetoric schedule, 376; exercises during correction, 379, 408, 428; in competition, 386, 401, 414, 424; theologians' academy, 488; grammar academy, 522, C57,

active expressions, 433

Acts of the Apostles, 65, 128

Actus generales, 16n

Actus peculiares, 16n

adage, 386

Adam, 176, C84, C123n, C125n

adequacy, of progress, 247

administration, administrative units, 2n; of the Society of Jesus, 5n; of law and →

aptitude, for rhetoric, 24, C101

Aquila, 153

argument, prefect not to resolve, 104; making disputations sharper, 123; significance, not number important, 135; in Jesuit in-house reviews, 140; pressing, 144; participation of external academics in, 144; professor's guidance in, 146; theologians on Immaculate Conception, 176n; open to any person, 196; in weekly disputation in cases of conscience, 202; opposed to the faith, 208; *loci* as *topics* shaping an argument, 220n; in the study of important passages, 227; Aristotle's 228; monthly disputations in philosophy, 231; review of argument by respondent, 234; in exercises in rhetoric during the correction, 379; in interpreting a composition, 382; invention and expression, 382n; in private classes for those reviewing theology, 451; beadle's office for public Acts, 464; rector of theologians' academy 488; structure of the reviews in the academies of theologians and philosophers, 500; in academy lessons, 504; and outsiders at Acts, 506; in exercises of academies of rhetoricians and humanities students, 515, C7, C16, C25, C33, C40

argumentum (theme), 266n

army, in compositions (rhetoric and humanities), 392, 404

arrangement, as a meaning of *institutio*, 1; of rector's time, 77; membership in sodality as prerequisite to membership in an academy, 97; of the schedule of studies, 125; of alternation of New and Old Testaments, 165; of questions in cases of conscience, 200; of three-year comprehensive philosophical course, 213; of *loci* and fallacies from the *Topics* and *Refutations*, 220; of teaching of the *Meteorologica*, 223; of solemn disputations in philosophy, 233; definition of *syntax* and *constructio*, 250n; splitting lowest class, 251; of examination boards, 268; of removal from class, 275; alternative for expulsion, 291; of awards, 312; in interpreting a composition, 382, 382n; of scrambled poems, 403, 408; biennials students' review, 448; biennial survey, 449; beadle and classroom order, 460; beadle and preparation of seats for guests at the Acts, 464; academy prefect and scheduling, 497; moderator and grammar academy's content, 520

ars metrica, as prosody, 337n

arts, 2n; executive assistant skilled in, 8, 8n; Master of 16n; *bonæ artes*, 99; as preparation for theology, 207, C34n

Ascension, 68n

Ash Wednesday, 63, 63n

assembling, for prizes, 314

assembly, 95, 110, 136, 282, 322, 381, 390, 497

assignment, of prefect of studies, 8; to scriptural studies, 14; to confession, 21; of books for the library, 26; to philosophy or cases of conscience by examination, 27; to case studies, 28; to philosophy or theology cancelled by low achievement, 34; decision left to provincial, 37; of career teachers, 47; to theology from the course of studies, 50; teaching assignment, 51; of substitutes for regularly assigned teachers of philosophers and theologians, 80; of speech at the inauguration of studies, 89; of the prefect of the courtyard, 96; finishing assigned material, 103; of examiners in metaphysics, 118; of student examiners in examinations of day and boarding students, 119; of material for exam, 121; of student to explicate passage of Scripture, 168; of material for the year, 186; authors assigned by presider in cases of conscience, 204; of professor of philosophy and the *Meteorologica*, 223; of professor of moral philosophy, 235; review of student work by prefect of lower studies, 247; review of assigned work, 257; of substitute for examinations, 266; of places and partners and seating in class, 279; of time for composition, 314; completing the prize composition, 316; of matter and time periods, 339; of exercises on break day, 341; names on the reverse of assigned work, 347; corrections of, 347; going beyond the daily assignment, 364; of exercise in rhetoric, 376; in schedule for rhetoric, 396; of literary passage for imitation, 397; in schedule of highest grammar, 406; in schedule of middle grammar, 416; in schedule of lowest grammar, 426; of classes by superior, 436; beadle's duties, 459; of benches for Jesuits, 460; of classes by the prefect, 467

assistance, of career teachers, 47; of the arts and natural sciences, 207; of divine grace, 374; withheld in composition exercise, 410; withheld in formal lessons in the academy of theologians and philosophers, 504

assistant, authors of the *Ratio*, 2; general →

authority, 1; synthesis of theology *(Summa)*, 15; of the prefect, 76; competent ecclesiastical, 97; needed for opinions, 134; and the meaning of *doctor*, 134n; limited citation of, 136; importance of reading, 136; and meaning of holy Fathers, 136n; Vulgate, 150n; Septuagint, 153n; canons 154n; and rabbinical writings, 157; of St. Thomas Aquinas, 175; some excluded, 179; defense of Aquinas's, 195; explanation of in disputation, 202; concise report of in disputation, 205; to be diminished, 211; of famous interpreters, 227; of teachers, 245; sources of scholarly learning, 375

award, annual public distribution, 88; in lower studies, 285; number of, 312; criteria for, 320; ceremony for, 322; for knowledge of entire book, 350; in class, 355; for officers, 359; as motivating force superior to punishment, 363; private (academy of rhetoricians and humanities students), 517; public, 518; private (academy of grammar students), 525. *Also see* prize

axiom, of the Doctors, 134; defined 134n; in choice and order of questions, 228

Azor, John, 2

babies, male babies killed by Herod, 62n, C127

baptism, 182, 185, 198n, C104, C127, [H14]

Basil, 15n, 387, 403n

beadle, [H33]; conferring with, 147; defined, 147n; and the secretary of the academy of theologians and philosophers, 490

beatific vision, C1n, C22

Bede the Venerable, 136n

behavior, moral, 325, 368; violent, 471

being, human, 30, 176n; states and duties of human, 198; spiritual (guardian angels), 331n, C10, C18, C19, C23, C25, C83, C93, C111, C122, C125

belief, 5, 72; and heretics, 164n; contradiction of orthodox, 208; Christian, 211, C95

benefice, 198n

Benedict, 19n

Bernard, 136n

Bible, and positive theology, 11n; for each theologian, 128; defined, 128n; Vulgate, 150n; Hebrew Bible in Greek, 153n; Ten Commandments in, 198n. *Also see* Sacred Scripture

board (examination), 268

boarder, 8; boarding colleges, 8n; and rhetoric, 86; examinations of (philosophy), 119, 120; assignment of place, 279; schedule for, 280

Bologna, 2n, 16n

bonæ artes,, 99n. *Also see* arts and liberal arts

book, languages in scriptural books, 13; allowance of special books, 26; for examination, 27; decision against theology studies, 37; provincial's, 48; sufficient supply of books, 56; avoiding unseemly books, 57; following the manual of studies, 71; record of public presentations by Jesuits, 90; distribution of books, 91; of the plan of studies, 102; selection and quantity of books, 127; which books distributed to which people, 128; Book of Revelation, 128n; limitation on use of books in teaching, 132; new book studied each year, 166; of Scripture (professor of Hebrew), 171; interpretation of sacred books, 172; Book of Genesis, 176n; Books of Exodus and Deuteronomy, 198n; Aristotelian works, 218, 219, 221, 222, 224, 225, 228, 235; division of grammar into three books, 250; finishing each class's book in the first semester, 251; record book, 263; reviewing teacher's record book, 270; examination on class's text books, 271; teacher to be shown his own record book after examination, 274; not keeping a record of those sent back, 275; listing and deciding on books to be taught, 277; adequate supply of books, 278; rules for Academy at the end of the *Ratio*, 284; learning an entire book, 286; distribution of books to Jesuit students, 300; arriving with books at examination, 303, 311; turning in composition with one's books, 309; *rosarius* as title, 329n; breviary defined, 329n; restriction on books in teaching, 335; delivery of book aloud in lower classes, 343, examination on all material, 350; teacher's reading entire book in advance, 351; notebook record of decurions, 360; Cicero's books on rhetoric, 375; Cicero's books on moral philosophy, 395; Cyprian's third book, 396; of Pliny's letters, 400n; Cyprian's Rhetoric, 402; in highest grammar, 405; entire book recited, 406; in middle grammar, 415, 416; in lowest grammar, 425, 426; limitation of books, 436; abstaining from harmful and useless books, 477; secretary and acade- →

good, C109

charge, in charge, 8n, 9, 14, 51, 84, 104, 134, 203, 230, 300, 306, 315, 439, 481, 484, 500; duty, 19; of heretics, 189

charity, work of, 39n; spirit of religious, 94; and sodalities, 97n; in accommodation to others, 179; faith, hope, and, 181, 184; in serious incidents, 291; in undertaking studies, 435, C78, C96, C99, C100, C106

charm, in the interpretation of a composition, 382

charter, first of the Society (Formula of the Institute), 7; of a teaching institution, 44

cheating, avoiding in examinations, 306; penalty for, in prize competition, 324

checking, time allowed for during examination, 310; of decurion's marks, 396, 416, 426

children, in Formula of the Institute, 7n; allegory of Hagar, 154n, C104

chria, 396; defined, 396n; composition of in humanities, 400

Christmas, starting a vacation, 62; defined, 62n; Acts at, 505

chronology, of the Fathers of the Church, 136n; not to be lingered over, 162

church, preaching sermons in, 79; and time for sodality meetings, 97; Lateran, 208n; attendance of students, 295; and confessions, 296; and litanies, 331; and exercises, 379, 392, 404; public declamation in, 391, 394; behavior in, 479

Church, Doctors of, 15, 25; reform of, 128; doctrine of, 136n; Fathers of, 136n; and Vulgate, 150, 170; consensus of, 155, 178; as subject for study, 184; and censures, 198n, 295; litanies and common necessities of, 331n, 387; Church-related learning, 455; ecclesiastical material, 457; ecclesiastical power, C105; membership in, C115

Circumcision, feast as end of vacation, 62; defined, 62n

circumflex, verbs, 337, 337n; accent mark, 406n; verbs in -mi, 415

citation, of main reasons for objections to Ratio, 2; restraint in, 133; avoid excessive, 136; only from authors read, 136; explanation rather than dictation, 138; from Hebrew or Greek text, 152; insufficient without expression of teacher's own opinion, 195; from Averroes, 210; of the rule broken, 346; of rhetoricians' rules, 381; in the interpretation of compositions, 382; of ver-

nacular expressions, 399; of rule or passage in competition, 401, 414

city, descriptions of in compositions, 392, 404

civil power, C105

Civil Wars, of Julius Caesar, 395

class, scheduling, 6; of college, 8n; management of, 9; on Sacred Scripture, 12; of cases of conscience, 18; public class on cases of conscience, 19; covering enough theology, 30; mathematics, 38; how many lower, 39; having the right number, 40; two levels in, 41; keep higher, 42; multiplication of, 43; assignment to, 51; starting point for assignment, 52; schedules maintained, 58; vacations for, 60–67; and public supplications, 68; different breaks for, 70; oversight of following rules for, 71; admission to theological, 74; rector's visitation of, 77, 115; substitutes for teachers, 80; to train teachers of rhetoric, 84; consultation on classes below logic, 92; weekly break in lower classes, 93; exhortations to, 95; prefect's function regarding, 99; theses when classes resume, 109; audience for non-Jesuit's examinations, 120; philosophical Acts and class time, 122; and the teachers' special intention (higher faculties), 129; prayer before class, 130; class discipline, 132; teacher in time after class, 139; reviews of, 141; disputations on Saturday, 142; value of disputation over against, 146; conferral about class's progress, 147; interest in, 148; in dining hall, 167; student presentation in place of, 168; cancellation for Saturday disputation, 202; not to include anti-Christian interpreters of Aristotle, 209; on entire range of philosophy, 213; time for Meteorologica, 223; time for related questions, 229; review in, 230; division into decuriæ, 230, 230n; defense of theses on Saturday, 232; of moral philosophy, 236; metaphysicians disputations, 238; of mathematics, 239; goal of prefect of lower studies, 242; moral discipline in, 243; prefect's visitation of lower classes, 247; prefect and oversight of schedule, 248; five grades of, 249; division of grammar, 250; split arrangement for lowest class, 251; college of five classes, 253; of four classes, 254; of three classes, 255; of two classes, 256; review of work in classes of two levels, 257; material taken in classes where there are two levels, 258; placement in class, 261; to be excluded →

medical matters avoided, 224; into theology by professor of moral theology, 235; in correcting compositions, 378

diligence, of faculty, 10; in promoting study of sacred texts, 11; in fostering the enthusiasm of teachers, 94; in carrying out provincials' decisions, 98; of non-Jesuit students, 147; of professors (higher classes), 148; of professors of philosophy, 207; as a factor in examinations, 273; correction of shortcomings, in by disciplinarian, 288; in encouraging devotions, 331; of professors (lower classes), 374; of Jesuit students, 435, 437; in practicing style, 442; in maintaining a love for the essential virtues, 445; of the study of biennial students, 448; of beadle, 459; of non-Jesuits, 473, 474, 479; of academy members, 483; of rector of an academy, 488; of prefect of an academy, 494, 496; oversight of, in academies of theologians and philosophers, 510; correction of shortcomings in, 526

dining hall, reviews and in-house classes, 167; delivery in, 394; biennial students' presentations in, 451, 456

dining, as a subject of scholarly learning, 389

direction, of the general prefect, 9; *Ratio* directing the provincial on membership, 48n; of classes by the prefect, 99; prefect of lower studies, 242; of day students and boarders, 279; of biennial students, 450; of philosophers in an academy, 488; by the prefect of the academy of theologians and philosophers, 510

directive, canons, 154n; of provincial, 203

disagreement, with Thomas, 15; with heretics, 164

discernment, 37

disciplinarian, non-Society, 288; when insufficient, 290; and whipping, 364; disclosure of function to non-Jesuit students, 472

discipline, teaching, 7, 16n; in class, 132; Doctors and, 134n; Church, 136n; questions of moral, 243; matters of class discipline and prefect; importance of observing the rules, 363

discourse, and meaning of *collatio*, 19n; meaning in formal, 155; in house conference, 203; and use of topics, 220n; and interpretation, 382; scholastic, C1n, C105

discretion, superior's, 16; provincial's, 23; teacher's, 386, 401, 414, 424, 433

discussion, in writing of the *Ratio*, 3; of individual cases, 19n; on angels, 30; limited, 134, 221; in councils, 136n; of Scriptures, 155; of contracts, 198; in-house conference, 203; in doubtful cases, 273; open to biennial students, 447, C16, C45, C47, C56, C62, C63, C68, C69, C70, C83, C102, C106, C121, C123

dismissal, for public prayers, 248; of students only with consultation of the prefect, 335; quiet, 368; from our schools, 472, 486

dispensation, provincial's power of, 74; prefect's, 101; from law of celibacy, 198n

display, in Acts, 16n, 506; in solemn disputations, 233; of poems and emblems, 244

disposition, towards Thomas Aquinas, 15, 175; towards rabbinical authors discouraged, 157; of intellectual talents for theology by arts and sciences, 207; towards anti-Christian writers discouraged, 209; personal, C129

disputant, 104, 146, 439, 462, 463

disputation, mentioned in the *Constitutions*, 6n; in General and Special Acts, 16; diversity in, 72; defined, 72n; rector attending, 77; importance of students' attendance at, 78; biennial students presiding at, 80; prefect's oversight of, 104, 112, 113, 114, 117, 122, 123, 124, 125; in common rules for teachers (higher faculties), 132, 140, 142, 143, 144, 145, 146; Vulgate authoritative for, 150n; and the professor of scholastic theology, 174, 190, 191, 192, 196; in cases of conscience, 202, 205; in philosophy, 216, 217, 219, 221, 227, 228, 229, 231, 232, 233, 234; adding ethical propositions to, 238; in mathematics, 240; and prefect of lower studies, 283, 284; in humanities, 396; and Jesuit students, 438, 439, 444; and biennial students, 446, 447, 449; and beadle, 461, 462, 463, 464, 465; and the academies, 497, 498, 499, 501, 503, 506, 509, 512, 515, 522; disputing particular questions, C2, C4, C16, C22, C23, C28, C30, C33, C41, C42, C43, C44, C47, C48, C52, C65, C88, C90, C97, C101, C108, C111, C112, C115

distinction, Saint Thomas's, 193; in disputations, 234; of grades and grammar, 250; in grammar lesson when there are two levels, 258; of poets and prose writers, 352; in the register, 362; of different interpretations of a composition, 382; of figures of speech in a composition, 386; in Thomas Aquinas, C24, C42, C79, C106, C109

322, 323; for confession, 333; with name of rival, 347; of rank of officer in class, 359; calling by, 364; patronymics, 406n; in academy register, 490, 492; of those not performing well in an academy, 526; name of God, C27

narration, *collatio*, 19n; and Bible, 128n; and composition, 354, 400; in the interpretation of a composition, 382; and epic, 389n; prose compositions posted, 392, 404; *Metamorphoses*, 405

native language or tongue, 354, 409, 420, 423

natural good, C90. *Also see* vernacular

natural inclination, 458

natural philosopher or philosophy, 231, 502, C34, C45

natural qualities, C16

natural reason, 153n, C55

natural science, 207

nature, of the material, 57; personal, 261

nature, of science, C1; and substance, C2, C10, C39, C109, C111; of propositions, C41;

nature (creation), C46; fallen nature, C84, C84n; in Christ, C116; law of nature, C125, C125n

neighbors, 7, 7n, 75; Bible, 128n

Nerva, 400n

New Testament, 13, 65n, 128, C43, C86, C121

Nicomachean Ethics, C49n

non-existence, C61

noticing, 2; in class visitations, 115; digressions, 146; expressions in Scripture, 151; feast days, 248; notice to parents or guardians, 275; by censor, 287; vocational interest, 330; failings of Jesuit students, 465

notion, summary (rhetorical rules), 395

noun, 337, 337n, 414, 414n, 415, 416, 416n, 424, 425, 429, 433

oaths, C66

obedience, to the general prefect, 8, 132, 335; holy, 48, 48n; vow, 48n, 82n; to God, 129; and the effort of study, 435; of Jesuit students to the one in charge, 439; beadle's, 459; of non-Jesuit students, 473; and God's laws, 479

obediential potency, C109, C109n

object, C20, C55, C70

objective existence, C112

obligation, to observe *Ratio*, 5; of the provin-

cial, 7; to train teachers in an academy, 53; those refusing, 86; Divine Office, 329n

observance, of rules for conferences on cases of conscience, 19; of cloister, 26n; of rule for recording publications and presentations of Jesuits, 90; failings in, 92; of rules of the *Ratio*, 102; of meaning in other passages, 227; lower prefect and rules, 245; of the practice of speaking Latin, 342; of the rules and concern for discipline, 363; of rules by biennial students; of modesty, 479

observation, 2, 3, 5; of teachers, 115; about the Latin language, 420, 430

occasion, 19n; confessors, 21; feast days, 61n; for Literature, 323; of alternate Saturdays, 357; and posting of poems, 392, 404; beadle and disputations, 462;

ode, 384, 389; defined, 389; of Horace, 395, 396

Odyssey, 387n

offense, to Catholics, 179; too serious for expulsion, 291; in material needing expurgation, 395; to other students, 486

office, rules for provincial's, 26n; of prefect, 76; of rector, 94, 94n; and *depositio* or *degradatio*, 198n; of disciplinarian, 290; of the Blessed Virgin, 329, 329n; divine, 329n; of decurion, 343; award of, 359; political, 400n; of rational philosophy, C34; of the Mediator, 123

officer, and meaning of an academy, 14n; and competition, 355; for the class, 359; announcing, 392, 404; appointing, 410; selecting in an academy, 487; names kept by secretary, 490

official, highest, and seating, 359; of an academy, 491

omission, easier items, 160; of allegories and moral matters, 163; of questions that can not be finished, 186; of nothing noteworthy in individual articles, 192; of questions that can not be defended, 195; of parts of *On the Heavens*, 222; of parts of *Metaphysics*, 225; of attention and care to lower levels, 255; of words on examinations, 304; of Saturday's lessons, 376; of grammatical review forbidden, 427; of exercises in an academy, 515

omnipotence, C109, C109, C123

On Friendship, 405

On Old Age, 405

On the Elements, 219n, 222

opinion, about talent, 37; selection of opinions; respect for contrary, 133; avoiding novelty of, 134; avoiding opinions lacking authority, 134; no useless, out-of-date, absurd, or false, 135; confirming one's own, 136; about the day devoted to disputation, 146; on Immaculate Conception and on solemnity of vows, 176; of Saint Thomas when unclear, 177; offensive to Catholics, 179; citing academic authorities not sufficient, 195; indication of valid contrary opinion, 201; in disputation, 205; of the ancients, 221, 224; of interpreters of rules of rhetoric, 381; and Roman method, 415n; defense of student's own, 454; diversity of, C41

oral examination, 273

Oratorical Training, p. 3, unnumbered notes

orator, Cicero, 258n; skill of, 382; and Greek lesson, 387, 387n; teaching Cicero, 395, 405

oratory, as a subject, 375; oratorical rhythm, 396; in argument in an academy of rhetoricians and humanities students, 515

order, of classes, 6n; approach the order of the *Ratio*, 6; of the Father General, 7; of the course of studies, 8; orderly management of the classes, 9; diversity in, 72; religious, 82n, 122, 233; following the levels in order, 92; academic, 99; of studies, 101; schedule, 121; of the theses, 122; of explanation of Thomas's articles, 193; in the house conference on cases, 203, 205; in philosophy, 228; and *decuriæ*, 230; alphabetical, 267, 269, 276, 308, 362; of seating, 279; in the courtyard, 293; in church, 295; daily, 336; of exercises, 339; word order, 351, 398, 362, 408, 428; well-ordered learning, 363; in producing the grammatical material, 419n, 424, 433; of notes, 456; in the academy's register, 490; order in nature, C8; providential ordering, C29; in natural philosophy, C34; order of acts in justification, C97

Order (Society of Jesus), 7n, 82n

orders, 198n, C127

ordination, 182, 198n, C30

Organon, 215n

Origen, 154n

origin, of master's degree, 16n; countries of, 261; of rosary, 329n; of expressions, 409

original, text of Scripture, 152, 169; context, 188n

original sin, 176n, C127

ornament, and rhetoric, 375; of scholarly learning, 399

orthodoxy, 174, 208

outcome, 31

outsider, 23n, 280, 506

overview, of refutations, 220; of material, 229; general, 232, 375, 507; of Cyprian, 263; of rules of rhetoric, 395

Ovid (Publius Ovidius Naso), 405, 405n

Oxford, 16n

Palm Sunday, 64, 64n

paper, for composition, 308; with names of competitors, 318, 321; for confessions, 333; correcting, 418

parable, C6

paradigm, 415

paradox, 392, 404

Paradoxes, 405, 405n

paraphrase, 352

parent, 86; first, 176n, 259, 261, 275, 370

parish, 94n, 197

participation, in the Acts, 16; in language academy, 81; in Special Acts, 105; of academics from elsewhere, 144, 233; in choice of books, 277; of biennial students in Acts, 453; of rector of an academy, 488; of outsiders, 506; and practice, 511; participatory government, C73

parts of speech, 250, 250n, 337, 405, 414, C34

passage, scriptural, 17, 151, 154, 160, 162, 164, 168, 19n; and *loci*, 200n; 227; on examinations, 271; and lesson, 351, 399, 420, 430; and schedule, 376; and composition, 378, 382, 397; and exercises, 379, 398, 418, 428; and the interpretation of the rules, 381; and competition, 401, 414; and theme for the composition, 421

passion, 64, 64n; in argumentation, 144; for the virtues, 480

passive voice, 433

past tenses, 433

patristic, 11n, 136n; interpretations, 168

patrius sermo, 271n

Patrologia Græca, 136n

Patrologia Latina, 136n

patrology, 136n

patronymics, 406, 406n

Paul, Saint, C86, C88

Peloponnesian, 387n

penalty, 198n; for cheating, 324; method →

sultation with teachers, 92; and exhortations, 95, [H3]; obedience to, 132; and prize competitions; approval of public declamation; and biennial students, 450, 454; and disputations, 454, 462, 463; and the Acts of an academy, 506

prefect, lower 9; 41; and consultation with teachers, 92, [H22]; obedience to, 335; competitions with closest class, 358; being informed of student excellence, 361; and register of students, 362; and the more severe penalties, 364; and frequently absent students, 365; and meeting with parents, 370; and the Greek lesson, 413; and course material, 415; and schedule, 436, 448; and books, 436; assignment to class, 467; and what is forbidden, 471; and entertainments, 478

prefect, for examinations, 302, 306, 307, 308, 309

prefect, for prize competitions, 317, 318, 321, 322

prefect of courtyard, 9, 92

prefect, of an academy, [H36], 500, 503, 504, 505, 507, 508, 512

preparation, for priesthood, 8n; pastoral, 19n; of humanities teachers, 45; of career teachers, 47, 48; teacher training, 53; for solemn profession, 82n; for the Act, 119; for theology, 207; preparatory sections of logic, 216; and theme or *argumentum*, 266; for spiritual life, 325; in competition with the closest class, 358; for the examination, 361; of the ground for eloquence, 395; preparatory exercise, 396, 396n; of Jesuit students, 434; of sermons disallowed, 456; of classroom for the Acts, 464; lessons given in an academy, 504; of academy members for an Act, 511; in review at an academy meeting, 521; of memorized material, 523

prescription, of *Ratio*, 5; two-year period, 14; as *Constitutions* prescribe, 16; for the conference on cases, 19; of vacation times, 59; circumcision, 62n; concerning morals and religious devotion, 73; in the practice of rhetoric, 84; for rector in encouraging teachers, 94; for theologian concerning the teaching of Saint Thomas, 102; for weekly disputations, 114; for the Acts, 123; of the schedule of studies, 125; of classes in the dining hall, 167; by rector and general prefect, 243; for grades, 255; for disputations, 283; for examinations, 304; of schedule and

study plan, 436, 448; procedure for biennial students, 450; of content, 458; of study plan by teacher, 473; following what has been prescribed in an academy, 496

presence, of rector, 25, 74, 77; of entire community for public supplications, 68; of both prefects, 92; of general prefect, 92; at examination of Jesuits in metaphysics, 118; of others in public examinations, 120; for degree conferral, 123; teacher, 202; of Jesuits and other religious, 279; of prefect of lower studies at class disputations, 283; mischief in absence of teacher, 287; of prefect of lower studies, 294; of teacher for attendance at Mass, 295; for examination, 301; of large assembly for awards, 322; required to receive prize, 322; attendance at Mass and sermon, 327; of teacher or another for Jesuit reviews, 394; of Jesuit students at disputations and reviews, 438, 439; of biennial students at conference on cases and disputations, 446, 447; of academics for private classes, 451

presentation, public, 16; scholastic, 200; of lessons and disputations and such, 284; in the lesson, 380; public declamation, 391; in humanities schedule, 396; beadle's reminding for, 461

preservation, of the understanding of humanistic literature, 45; of peace and charity, 291; of the word order, 351; of well-ordered learning, 363; of silence and modesty, 367; teaching of Saint Thomas, 449

presider, for conference on cases, 19, 204, 205, 206; rector, 94n; of Acts, 454; over disputations in an academy, 503, 512

presiding, for teachers, 80; over Acts, 111, 146, 505

pretense, disallowed, 146

previewing, of class material in an academy, 520

priesthood, 8n; of Melchisedech, C121, C121n

principle, axiom, 134n; in refutations, 135; of morality, 149; solid and lasting, 178; in defense of thesis, 189; general principles of moral issues, 191; in the house conference on cases, 203; first principles, 229; grammatical, 250n; essential, 450; in Acts, 454; of individuation, C9, C9n, C34n; and form, C100n; of justice, 108. *Also see* holy orders

printing, 102, 108

private (rank), 355

private academy, 14, 30, 53

the composition, 421, 431; purity of heart and intention, 434; Jesuit and non-Jesuit students, 441, 445; beadle to remind students, 461; and weapons, 470; and academies, 481, 482, 483, 485, 488

study, of Sacred Scripture, 11; no exemptions from scriptural study, 14; quiet study for reviewing theology, 16; of cases of conscience 18; time period for humanities, 24; of logic, 25; third year of theological study, 30; privilege of study, 33; removal from, 34; teaching assignment and study, 51; diversity in study hours, 72; of rhetoric, 86; Ignatius and language study, 99n; schedule of, 125; private study, 128, 204, 280, 444; of Aristotle, 226; grammar course, 336; of historian or poet, 376; grammatical study, 395; catechism study, 396, 406, 416, 426; great merit of, 435; direction in, 436; limits on continuous study, 443; plan of study and those reviewing theology, 448, 449, 456, 457, 458; and disciplinarian, 472; obedience in, 473; study circle's rector, 487n

style, in examinations, 304; criteria for judging, 320; practicing, 345, 442, 522; differences of, 352; and rhetoric, 375, 380

Suarez, Cypriano, 230n, 263n

subalternation, 219, C2, C2n

subject, of an action, C34

subject matter, unseemly, 57; of tragedies and comedies, 87; in beginning logic, 216; overview of, 229; for writing, 410; and classes given by biennial students, 452; and Acts, 505; and academy exercises, 515

subjection, C65

substance, of grammar, 46; and On the Heavens, 222

substance, philosophical, C10, C11, C16, C39, C39n, C109, C128; of a vow, C130

substitution, for teachers, 80; for prefect, 302; for Latin words, 351

subtlety, in disputation, 174; in cases of conscience, 191;

summary, 192; argumentum, 266n, 306, 315, 383, 396, 400, 409, 411, 420, 430, 431; overview of rules of rhetoric, 395; final summary in Acts, 506

superior, of the Society of Jesus, 1n; and responsibility for the Ratio, 6; at the superior's discretion, 16, 21, 30n, 456; and the time devoted for the study of humanities and rhetoric, 24; and consultors, 31n; and grammar, 46; and professional teachers, 48;

and rector, 94n; reporting deviations to, 101, 465, 496; and Acts, 105; and awards, 285; and assignment of studies, 436, 458

supernatural, C16, C30, C129

supervision, 1n, 266

supplication, 68, 68n

supply, of books, 56, 127, 278; of prizes, 286; of phrases and helps, 354; of rules for prose composition, 380

Suppression (of the Society of Jesus), 1n

surname, at admission, 261; in examinations, 308; in contest compositions, 317; at confessions, 333; and addressing students, 364

swearing, 293, 471

swords, 470

syllable quantities, 250n, 401, 414

syllabus, 43

symbols, 386, 515

Symmachus, 153, 153n

Synesius, 403, 403n

syntax, introduction to, 250, 250n, 337; Greek, 376, 388, 395, 403, 400, 405; rules of 408, 410, 413, 418, 421, 412, 416; beginner's knowledge of, 425, 425n, 426; in exercises, 428, 431; in competition, 433

system, p. 3, title and unnumbered notes; in theology, 15n, 211n; Aristotelian, 229; of Greek syllables, 403; of accents, 406n

table, speeches and poems at, 85; of forms, 419n

Table of Cebes (Tabula Cebetis, Pinax Cebetis), 415, 415n

talent, and biennium, 16; and literary studies, 24; and two years of theology, 29; and three years of theology, 30; average talent described, 35; decision about, 36, 37; for teaching, 48; and admission into theology, 74; for participation in the General Acts, 105; disposing for theology, 207; and advancement, 252; and examinations, 273; and special exercises, 356; and the rector of an academy, 488

teacher, word for, 2n; and correcting compositions, 6n; of Sacred Scripture, 11; of theology, 15; and selecting students for the review of theology, 16; and examinations, 25, 118, 119, 121; multiplying, 43; preparing outstanding humanities teachers, 45; and grammar book, 46; career teachers, 47; academies for training, 53, 83; not employed in household duties, 55; and →

425; Greek, 421; producing tenses in competitions, 424, 424n, 433

Terence, 57, 57n

term (the school year), 109

tertianship, 50n

testimonies, 136

testing, 32, 396; tested, 16, 16n, 50, 74. *Also see* examination

text, of Quintilian, 1n; of the *Ratio*, 2n; foundational text for the Society of Jesus, 5; sacred texts, 11, 128n, 149, 152, 171, 188; for theologians, 128, 128n; Hebrew pointing, 159; texts given, 221, 222, 225; importance of the text of Aristotle, 226; which texts to be taken, 227; choice and order of questions, 228; questions inserted, 229; Aristotle's *Ethics*, 235; in highest grammar, 405

theme, and commonplaces, 220n; in classes with two levels, 258; given for examinations, 266; defined, 266n; Greek theme, 344, 385, 412; manner and content, 354, 400; for composition, 384, 421; in schedule, 396, 406, 416, 426; as exercise in the academy, 515

Theodore Roosevelt, 16n

Theodore the Studite, 136n

Theodotion, 153, 153n

Theognis, 403, 403n

Theogony, 387n

theologian, and study of Sacred Scripture, 12; and teaching Hebrew, 13; Saint Thomas Aquinas as preeminent, 15n; usage of the term *theologian* as a Jesuit formational term, 20n; disputations of, 77, 104, 231; substitute teachers for, 80; and poetic compositions, 82; prefect's oversight of, 102; finishing material, 103; and Acts, 105; books distributed to, 128; proving dogma from Scriptures, 156; exceptions to following Thomas, 176; Alexander of Hales, 211n; Francisco Toledo, 215n; Pedro da Fonseca, 215n; and mathematical problems, 240; biennial students and cases and disputations, 446, 447; biennial students giving classes, 451, 452; competence, 455; in academies, 485; rector of theologians' academies, 488; beadle's office for theologians' academies, 490; running the reviews, 500; academy disputations, 501, 502, C16, C18, C19, C29, C94, C123n, C124, C124n

theology, and terms for teacher, 2n; in colleges and universities, 8n; and teacher of Sacred Scripture, 11; scholastic theology, 11n; theology studies, 12; no exemption from scriptural study, 14; course and teachers, 15; two-year review of, 16, 29, 79, 80, 98; and Acts, 16n, 105, 106, 107, 110, 123; and cases moral theology, 19n, 20, 21; and professors of philosophy, 22; professors and examination of students of logic, 25; years given, 30, 31, 32; removal from course, 34; average achievement in, 35; and decision about talent, 36; and career teachers of grammar and rhetoric, 47; selecting for, 50; promotion to the study of scholastic theology, 74; in-house courses in, 105n, 107, 110, 113; disputations in, 113, 114; examinations of day students and boarders, 119; and philosophical Acts, 122; and external disputations, 124; books distributed, 128; Saint Thomas followed, 175; time for, 180; division of course, 183, 185; questions avoided in, 187; relation of arts and sciences to, 207; biennial students of, [H32]; reviews in the academies, 500, 512, C3

thesis, defense of in Acts, 16n; theses on scriptural passages and promotion, 17; disputation (defined) 72n; oversight of, 102; and theological Acts, 105; publishing theses, 108; schedule of, 109; number of, 112; respondent's assertion of, 113; examining theses, 116; in philosophical Acts, 122; prefect and, 132; and medieval schools, 134n; proving, 135; focused defense of, 189; explaining, 193; presenting difficulties through problems and theses, 200; weekly disputations, 202; monthly disputations, 231; and Saturday defenses, 232; metaphysics students and ethical propositions, 238; biennial students and presentation of, 450; beadle's reminders about, 461, 462; in academies, 488, 490, 498, 502, 505, 508, 509, 512, 515, 516

Thucydides, 387, 387n

Thursday, 65, 66, 69

Tibullus, 405, 405n

timepiece, 463

times, adaptation to, 6, 72, 470; starting and ending, 58; for language academies, 81; for speaking and writing Latin, 82; for teacher-education academies, 83; for humanistic reading, 128; of Christ, 157; for solemn disputations, 233; for competition with closest class, 358; of falling short in mem- →